More Advance Praise for *God's Red Son*

"With *God's Red Son*, Louis Warren has written yet another book that is going to rearrange the mental furniture in our heads. His wonderfully clear prose pulls us effortlessly through a story that has western Indians emerge as entirely modern, and their nineteenth-century Ghost Dance religion as an endeavor many readers will find not just freshly understandable, but spiritually familiar. As was the case with his biography of Buffalo Bill, this book is Warren at the absolute top of his game."

> —Dan Flores, author of *Coyote America: A Natural and Supernatural History*

"I can't remember the last book I read that so persuasively rewrites what I thought I knew about a much studied topic. Louis Warren's book does that for the Ghost Dance, and, more than that, it allows readers to see anew the history of the era and of all American religions. *God's Red Son* is truly a revelation."

> —Stephen Aron, professor of history, UCLA

"This eye-opening book is rich with empathy-stirring insights into the Indian Ghost Dancers' dilemmas, hopes, ecstatic experiences, and practical precepts for survival in the modern United States. Importantly, it shows us Indians who reacted to the jarring consequences of US expansion and industrialization much as many other Americans did—with a mix of hope-inspiring religious fervor and pragmatic economic adjustments. This is American Indian history at its very best, vividly illuminating not only its distinctiveness and captivating complexity but also its inseparability from the larger story of Americans at a time of rapid, wrenching changes. With an abundance of compelling evidence woven into an accessible, absorbing narrative, Warren convincingly refutes the all-too-common assumption that the Ghost Dancers, and most American Indians in the 1880s, were irrational dreamers, futilely resisting their culture's inevitable demise."

> —Alexandra Harmon, author of *Indians in the Making* and *Rich Indians*

"Louis Warren's *God's Red Son* is a truly powerful re-envisioned (not revisionistic!), trenchant analysis of the Northern Paiute's revitalization movement by a leading American historian, whose keen understanding of those pulverizing industrializing engines of the late-nineteenth-century American West, compellingly forces our shift from romantic notions about the 'dying Indian race' resulting from the Wounded Knee Massacre that followed Wovoka's teaching into this undying religion's twentieth- and twenty-first-century legacy: its spiritual and political semiotics in the Great Basin, as well as where it formerly spread. From Nevada to the northern and southern Plains, its descendants today face late-capitalistic environmental crises staining our late nights—the Dakota Access Pipeline the most recent of these, and unhappily surely not the last."

> —Michael Hittman, author of *Wovoka and the Ghost Dance*

"In *God's Red Son*, Louis Warren tells a wonderfully compelling and justly insightful story about the Ghost Dance religion, a tradition that is close to the hearts of so many Native peoples. Staying true to the moving 'perspectives of the faithful,' he weaves a tapestry of multi-situational complexity that sharpens our understandings of how this important indigenous religion contributes to the making of modern America, as well as demonstrating his vision of the possibility of a pluralistic society that values and affirms Indian autonomy."

> —Ines Hernandez-Avila, professor of Native American studies, University of California, Davis

"Many people consider the Ghost Dance and the Wounded Knee Massacre as an end of American Indian history. In *God's Red Son,* an engagingly written and meticulously researched book, Louis Warren tells of a Ghost Dance that endured Wounded Knee. Warren makes readers understand the origins of the Ghost Dance in Gilded Age Nevada, its attraction among Plains Indians, and its influence on the development of the social sciences. After consulting this book, readers will no longer consider the Ghost Dance a backward-looking effort to regain a primitive past, but a forward-looking religious movement that engaged with the modern United States."

> —William Bauer, Wailacki and Concow of the Round Valley Indian Tribes, Associate Professor, University of Nevada

GOD'S RED SON

GOD'S RED SON

THE GHOST DANCE RELIGION AND THE MAKING OF MODERN AMERICA

———⊷❧⊷———

LOUIS S. WARREN

BASIC BOOKS

New York

Published by Basic Books, an imprint of Perseus Books, LLC, a subsidiary of Hachette Book Group, Inc.

Books published by Basic Books are available at special discounts for bulk purchases in the United States by corporations, institutions, and other organizations. For more information, please contact the Special Markets Department at Perseus Books, 2300 Chestnut Street, Suite 200, Philadelphia, PA 19103, or call (800) 810-4145, ext. 5000, or e-mail special.markets@perseusbooks.com.

Designed by Trish Wilkinson

Library of Congress Cataloging-in-Publication Data
Names: Warren, Louis S., author.
Title: God's red son : the Ghost Dance religion and the making of modern America / Louis Warren.
Other titles: Ghost Dance religion and the making of modern America
Description: New York : Basic Books, [2017] | Includes bibliographical references and index.
Identifiers: LCCN 2016045328| ISBN 9780465015023 (hardcover : alk. paper) | ISBN 9780465098682 (ebook : alk. paper)
Subjects: LCSH: Ghost dance. | Indians of North America—West (U.S.)—Religion. | Indians of North America—West (U.S.)—Government relations. | Lakota Indians—Religion. | Wovoka, approximately 1856–1932. | Mooney, James, 1861–1921. | Wounded Knee Massacre, S.D., 1890. | Indians of North America—Great Plains—History—19th century. | Indians of North America—Great Basin—History—19th century.
Classification: LCC E78.W5 W35 2017 | DDC 299.7/85244—dc23 LC record available at https://lccn.loc.gov/2016045328

10 9 8 7 6 5 4 3 2 1

For my parents, Claude N. Warren Sr. and Elizabeth Warren,
who taught me the Great Basin,
the Mojave, and Snake River Canyon.
Great teachers, great classrooms.

And in memory of my sister, Susan Elizabeth Warren Kunkler,
1961–2015.
Still she rides, across the sagebrush sea.

CONTENTS

FIGURES

MAPS

AUTHOR'S NOTE ON TERMINOLOGY

THIS IS A BOOK ABOUT INDIANS. READERS WILL NOTICE THAT I refer to the antagonists of Indians as "Americans" at least as often as I call them "whites." There are two reasons for this. First, I use the term "American" to refer to US citizens, and until 1924 Indians were not citizens and could become so only in limited circumstances, usually by surrendering tribal identity. Thus, in the period with which this book is concerned, Indians were not Americans, and many did not consider themselves as such. A great question of the era, for Indians and non-Indians alike, was whether and how Indians could, would, or should become Americans.

A second, subsidiary reason for my terminology concerns the racial variability of Indian opponents. The diversification of the citizenry was a hallmark of modern America, particularly after the Civil War. Although the power structure of the American state continued to serve white interests, by the 1880s and 1890s many of the non-Indians with whom Indians competed for land, employment, water rights, and other social goods were European immigrants, whose whiteness was often ambiguous, or black and Mexican American settlers. In the pages to come, these latter groups are often categorized as "Americans" because, unlike Indians, they were American citizens or could choose to become citizens.

A HOLE IN THE DREAM

THE BODIES WERE FROZEN AND COVERED IN SNOW. IN PLACES, they clustered together, but some of the Indians—from the Minneconjou and Hunkpapa tribes of the Lakota, or Western, Sioux—had scattered across miles of prairie before being cut down by soldiers. The men of the burial party, led by a civilian, a Lakota-white mixed-blood named Paddy Starr, searched out their corpses in earnest, some we may assume because it was a somber task, and others because for every Indian they put in the grave they received $2. The more they recovered, the bigger the payout. Starr's gravediggers turned up most of the dead in the ravine of Wounded Knee Creek, where the village had camped alongside the US Seventh Cavalry the night before. There, at the site of the council where they had been ordered to appear before the commanding officer, Colonel James Forsyth, eighty Lakota men had died after handing over their weapons to the soldiers, who then killed them. Others had run far in a desperate bid to escape, but the soldiers showed no mercy. Boys and girls, women and men lay in heaps for hundreds of yards up the ravine. A woman and three children had been shot to death a full three miles from the bloodbath at the council circle. Occasionally a shout went up when a survivor was discovered, and these were left in the care of Indians who had come along or who lived nearby.[1]

1

FIGURE I.1. Placing frozen bodies in the mass grave at Wounded Knee, January 1891. Denver Public Library, Western History Collection, X-31292.

Into the wagons the gravediggers loaded the corpses, all that remained of 146 women and men, old and young, including many children. Then, steering the wagons to the top of a nearby knoll, they lowered the bodies into a long trench.

The victims had been part of a village that took up the Ghost Dance, a new religion that swept dozens of reservations with remarkable speed in the brief period of 1889–1890. Promising Indians redemption from the agonies of American conquest on a newly restored earth teeming with buffalo and horses, it drew believers into dance circles where some fell into unconscious trance visions in which they encountered their deceased kin and, sometimes, the Creator himself. Even at its peak, only a minority of Indians were believers; among Lakotas, for example, it was estimated that at most one in three joined the Ghost Dance circle. Initially the public remained indifferent. But growing alarm in the press and among officials about a potential Indian "outbreak" eventually inflamed opinion. Late in

1890, the US Army arrived among the Western Sioux to suppress the religion on the orders of President Benjamin Harrison. At Wounded Knee Creek, on the morning of December 29, the army veered into massacre.

In what is perhaps the most famous rendering of the event, the venerated Oglala Lakota holy man and sometime Ghost Dancer Nicholas Black Elk recounted coming upon the killing field soon after the shooting stopped. The army had left for shelter from the approaching storm. "I can still see the butchered women and children lying heaped and scattered all along the crooked gulch as plain as when I saw them with eyes still young. And I can see that something else died there in the bloody mud, and was buried in the blizzard. A people's dream died there. It was a beautiful dream."[2]

The rhetorical power of Black Elk's elegy has inspired generations of filmmakers, poets, painters, and authors, including most famously Dee Brown, whose *Bury My Heart at Wounded Knee: An Indian History of the American West* became a best-seller upon its publication in 1970. Ever since, *Bury My Heart* has remained perhaps the most influential history of what we label "the Indian Wars"—the overlapping invasions, battles, skirmishes, massacres, and murders by which the United States claimed the West. The book ends with the holy man's lament, as if Black Elk is announcing the death not only of the Ghost Dance but of Indian history itself—"a people's dream died there." Down to the present day, the holy man's vivid regret captures a still widely held sense that the massacre marked the end of the Indian Wars and Indian resistance and killed the Indians' religion. As the interpretive sign at the massacre site explains, "Ghost Dancing ended with this encounter."[3]

In many ways, there was nothing exceptional about Wounded Knee, which was one in a long series of nineteenth-century mass Indian killings. The massacre devastated Lakotas, but compared to the vast slaughter in the Civil War or World War I, it can seem like a relatively small, remote military event.

But in that face-off between an industrialized army and overwhelmed, exalted natives, Wounded Knee came to represent a central confrontation not only in American history but in world history. While many saw it as a signature moment in the ending of Indian freedom and the frontier, others presented it as a window into the spiritual longings of all humanity. This tradition began in the 1890s and only grew stronger in subsequent decades. In 1956 the anthropologist Anthony F. C. Wallace argued that the Ghost Dance was exemplary of many "revitalization movements" through which colonized peoples around the world tried to create new cultures, and in 1970 another scholar, Weston La Barre, presented the religion as a template for the psychological and philosophical underpinnings of all spiritual thought. To La Barre, the Ghost Dance was a cult anticipating the end of the world, comparable to the Xhosa cattle killing of 1856 in South Africa, the "Vailala Madness" that began in Papua New Guinea in 1919, and scores of other "crisis cults" characterized by "spectacularly unrealistic and bizarre beliefs" (including Western religions; to La Barre, "Christianity itself was a crisis cult"). Dee Brown and Weston La Barre are but two among a multitude of authors behind a vast Ghost Dance literature in history, anthropology, psychology, theology, and other fields that has compared the Ghost Dance to other millenarian, anticolonial movements in Asia, Africa, Europe, Australia, and the Americas. Today the Ghost Dance, a movement that is usually understood to have briefly gripped remote regions of the American West, sits at the center of American, and indeed world, understandings not only of Indians and their spirituality but of all religions and their place in modern societies.[4]

But as the Ghost Dance has become ever more relevant, it has never escaped the burial shroud in which the Wounded Knee massacre seemed to enfold it. In most studies, the religion represents not merely a native effort at cultural and political restoration, but a failed effort. To invoke the Ghost Dance has been to call up an image of indigenous spirituality by turns militant, desperate, and futile—a beautiful dream that died. So associated is the Ghost Dance with tragedy that it becomes hard to imagine it could have met any other fate. In most of our books, the religion represents a primitive effort to go back to the past, to exit history. Much like Indians themselves who were also fated to disappear, the Ghost Dance seemed backward and foreordained to fail. Seldom has any historical development seemed more doomed. That impression has been reinforced by the many accounts in which the Wounded Knee Massacre has come to stand in for the entire history of the religion, as if the hopes of all its devoted followers began and ended in that fatal ravine. Almost invariably, where the religion itself appears in our history books, it does so in order that it may die.

As the religion has come to represent failure and the past, the ravine at Wounded Knee Creek has come to embody the abyss between primitive and modern. It is as if, in looking into its shallow trace, one could see the twilight of an epoch, the death struggle of all the ancient ways, the eclipse not only of Indians but of all the colonized people of the earth in the violent blast of the machine—especially the machine gun—wielded by the modern state. So Wounded Knee has become a metonym for conquest, and the Ghost Dance a ritual that marks the terminus of an era, separating the end of the American frontier (famously closed by the US Census Division that very year) from the beginning of the twentieth century. So the sacrifice at Wounded Knee marks America's passage into the modern age.

But telling stories about benighted savages in order to make Americans seem more advanced is one of the oldest clichés in historical writing, one that even now threatens to trap us in the same assimilation stories, the same evolutionary narratives that present Indians as primitive in order to make ourselves modern. And the story of how believers yearning for the past met a bloody, tragic ending at the hands of the world's most industrial and modern nation has proved so compelling, and so useful for conveying so many different messages, that—a few recent, notable exceptions aside—generations of historians have overlooked its obvious flaws. Perhaps the most telling of these has been the peculiar determination to analyze the Ghost Dance—a messianic, millenarian religion—almost entirely by its representation of the postmillennial world, the visions of buffalo and horses and the restoration of old ways that exhilarated many Ghost Dancers.[5]

To treat Protestantism in this way, by focusing exclusively on visions of the postmillennium or of heaven, would run the risk of reducing all Protestant experience to a longing for the heavenly reward of eternal youth, as promised in the Gospel According to Luke (23:43). Although such images of the afterlife are telling clues to the meaning of Christianity, they are only clues, and to rely on them exclusively to interpret the religion would beggar the history of billions.

In fact, Ghost Dance teachings extend far beyond the promise of a millennial paradise and are intimately connected to the religion's larger significance for believers and the question of how and when it "died." These issues lie at the center of this book. Poetic allusions and cultural presumptions notwithstanding, the massacre at Wounded Knee did not kill Indian culture or Indian religion, and evidence even for the death of the Ghost Dance has proved elusive. As scholars have known for some time now, Black Elk's elegy for the "people's dream" was actually composed not by the holy man but by John Neihardt, the poet laureate of Nebraska who was essentially Black Elk's coauthor. A close review of stenographic transcripts of Niehardt's interviews with Black Elk reveals that although the holy man had much to say about the practice of the Ghost Dance, he neither mourned the religion's death nor speculated about its fate after the massacre. On the contrary, the Ghost Dance had a curious power over Black Elk that he could not shake. More than forty years later, sitting near Wounded Knee Creek on a spring afternoon, he recalled that the Ghost Dance had brought him visions in which he had "seen the son of the Great Spirit himself." Where Niehardt's version of Black Elk's memory emphasizes the vanishing of the Ghost Dance, in Black Elk's own account the fate of the dream remains uncertain, as if it might not have died at all.[6]

THIS BOOK NOT ONLY TRACES THE ORIGINS AND PROPAGATION OF the Ghost Dance religion across the US Far West but advances a major reinterpretation of the religion and the crisis that swirled around it. In marked contrast to contemporary accounts and much scholarship on the Ghost Dance since Wounded Knee, this book shows that the Ghost Dance was no romantic "last stand" by Indians desperate to return to the past, and that it did not die at Wounded Knee. It was, rather, a forward-looking, pragmatic religion that had a long life after the notorious atrocity in South Dakota.

According to Ghost Dance teachings, the Messiah—at times called Christ, and sometimes even Jesus—would arrive to save the faithful and transport them to an earth renewed, and Indians could hasten the event by dancing and right living. Some believers, famously but not exclusively among the Lakota Sioux, donned "ghost shirts," muslin garments that were painted with dragonflies, eagles, and other symbols seen in visions and that some alleged to be bullet-proof. These believers and many more besides were often seized with millennial excitement, and their spectacular, ecstatic behavior preoccupied not only contemporary observers but generations of writers who have focused on the dancing at the expense of the code for day-to-day conduct propagated alongside it. That the paradise said to be coming with the Messiah looked much like the past (as most imagined paradises do) has contributed to a widespread belief that the Ghost Dance promised only a return to a premodern era. But the religion also offered believers hope of sustaining themselves in this world by engaging the modern, industrial Gilded Age in which they found themselves. The prophet of the religion, a Northern Paiute visionary named Wovoka, taught that Ghost Dancers were obliged not to steal, to tell the truth, to keep the peace with Americans and other Indians, to love one another, and to "work for the white man," that is, to work for wages or engage in commerce for money.

That last teaching in particular has been widely ignored by scholars, and all of the teachings have been broadly overlooked by historians and writers fixated on the Indian paradise that was prophesied to follow after Indians took up the new dispensation. These teachings were central to Ghost Dance practice, and as we shall see, they made a great deal of sense to Indians who followed the prophet into the first Ghost Dance circles.

Disciples, then, preached about the glorious millennium in which the old ways would be resurrected, with buffalo and horses, but they also taught their followers that they must take up paying work and abandon war. Indeed, as the dance proliferated, these commandments were expanded. By the time the Ghost Dance reached the Plains, some were preaching that followers must send their children to school, attend Christian churches, acquire farms, and cooperate with authorities. Only in this way could the Indian redeemer descend from heaven, bringing the millennium.

For all the fascination with ghost shirts, most dancers never wore those garments. In the other, more conventional clothing of these believers lie clues to the complexity of Ghost Dance belief and practice, and to their earnest efforts to embrace modern life. At Wounded Knee, eight boys were playing leapfrog near the council circle when the shooting erupted. In the first volley the boys fell, "like grass before the sickle" in the words of a journalist. Their bodies went into the mass grave in the clothes they were wearing when the army opened fire—not painted muslin shirts and moccasins but gray woolen pants and shirts, the uniforms from the reservation day school.[7]

Indeed, while historians and anthropologists have interpreted the faith as an outright rejection of modernity, the Ghost Dance promised to help Indians address the implications of American conquest and to live in the nation as Indians. Much of the religion's allure came from its promise to help Indians of the Industrial Age who sought futures both modern and traditional, prosperity and health in modern pursuits, and vibrant, enduring Indian culture.[8]

Religion is an affair of the heart, but it offers relief and guidance for people living in a hard-edged world. Indians became Ghost Dancers partly in response to changing material conditions that had created an existential crisis. By 1889, Indians had been uprooted and dispossessed, consigned to reservations, and stripped of almost all their land. Some had been cast into wage work that required long absence from home. The furious pace of western settlement and industrial development had nearly eradicated many wild creatures and plants that not only once provided food but were themselves embodied spirits that provided counsel and support, allowing Indian people to locate themselves and one another in relation to the cosmos. Federal proscriptions against ceremony and ritual had alienated many Indians from prior religions. In many places, the destruction of customary food and trade networks had reduced native peoples to dependence on what were known as "rations"—actually payments in kind for land cessions—doled out by the federal government. Their survival depended less on local creatures and their own people than on faraway strangers in the Office of Indian Affairs, the White House, and the halls of Congress. To Ghost Dancers, the new teachings were not human creations but gifts from spirits who had intervened for mysterious reasons, and their popularity stemmed in part from the way they addressed these primary challenges of the reservation era.

Those challenges might have inspired a purely nostalgic religion, one preoccupied only with the old ways, but in both its teachings and the means by which it spread, the Ghost Dance was clearly innovative and modern. Although some white observers were mystified as to how so many Indians, people bound to the wheel of the past, could have communicated the teachings over such vast distances, the answer was hidden in plain sight. The Ghost Dance was no atavistic impulse, but a religion born of steam and steel—on the railroads that carried seekers to the prophet and back to their home communities; in the boarding schools where Indian students became literate in English and capable of instructing one another and their intertribal audiences in the new teachings; in the newspaper accounts of the dance and its prophecy read by educated Indians; and in the pencil factories and paper mills that produced the implements for a primary Indian method of communicating the new gospels, the letter, sent through the US Postal Service.[9]

And so, too, were the ambitions of Indian believers distinctly modern. As we shall see, the dance itself was accompanied by demands for jobs, money, and the expansion of religious freedoms. The dance fomented Indian nationalism and, in calling on Indians to "be Indians" again, helped turn Indians into a far more unified bloc of agitators than ever before, laying the foundation for the truly pan-Indian politics that would characterize the twentieth century. The Ghost Dance, it turns out, was no last gasp of Indian resistance, but rather a movement that promised believers a means to persist as Indians while surviving conquest and the reservation era.

To see Ghost Dancers for what they were, as people in pursuit not of oblivion but of modern health and prosperity, requires us to readjust our expectations. We must, as the historian Philip Deloria has urged us, abandon our preconceptions, broaden our vision, and prepare ourselves to see "Indians in unexpected places," not only in the dance circle but at work, in school, and on the train. Like other Indians, Ghost Dancer wrote and read letters, farmed, logged, and drove freight wagons; they performed in "Wild West" shows and regularly engaged in a whole range of activities alongside other Gilded Age people. Ghost Dancers were caught up in modern struggles for survival, and so their religion became infused with ongoing debates about the meaning of Indianness and the proper place and form of Indian spirituality in a postconquest world.[10]

The Ghost Dance creed was through and through a peaceful one. Since the weeks before the Wounded Knee Massacre, when army officers began to circulate rumors that the Ghost Dance had been hijacked by "hostiles" out for blood, generations of scholars have wrestled with the specter of "warlike" Ghost Dancers. And yet the evidence remains overwhelming that the new religion preached not armed resistance but a path toward accepting many government demands while, at the same time, retaining Indian identity and community and resisting assimilation.

Beyond that, the Ghost Dance addressed a pervasive need for new forms of ritual expression in Indian communities. Dancing, a mode of expression that simultaneously allowed Indians to create community with one another and establish communication between the world of the living and the world of the spirits, had deep social and religious meanings and was integral to many religious rites. During the 1880s and 1890s, Christian missionaries and the US government increasingly sought to suppress Indian religion, and especially ceremonial dances. In resisting these proscriptions, Indians often reformed earlier Indian religious practices and hierarchies. New beliefs and ceremonies, including the Dream Dance, the Peyote Religion, and others, spread across the interior West at the very moment the Ghost Dance took hold. To be sure, this wave of religious change was, in a sense, also traditional. Since Native American religions did not usually adhere to doctrinal texts, Indian peoples often revised ritual practices. Sacred encounters and spirit visions were always possible, and throughout Indian history they had inspired new dances and rituals. In this sense, the appearance of the Ghost Dance religion could be seen as in keeping with older customs of renewal and revival. In the closing decade of the nineteenth century, the Ghost Dance emerged in many places, in different ways among distinctive peoples, as a means of making Indian religion more responsive to the realities of reservation life.

Many scholars have concluded that Christianity's influence determined much of the form and content of the Ghost Dance, but in its day such claims raised complex questions. Discussions about the religion's origins and meaning sometimes provoked lively disputes among Ghost Dancers themselves, as well as between them and their critics, both Indian and white. Indian peoples of the Far West had been objects of missionary attention for generations by 1890, and Christianity had attracted followers among them. Since the colonial period, Indians had adopted some Christian practices and mingled them with those of older religions, engaging or even affiliating with one or another denomination without undergoing what missionaries considered full-fledged "conversion." In some places, well before the Ghost Dance appeared, Indian congregations were attending Indian churches. Perhaps not surprisingly, where missionaries denounced the Ghost Dance in favor of Christianity, some Indian believers appear to have felt that the Ghost Dance was a Christian religion. But even at the time, other Ghost Dancers rejected such claims. As we shall see, there were Indian precedents for the Ghost Dance prophecy, some of which apparently predated missionary efforts, and some believers maintained that the religion was the fulfillment of a distinct, authentic Indian vision. To these Ghost Dancers, the Messiah was not Jesus but another, Indian figure.[11]

And yet, whatever the connection between Christianity and the Ghost Dance might have been, it remains undeniable that the Ghost

Dance religion functioned in many ways like evangelical Christianity. Partly for this reason, I use Christian terms to describe some aspects of Ghost Dance practice, even though I do not weigh in on whether the Ghost Dance constituted a Christian ritual. So throughout this book we will meet Ghost Dance "evangelists" and "apostles" carrying "gospels" to gather the faithful.

Indeed, the religion bore some resemblance to Christianity not only in content but in its appeal and effect. Like Methodism and other reform denominations in Europe, the Ghost Dance helped believers adjust to new economic realities and accept the painful contradictions of life in a countryside turned over to ranching and farming and other forms of resource extraction. Much of the religion's allure came from how it addressed a radically shifting material world and helped Indians cope with the Industrial Revolution and its accompanying juggernaut of modernity, the rise of corporate structures to economic dominance in the United States, and the expanding bureaucracy of the state and modern education. The Ghost Dance served the needs of Indians hoping to adjust to life under industrial capitalism in a nation where literacy was key to negotiating courtrooms and the government offices that administered so much of Indian life. In other words, in the aftermath of American invasion, the Ghost Dance helped believers find ways to negotiate and assert new dimensions of control not only over their own spiritual lives but also over their governance. In this sense, the massacre at Wounded Knee marks a brutal suppression not of naive, primitive Indians but of pragmatic people who sought a peaceful way forward into the twentieth century.

It is testament to its modernity that the religion was not so easily killed. The promise of the Ghost Dance was so great that Indian people carried on its devotions long after Wounded Knee. It survived on the Southern Plains and in Canada well into the twentieth century. In many places, it made lasting contributions to Indian ritual, some of which survive to the present day.

BEYOND ITS INFLUENCE IN INDIAN SOCIETIES, THE GHOST DANCE also had a significant impact on American culture, primarily through the work of the religion's first anthropologist, James Mooney. If anthropology has taught us most of what we know—or think we know—about the Ghost Dance, then studying the Ghost Dance and the response to it can teach us much about the social sciences and especially anthropology, a discipline that owes significant parts of its development to scholarship on this religion. All books about the religion (including this one) rely to a significant degree on Mooney's classic 1896 study, *The Ghost Dance Religion and Sioux Outbreak of 1890*. Less acknowledged is that Ghost Dance teachings inspired Mooney to rebel against the intellectual strictures of the period, casting aside ideas of psychological and religious evolutionism in favor of a broader, more inclusive, and more contingent view of religious thought. His position was so radical that his superiors debated suppressing his work.[12]

His own biases about the essential primitivism of Indians led Mooney to make errors that continue to plague our understanding of the Ghost Dance. Nevertheless, his study occupied the forefront of a contemporary shift in American thought about race, religion, and tolerance. *The Ghost Dance Religion* was one of the first government reports to question the reigning policy of assimilation—the decades-long effort to obliterate Indian culture and make Indians over into white people.

Connecting Ghost Dancers and anthropologists threatens to lead us into the trap of pitting "spiritual" Indians against "scientific" Americans, but to fully separate spirit from science in either group will prove harder than we might first imagine. If the Ghost Dance was a decidedly spiritual program for renewing the earth, the Ghost Dance prophet himself had a political agenda, and Ghost Dancers also had political motivations. Amid the mounting crisis of government hostility, some believers helped Mooney compose an official portrait of the religion as peaceful and deserving of protection, and many developed a language of religious devotion that allowed them to demand religious freedom. This in itself marked a decidedly cultural innovation. The word "religion," after all, signifies a Western ideal, "a set of beliefs, practices, and institutions that can be separated from other spheres of life," in the words of historian Tisa Wenger. Of course, within the traditions of the Indians who took up the Ghost Dance there was no clear division between spiritual devotion and daily life, no hard line between the religious and the secular. But as the crisis of 1890 mounted the Ghost Dancers increasingly claimed the ceremony as the central element of what they referred to as their "church, "the new religion," or "our religion." Although none appears to have invoked the First Amendment explicitly, Ghost Dancers proved adept at evoking American traditions of religious tolerance and thereby staked a claim to protection under the US Constitution. This marked a turn that would have profound consequences in the decades after 1890 as Indians increasingly and sometimes even suc-cessfully demanded federal protection of customary rituals and reli-gions, as well as sacred landforms and landscapes. In many ways, the Indian fight for the Ghost Dance prefigured these later campaigns.[13]

Just as Indians commonly blended religion with daily life, white people also did not easily compartmentalize their beliefs. Social sci-ence itself—like the assimilationist dreams that sometimes motivated it—could be inflected with millenarian thinking: even the most ra-tional anthropologist could utilize science in pursuit of profoundly unscientific, even religious ends. That the Ghost Dance erupted into public view at the same time that anthropology itself began to co-here as a freestanding social science was more than coincidence. The religion and the primary intellectual method through which Amer-icans came to know it were both, in distinctive ways, responses to the peculiar conditions of the Gilded Age and the profound intellec-tual, spiritual, and economic crises that epoch generated for Indians and non-Indians alike. New religions and new scientific approaches to understanding complex societies were, as we shall see, connected projects that engaged contemporaries from all racial and ethnic groups.

How is it possible that a religion extolling wage work, farm-ing, and education could be stigmatized as dangerous savagery in 1890? One answer is that popular racial prejudice presented Indians as "primitives" incapable of modernity. By these lights, no Indian religion could be anything but barbarous and backward—if any of their "superstitions" could be said to amount to a religion at all.

Alongside racial stereotypes, popular biases against new forms of religious expression were also partly responsible for the widespread failure to recognize the complexity of the Ghost Dance. Indeed, it is in the fights over new religions, and over scientific "progress," that we can begin to grasp the larger significance of the Ghost Dance for American history and religion. Indians were hardly alone in taking up new religions. The decades between 1800 and 1920 saw rapid proliferation of new forms of religious devotion across the American landscape as believers sought relief and spiritual intimacy that were less available in older churches. These dynamics fueled the so-called holiness movement and other expressions of "incipient Pentecostalism," which featured charismatic preaching, faith healing, and, among followers seized by the spirit, speaking in tongues and bodily exaltation to the point that some rolled on the ground (giving rise to the epithet "holy rollers"). These outpourings of religious sentiment might seem quaint to modern readers, but to contemporaries they often seemed like the dangerous exhalations of some noxious spirit. In the minds of many, the explosive movements of bodies in the grip of the Holy Ghost too easily suggested other kinds of explosions, notably the brewing storm of worker unrest and racial strife that seemed always about to erupt in these years. The suspicion was not limited to holiness believers. "Are spiritualists insane?" asked the *Chicago Daily Tribune* in 1885 after a judge threatened to commit to an asylum a woman who had dabbled in séances to contact the spirits of the dead. In this moment, the adoption of ecstatic religion by Indians, many of whom also claimed to speak with the dead, created a kind of cultural conflagration as suspect bodily movements and beliefs were taken up by brown-skinned people already thought to be savages. Such biases made it extremely unlikely that most white people would grasp the significance and pragmatism of Ghost Dance belief.[14]

By understanding the anticharismatic leanings of many Ghost Dance critics, we can begin to place the religion in its proper context in the broader history of American religion. Elite and middle-class observers seemed less concerned with the validity of spiritualist, holiness, or Ghost Dance beliefs than with how they might inspire dangerous unrest among those who believed. To many, unconventional religious beliefs were more likely to inspire workers and Indians to rise up, and anxiety over the "unreason" of lower-class and disparate ethnic beliefs helped drive intellectuals of the day to explore religion and the meaning of belief in new ways.[15]

Scholars have pointed to a variety of reasons for the appeal of the holiness movement and spiritualism among believers, and we shall see how some of these extend, in a qualified way, to the Ghost Dance. To put it briefly, the increasing rationalism of work and daily life created longings for the experience of religious feeling that seemed to be disappearing from the modern world. Of course, the Ghost Dance, as an Indian religion, differed in many ways from incipient Pentecostalism, but the movements shared certain devotional forms and attributes, including trance visions, an insistence on the body as a site of "holiness" or wonders, a longing for health and prosperity, and enthusiastic anticipation of a messiah. And the two religions also shared certain inspirations. No people, after all, had been more "rationalized" by 1890 than Indians, whose communities, families, and bodies had been made subjects of scientific inquiry and reforms, both religious and technocratic, for decades. Moreover, the broader cultural push toward alternative religious expression, from Mormonism to spiritualism, had a profound effect on Indians, who at times adapted these nascent traditions to their own uses, and some believers may even have integrated some of these practices into the Ghost Dance itself. Holiness, spiritualism, Mormonism, and the Ghost Dance were all radically different expressions of belief but nevertheless developed in conversation with one another. Seen in this light, the Ghost Dance becomes a window not only into Indian history but also into contemporary religion and social anxieties, as well as the place and meaning of science and social science in American life, at the end of the nineteenth century.

A BOOK THAT CONNECTS INDIAN RELIGION AND AMERICAN social science to economy, politics, and culture is inevitably complex;

therefore, in the pages that follow, we trace a path via the stories of selected Ghost Dancers. The foremost of these is the charismatic founder of the movement, the Northern Paiute visionary named Jack Wilson, or Wovoka. In his wake follow apostles and evangelists, including Porcupine of the Northern Cheyenne, Short Bull of the Lakota Sioux, and Black Coyote of the Southern Arapaho. Among this company, too, is James Mooney, who in the course of his investigation joined the circle and became a Ghost Dancer. A rigorous social scientist, Mooney himself disavowed belief. But in a grand irony that demonstrates anew the connectedness of the Ghost Dance and anthropology, his ostensibly detached, rational study inadvertently enhanced the appeal of the religion for some Indians. In general, it was the power of the circle to draw in the faithful and the curious that helped make the Ghost Dance so alluring to contemporaries. So we take up the trail of the movement and its joyous circle through disparate regions and peoples of the Far West and follow the Ghost Dance as it occasioned revival and reform, encountered both elation and opposition, and left a profound legacy that would have implications for American and world understandings of spirituality and tolerance.

Our story is divided into three parts. Part 1 recounts the gathering crisis around the Ghost Dance in 1890, especially in South Dakota, before turning to the mystery of the Ghost Dance origins in Nevada, far from the Great Plains. In Part 2, we learn how the religion took root on the Great Plains in the reservation era, why it appealed to so many Indians in Oklahoma and South Dakota, and what internal and external frictions laid the groundwork for the catastrophe at Wounded Knee. In Part 3, we follow the life of the religion after Wounded Knee, including not only its ceremonial development but its inscription into James Mooney's scholarship in a book that inspired generations of Ghost Dance research and began the tradition of comparing the Ghost Dance to other world religions.

Throughout I relate trance visions and spiritual encounters the way believers related them—as if they were real—because whatever nonbelievers might think, to believers these experiences were real. An "objective" historian might try to qualify every spiritual event as an expression of subjective emotion or belief, but understanding the excitement that drove this religion requires that we consider always the perspectives of the faithful.

In keeping with the spiritual and intellectual rebelliousness of the religion, this book, too, represents a provocation and an invitation, opening the door to thinking about Indian religion, American spirituality, and social science as entangled threads in a single fabric. Where the Ghost Dance has stood in our histories as an endpoint for the frontier, for Indian autonomy, and for an era, a primary goal of mine in writing this book has been to recast it as a beginning— or perhaps a whole series of beginnings—as Indians and Americans ventured forth into the twentieth century. By rethinking one story and changing its ending, we alter not just perspectives on the past but the sense of our collective present and future. In so doing, may we rethink perceptions of all peoples and all religions, remaking our society and ourselves.

PART 1

GENESIS

CHAPTER 1

1890: THE MESSIAH AND THE MACHINE

B Y THE SPRING, THE RUMORS HAD REACHED THE CITIES AND the daily papers had begun to report something strange out west among the Cheyenne Indians of Montana, who, it was said, were "greatly excited over the expected appearance of a Savior." Christ was in the mountains, claimed the Cheyenne, and he wanted all the Indians to come to him, so that he could put them behind him and then roll the earth over on the white people and destroy them. Some Indians even claimed to have visited Christ and to have seen scars on his hands and feet and a spear wound in his side.[1]

The story may have struck many as "strange and interesting," in the words of one correspondent, but it inspired little concern. Americans were busy. They read the odd newspaper accounts as they rode electric trolleys to work in Cleveland or St. Louis, or sitting under the glow of new electric lighting in their homes in Chicago and New York. On the prairies of Iowa and Kansas, they surveyed the tender shoots turning their fields bright green and wondered if that year's crop would pay for a new stove or some ready-made clothing from the Sears Roebuck catalog, whose goods arrived so conveniently on the new railroads. Others were learning the new technology of the typewriter in secretarial colleges or tending shop in small towns. In the cities, vast ranks of immigrant workers churned out textiles, laid

down pavement, or hammered together new buildings, new machines, and new lives. This age of prodigious industrial growth daily
announced new wonders, among them technologies like the sewing
machine, the telephone, the internal combustion engine, and even
a newly discovered metal, aluminium, which some dreamers said
might be light enough to craft into a flying machine. Society papers
were transfixed by a new class of millionaires whose consumption
was so conspicuous (hosting formal dinners at tables big enough to
have ponds in the middle—with live swans) that Mark Twain would
christen the era "the Gilded Age." The West and its Indians seemed
far away.[2]

Caught up in the churning present and absorbed by the prospects
for their presumed future, Americans were accustomed to thinking of
Indians as history even before the Indian Wars were over. To most,
those conflicts appeared to have ended. After General George Armstrong Custer's fall at Little Big Horn in 1876, the US Army had
forced Crazy Horse to surrender and then killed him. They harried
Sitting Bull into Canada. The old warrior had returned in 1881, but
for years now he had been living quietly at Standing Rock Reservation, on an isolated patch of South Dakota prairie. Americans still
killed Indians here and there, and there were always rumors of bigger
trouble, but the last chance for a real fight seemed to have vanished
when Geronimo turned himself in. By 1890, the scourge of the Sierra
Madre was confined to military barracks at Mount Vernon, Alabama,
and from there he would soon be on his way to farming melons under
the watchful eye of troops at Fort Sill, Oklahoma.[3]

A month later, in May 1890, came a report that further encouraged the public to ignore the strange news from the West. An Indian
delegation sent to meet the Messiah had returned without him. Indians sank into despondency, and officials breathed a collective sigh of
relief. The Indians had been "restless" for some time, "holding dances
and religious pow-wows," explained the *Chicago Daily Tribune*. Now
perhaps they would prove "tractable."[4]

But those hopes soon were disappointed. Before the eyes of the
government agents and military officers in Indian country—if be-

yond the sight of most of the nation's public, including most of its journalists—the messiah rumors continued to circulate as spring gave way to summer. On May 29, a businessman in South Dakota warned the government that something peculiar was happening among the Sioux. Three missionaries at the Sisseton Sioux Reservation had complained about a recent spike in Indian dances. In back-channel correspondence, an official acknowledged "some little excitement" at the Cheyenne River Reservation "over the coming of the Indian messiah."[5]

By June 1890, the US Army had begun to scan Indian country for the source of the messiah prophecy. Not long after, Lieutenant S. C. Robertson of the US First Cavalry in Montana submitted a startling report, kicking off a sequence of events that would turn the odd tales of whirling Indians into a prologue for bloody tragedy.

At the Tongue River Agency among the Northern Cheyenne, Lieutenant Robertson had tracked down a Cheyenne man called Porcupine, who had recently completed a mysterious journey in the West. Ever since his return, he had been preaching fervently to the Indians, extolling a new messiah and exhorting his listeners to dance a new world into being.

When confronted, Porcupine happily agreed to describe his travels. He spoke before a rapt audience: a translator, a secretary, the lieutenant, and a group of Cheyenne men in broad-brimmed hats. The secretary was meticulous in his transcription, and Robertson sent every word of the Cheyenne's haunting testimony to his superiors in Washington.[6]

As Porcupine told it, he had gone traveling the previous November, in 1889, more for recreation than anything else, "to meet other Indians and see other countries." He had known nothing of any messiah and was most concerned with the logistics of traveling. It was illegal to leave the reservation without an official pass from the federal agent who supervised it. But passes were hard to get, and like many others in that time, Porcupine had decided to leave without one.

With two friends, Porcupine had left Montana and headed for Rawlins, Wyoming, where he boarded a Union Pacific train for an all-day journey to Fort Bridger, Utah. After changing trains at that point, he headed northwest to Fort Hall, Idaho. He and his two companions disembarked there and spent the next ten days at the Bannock and Shoshone Reservation, making new friends among their former enemies, talking about the need "to be friends with whites and live at peace with them and with each other." When the Indian agent at Fort Hall discovered that Porcupine was traveling without permission, he gave passes to the Cheyenne and his companions and then provided more for some of their new Shoshone and Bannock friends.

Together the group boarded the train and headed south, "to a town on a big lake"—probably Salt Lake City—where they changed trains and headed west to Nevada. Over the next two days, they saw various "Indian towns" and white settlements, stopping to eat and visit occasionally before arriving in the evening of the second day among "the Fish Eaters"—Paiutes who lived on the shores of Pyramid Lake.

Here, in a desolate and harsh terrain seemingly in the middle of nowhere, Porcupine's journey grew truly strange. Even before he arrived, these Paiutes seemed to have had a plan for him and his companions. Providing Porcupine's party with four wagons and teams of horses, the Paiutes led them south, away from the main railroad line and into a vast desert. "We traveled all day, and then came to another railroad"—another railroad spur line that was probably in Wabuska, Nevada. Here they left their wagons and boarded the train, "the Fish-eaters telling us there were some more Indians along the railroad who wanted to see us."[7]

By this point, Porcupine's story had already raised troubling questions. How did these Paiutes know he was coming? What were they planning? Perhaps a clue dangled in his almost offhand remark that during much of the journey from Fort Hall to the place of the prophet, "all the Indians . . . danced this dance." Lieutenant Robertson wondered what the dance meant. Was it announcing a war? Was there a conspiracy among Indians to rise up?

Porcupine reminded the officer that he had not gone in search of this dance. "I knew nothing about this dance before going. I happened to run across it, that is all." Sensing that he was still concerned, Porcupine announced, "I will tell you about it."

In one motion, the Cheyenne listening to Porcupine then removed their hats. The preacher was about to speak holy words.

"There is no harm in what I am about to say to anyone," he reassured the army officer. "It is a wonder you people never heard this before." And patiently, like the teacher he had become, he explained the new gospel.

THUS FAR THE CHEYENNE'S QUEST MIGHT HAVE SEEMED PECULIAR, but perhaps nothing could have prepared Robertson for what was next revealed. The train journey had ended at an Indian reservation even deeper in the desert, where Porcupine waited with hundreds of other Indians from fifteen or sixteen tribes. "There were more different languages than I ever heard before, and I didn't understand any of them," recounted the preacher.

Why had so many gathered there?

Because Christ had summoned them, not from heaven but from earth, for he had returned and "eleven of his children were coming from a far land."

At first Porcupine did not realize that Christ had called him to this place. But after several days waiting at this even more remote setting, a man appeared whom Porcupine called the "White Father." Porcupine could not tell if he was a white man or an Indian, but he was "a good looking man" who preached to them before falling into a trance. "I have sent for you and am glad to see you," the man announced to the crowd. He told them to dance, and then he sang— and sang and sang—until late in the evening, as Porcupine and his new friends and hundreds of strange Indians danced in a great circle in the desert beneath the wheeling stars.

The White Father returned to them the following day. He revealed that he had been sent by God to earth once before, but "the people were afraid of me and treated me badly"—here he showed his scars. So he had gone back to heaven, promising to return "in many hundred years." Now he had come. "My father told me the earth was getting old and worn out, and the people getting bad, and that I was to renew everything as it used to be, and make it better."

A better earth, with more people to love, for all the Indian dead were to be resurrected. Since the earth was too small for both the living and the newly risen, God would "do away with heaven and make the earth itself large enough to contain us all."

To ensure this outcome, all Indians were to live by new rules. Fighting was evil and was to be avoided. All people were to be friends. The whites and the Indians were to be one people, a sentiment that Porcupine found truly marvelous. "Where I went there were lots of white people, but I never had one of them say an unkind word to me."

Since his return, Porcupine reassured Robertson, he had preached only peace among the Cheyenne. "I knew my people were bad and had heard nothing of all this, so I got them together and told them of it and warned them to listen to it for their own good." He had preached for days and nights, warning them against evil deeds and urging dance and celebration of this joyful gospel.

Now, back in Montana, Porcupine still saw the Christ in his dreams. "You can see this man in your sleep any time you want after you have seen him and shaken hands with him. Through him you can go to heaven and meet your friends. "

Robertson left the interview thinking we know not what. But soon after, an army typist at Camp Crook recorded the story on paper. The strange words of Porcupine and his news of a messiah in the wilderness were then carried in a mail satchel that made its way from Montana to Cheyenne, Wyoming, and then east on the railroad to Chicago, and then to Washington, DC.[8]

Porcupine, for his part, went traveling again, taking the gospel to the Crow Reservation. There he preached not only to his former enemies among the Crows but also to an audience of "officers and ladies of the post" at Fort Custer. We can detect a glimmer of his passion in the brief account of an eyewitness: "The apostle stood with outstretched hands in silence for several minutes before he began speaking, and then broke forth like one inspired."[9]

Astonishing as it was, the gospel of Porcupine met with silence from the nation's capital. Perhaps the humid heat of summer was forcing the wheels of government to turn more slowly even than usual. Or maybe officials, however well versed in language and policy, could find no words to respond.

THE NEWSPAPERS BARELY MENTIONED ANY OF THESE EVENTS, and even when they did, almost nobody paid attention, captivated as they were by seemingly more relevant stories about railroad rates, industrial accidents, local politics, crime, and scandal. If they focused on the West at all, journalists conjured rich mines and ranches and thriving cities with universities and opera houses in the largely empty new states of Montana, North and South Dakota, Idaho, and Wyoming, all admitted to the union during the previous year. In Chicago, organizers were scurrying to prepare for the World's Fair, a celebration of the 400th anniversary of Columbus's arrival in the New World. Nationwide, pulses rose over the political debates of the day—whether to raise tariffs to protect American manufacturing from foreign competition or lower them, and whether to abandon the gold standard. Even the impending decennial census was more exciting than Indians dancing strangely in the West.

Indeed, the census, which enumerated the nation's rapidly growing disparities and distinctions, provides what might be the best window on the growing anxieties of the age. Examining the public's preoccupation with the census in 1890 sheds light on why the citizens of such a rich and powerful country, who at first ignored the hopes for redemption among a few poor Indians, would soon resort to terrible violence to crush them.

Modern readers might find it hard to imagine so much public interest in an event as banal as the government's regular count of its people. But Americans were preoccupied with the census because they fully expected it to confirm their power and success. They knew their country was growing, and they wanted to know how much it had grown, and how fast. Would New York remain the only city with a million people? Would Chicago displace Philadelphia as the nation's second-largest city? How many villages of yesteryear had grown into cities of 100,000 or more? In 1880 the geographic center of the American population was Cincinnati. How far west had the center of the country moved?[10]

Such questions might have energized the population count in any year, but Americans of 1890 found them particularly compelling. A full century had passed since the first census, in 1790, the year after the US Constitution sealed the young republic and sent it forth into the community of nations. The growth in US power and treasure had been prodigious since then. Surely the results would be cause for celebration. "Our males of arms-bearing age will make every civilized nation bear to us a pigmy relation," predicted one patriot.[11]

And if the precise contours of the American dynamo remained uncertain, signs of American greatness abounded, not the least of them being the technology of the census itself. "It is likely," a breathless *New York Press* contributor predicted, that "the next census will be tabulated by electricity."[12]

Indeed, although enumerators would go door to door with pencil and paper, much as they always had, the numbers on the forms they submitted to headquarters in Washington would be processed very differently. Information about each individual would be transferred to cards, not in the form of ink but as a combination of holes created with a new device called a punch card machine. The brainchild of an engineer and former census worker named Herman Hollerith, the punch card machines would translate data to tens of millions of cards, one for each individual or family in the census, and to more cards for businesses and other entities.

But the cards themselves were mere auxiliaries to Hollerith's greatest invention, the mechanical wonder that would read the cards: the Hollerith Electrical Tabulating Machine. Standing at this contraption, which resembled an upright piano, a census worker inserted each card—the exact size of a dollar bill—into a press. As the worker lowered the top of the press onto the card, a set of 240 steel pins slid onto the stiff card paper. Those pins that encountered holes (rather than the card) slid through and into a pool of mercury in a basin beneath. The contact of the pin with mercury completed an electrical circuit, causing a counter on the machine, in whichever category the hole enumerated, to increase by one: race, age, national origin, mortgage debt, health, marital status, family size, and many more. Each time a pin touched mercury and closed a circuit, a single bell rang.

In this way, not only would the electrical tabulating machine clamorously total the details of American population and industry across dozens of categories for a population far bigger than had ever been measured in the United States, but it also promised to produce new orders of statistical data at a much higher rate. The 1880 census had taken almost ten years to tabulate. The 1890 census would take only four and a half, despite counting millions more people across far more metrics. "The apparatus works as unerringly as the mills of the Gods," wrote an enthusiastic commentator, "but beats them hollow as to speed."[13]

And indeed it seemed to work like a heavenly machine. By late June, about the time Lieutenant Robertson was transmitting the gospel of Porcupine to his superiors, the census operation on the third floor of the Inter-Ocean Building in Washington, DC, resembled "a very tidy and airy machine shop," as one visitor put it, "where nice-looking girls in cool white dresses are at work at the long rows of counting machines." The flurry of hands, the punching of keys, and the ringing of bells inspired one Michigan reporter to dubious verse:

> *Hear the Census with its bells*
> *Electric bells!*
> *What a world of work*
> *Their wild confusion tells*[14]

Indeed it was a "world of work." With its ranks of wage labor attending an information assembly line, the census resembled the industrial factories of the day. But while the census machinery was an expression of the ongoing Industrial Revolution, the census effort represented something more. That "tidy and airy machine shop" twenty feet above street level in downtown Washington that summer of 1890 was the birthing chamber for something radically new in human experience: the mass production of data.[15]

The implications of that development were hardly visible to the workers, to their supervisors, or even to Herman Hollerith. But they are to us, in the story of Hollerith's business. The electrical tabulating machine made Hollerith wealthy, and it became the foundation of his successful new enterprise, the Tabulating Machine Company. In years to come, this outfit produced reams of data for governments, railroads, and insurance companies. Hollerith sold the company in 1911, and the new owners ultimately changed its name to International Business Machines. We call it IBM.[16]

Americans in 1890, like Americans today, were prone to separating their technological wonders and modern problems from the rustic past, including the primitive gyrations of exotic people like Indians. Thus, little news was reported in the summer of 1890 about Indians, who were not just poor and remote but were also, as far as most Americans were concerned, people of the past and much diminished in numbers. (The census would record a total of not quite a quarter-million Indians in 1890.) Practically everybody assumed that the teeming mass of Americans (252 times as numerous) would any day now engulf Indian villages and usher the native peoples, finally, into oblivion.

THAT SEPTEMBER THE TABULATING MACHINES BEGAN TO PRODUCE their results, and by 1895, when the US Government Printing Office released the last of the census bulletins, Americans had learned that the nation's wealth and industry had indeed grown at impressive rates. The same railroad network that took Porcupine to the Messiah and back spanned some 163,000 miles of American earth in 1890—almost double the trackage of 1880 and more than triple that of 1870. American industry produced goods valued at almost $9.4 billion in 1890—almost 70 percent more than in 1880—and iron and steel production rose by more than 150 percent in the previous decade alone. And so it went: the census stacked up statistics like bullion in acres tilled, goods produced, and skyrocketing dollar values.[17]

But by the time most of the facts were known, the slumping American economy had dispirited the public almost beyond any ability to be inspired by such happy news. Even before that, in that summer of 1890, the shiny promise of the census had faded almost as quickly as newspapers published its initial findings. New Yorkers, residents of the biggest city, were certain that they had been undercounted by perhaps 100,000 people and soon demanded a recount. Philadelphians, Chicagoans, and other metropolitan residents made similar demands.[18]

The spat had wide ramifications. The census was the key yardstick for apportioning congressional representatives, and it was also the work of a temporary bureau staffed by political appointees. Census jobs went to acolytes of the ruling party, in this case Republican followers of President Benjamin Harrison. Democratic New York cried foul, and allegations of crass partisanship tarnished the gleaming image of the "light and airy machine shop."

Worse was still to come. In December, with the announcement of the nation's total population, charges of partisan bias gave way to cries of incompetence. Hollerith's machines counted just under 63 million Americans, dramatically fewer than authorities had predicted. As one wry observer remarked, the new number "sent into spasms of indignation a great many people who had made up their minds that the dignity of the Republic could only be supported on a total of 75 million."[19]

Although the populace had continued to expand—at a rate of 25 percent over the previous decade—Americans were accustomed to still faster growth. In tallies before the Civil War, populations had advanced by 33 percent or more. The new results suggested a slowdown so precipitous as to strain credulity. How could the population be growing at a slower pace than at any time since the bloody decade of Shiloh and Gettysburg? Americans had become more numerous than ever, they lived longer than their ancestors, they amassed more

wealth, and they produced so much more. How could they be reproducing less?[20]

MEANWHILE, IN THE WEST, DROUGHT HAD BAKED THE EARTH
bare. Indian reservations occupied poor land that had little game and
few wild plants of any use. In the withering heat, what grass was left
by cattle and sheep (most of them owned by white ranchers) quickly
shriveled. Scarce game vanished. By 1885, many Indians had turned
their hand to farming, but in 1890 their crops wilted. Starvation, that
old monster, circled the camps. It was thus not surprising that some
Indians had turned to a new faith, the savior announced by Porcupine and others across the Indian reservations of the interior West.
In doing so, Indian believers unwittingly launched upon a collision
course with the anxious American public.

What swept the West that summer was an evangelical revival that
synthesized ancient Indian beliefs with new millenarian teaching.
Strange stories made their way from neighbor to neighbor, from one
people to the next, stories of distant laughter on the breeze, dead
loved ones brought back to life, and an earth again made green and
bountiful. The believers claimed remarkable providences. A small
party started from Montana in search of the Messiah, heading first to
the camp of the famed Hunkpapa Sioux leader Sitting Bull in South
Dakota. Along the way, one of their number—Yellow Hawk—
announced that he would prove the resurrection prophecy. He committed suicide. When his friends arrived at Sitting Bull's compound,
there was Yellow Hawk, alive and happy. He had been carried to the
compound, he said, by the Messiah.[21]

Talk of resurrection extended to the earth itself. Bison hunting
had ceased by the early 1880s, for the animals were nearly extinct.
The only survivors of the great herds were living in Yellowstone National Park in Wyoming, on a few private ranches far to the south or
in Canada, and in zoos and traveling Wild West shows. But in 1890,
in the midst of the drought, a few of the shaggy beasts appeared
suddenly on one of the Sioux reservations in South Dakota. Had the

spirits returned their favor? How else could one explain this miraculous event?[22]

Stories like these spread among friends and acquaintances, raising unanswerable questions and inspiring new faith. And all that fall, Indians danced. They danced from the deep Southwest to the Canadian border and into Alberta. They danced from the Sierra Nevada to eastern Oklahoma. They danced in southern Utah, and in Idaho. They danced in Arizona.

In Nevada, a thousand Shoshones danced all night, and as the eastern sky turned pale shouts rang out that the spirits of deceased loved ones were appearing among the faithful. A thousand voices shouted in unison, "Christ has come!," and they fell to the ground, or perhaps to their knees, weeping and singing and utterly exhausted.[23]

Although many had dismissed the springtime talk of a messiah somewhere in the mountains of western Montana, the rumor seemed only to grow over time. From the Southwest to the Wind River Mountains of Wyoming and on into the plains of South Dakota, Indians spoke of a redeemer to the north—suspiciously close to where, back in the spring, the Cheyenne of Montana had placed him.[24]

By the fall of 1890, authorities who read the telegrams and heard the reports had become uneasy. Thirty Indian reservations were transfixed by the prophecies of the Messiah, but the teachings had a particularly enthusiastic following among the Lakota Sioux, also known as the Western Sioux. Because of the relatively recent history of US hostilities with these people—the notorious Sitting Bull was learning the new faith—it was there that government agents soon focused their attentions.

SIOUX DISCONTENT HAD MANY SOURCES—AND AN ODD connection to Hollerith's device 1,500 miles away. In 1889 the government had forced a new treaty on the Sioux, a successor to the 1877 treaty (which had been foisted on them by means so foul that the Supreme Court would invalidate it a century later). Under the terms of this new purported agreement, the Sioux gave up a vast tract of land in exchange for paltry payments of beef, flour, coffee, and sugar. But even these rations proved ephemeral. Within weeks, Congress, in a fit of economy, slashed appropriations for Sioux subsistence by 10 percent. The beef ration at Rosebud Reservation plummeted by 2 million pounds, and at Pine Ridge by 1 million.[25]

At the same moment, authorities, in a push to index rations more tightly to population, initiated a special census of Rosebud and Pine Ridge Reservations in 1889. Being counted had never sat well with Sioux people, who resisted it from the days when the first bands began to submit themselves to US Army authority in 1872. They invariably saw the process for what it was: an attempt to better confine and control them. Resistance to this new census was bitter. At Rosebud, Chief White Horse flat out refused to let his people be counted. The agent threw him in jail and withheld beef from his followers until he relented. When it was over, White Horse and the other critics were proved right: enumerators counted 2,000 fewer Sioux among the Brule (one of the seven Lakota tribes) than had been on the rolls. In April 1890, the inevitable result became clear: rations would be permanently lowered.[26]

The special census of 1889 was not directly related to the 1890 general census, but in its precision and its purpose—gathering data to inform policymaking—it expressed the same faith in tabulation as a path to benevolent, moral governance. And one of its effects was to prevent Sioux families from escaping poverty and near (if not outright) starvation.

Ever since 1890, scholars of these events have debated how militant the Sioux dancers were. Did they actually plan a war? In fact, to the dancers and even some officials on the scene, it was eminently clear that, to believers, the dance was a prayer for peace. The new religion barred them from violence, which threatened only when authorities (or other Indians) tried to prevent believers from dancing in what they saw as a direct attempt to prevent the fulfillment of prophecy.

It is almost impossible to overstate how vehement officials and other Americans eventually became over the need to break up the dances. Writers and scholars have spilled oceans of ink (and with this book, I add my share) exploring what made the Indians dance. They have largely overlooked an equally large mystery: after initially ignoring the dance, why did Americans come to care so much about it?

Indeed, even for a famously determined people, Americans' fixation on the dance seems peculiar. Few mistook it for a war dance. Indians were not massing for combat. Popular histories point to the special clothing that some dancers wore, the so-called ghost shirts. It is true that some of the Sioux believed these shirts to be bulletproof, and perhaps there were a few who fancied themselves redeemers-in-arms. But the ghost shirts appeared only among some dancers and only late in 1890, after the dance was already entrenched. Most followers of the new religion were apparently dressed in "Indian" clothing—leggings and moccasins for men and dresses for women— or, like other poor westerners, in faded dungarees or dresses and cotton shirts. They often painted their faces, but this practice was hardly unique to the Ghost Dance. To explain the discomfiture of officials we have to look elsewhere.[27]

Of all the features of the new ritual that garnered commentary, the physical excitement of the dancers received the most attention. The central feature of the Ghost Dance everywhere was a ring of people holding hands and turning in a clockwise direction—"men, women, and children; the strong and the robust, the weak consumptive, and those near to death's door," as one observer described them. Lakotas had grafted onto the Ghost Dance some symbols of their primary religious ritual, the Sun Dance. Thus, Sioux believers felled a tree, often a young cottonwood, and re-erected it at the center of their dance circle. On it they hung offerings to the spirits, including colored ribbons and sometimes an American flag. Near the tree stood the holy men, supervising the event and assembling the believers, who began by taking a seat in the circle around the tree. There was a prayer, and sometimes a sacred potion was passed for participants to drink. Then dancers might together utter "a sort of plaintive cry, which is pretty well calculated to arrest the ear of the sympathetic." Once these preliminaries were completed, the dancers rose and started singing—unaccompanied, without drums or other instruments—and the circle began to turn.[28]

Although other tribes' dancers rotated at a constant rate, among the Lakota and other Plains tribes they gradually picked up speed. "They would go as fast as they could, their hands moving from side to side, their bodies swaying, their arms, with hands gripped tightly in their neighbors', swinging back and forth with all their might." Those who stumbled were pulled upright by their neighbors.[29]

Before too long some individuals might collapse, often spectacularly. Some stumbled away from the circle, and some ran. Others high-stepped, pawing the air. An observer described a woman who burst out of the ring, her arms moving "wildly," her hair falling over her face, "which was purple, looking as if the blood would burst through." She "went down like a log," on her back, motionless and apparently unconscious, "but with every muscle twitching and quivering."[30]

The circling and singing continued for a time, sometimes until dozens of people had fallen unconscious in similar fashion. Then the singing stopped, and the dancers sat down in their circle and waited for the fallen to awaken. As they did, they were ushered to the center of the circle. There they related wondrous visions—of camps filled with long-gone family members feasting on fresh buffalo meat, of joyous reunions amid green hills and tumbling streams—and ceremonial leaders proclaimed these happy tidings to the assembled crowd.[31]

Astonished and disturbed by the enthusiasms of the ritual, some American witnesses were moved to dire warnings. One agent reported that the Indians favored "disobedience to all orders, and war if necessary to carry out their dance craze." "The Indians are dancing in the snow and are wild and crazy," hyperventilated the agent at Pine Ridge. Another denounced the actual dance as "exceedingly prejudicial" to the "physical welfare" of the Indians, who became exhausted by it. "I think, " the agent went on, "steps should be taken to stop it." Fearful that unconscious women might be molested, one white witness at Pine Ridge claimed that women "fall senseless to the ground, throwing their clothes over their heads, and laying bare the most prominent part of their bodies, viz., 'their butts' and 'things.'" Concluded still another, "The dance is indecent, demoralizing, and disgusting." If there was a "messiah craze," it was this unreasonable conviction that messiah dancing was a threat, and it was Americans, not the Sioux, who were afflicted.[32]

For these observers, the dance was a physical manifestation of irrationality, a refusal to be governed in body or in spirit by the codes of Victorian decorum handed down from missionaries. In one sense, at least, this view was substantially correct. For the Lakota and for other Indians, however, the Ghost Dance was both strikingly new—even radical—and reassuringly familiar. Ghost Dancers were searching for a new dispensation, seeking to restore an intimacy with the Creator that seemed to have vanished. And for followers, the religion's key attractions included the chance to worship in a form that reconstituted Indians as a community and expressed their history, families, and identity—in a word, their Indianness. The Ghost Dance invited believers, as one Sioux evangelist put it, to "be Indians" again.[33]

In many ways, the Ghost Dance bore little resemblance to older Lakota rituals. Dances in the old days segregated women and men. This new circle of dancers, holding hands across generational and gender divides, reconstituted the entire community in a single ceremony. It may have borrowed from Christian traditions. Lakotas had become increasingly familiar with Catholics, Episcopalians, and others during the 1880s as the number of churches on the reservations rapidly increased. The influence of these Christians may help explain the development of the messiah idea. Traditional Western Sioux religion is populated by a panoply of spirits, including Grandfather Buffalo, Sun, Elk, Bear, Rock, North Wind, and many others. But only one of these, White Buffalo Calf Woman, is an anthropomorphic figure. In a startling shift, Ghost Dancers added to these spirits both Christ, or the Messiah, and the Father—spirit presences who appeared as people.[34]

But if it was innovative, even radical in its break with convention, this dance came also from the Indian heart. Its earnest hymns and prayers to an Indian redeemer were inflected with visions of animal spirits and long-vanished family:

> *You shall see your grandfather*
> *The father says so*
> *You shall see your kindred*
> *The father says so*
>
> *It is your father coming, it is your father coming*
> *A spotted eagle is coming for you*
> *A spotted eagle is coming for you*
>
> *The Eagle has brought the message to the tribe*
> *The father says so, the father says so*
> *Over the whole earth they are coming*
> *The buffalo are coming, the buffalo are coming*
> *The Crow has brought the message to the tribe*
> *The father says so, the father says so*[35]

Why were Americans so frightened of singing and dancing? A vital clue lies in the invidious comparisons to which they subjected the Ghost Dance. One commentator, for example, thought it resembled a Methodist love feast; another called the ritual a "séance." Anxieties about the Ghost Dance shared key features with the American response to other unconventional religious practices, from ecstatic camp meetings to Spiritualism.[36]

The appeal of unconventional religion for increasing numbers of Americans stemmed partly from its promise of individual, authentic experience of the miraculous and the providential in an age of stifling rationalism. Contemporary science had distanced God from everyday life, as Charles Darwin unmoored age-old faith with his postulate that species—including people—were not made perfect but rather were continually changing through natural selection. A popular, derivative theory known as social Darwinism extended these arguments to society as a whole, presenting economic inequities as "natural" features of a competitive society, impervious to reform, and consigning the poor to irredeemable misery. Industrial forces seemed also to alienate Americans from spiritual experience and leave them at the mercy of machines and their elite owners and managers. An expanding technocracy, the mechanization of work, the loss of individual control over production, and a new economy of consumption all played a role in the rise of the "holiness movement" and spiritualism.[37]

Thus, influential revivals of "holy rollers" and holiness believers, replete with unorthodox behaviors, were contemporaneous with the Ghost Dance, and it is likely that some Ghost Dancers, including those recently returned from government boarding schools, were exposed to them. Perhaps chief among the outpourings of holiness sentiment in this period were the "trance revivals" of Maria Woodworth. The Ghost Dance spread eastward in the first half of 1889–1890 as if synchronized with the westward-moving wave of Woodworth's visionary faith healing that gripped the Midwest and California in the same period. A self-made, fire-and-brimstone revivalist preacher, Woodworth drew hundreds and even thousands of earnest seekers and curious passersby to her sermons. Many of these people fell into trances (which Woodworth said were manifestations of the Holy Ghost) for as long as several hours. Upon waking, they often related visions of heaven and hell in vivid color.[38]

These revivals, like many others, were not without controversy. Some critics expressed class suspicions of the overexcited "rabble," but it was gender anxieties that seemed to rise to the surface more often. Trance revivals inspired fears that bodily excesses such as spasms and fainting by young girls would leave them vulnerable to moral outrages on their unconscious bodies—the same anxiety that troubled some white observers of insensate female Ghost Dancers. In Oakland in January 1890 at one of Maria Woodworth's trance revival meetings—which drew upward of 8,000 people every night for months on end—a fourteen-year-old girl fell unconscious for at least four hours. When revivalists refused to allow her anxious uncle to carry her home, he returned with police and commandeered her still-somnolent body. Press accounts of the revivalists keeping a male relative from protecting the incapacitated body of a young girl enraged portions of the public. The next day crowds of antagonists who had assembled to denounce the "frauds" and "humbugs" flooded toward the tent. Believers (and the off-duty Oakland police hired by Woodworth to protect her flock) mounted a ferocious defense. The furious brawl ended only when a deputation of regular police arrived (having been summoned by the claxon of Oakland's first-ever riot alarm). The events reminded revivalists (as if they needed a reminder) of the volatility surrounding any gathering at the intersections of gender, bodily comportment, and charismatic religion.[39]

If the appearance of young white girls in the grip of charismatic faith was provocative for authorities and many members of the public, the news that Indians were similarly possessed threatened to unhinge public sentiment. Religious unorthodoxy combined with race, and in particular with Indianness, has perhaps always been an explosive mix. But in 1890, America's racial fears made public sentiment on such matters particularly volatile, owing at least as much to events in the East and Midwest as in the West. The most important was the radical diversification of American society, a trend that, already hard to miss, was made strikingly clear by the census. Back in 1881, as the United States was preparing to receive the Statue of Liberty from the people of France, a Russian-American poet named Emma Lazarus donated some new verse at an auction to raise funds for the monument's pedestal. Although her words would not be inscribed at the foot of the statue until after 1900 ("Give me your tired, your poor, your huddled masses yearning to breathe free"), apparently the world had already complied. In 1890 census enumerators turned up astoundingly large numbers of foreign-born immigrants. Almost 5.3 million new arrivals—fully one-third of the total number of immigrants to the United States since 1820—had arrived since 1880.[40]

Most alarming perhaps was the shift in the identities of the newcomers. Although most immigrants were former peasants, their American homes were overwhelmingly urban. Their origins were different too. Sometime around 1880, the mostly northern European arrivals at America's docks gave way to immigrants from eastern and southern Europe, including Poles, Italians, Slovaks, Czechs, Hungarians, and Russian Jews.

The conjunction of newspaper stories about recalcitrant Indians and the impossible-to-miss evidence of increasing numbers of immigrants left some white Americans convinced that their nation was being torn asunder. That very November, as newspaper reporters spun ever more lurid tales of whirling dances and conspiracies of red men, a book packed with forty photographs of New York's tenement districts appeared in city bookshops. *How the Other Half Lives* by the photographer and social reformer Jacob Riis advanced the case for better living conditions among the poor. But it also portrayed the dizzying complexity of the city and the alien, international society that occupied it. To Riis, the tenement districts constituted a frontier of savagery that rivaled the all-but-won West. For the Victorian middle-class public, the dark-skinned Italians, Jews, Chinese, and African Americans who stared out from the pages of Riis's book looked less like pitiful objects of charity, in their stark poverty, than a barbaric horde, possibly even the vanguard of a workers' revolution.[41]

Riis's book only underscored the sense of emergency that accompanied the census figures. In the view of one prominent statistician, the invasions that toppled Rome "were no more than a series of excursion parties" compared to the "rising flood of immigration" that now threatened the United States.[42]

The kaleidoscope of peoples gathering on America's shores might have been less worrying in a different context. The Civil War had sealed the union (again), but to many it seemed ready to split apart along lines of race and class. The rapid extension of industrial working conditions, the growing disparities between rich and poor, and repeated financial panics together would have made America a nation of widening social divisions and bitter labor unrest even without the surge in immigration that helped define the era. For a nation that still imagined itself to be a country of independent farmers, the last quarter of the nineteenth century brought an ugly confrontation with urban industrial working conditions. The aftershock of the financial panic of 1873 saw wage cuts and a spontaneous nationwide series of strikes by railroad workers in 1877. Thereafter, for three decades, tens of thousands of labor actions and company shutdowns would paralyze commerce, and pitched street battles between cudgel-swinging strikers and pistol-packing corporate guards would sometimes close whole city districts. In 1885, at a demonstration to support a strike at Cyrus McCormick's plant in Chicago's Haymarket Square, somebody threw a dynamite bomb into the ranks of police. Seven people died in the ensuing melee, and dozens were wounded.[43]

Growing radicalism, primarily in the form of the anarchist movement, swept up native-born and immigrant alike. Americans associated the most radical forces with foreigners in part because Irish, Germans, and other immigrants flocked to the nascent labor unions (although native-born Americans did too). In the wake of the Haymarket bombing, the national panic over foreign-born anarchists created America's first "red scare" and its first terrorist panic. Business elites and their middle-class supporters organized militias and built armories in many of the nation's cities.[44]

To a public convinced that organized laborers were exclusively foreign, the continuing flow of migrants was a terrifying specter. "Every steamship unloading upon our shores its motley horde of Germans, Bohemians, Hungarians, Poles, and Italians," warned one observer in 1887, "prepares the way for . . . [an] attempt at revolution."Another, bemoaning these "hordes of barbarians," concluded, "We are undergoing changes similar to those which have been the ruin of ancient peoples."[45]

American whites worried not only about changing immigrant populations but also about changes in themselves that might have left them unworthy of the task of subduing industrial labor. For instance, believing fervently in America's rural majority as the bulwark of republican virtues, many American whites were worried by the results of the census of 1890, which showed that fully one-third of the nation was now urban. If the trend continued (which it did), in another generation or so Americans would become a majority-urban people (which they did). White men might manage or even own the new factories, but increasingly they complained that their office jobs and white collars had alienated them from nature and sapped the innate racial energy that—in their minds—had once empowered their forebears to conquer most of North America.

Fixated on their own decline, the middle and upper classes—the managerial classes—claimed to be afflicted with an array of debilitating disorders stemming from "overcivilization." In 1868 the neurologist George Beard even diagnosed this condition: neurasthenia (literally, the lack of nerve strength) was a psychiatric malady whose symptoms included almost every imaginable anxiety: "fear of responsibility, of open places or closed places, fear of society, fear of being alone, fear of fears, fear of contamination, fear of everything." By the 1880s, his textbook on the subject was widely read and middle-class Americans were conversant with the notion that their conquest of the primitives had succeeded all too well. In the words of the good doctor, "The prime cause of modern nervousness is modern civilization with all its accompaniments."[46]

In Beard's reckoning, the "lack of nerve force" that characterized neurasthenics left them unable to "go through the process of reproducing the species." Neurasthenia was thus seen to have contributed to the declining American birth rate, and the 1890 census amplified the concern. If so many of the people counted in 1890 were new arrivals, that must mean that native-born Americans, the so-called old stock, were reproducing even more slowly than it seemed. Dire warnings about birth control as "race suicide" were not far behind.[47]

Although few recognized it at the time, such fears—along with the demographic trends that inspired them—were emerging elsewhere. All over the Western world, rates of population growth were slowing, to great consternation. Decrying the "systematic sterility" that seemed to have befallen "the French race," a census official in Paris surmised that "we can only derive consolation from the fact that all other civilised nations appear to be tending in the same direction." Defending himself against charges of manipulation and mismanagement, the director of the US census soberly observed that his counterparts in other countries had been likewise slandered. "The decades ending 1890–91 have been ominous ones for officials in charge of census work."[48]

Thus, the "electric census" limned a smaller, more crowded earth. In America's cities, the space between the world's peoples collapsed. Bohemians took up residence beside Irish, just up the street from African Americans and Chinese. In the West, the vanishing frontier made Americans even more covetous of Indian land. Native peoples grew more vulnerable to white and immigrant neighbors, like the Germans and Scandinavians who populated the Northern Plains and the heavily Irish and Anglo-American settlements of the Southwest. Regulations confined many Indians to reservations, and when they managed to leave to find work, they had to compete with the Chinese, Mexican, Czech, Greek, and Basque laborers who migrated from one payroll to the next between Sinaloa and Seattle, Los Angeles and Ottawa.

Even before 1890, the uncomfortable sense of being cheek by jowl with so many aliens had stoked the public commitment to erasing the differences between all these peoples. Through the late nineteenth century, reform movements were infused with a fierce public devotion to imposing sameness, to recasting the polyglot nation and recapturing a mythical past of social uniformity. Countless pamphlets and polemics by reactionary and reformer alike expressed the dream of creating "one great, free, common nationality" of people obedient to the same god and conversant in the same English. Such a people, it was thought, would idealize as one the capitalist economy, from which they would retreat nightly together to the detached homes where they sheltered families composed of monogamous parents embodying the same notions of manliness and womanhood to their children. A nation of disparate origins would be rendered equally patriotic and equally deferential to law and Anglo-American custom.[49]

The name for this policy of imposed sameness was "assimilation," and if it seems wrongheaded in retrospect, it is worth recalling that its advocates were seeking to guarantee the equal access of all peoples to the instruments of governance. In a democracy that threatened to split apart over racial and ethnic differences, erasing those differences seemed the only viable path to social harmony and greater equality of opportunity.[50]

But immigrants were only assimilation's newest subjects; Indians had been its first. Americans had been promising to gather Indians under the umbrella of the republic as full citizens at least since the Revolution. They had failed. As Cherokees and others learned all too well in the 1830s, citizenship was restricted to white men, and even when Indians assumed vestments of white "civilization" like private landownership, black slavery, and a plantation economy, their land was forfeit.[51]

After the Civil War, reformers energized by their success with the cause of abolition took up the challenge of the nation's persistent Indian conflicts. Offended by the violence of the Plains Indian Wars and scandalized by their bloody excesses, they settled on a series of radical reforms to bring Indians into the fold of civilization once and for all. The only way to do this, they calculated, was to make Indians just like white people. The reformers persuaded President Ulysses S. Grant to appoint Christian missionaries to administer Indian reservations. Through their representatives in Congress, they championed government policies to send Indian children away to boarding schools, end polygamous marriage, ban Indian ceremonies, and begin aggressively breaking up those same reservations on the grounds that communal property undermined the process of civilization. Before 1880, Indians owned 138 million acres of reservation land. By allotting parcels to make Indians into independent, freehold farmers and selling the remainder to settlers, the new policy would eventually strip away all but 48 million acres of the Indian estate.[52]

Indians were thus cast onto the anvil of assimilation, hammered by policies meant to make them free individuals in a laissez-faire economy, strip them of their customary beliefs, and break down their ties to land and one another.

THE REAL "MESSIAH CRAZE" OF 1890 WAS THE FIXATION OF Americans on Indian dancing and their relentless compulsion to stop

it, and the root of that craze was this American passion for assimilation, which was, after all, every bit as millennial a notion as the
Second Coming itself. What more utopian a dream could there be
for a rapidly globalizing society riven by fractures of race, culture, and
class than that a day would come when differences between people
had simply disappeared?

So it was that, in a show of hostility to physical exaltation reminiscent of the Puritans, policymakers waged war on Indian dances. In
1882 US Secretary of the Interior Henry M. Teller issued new orders
to suppress "heathenish dances, such as the sun dance, scalp dance,
&c.," in order to bring Indians into line with conventional Christian
practice.[53]

In the assimilationists' relentless quest for erasure of all social differences, Indian country had already become a kind of vast social
science laboratory, a testing ground for their (thus far unsuccessful)
attempts to scrub away racial and cultural distinctions. In 1887, Senator Henry L. Dawes puzzled over the public failure to resolve "the
Indian question." How could tens of millions of English-speaking
Americans, "a civilization that was otherwise irresistible," find themselves unable to answer the query, "What will you do with 300,000
Indians?" In 1890, finding an answer, given the increasing diversity
of American society, seemed more urgent than ever.[54]

The situation was all the more frustrating because it should have
been easy. Indians had practically no power. They held no citizenship
and remained federal subjects unable to vote. With no political representatives, they depended on appointed officials—reservation supervisors known as "Indian agents"—for their very survival. Dawes and
others believed that education, example, and compulsion could turn
Indians into good citizens. If Congress would mandate (and Indians
agents would follow) a stern policy of assimilation, surely it would
"kill the Indian and save the man," as one prominent assimilationist
put it. Thus would Indians enter the fold of the civilized, pointing the
way for millions of immigrants and African Americans and preparing
the ground for that glorious day when all dark skins would somehow
whiten and racial strife would vanish.[55]

For Americans, then, the challenge of assimilation was the great social question whirling at the center of the Ghost Dance of 1890. A millennial enthusiasm for assimilating others, as well as a deep anxiety that they might refuse to be assimilated, explains much of what made the Ghost Dance so troubling. To most white Americans, the dance itself was proof that assimilation had failed to dampen the savage impulse and that America's irresistible conquest might prove resistible after all. In this light, the dances in South Dakota were more than just dances, and more than another Indian uprising. For Americans, something more, much more, was on the line.

The dazzling technology of the census could not banish these dark shadows and lingering questions, even as the returns streamed in and the abstract columns of data flowed out of the census building all that summer and into the autumn. All that mass-produced information created a composite reflection of a society that Americans realized they knew both more about than ever before and yet too little. And all that fall, Indians danced to renew the earth and resurrect their ancestors.

The Ghost Dance and the census may seem unrelated—the one primitive, spiritual, and tragic, the other modern, technological, and practical—but there was a profound and troubling correspondence that hung about them. Indians danced to restore their populations at the very moment when the census breathed fears of population decline into the American air. The Ghost Dance messiah promised a new, larger earth for the restored Indian multitudes at the very moment when officials throughout the Western world were wondering why their populations were growing so slowly ("Where did all the people go?"). And Americans, as we shall see, were looking to expand arable lands and restore the abundance of a vanished frontier.

STILL, WELL INTO THE FALL OF 1890, GHOST DANCES WERE nothing more than a curiosity, titillating fare for newspaper readers in distant cities. Although the dances had increased in intensity early in the fall, officials on the scene were mostly unconcerned. As late as the first week of November, only one Indian agent in South

Dakota had requested military intervention; the others believed that the dance would die out of its own accord. Most local newspapers carried little to no news of the Ghost Dance.

But on November 13, President Harrison ordered the army into the Sioux reservations to shore up beleaguered officials and prevent "any outbreak that may put in peril the lives and homes of the settlers of the adjacent states." Since only one agent had requested military help, why Harrison sent the army remains something of a mystery. But given that settlers in the region had remained mostly calm, Harrison's concern probably stemmed in large part from the upheaval in national politics. Republican control of the US Senate hung by a thread. A South Dakota seat was being contested in an upcoming election, and its loss might tip the balance against the president's agenda in Congress. Sending in the army would be popular with settlers because large numbers of soldiers meant profits for local merchants and military contractors.[56]

Executing the president's order was the duty of General Nelson A. Miles, commander of the Division of the Missouri. Miles had made his name fighting Crazy Horse, the Lakota war leader who defeated Custer, and Chief Joseph, leader of the Nez Perce in their last valiant effort to secure freedom in 1877. Now he was an ambitious officer in a post–Indian War world. Initially, he counseled peace, urging patience with the Ghost Dancers. But the smell of opportunity soon overpowered him. He was anxious, even desperate, to prove that the western army still had a purpose and, his critics would say, to gin up a war that might earn him a third star or even launch a presidential bid. He began battling bureaucratic inertia and leaning on superiors to send in the troops. In the end he won. It was a victory he would come to regret.[57]

Eager to present the military as an irresistible force, he dispatched more troops than had gone after the Sioux when they whipped Custer and were actually a formidable adversary. With one-third of the entire US Army descending on some of the most remote and impoverished communities in the United States, the "Ghost Dance War" quickly became the largest military campaign since Lee's surrender at Appomattox.[58]

The arrival of columns of soldiers panicked the Indians and, in conjuring the possibility of war, terrified many settlers, who until that moment had not felt threatened. After treating the Ghost Dance mostly as a curiosity, the press now sank to new lows, riveting a considerable portion of the nation's 63 million people with stories about imminent "outbreaks" by bloodthirsty savages—never mind that fewer than a quarter of a million Indians remained in the United States, and only 18,000 of these were Lakota Sioux. Never mind that there were only about 4,200 Ghost Dancers, and that most of them were children, their mothers, and the very old. *The New York Times* quoted Miles's estimates of 15,000 "fighting Sioux," and others picked up rumors of an impending Sioux "outbreak." Some even reported that thousands of armed Indians had surrounded the reservation and killed settlers and soldiers.[59]

In mid-December, James McLaughlin, the agent at Standing Rock Reservation (some 275 miles north of Wounded Knee), sent the Indian police to arrest Sitting Bull, the most renowned Lakota chief still living. McLaughlin had long harbored a personal grudge against Sitting Bull. Now, since Sitting Bull had allowed Ghost Dances to take place at his camp, McLaughlin hoped to exploit the Ghost Dance tumult to have him removed from the reservation. When the detachment arrived at Sitting Bull's home at dawn on December 15 and took him into custody, however, some of Sitting Bull's enraged followers opened fire, and in the conflagration that followed the police shot the famed chief in the head and chest. The killing of Sitting Bull sent waves of panic and fear across the reservation, and when Lakota Indians there and at other reservations heard the news, they began to crisscross the countryside looking for refuge from the troops.[60]

So it was that on December 28 a starving band of Ghost Dancers who had fled their homes on Cheyenne River Reservation surrendered to Colonel James Forsyth's Seventh Cavalry at Wounded

Knee Creek. The next morning troops upended Sioux lodges in a hunt for weapons. Two soldiers were attempting to seize a weapon from a Lakota man when it discharged. No one was hurt, but it did not matter. The ranks of soldiers opened fire. With four rapid-fire Hotchkiss guns on the edges of the ravine, Custer's old regiment loosed an exploding shell nearly every second from each of the big guns—and a fusillade of rifle and pistol fire besides—into the mass of mostly unarmed villagers below. Indian men who were not instantly cut down did their best to fend off the troops with a few guns, some knives, rocks, and their bare hands as the ranks of women, children, and old people fled up the creek.

Among the Sioux men at Wounded Knee were a handful of the continent's most experienced close-range fighters, and when the conflict was over, the army did not emerge unscathed. The Seventh left the field with dozens of wounded, and thirty troopers died. The army took thirty-eight wounded Indians with them but left the Indian dead and more of their wounded to the mercy of the Dakota sky.

As night fell winter descended in all its high-country fury. Temperatures dropped far below freezing, and a fierce blizzard howled in from the north. Corpses turned to ice. When soldiers and a burial party returned three days later, they found several wounded Lakotas yet clinging to life and some surviving infants in the arms of their dead mothers. All but one of these babies and most of the others soon succumbed.[61]

Soldiers heaped wagons with the Indian dead, who looked eerily like the haunting plaster casts of the Pompeii victims of Mount Vesuvius, some having frozen in the grotesque positions in which they had hit the ground. Others were curled up or horribly twisted, their hands clawing at the air and mouths agape, each a memorial to the agony of open wounds, smothering cold, and the relentless triumph of death. A photographer arrived to take pictures (which immediately became a popular line of postcards).[62]

The gravediggers lowered the bodies of eighty-four men, forty-four women, and eighteen children into the ground. More had died, but many had been taken by kin or managed to leave the field before dying, perhaps in another camp, or alone on the darkling plain. We can look at old photographs, read crumpled letters, and scan columns of crumbling newspaper, but death is final and pitiless, and its tracks soon vanish. We cannot account for all who were killed at Wounded Knee.[63]

AMERICANS RESPONDED TO THE MASSACRE WITH A CONVENIENT ambivalence, cheering the alleged heroism of their troops while decrying the violence. Eighteen soldiers received Congressional Medals of Honor. The newspapers, predictably, turned against the slaughter that so many of them had helped to set in motion. The US Indian Service, a division of the Department of the Interior, gathered all the correspondence it could find to reconstruct the chain of events that had led up to the killings. General Miles, horrified that his showcase Indian war had gone wrong, ordered a court-martial of Colonel James Forsyth, the Wounded Knee commander. The army compiled more documents and testimony, including the eyewitness accounts of two Indians, before the court acquitted Forsyth. Miles ordered another court-martial, but Forsyth was soon returned to his command.[64]

Not quite a year after the calamity, another government agent arrived at Wounded Knee Creek to conduct another, quite different inquiry. He was a small man, only five-feet-four, with bright blue eyes and dark hair that flowed to his shoulders. He walked around the burial ground, which Lakota survivors had encircled with a simple post-and-wire fence. The corner posts were smeared with a dry red substance—sacred clay from the land of the prophet. When the Messiah returned to resurrect the dead, the victims of Wounded Knee would be first.[65]

A short distance away from the burial ground, the man carefully positioned a tripod and camera. Sighting through the viewer, he triggered the shutter.

Before finishing, he took another photograph of the killing field. Mourners or gravediggers had thrust stakes into the earth to mark each spot where a Sioux body fell, until the grassy bottomland bristled with markers of each life surrendered, like a field of spears.[66]

Pictures taken, the man packed up his camera and left.

His name was James Mooney, and he was an investigator from the US Bureau of Ethnology, a small office under the Department of the Interior, located at 1330 F Street in the nation's capital. The work of the office was testament to the nation's growing reliance on the social sciences, disciplines that, it was hoped, would allow the nation to grapple with many of the problems the census had revealed. The bureau, which had been in existence for only a little over ten years, employed a small group of anthropologists who sought to record and understand Indian societies, partly with the aim of better managing Indians and preventing conflict with and among them, and partly to better understand how to assimilate them into American society.

Unlike the other investigators who examined the violence at Wounded Knee, Mooney sought to explain the origins and meaning of the "messiah craze." What he eventually had to say about the Wounded Knee massacre—good work takes time and his report would not appear until 1896, a year after the last census report rolled off the press—would change the way government officials and the general public thought about the killings and much else besides. His study would initiate not only a new way of seeing the Ghost Dance that led up to the killings but also new ways of understanding Indians and every other people who did not share western European origins. To an unusual and perhaps unprecedented degree for a government report, Mooney's study would challenge assimilation policy. It would also mark a shift in the way Americans comprehended themselves and the place of religion in American life.

Mooney's insight that the Ghost Dance was a religion, not a "craze," opened up for him a world of Indian cosmology. After learning that the Ghost Dance had propagated on the Southern Plains alongside another new religion that involved the eating of peyote, he would begin a study of the Peyote Religion. The bold conclusions he reached about the need for religious freedom led him into confrontations with his superiors at the Bureau of Ethnology and with representatives in the halls of Congress. Mooney's investigation also kicked off a vigorous tradition of Ghost Dance scholarship that continues to the present day. Most notably, he was the first Ghost Dance scholar to trace the prophecies to their source, the visions of a Paiute ranch hand from the nation's most impoverished state.

For all the triumphalism of the census taker, for all the miles of railroad track and acres of wheat and mortgage debt, for all the frontier that was won, the American West of 1890 was hammered by drought and sagging under the failed dreams of its conquerors. The Ghost Dance prophet, as we shall see, stood not only at the center of an Indian community but at the heart of an American crisis. His religion was meant for Indians, but he also had something to offer Americans in general. Only when we understand the man who promulgated the prophecy and the broader crisis to which he spoke can we grasp what happened at Wounded Knee, how James Mooney and the nation responded to it, and what it meant for the dawn of the twentieth century.

CHAPTER 2

GREAT BASIN APOCALYPSE

I N THAT ANXIOUS FALL OF 1890, AMID THE CATARACT OF RUMOR and speculation that would soon sweep officials and the army to Wounded Knee and Lakota believers over the precipice, there was no greater mystery than the question of who originated the Ghost Dance. Theories abounded. One Indian agent said the teachings came from a Paiute in Utah named Pan-a-mite. Another announced that the Indian Christ was one "Bannock Jim" of Fort Hall, Idaho. "The astonishing thing about the business," remarked another official, "is the fact that all the Indians in the country seem to possess practically the same ideas and expect about the same result." Noting how similar the teachings were from one tribe to the next, he could only suspect that "some designing white man" was "at the bottom of the whole matter."[1]

This idea that a white mastermind had duped Indians into an uprising proved one of the most popular and tenacious of explanations for the Ghost Dance. Their cultural blinders made it impossible for many white people to credit Indians with authentic religion, or indeed with anything significant. If Indians were up to something big, whether a rebellion or a revival, it had to have been initiated by a white man.

This strange paranoia drew support from the curiously warm reception of the religion in Utah, where the rumors took a decidedly different form: the inspiration for the movement was not some imitator of Jesus, it was said, but Jesus himself. The timing was fortuitous, especially for those Mormons distressed by the recent, epochal decision of the church hierarchy to give in to federal pressure and abandon plural marriage. In 1843, Joseph Smith, the founder of the Church of Jesus Christ of Latter-Day Saints, had prophesied that when Jesus returned, he would appear first to the Indians and convert them to Mormonism. Smith had even forecast the date of this event—1890.[2]

Taken aback by the joyful reception of the Ghost Dance among Mormons living near Nevada, and recalling that Mormons had conspired with Indians to attack other white settlers in the Mountain Meadows Massacre of 1857, some influential voices speculated that the Mormon church had created the Ghost Dance as part of a larger conspiracy. Some Plains evangelists, including Porcupine, reported seeing white Ghost Dancers in Nevada. In actuality, the evangelists probably saw some of the scattered white settlers who joined Indian dances and celebrations—not just in 1890 but for decades after—without always realizing their ceremonial import. But General Nelson Miles read these reports, considered other clues, and then announced, "It is the Mormons who are the prime movers in all this." Others concurred. Even an educated Dakota Sioux was persuaded that "in my opinion this whole business is started or originated by the spies of missionaries of the Mormons."[3]

And yet, for all the certainty of General Miles and those who agreed with him about Mormon "spies," perhaps it was a sign of the nation's growing reliance on data collection that the first indication of the prophet's true identity came from the census. John Mayhugh, a special census agent, had been enumerating Nevada's inhabitants the previous summer when he met the prophet. That fall, in an effort to quell the wild surmisals he was reading in the newspapers, he put pen to paper and explained the whole matter to authorities.

According to Mayhugh, there was little intrigue about the seer's identity in his home country: "The prophet resides in Mason Valley, Esmeralda County Nevada close to the Walker River Reservation."

Many people knew him, and he was neither a white man nor a Mormon. An "intelligent, fine looking Indian of about 35 years of age," he was "known among all Indians by the Indian name of We-vo-kar and also Co-we-jo," and by whites as "Captain Jack Wilson." Surrounded by crowds of Indians, he would go "into trances or seemingly so from 12 to 14 hours." Upon waking, he would prophesy that Indians would soon gain "possession of the country," explaining that he had seen many Indians in heaven and that a messiah would soon arrive at Mount Grant, a sacred mountain. His teachings were peaceful: "He counsels the Indians not to disturb the white folks, saying that the blanket of rabbit skins that was put over the moon by the Indians long ago will soon fall off and then the moon which is now a fire will destroy the whites." To Mayhugh, as to many other white Nevadans, these prophecies were harmless superstitions. Concluded the census taker: "I think if the Indians are let alone at the various agencies the whole thing will die away."[4]

Perhaps the most surprising aspect of Mayhugh's report is its tone, which is simultaneously amused, fascinated, complimentary to the prophet (describing him as "intelligent" and "fine looking"), and not at all alarmed. Government investigators who followed Mayhugh's directions to the prophet's residence were prepared to find a malevolent charlatan or a scheming fraud, but even they ended up describing him in similar terms, noting his good looks and conviviality and adding that he was a "hard-working Indian" with "a reputation for industry and reliability."[5]

Mayhugh's report proved accurate in almost every detail, and if it did not stop the rumors of white renegades in Indian country, it did suggest how prominent the tall, broad, charismatic young prophet had become, even among Nevada settlers, by the time of the Ghost Dance troubles. Jack Wilson was a photogenic man: in numerous photographs he appears as a man of powerful build, often leaning slightly forward into the camera and wearing an enigmatic smile, a suggestion of the good humor for which he was renowned among Indians and settlers alike even before 1890. Ranchers appreciated not only his equanimity but his willingness to work, whether it was

FIGURE 2.1. Wovoka (Jack Wilson), ca. 1914. Milwaukee
Public Museum.

stringing barbed wire, clearing sagebrush, digging irrigation ditches,
or cutting and stacking hay. It is a telling fact that one of his names,
Wovoka (most likely a poor transliteration of Wykhotyhi), means
"cutter," reflecting his skill as a prodigiously hardworking woodcut-
ter who trafficked in firewood among the ranches and merchants of
Nevada. His English name was also associated with his work: Wilson was the surname of the ranch family for whom he worked from
childhood, alongside his father, Numu Taivo, and his mother, Tiya,
a domestic laborer in the Wilson home. Jack was the name bestowed
upon him by the ranch owner, David Wilson, whose Presbyterianism
may also have been important to the prophet's development.

A man of means as modest as Wovoka's seemed to Mayhugh and
other authorities an unlikely inspiration for a religious movement. But
people who knew him better, Indians and whites alike, acknowledged
that there had long been something peculiar about him. Beginning in

the mid-1880s, they heard him say strange things and exhibit curious powers. Indians said that he could make it rain, snow, or clear and that he could bring wind and fog. Many white people also ascribed to the ranch hand a peculiar ability to predict the weather. Years later, one local rancher remembered that Wovoka's ability to forecast storms proved so accurate that "I used him for a weathervane."[6]

Then his strange powers advanced into prophecy. By 1889, Jack Wilson was recounting a visit with God and the instructions given him to end his people's troubles and re-create the earth. A group of visiting Bannock Indians picked up the word and took it back to their reservation in Idaho, and so began the meetings, letters, whispered stories, and telegrams that would carry the news far and wide, until believers whirled the sacred circle from Nevada to New Mexico and from Oklahoma to Saskatchewan.

WOVOKA'S HOME WAS IN THE DRIEST OF AMERICA'S STATES, AND it was a fitting place for the Ghost Dance to originate. All the reservations where his teachings took hold were located west of the 100th meridian, the line that forms the eastern boundary of the Texas panhandle and, extended north to Canada, would mark the boundary between the relatively well-watered eastern prairies—lands that receive sufficient rain for farming—and the drier lands that stretch west, where less rain falls and crops usually fail without irrigation.

In the mid-nineteenth century, the arid Great Plains grew not only buffalo grass but the verdant visions of boosters who imagined transforming it into a thriving landscape of farms and small towns. In the decades after the Civil War, however, more and more Plains farmers had to surrender to the climate. The unsuitability of the region for agriculture was one reason settlers acquiesced to placing Indian reservations there: the Lakota reservations, home to so many fervent believers, sat mostly just to the west of the 100th meridian. Westward, as the meridian numbers increased, more believers could be found as the terrain grew drier still.

The Great Plains slope gradually upward for about 400 miles to the Continental Divide. Another 200 miles west of the Divide in Utah and southern Idaho the land plummets down the steep face of the Rocky Mountains and into the Great Basin, which stretches 400 miles between the Wasatch Front on its eastern edge and the Sierra Nevada to the west. At the foot of the Wasatch lies the Great Salt Lake, a body of water more salty than the ocean. Beyond the lake lies a vast, silent desert, an austere landscape that makes the arid plains seem positively bountiful. Indeed, if the Great Plains tested American dreams of conquest and empire, this was the place that shattered them.

Between 1860 and 1890, the precipitous rise and equally sudden collapse of American settlement and modern industry would turn this sagebrush desert upside down and bring on what we might call a cross-cultural crisis of authority: in different ways, both Americans and Indians were confounded by the unruly, unpredictable economy of the new settlements. Both peoples struggled to create new kinds of specialists, new cultural brokers with the know-how to manage the radically unsettling effects of American expansion. Thus, most of the basin's western half became the state of Nevada in 1864. A few decades later the Americans designated much of it national forest, turning the area into a kind of laboratory for modern ideas of social science and managed development. Among Indians, this crisis of authority helps to explain how Jack Wilson's development of an older prophetic movement took hold in the late 1880s as he struggled to reformulate Indian religion. Although Wilson's aims were otherworldly, a quest for redemption and spiritual salvation, one effect of his teachings was to offer Paiutes and other Indians a path into the modern world and modern success—on Indian terms.[7]

Today the remote deserts between the Sierra Nevada and the Rocky Mountains are connected to the global economy by highways and electrical wiring and sporadic microwave telecommunications. These were preceded by other, more tenuous connections: wagon roads, railroad tracks, and telegraph wires, all of which bound this region to a different but no less global economy by the time of Wounded Knee. Through the power of the state and the ties of commerce—notably the gold and silver that flowed out of Nevada to lubricate the explosive capitalism of the Gilded Age—this homeland to dozens of Indian peoples was integrated into a more or less coherent region called the American West.

A stranger and more perilous place for Indians could hardly be imagined. New market connections had changed the land in ways that unsettled the balance of spirit and substance undergirding Indian economy and cosmology. Driven to desperate new measures by these changes, Indians had come to rely on the wage work they found in the American settlements. Indeed, they could not survive without it. In this long-overlooked fact about their circumstances we find a vital clue to the meaning of the Ghost Dance visions for believers and for American history.[8]

Indians were not alone in their travail: by the time Jack Wilson's visions began to circulate beyond the Great Basin, both settlers and Indians were in crisis in the American West. This context is critical to understanding the deeper meaning of the Ghost Dance prophecies. Jack Wilson was looking for a way out of the emergency that by 1890 had overtaken not only his people and his homeland but the entire West—a vast, dry land where the ever-expanding American nation seemed on the verge of retreat.

AMERICANS AND INDIANS PROPOSED RADICALLY DIFFERENT solutions to their mutual problems, but each people was influenced by the other. The Ghost Dance would become a primary lens through which Americans came to know Indians and to think about religion and modernity, while American visions would prove instrumental to Indians in shaping the new religion.

At least since the founding of Plymouth Plantation, English settlers had seen the colonization of North America as a sacred project commanded by God—the redemption of the garden from the wilderness. With the creation of the United States, American nationalism layered still more meanings on top of this sacred project. After 1848, when they wrenched the Great Basin away from Mexico and brought it within the national border, Americans were eager to add the sandy sagebrush country to the national story of savage wilderness being turned into yeoman farms in a republic of virtue.

According to this narrative, some version of which most Americans subscribed to, wildernesses like the desert, populated by savages, were destined to become fertile farmland for white Christians. When that transformation was complete—when the verdant farms of Christian Americans had reclaimed the plains and deserts from the Atlantic to the Pacific—then history would end. Some thought that Jesus would return at that point. Others believed that the world thus perfected would become the true and only heaven.[9]

That so many Indians across so much western space were captivated by the Ghost Dance, a millenarian religion, has everything to do with the calamitous failure of this equally millenarian American vision of western conquest. The religion that met with such violence at Wounded Knee emerged from a yawning chasm between American ideals and the complexities of North American nature and peoples. Militarily defeated, terribly impoverished, and socially marginalized, Indians had little choice but to invest themselves in the dreams of their conquerors. When those dreams failed too, they were more vulnerable than ever. The Ghost Dance of 1890 emerged in part as a prayer for deliverance not only from poverty and hunger but also from the wreckage of the American faith in perpetual progress—a faith that had been briefly adopted by Indians too.

To see how it all came to pass, let us begin with the Great Basin and the people of Jack Wilson.

To most who encounter it, the Great Basin—a desert bigger than France that encompasses one-sixth of the area of the forty-eight contiguous states—is a void. The basin is the most arid and least populous of America's physiographic regions. On its western edge lies Death Valley, its most famous landscape and in some ways its most exemplary: extremely dry and thinly populated, the valley alternates between baking heat and subfreezing cold. Throughout the Great Basin, the scarcity of water makes the development of cities impossible. Visitors seldom tarry. Haunted by the bone-dry land and dreaming of journey's end, they race along fast-track highways to air-conditioned rooms and swimming pools in the oases at the basin's edge in Salt Lake City, Reno, Boise, or Las Vegas. If dryness is the West's defining characteristic, then the Great Basin is the nation's most western place.[10]

The "arid West" might be considered a single region, but within its boundaries rainfall varies considerably. The Plains region stretches out in the rain shadow of the towering Rockies on its western border, while the Great Basin lies in a gigantic rain shadow cast by the even taller Sierra Nevada, the huge mountain range at its western edge. The high Sierras block virtually all Pacific moisture, leaving the basin even drier than the Plains. Tilting from north to south, the basin is warmest at its southern reaches, in Death Valley, where summer temperatures can exceed 120 degrees. In winter, its northern parts—the belt that runs through northern Nevada and northern Utah—can plunge far below zero. With scarce rainfall—less than six inches a year—it is a region defined by absences: of arable land, of people, of vegetation, and most critically of water. A visitor standing alone on the sagebrush plain can hear what also defines this place: Stillness. Silence.[11]

But the quiet is deceptive. The Great Basin sits atop tectonic plates in constant motion: in the years since the birth of the Ghost Dance prophet, Salt Lake City has moved several feet away from Reno. The crust of the earth stretches taut here, like a drum, allowing the release of tremendous pressure from the magma deep within the earth and pushing up blocks of crust that, over millennia, have formed hundreds of mountain ranges, with troughs of desert between them. These mountains rise in a north-south direction, like so many longitudinal islands in a sea of sagebrush. They are biological "islands" as well, home to deer, elk, and bighorn sheep, even mink and otters, with flowering summertime meadows in the midst of forests of piñon and juniper. Soaring thousands of feet from the desert floor, the mountains capture snow from passing clouds, and the melt trickles into streams that pour down their shoulders. On the very highest peaks grow the gnarled trunks of the bristlecone pine, among the world's oldest living things. The Great Basin is not one basin but many adjoining ones, large and small, nestled between these towering peaks.[12]

Of all its absences, the most peculiar one inspired its name, bestowed by the explorer John C. Frémont. The rivers of the Great Basin run into lowland lakes and marshes but, unlike anywhere else in North America, have no outlet to the sea. In Utah, on the eastern edge of the basin, streams flow out of the Rockies into the Great Salt Lake. In Nevada, on the western edge, the melting snows of the high mountains drain into the Humboldt, the Quinn, the Walker, the Carson, and the Truckee Rivers and collect in the desert before vanishing into thin clear air. Early explorers followed these rivers in hopes of reaching the Pacific or the Gulf of Mexico, only to end up beside reedy, saline pools in the baking sands.

Over millennia, the basin has at times been wetter or drier. Sometimes parts of it were submerged beneath a single body of water—called Lake Lahontan by geologists—that stretched across 8,284 square miles. Ghostly traces of this lake remain in the watermarks that still score the mountainsides and in relict bodies of water that endure in far-flung parts of the basin. All rivers carry salt eroded from the earth, making the oceans into which most of them empty saltier over time; the basin lakes, having no outlet, have also condensed salt over the millennia. Pyramid Lake and Walker Lake in Nevada and the Great Salt Lake in Utah are all like small seas: they retain salt as the water evaporates. Consequently, their waters are briny and not fit to drink.[13]

Visitors are alternately bored and terrified by the weird landscape of the Great Basin. The fear is well founded. More than any other place in North America, the basin challenged nineteenth-century American assumptions about progress and civilization, calling into question core beliefs about American exceptionalism and godly providence. The basin was a sinkhole for happy visions of frontier progress. Both practitioners of science and exponents of spirit sought desperately to repair that hole, or at least to reconcile it to the expanding agrarian nation.

ALTHOUGH MUCH OF THE GREAT BASIN WAS SPANISH OR Mexican territory until 1846, it remained largely unexplored by the

governments of those countries. Mexican traders opened a trail along
its southern boundary in 1830, linking the seaside village of Los Angeles with Santa Fe in northern New Mexico. But its deserts remained terrifying *jornadas del muerto*—journeys of death—to the few
outsiders who knew them at all.

Plains Indians of Porcupine's generation occasionally visited the
eastern fringes of the Great Basin through the 1870s as they traded
and warred with Shoshones and Utes, who came from the region.
But the first American travelers there were the so-called mountain
men—fur trappers seeking beaver pelts who were illegal immigrants
in this nominally Mexican province in the 1820s and 1830s. They
negotiated the low-lying routes on their way to the Pacific coast,
bypassing the verdant mountain slopes. They reacted with dismay,
even horror, to the desert and its salty lakes. In 1827 the fur trapper
Jedediah Smith, in two sentences, described the basin three times
as "extremely barren," a "desolate waste," and a "sand barren plain."
Frémont, who mapped the region for the US Army, was awed by its
foreboding silence in 1844: "Sterility . . . is the absolute characteristic
of the valleys . . . no wood, no water, no grass."[14]

So, too, with the emigrants who steered their wagons across the
basin en route to green Oregon or golden California. "The whole
country appeared so dreary and dismal, so forsaken and cursed of
the Almighty, that it reminded me every day of the curse pronounced
against Babylon." The "poorest and most worthless country that man
ever saw, a barren, worthless, valueless, d——d mean God forsaken
country." Or perhaps not exactly "God forsaken," "for He never had
anything to do with it." The landscape seemed to personally affront
its visitors. "A strange, weird land," wrote an 1869 observer. One
hundred years later, the judgments were scarcely less damning: "Geographic purgatory."[15]

TO AMERICANS, THE LANDSCAPE'S APPEARANCE WAS ONLY ONE OF
its drawbacks. Besides being sparse, parched, hungry, barren, vast,
and at the mercy of relentless sun, it also projected strange appari-
tions. The wind rose without warning, a hiss in the sagebrush and

sand in the eyes. It whipped dust into funnel shapes that danced across the desert floor like mini-tornadoes. Often, the blue sky reflected off the dry lake beds where the waters of long-vanished Lahontan once shimmered, creating spectacular, cool mirages that beckoned the thirsty, who moaned in desperation when they approached these phantom lakes only to see them vanish. Meanwhile, a cloudburst miles away could fill desert washes with an angry tide that boiled downhill. For pilgrims crossing this earthly hell, a sizzling summer day could come to a calamitous end in a galloping wall of water, sand, and rock.

Americans were thus stunned to find that in this place that "forbids the support of animals of every description"—a wilderness so forsaken that God could not have made it and where making a home was unimaginable—there were people. "I do not believe that we passed a single day without seeing Indians," wrote the fur trapper Zenas Leonard, "or fresh signs [of them], and some days hundreds of them."[16]

Indeed, a great many people lived in small groups in the oddest places. "Dispersed in single families," wrote Frémont, "without firearms; eating seeds and insects; digging roots." They had few if any horses. They were often naked. That so many lived in a place so poor was incomprehensible to American visitors, one of whom called them "the most miserable, if not the most degraded, beings of all the vast American wilderness."[17]

Although all these observers believed these remote Indians to be consummate primitives, untouched by European colonialism, the poverty they described was partly the result of decades of European slave raiding. After Spanish conquistadores founded Santa Fe in the future state of New Mexico in 1609, the Spanish and Mexican demand for Indian slaves drove a vigorous trade in captives across the Southwest. By 1700, mounted Indian raiders were driving deep into the basin for chattel to sell in Santa Fe, and the near-constant state of war resulting from the slave trade had scattered and impoverished many communities. In the 1830s, the opening of trails between Santa Fe and Los Angeles increased the commerce in Indian children, especially among Southern Paiutes from Utah and southern Nevada.[18]

Slavery continued to trouble the Great Basin peoples into the 1850s. By then, however, Indians of Nevada were reeling from a series of other calamities. It was among these people that visions of a new earth for Indians first took hold.

THE FIRST GHOST DANCES BEGAN AMONG COMMUNITIES OF Northern Paiutes living close inside the rain shadow of the sawtooth Sierra Nevada, on the western side of the Great Basin, where the Walker River flows eastward out of the mountains and into the desert. Near the headwaters, the river has two tributaries. The West Walker pours out of the mountains about sixty miles south of Reno and rolls through Smith Valley. Twenty miles farther south, the East Walker tumbles down the steep Sierra slopes, through the California town of Bridgeport and past the Pine Grove Hills. These two tributaries flow north and east into the basin, joining some thirty miles into the desert at Mason Valley, near the town of Yerington. From here the river curves east like a scythe, coursing another fifty miles or so, first north and then south onto the desert floor, before pooling in Walker Lake at the foot of towering Mount Grant. There, invisibly, the water rises into the blue vault of sky.[19]

Center stage for the events of 1890 was upriver from the lake, just south of the rivers' confluence, where the West Walker flows through Wilson Canyon, a series of low volcanic mountains and dramatic cliffs, before entering Mason Valley. Here it traverses a flatland beneath spreading cottonwood trees where emigrants from Missouri, the David Wilson family, staked their claim in the early 1860s.

This small piece of Nevada, from the split in the mountain to the flatlands that border the river, is in many ways a sacred space. Around it swirl stories of Wovoka and his great power. Perhaps none of them is more telling than the story of the day, more than twenty years after Wounded Knee, when he became a healer. He had been performing miracles for decades, but only then did he make the sacred journey required of men and women who sought to become shamans—or as his people called them, doctors. Sometime around 1912, after his father died, he entered a sacred cave to the north. There he communed

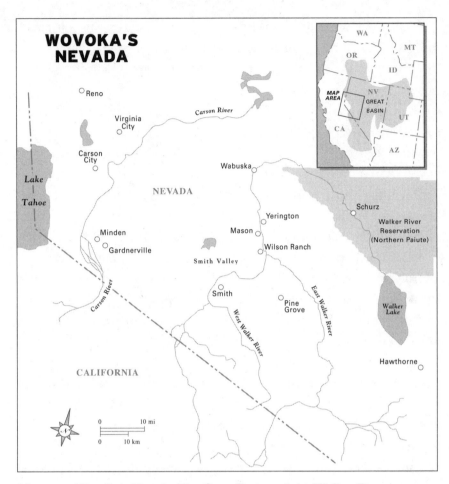

MAP 2.1. Wovoka's Nevada: The Great Basin and the Walker River

with spirits for an entire night. Only a person with the strongest character and purest heart could endure such an ordeal, for in caves the spirits approach. Alone in the darkness for hour after hour, he heard the singing of animals, the singing of clouds and thunder, the singing of ghosts. After hearing and learning the ritual songs that invoke the powers of the singing spirits, he could not refuse to become a doctor, for to do so would be to decline the spirits' gift, a gross insult that brings illness or death to the seeker.[20]

Having completed his all-night ordeal, Wovoka stepped out of the cave as the sun rose and mounted a white horse. As he rode down the hill the animal lifted into the air. Like Thunder, the spirit who rode a white horse to the heavens and brought the rain, Jack Wilson flew through the sky over the flatland all the way to Wilson Canyon, where the water rushed through.[21]

During this aerial journey the visionary passed over the land where he grew up working for the Wilson family and where it was said he convened the first dances inspired by his visions in 1889. Just as a river embodies a confluence of mountain streams, this land was emblematic of the convergence of work and spirit, labor and cosmic power, embodied in Jack Wilson. These attributes were Northern Paiute ideals that found expression in his Ghost Dance teachings, which spread up and down this river valley and ultimately far beyond.

Pilgrims have been coming to this site for a long time, at least since Porcupine crossed the sagebrush plain by wagon and train, and still they come. Some leave offerings—strands of ribbon, feathers, tobacco—out of respect for the prophet and his visions. It seems a fitting destination for seekers. After a hard, dry journey, few places on earth could have seemed more beautiful. On a hot day here on the old Wilson Ranch in the shade of the cottonwood trees, the rushing current sounds like music, and the canopy of leaves gives shelter from the unrelenting sky.

And yet, its natural beauty and association with Jack Wilson cannot completely explain why the Walker River became the origin point for all that happened there. This river birthed not only Wovoka's 1890 Ghost Dance but also its progenitor, an earlier, lesser-known prophecy. Not one but two successive waves of religious reform emanated from this valley to rock the Great Basin and the entire West. Like the people who occupied the banks of the Jordan River two millennia earlier, the small, isolated fishing communities of Walker River suddenly began to produce a series of prophets around 1870. Jack Wilson and his Ghost Dance of 1890 were the culmination of a generation of religious upheaval that would make the banks of a small river in the vast, ancient desert an Indian Holy Land.

CHAPTER 3

THE BIRTH OF THE PROPHET

Wovoka was born in 1856 near the banks of the Walker River in what is now western Nevada. His parents were Northern Paiutes, who call themselves Numu, the People. Paiute origin stories teach that the first Numu, "Our Father," emerged when this land was covered by a giant lake and the mountain peaks were like islands, and that Paiutes acquired fire on the island that is now the summit of Mount Grant. Indeed, archaeologists believe that this land first began to be occupied as Lake Lahontan was receding. When people arrived is a matter of some debate, but it may be that their original homeland was in Death Valley and that these forebears spoke what is termed a Shoshonean or Numic language (ancestor to the language still spoken by some Numu).[1]

As the landscape dried the people dispersed. As early as 4,000 years ago, and certainly by 1,000 years ago, they were spreading eastward across the desert to avoid exhausting its diminishing water and the ever-scarcer plants, game, and fish. Thus, the people of this region have always been not only few in number but far-flung. The desert slopes of western Nevada are crisscrossed with drive fences for the hunting of antelope, ornamented with petroglyphs on basalt boulders, and sprinkled with detritus from the manufacture of knives, spear points, and arrowheads. These flakes of stone glitter in the afternoon sun, silent witnesses to millennia of work and family.[2]

In time some of these Numic-speakers left the Great Basin and had the tribal identities imposed upon them that appear in history books. From eastern Nevada up into Oregon, Idaho, and Wyoming, some became the nomadic hunters and fishers called Shoshones. After Shoshones acquired horses from Spanish herds to the south, they became formidable horsemen and expanded their territory onto the Northern Plains. The Numic-speaking Utes also hunted and gathered and took to horseback, venturing east into today's Utah and out of the Great Basin into Colorado. Other Numic-speakers joined forces with Shoshones in southern Idaho and became known as the Bannock. One group of Numic-speakers broke away from the Shoshones to venture south and still farther east, leaving the Great Basin to become lords of the Southern Plains, the Comanches.

Though sometimes allied, these peoples also sometimes made war against one another. Utes contested Comanche dominance on the southern buffalo grounds, and they also abducted Paiutes for sale in the slave markets of Santa Fe. Nonetheless, the Paiutes and their Numic kin spread their beliefs and religious practices over one of the largest regions controlled by any single language group in the future United States. With their common origins and common language, many of these groups could speak to one another despite vernacular differences. The so-called Numic conquest of the Great Basin and adjoining areas is one of the most significant developments in the history of Indian America. When the 1890 Ghost Dance first began to spread, it moved eastward among Numic-speakers, from its origins on Walker River to the lands of the Bannock, Shoshone, and Ute, and eventually even to the Comanche living, by that time, on a reservation in Oklahoma.[3]

All the Numic peoples were nomadic, and the mounted Great Plains peoples inspired some admiration among Americans. In contrast, those who remained in the Great Basin became targets of derision, and even today most Americans know little or nothing about them. Where buffalo hunters on horseback seemed picturesque, Paiutes seldom hunted big game—it was scarce in the deserts—and they had few horses because there was too little grass to feed them. Because their survival in the desert required a stripped-down material culture, with few belongings, many white observers concluded that the Paiutes were intellectually inferior not only to Americans but even to other Indians. In reality, the peoples of the Great Basin were tremendously innovative, conjuring not only survival but often abundance from the most nutritionally desolate landscape in North America.

JUST AS JACK WILSON RETURNED TO THE RIVER AFTER HIS NIGHT in the cave, so Northern Paiutes continually returned to the rivers and lakes across western Nevada. The name "Paiute," bestowed on them by neighbors, comes from *pah,* the Shoshonean word for "water"; "Pah-Utes" were the Water Utes. Even now the map is sprinkled with the names of the streams or seeping springs where they gathered: Tonopah, Ivanpah, Pahranagat, Pahrump.[4]

However far afield Numu ventured for bunch grass or antelope, home was near the river and its terminal lake or marsh. Along the Walker River and the shores of Walker Lake in, say, 1830, before the American arrival, Numu flourished with an economy that was small in scale and remarkably resilient. They lived much of the time in small kin groups—"dispersed in single families," in Frémont's words—that usually numbered no more than six people. A few kin groups had as many as twelve members but seldom more than that because larger groups found it harder to gather enough food from the arid surroundings. Annual festivals and communal rabbit hunts or celebrations might draw more people together temporarily, but small communities were the order of the day. Family relations created the bonds between many of these otherwise dispersed people, and so anthropologists speak less in terms of Paiute "bands" or "villages" than of extended families, or "outfits." Each outfit was led by a senior man, and there was no central chiefdom. Making their own decisions and congregating or dispersing as the occasion demanded, Paiute outfits were a supple form of social organization, capable of relocating as needed in response to food shortage or abundance, war, or drought.[5]

As late as 1890, at least three distinctive Paiute communities, comprising a number of outfits, made their homes on Walker River. Each community was named after a major source of their food, not to point to differences between their diet and that of others (it is fair to say all ate similar food), but rather to distinguish one group from another according to slight regional variations in food. At the south end of Walker Lake lived the Pugwi Dicutta, the Fish Eaters. At the north end of the lake, where the river mouth emptied into Walker Lake, were the Agai Dicutta, the Trout Eaters. And upriver from them, where the river curved north through Smith and Mason Valleys before heading south to the lake, were the people of Jack Wilson, the Taboose Dicutta, the Grass Bulb Eaters.[6]

One reason for the rise of the Ghost Dance was the failure of the old ways—on which centuries of Paiute autonomy before the American conquest had been based—to provide a living for the outfits in the American age. In the middle of the nineteenth century, before the digging of hundreds of ditches to divert the waters of Walker River to fields and pastures, the crystalline blue of Walker Lake covered 69,000 acres, more than twice its size today, and the lake was 140 feet higher too. As a remnant of long-vanished Lake Lahontan, it was home to creatures that evolved there, notably the Lahontan cutthroat trout. Paiutes called the lake Agai Pah, or Trout Water, after the large schools of trout that made their way out of the lake and 100 miles up the Walker River to spawn each spring in the sweet streams of the Sierra Nevada, like salmon leaving a desert sea.[7]

The Numu year began in January and February when small numbers of fish began the journey up the river. Using weirs and fishing platforms they had built from willow, Paiute men hooked and netted the trout, some of them four feet long, hauling them onto the riverbanks where their spotted red sides writhed and glistened in the sun. In mid-February, Numu caught ground squirrels by smoking them out from their burrows, then roasted them on beds of hot coals. As the season warmed in March great flocks of Canada geese, mallards, pintails, and canvasbacks returned to Walker Lake from points south. Men and boys hunted waterfowl along the shore, collected eggs from nests, and netted ducks and mudhens, while women and other children gathered up desert candle and the carved-seed plants from the land that, having soaked up the snowmelt and winter rain, was now turning a bright, evanescent shade of green.[8]

By May, the primary trout run was on as thousands of trout made their way from the lake into the river. Paiutes gathered along the banks, catching the fish, roasting and drying their flesh, and meeting for the great feast that punctuated this happy season.

In June, women ventured out to gather various seeds ripening in the desert. Stripping the heads of wild grass between two sticks tied together like scissors, they threw the seed over their heads into winnowing baskets on their backs. The women gathered mustard and mentzelia, and some walked as far as fifty miles to glean the berries of the desert-thorn. In this season, men trapped squirrels or birds for meat.[9]

Like hunters and gatherers the world over, Paiute people shaped the landscape to produce what they needed. Their practice of burning old stands of brush to encourage new growth and broadcasting seed on the burned-over lands to boost food supplies made Walker River into more of a garden than a wilderness. These communal efforts even extended to irrigation projects. The Taboose Dicutta diverted streams into meadows to enhance wild plant growth, excavating communal ditches two and three miles long to water stands of *taboose* (nut grass, a kind of lily sometimes called earth almond), *pozeeda* (wild clover, eaten raw or boiled), and *mahaveeta* (an oval-shaped wild onion the size of a cherry that tastes like yam when roasted and whose spears of grass taste like a mild, nutty garlic).[10]

Tending these semi-domesticated patches of seeds and food was part of the seasonal round. In July, the Indian rice grass ripened, and the golden pollen of cattails could be baked into cakes. In August, families hid from the scorching sun in the shade of the buckberry groves in the river bottoms, where women thumped bright red berries into their winnowing baskets with long poles and men and boys hunted the robins and cottontails that fluttered and rustled in the brush.

But perhaps the most important of the wild foods was the pine nut, which fattened in the cones of the piñon tree and drew Paiutes upriver to the mountains as summer ended. After scouts had located the most productive groves in August, the whole community started moving slowly up the mountain slopes to gather cones when the pine nuts were ready—about the time the wild rose hips turned red. While some of the men hunted for squirrels and sage hens, the Numu carried the cones back to camp, cleaned out the nuts, and sometimes roasted them and ground them to a buttery paste.[11]

In November, the men might leave the mountains for the rabbit drive. The rabbit hunt captain selected a campsite in the lowlands and built a large fire for several nights in a row to call the dispersed hunters. Between bushes and forked sticks, men strung lengthy rabbit nets, three feet high and often fifty yards long, made of two-inch-mesh yucca fiber. Then they formed a moving line and drove the rabbits ahead of them into the net. The older men stood at the nets to kill and remove the trapped rabbits and to restring the nets as the rabbits pushed them over. After the rabbits were clubbed and skinned and the meat and pelts distributed among the participating families, the people returned to the mountains for the last of the nut gathering.[12]

When the first snow fell, the people returned to the lowlands, where they gathered the tiny seeds of nut grass. In a good season each family might have over 1,000 pounds of pine nuts, in which case they would camp close to the nut cache at the base of the mountains. They set aside bundles of yucca fiber for making twine and rabbit skins for weaving blankets—two activities for the long winter nights. The elevation along the Sierra front was high—over 5,000 feet—and blizzards and severe temperatures as low as 30 degrees below zero were not uncommon. As winter storms dumped snow across the landscape families drew close around the fires in their huts, or *kanas;* with rabbit-skin blankets pulled over their shoulders, they savored pine nuts and smoked rabbit meat and told stories of the making of First Man and First Woman and the creator-destroyer Coyote.[13]

Hunting and gathering in this manner, year after year, required labor, the manufacture and maintenance of tools, and a great deal of mutual cooperation to make the desert produce goods. To look at Paiute tools is to ponder the intimate linkages between people and land, passed from one generation to the next through careful lessons in craftsmanship and the ethic of frequent, dedicated work: fish weirs woven from willow branches, themselves cut with knives carved from rock; tule boats bundled and shaped from wild grass stems in the marshes; rabbit nets woven from the yucca fiber pounded and stripped from yucca leaves with tools made from stone; grass seed gathered in baskets closely woven from the stems of other grasses; bows, arrows, spears, and fishhooks all bent and carved and assembled from wood, horn, stone, gut, and feathers; hunter's arrows tipped with obsidian points that were dipped in poison extracted from rattlesnakes or red ants or derived from rotten meat; decoys made of duck skin stretched over tule rushes; and snares of twine and stone and brush. With their carefully crafted tools and vast knowledge about animals, plants, seasons, soil, weather, and water, Paiutes manufactured abundance, not so much finding it as coaxing it out of the desert.[14]

For Paiutes, flourishing in the desert, in every season, depended not only on tools, knowledge, and cooperative work but also on the favor of spirits to provide *booha*—the Numu word for the force that clings to life and animates all living things. To them, the basin was no wasteland of absences but a place crowded with powerful spirits—of animals, the wind, insects, even stones and mountains, and of course people. All Numus possessed at least some booha, which came and went depending on one's ability to manage relations with spirits. Any spirit could bring booha to a person, and any spirit could take it away. Booha manifested itself for people in the form of good luck. Having booha enabled one to produce many children, enticed animals to give up their bodies, led one to nourishing food plants, and persuaded the heavens to open and water the desert.[15]

Thus, the good life had to be conjured as well as crafted. A person survived partly through skill and fortitude, but booha moved through the sky and air like water, and keeping self and family alive required magic to capture it or direct it into one's body. Because it was so easily lost, booha had to be cultivated and protected. One kept an eye out for dreams in which spirits might offer new power (and spurning such an offer was a grave offense to the spirits, who might take one's booha away). In a seemingly empty landscape, the spectral presences gathered around, watching, and all of them had to be appeased to ensure survival. For every Paiute, finding booha and keeping it was the prime spiritual requirement of daily life.[16]

Of course, booha was particularly plentiful near sources of good water. The tallest mountain peaks were especially powerful places infused with booha, as was evident in their mantles of snow that remained all summer, filling springs and rivers in the driest time of year, creating places below where people could gather in an otherwise inhospitable terrain. As one Southern Paiute man explained, booha "flows into and down the sides of mountains."[17]

Booha expressed moral and ethical balance, not only among the living but between the living and the dead. Key to maintaining that balance were rituals to give thanks to the spirits and ensure their favor. Every antelope drive, rabbit drive, or fish harvest began with a Round Dance, a gathering of the often far-flung family in which they held hands in a circle and turned clockwise as they sang in prayer for plenty, health, and well-being and gave thanks to the spirits of antelope, rabbit, trout, or others.[18]

ELSEWHERE ACROSS THE REGION, PAIUTE OUTFITS LIVED BY MEANS similar to those of the people of Walker River, but by the first half of the nineteenth century many had gathered into larger bands to defend themselves, first from slavers and then from violent Americans, whose arrival signaled great change and new hardships to come. The mountain man Joseph Reddeford Walker, in a futile search for valuable sources of beaver, sallied through the valley of the river that eventually carried his name in 1833. With Zenas Leonard and other trappers, he slaughtered dozens of Paiutes in a series of skirmishes and massacres orchestrated to terrorize the Indians.[19]

Almost immediately afterward, in the mid-1830s, westward-bound overland emigrants began to trickle through the region. These Americans were crossing northern Nevada on their way to the contested region of the Oregon Country or Mexico's Pacific province of California. Paiutes, apparently hoping that these people would prove to be trading partners and allies, generally avoided fighting them. But they could not ignore what these migrants and their animals were doing to the desert. By 1868 hundreds of thousands of California-bound migrants and their draft animals had made their way through the Numu homelands over two sets of overland trails cutting through the center of Nevada. One trail ran southwest along the Humboldt River and connected with the Carson River, and the other went across central Nevada, also to link up with the Carson. These were the very rivers on which many Numu relied for sustenance, and now they found themselves in an unprecedented competition for scarce resources. American oxen, mules, and horses depleted the wild grasses, and the migrants themselves consumed large quantities of perpetually scarce game and firewood. For overlanders, the Great Basin sections of the trail were fraught with peril as water, food, range, and firewood ran low or ran out. For Indians, the migrants were often belligerent and best avoided. In an effort to make up for the food and resources that were lost to the foreigners, a few Paiutes took to selling them firewood or offering their services as livestock guards or trail guides.[20]

With this heavy stream of migrants along the Carson and Humboldt Rivers, many Paiutes were displaced. Some of these (perhaps most) went to the Walker River, the next valley to the south.[21]

In contrast to the Carson and Humboldt Rivers, for a time the Walker River remained relatively protected because it lay twenty miles or more to the south of the main trail, with a forbidding stretch of high desert separating it from the flood of California-bound emigrants. Using the skills they had acquired over the millennia, Paiutes along the Walker River continued to draw sustenance from the desert. But soon Americans began to covet the Walker River country for something more than an emigrant trail. In 1859, the U.S. government set aside a reservation at Walker Lake where they intended Numus to gather that same year. California ranchers seeking new pastures for their herds colonized the river and took a battering ram to the Numu economy. Colonel T. B. Rickey began carving out a

42,000-acre domain for his Antelope Land and Cattle Company near the Walker River headwaters, while a short distance downriver H. N. A. "Hock" Mason claimed what became known as Mason Valley and turned his cattle herds loose along the riverbanks. Soon after, two other Californians, R. B. Smith and Timothy B. Smith, drove herds into what became known as Smith Valley and took up permanent residence.[22]

At the very same time, in 1859, prospectors discovered rich veins of silver and gold ore at Sun Mountain near the Carson River, a short distance to the north. By 1860, there were 7,000 European immigrants and Euro-Americans working the slopes of what soon became known as Mount Davidson, clustered around an urban core of explosive growth that came to be called Virginia City.[23]

Wovoka was three years old the year the Walker River was occupied and Virginia City began to boom; the key context for his childhood, as well as for the development of the Ghost Dance, was colonization. The boy's given name, apparently, was Wovoka. His father Numu Taivo was a minor leader, or *capita,* and a shaman who had powerful visions and was said to be invulnerable to gunfire and to have control over the weather. The boy's mother Tiya remains a mystery. Her origins are unknown, and her name has no known translation. She came from a distant community; except for her own children, she had no kin along the Walker River and remained an outsider.[24]

The Walker River and every one of the scarce rivers and streams of northern Nevada were soon swallowed in an emigrant rush that sprouted ranches and towns. Dispossessed, Paiutes united with Bannocks from Fort Hall, Idaho, and rose up against the Americans in 1860. There are hints that Numu Taivo fought in this conflict, or perhaps a later one. The translation of his name, "Northern Paiute White Man," suggests that Wovoka's father was one of the group of Northern Paiute warriors who were kept prisoner among the Americans for some years after the fighting ended. Indians won the biggest battles of the Paiute War, once even cutting down dozens of American militiamen in a running fight along the Truckee River. But in this as in subsequent conflicts across the region—in Owens Valley in 1862, and farther east in Nevada and Utah through the mid-1860s—Indian victories proved fleeting. Despite some remarkable triumphs, the Paiute warriors could not dislodge the newcomers from their armed settlements along the watercourses.[25]

So Paiutes had to accommodate themselves to the new American order. That regime was marked by ecological change and dispossession that increasingly pushed Indians out of their traditional work, which they had controlled themselves, and into modern wage labor, a tedious, exacting, and exhausting activity over which they had comparatively little control.

Nowhere was this process more evident than in what was then Nevada's largest city and the countryside surrounding it. Today much of Virginia City is abandoned, and the desert wind whistles through its ruins with a lonely wail that makes it all too easy to forget its former influence and power. Shortly before the Paiute War, prospectors realized that Mount Davidson harbored not only gold but silver beyond the dreams of men. In 1864, the year Nevada achieved statehood, the booming mines of the Comstock Lode drew over 60,000 settlers. By 1875, the conjoined towns of Virginia City and Gold Hill, with 25,000 residents, had become one of the largest settlements west of the Mississippi, and the Comstock mines among the largest and deepest mines in the history of the United States. The concentrated industrial and economic power produced on the dry slopes of the river valley immediately north of Walker River seemed to come from another world, as if a vast futuristic social machine had burst into the ancient desert through a crack in time.[26]

Except for a few brief years in the early 1860s, this was no rustic miners' camp with small pick-and-pan outfits scratching color from the dirt and grizzled pioneers yelling "Eureka!" The Comstock was more like a factory built into solid rock with dynamite, blood, German engineering, and forests of wood. Reaching the quartz-encased silver required 3,000-foot-deep tunnels, explosives by the ton, and armies of wage-earning miners to wrench treasure from the depths. Comstock workers loaded their haul into iron railcars that traveled via elevators up the shafts to the mine entrances. From there the ore was ferried to round-the-clock mills where other workers crushed it beneath steam-driven stamps that rose and fell like pistons, then poured the pulverized rock into solutions of mercury to separate the silver ore from the worthless granite. Virginia City whistled, roared, stamped, rumbled, and belched smoke twenty-four hours a day.[27]

In ways that have been too long overlooked, this urban indus-revolution in the lands of the Numu provided a vital context for the cycles of Indian prophecy that birthed the Ghost Dance. Aside from the relentlessly mobile overlanders, the money-hungry, cosmopoli-tan people of Virginia City and its outlying settlements comprised the first substantial American society to which Nevada Indians were exposed. This contact would reconfigure not only their societies but their sense of earthly possibility and torment.

VIRGINIA CITY WAS LIKE A VOLCANO THAT ERUPTED AND consumed much of the countryside's scarce resources, scattering smaller mining towns across the region like so many embers. In the subsequent experience of Wovoka's people along the Walker River, we can trace the dynamics that remade the Numu world during the prophet's childhood years and drove the Ghost Dance movement. The city's rise asserted a new division of Paiute homelands into mar-ket center and resource hinterland, urban center and rural space. Where the desert's scarce resources had compelled the dispersion of peoples, the city's market sucked wood, water, and food into its maw like a vortex, and the Comstock Lode and the markets that fueled it hammered away at the old hunting and gathering networks for vast distances.

Starting in the 1860s, the mining boom took a severe toll on Ne-vada's mountain woodlands. "The great development of the mining interests of Nevada has already nearly exterminated its scanty and stunted forests," reported one forester in 1880. One Indian agent noted the hardships that befell Indians as a result: "Where in former times they obtained Pine Nutts [sic] the discovery of the mines has brought the wood into demand and where the forests of that kind of wood grew five years ago nothing but stumps are left." Pine nut harvests continued to vary from one year to the next, but the documentary record suggests that pine nuts were generally becoming scarcer. At the same time, with the spread of ranching, cattle and sheep consumed much of the remaining landscape on which Paiute autonomy depended. The animals devoured native bunchgrasses—whose seeds were a critical source of Paiute food—and over decades of heavy grazing not only did bunchgrass disappear, but the seeds that remained in the soil had few chances to germinate. Unable to endure heavy grazing and trampling, bunchgrasses soon gave way to woody brush.[28]

The nascent cattle industry along the Walker River would grow by leaps and bounds as it supplied beef and hides to miners at Dogtown, Monoville, and Aurora, which sprang up south of the river in the late 1850s and 1860s, and at the gold-mining town of Bodie, founded near the headwaters in 1877. Ranches expanded across the state as demand for beef, leather, and alfalfa in the mining towns increased. By the 1870s, the high desert grasslands and meadows from the high Sierra down into the valleys of the Walker, the Carson, and the Truckee teemed with cattle.[29]

The cattle devastated the nut grass and wild clover meadows maintained by Paiutes with their communal ditches. In 1859, when Timothy Smith's cattle first overran the pozeeda meadows along Desert Creek, a Paiute leader named Horseman led his enraged people in confronting the rancher and demanding that he leave the valley. But in this and similar face-offs, the Paiutes acquiesced to gifts of cattle. Until other options appeared, they settled for stealing more of them to make up for the food that the animals and their owners had taken. Other biotic communities that provided Paiute food fared no better than the nut grass. Livestock grazing and upriver diversions of water for irrigation caused serious declines in buckberry and grass bulbs—the very taboose from which the Taboose Dicutta drew sustenance and their community identity. When erosion from irrigation and grazing led to sedimentation of the river, freshwater mussels were

suffocated and the Lahontan cutthroat trout debilitated. The large
ranches at the headwaters of the Walker River diverted even more
water over time, causing the lower reaches of the river to dry out
completely in the fall of 1882 and destroying fish habitat.[30]

The traditional year had begun with trout, and the end of the traditional era would be marked by the near-destruction of fish in the
Walker River. The 1860s saw a terrible drought, accompanied by
trout die-offs in the river as ranchers diverted large volumes of water
for irrigation. In 1868 and 1869, the trout migration was especially
poor. Starvation loomed for Paiutes, and fast on its heels came a
series of epidemics: typhoid fever and measles swept away at least
125 Walker River Paiutes over a two-year period. Those deaths were
catastrophic for the outfits, which critically relied on family labor to
gather the wild grass seeds that were a key traditional food source.
Instead of going to the mountains for pine nuts, as they normally
would have done, many Paiutes went to Virginia City to hustle and
scrape for cash and food to make it through the winter.[31]

In these ways, in urban space and hinterland alike, environmental
changes radically reoriented the Paiutes' economy and shifted them
away from hunting and gathering and into wage labor. In 1866,
Nevada's sole Indian agent, posted at Pyramid Lake Reservation,
praised the work ethic of Nevada Paiutes: "Many of them are employed as laborers on the farms of white men in all seasons, but they
are especially serviceable during the time of harvest and haymaking."
With their wages, they bought modern goods such as woolen clothes
and horses, and by the 1870s Paiutes were largely dressed in Western clothing and many drove wagons. In subsequent decades, Paiute
industriousness was often a subject among Nevada officials, one of
whom estimated in 1870 that 12 percent of Paiute men labored for
wages, a figure that is impressive but nonetheless probably low.[32]

About the time fish began to fail in the Walker River, Wovoka
joined the workforce. By the age of eight, he was working for David
Wilson, for whom his parents already labored and whose family arrived in Nevada from Missouri about 1864. The labor and social relations of Nevada were somewhat akin to those of the South: Indians

worked and lived alongside white landowners, who simultaneously needed their labor and socially rejected them. And just as black and white children played together during and after slavery in the South, young Jack played marbles, swam and fished in the Walker River, climbed trees, and hunted for birds' nests with the white Wilson boys, Billy and Joe. From Jack the Wilson boys learned to speak passable Paiute, and from the Wilsons Jack grew to understand English (although he was never comfortable speaking it). All three boys became practical jokers. (In later years, the Wilson brothers remained respectful of their boyhood friend and longtime employee, but like many of their contemporaries, they attributed Wovoka's miraculous powers to his formidable skills as a prankster.)[33]

So it was that by 1880 much of the Nevada working class was Numus—along with Chinese, Greeks, Italians, Basques, and some others. The Indians' willingness to work was widely praised, and contemporaries observed that without Paiute labor many business concerns could not have functioned. Rancher Timothy Smith—for whom Smith Valley was named—recalled that Paiutes initially ran off his livestock, "yet a few years later I do not see how we would have managed without their assistance in the harvesting of our large crops of hay as well as in some other lines of work."[34]

The centralization of work in towns and ranches created a new geography of Paiute labor, and as the biggest settlement and the center of the regional economy, Virginia City was a frequent destination for Paiutes in need of employment and goods. The city's vigorous newspapers (a young Mark Twain was employed by one of them) provide a glimpse of what Paiute urban work was like. Some Virginia City Paiutes were local, from the Carson River Valley, but others arrived from Walker River, Pyramid Lake, and other Paiute communities to find work when resources in their home communities became scarce. They joined a global wave of migrants from as far afield as Ireland, Germany, and China.[35]

Camped in small communities on the city fringes, Paiutes came to treat the city as part of their seasonal food-gathering round. Beginning at dawn, Paiute women walked the city streets with burlap sacks

FIGURE 3.1. Living by the river of money: Northern Paiute family at home in Virginia City, ca. 1900. Among the first followers of the Ghost Dance religion were wage-laboring Northern Paiutes who had settled in Nevada cities and towns. Nevada Historical Society.

for collecting bits of firewood, merchants' cast-off fruit and fish heads and tails, and even stray pieces of hay for their thin horses. At virtually any time of day their husbands, brothers, fathers, and sons could be found on the steep streets of Virginia City sweating every kind of casual labor, from hauling firewood to raising buildings. In an urban, concentrated version of their customary practice of dispersed hunting and gathering, they survived on a mix of wages from work and food foraged in town dumps and alleyways. They scavenged firewood from broken timbers and from boxes outside dry goods stores. They bought beans, flour, and coffee with the cash they earned, but they also combed through refuse piles, butchered dead horses and oxen on the streets, begged from other residents, and accepted church charity.[36]

The number of Paiutes living in Virginia City itself seems always to have been small: the 1880 census counted 127 Paiutes, including 35 women and 44 children, residing there. But for surrounding bands and outfits the city became a central node for acquiring food and other necessities and for exchanging goods as well as ideas and news.

FIGURE 3.2. Gathering firewood in Nevada, ca. 1905. An Indian woman carries railroad ties. The destruction of Nevada forests, rivers, and grasslands drove many Indians into the towns and cities for food, firewood, and paying work. Nevada Historical Society.

Although Indians from different areas apparently lived in distinctive camps around the city, they worked many of the same jobs and congregated daily in vacant lots, storage yards, and streets to gamble and socialize. We cannot know what they said to one another. But given city newspaper accounts of assembled Paiutes talking, gesticulating, and laughing, we may presume that they exchanged news about work opportunities, family, and events in the hinterland.[37]

The city was also a market, a focal point for those Numu who, compelled by their need for clothes and other goods, behaved like Americans and turned the desert into dollars. In 1887, Paiutes sold an estimated 75,000 pounds of pine nuts on Virginia City streets. Each year Pyramid Lake Numu also shipped between 40 and 100 tons of fish to city merchants. Paiute men arrived from the marshes of the Carson and the Humboldt to peddle game meat—rabbits, ducks, geese, even the odd rattlesnake. As wild species changed,

Paiutes altered their habits. When white sportsmen introduced trout and catfish to local streams or released quail in adjacent areas for their own hunting enjoyment, they were distressed to find Paiute men industriously harvesting the animals. At least once, Paiutes transferred fish to the man-made pool at the mouth of the Sutro Tunnel, four miles southeast of Virginia City, to eat them later.[38]

Enthusiasm for the market made Paiutes entrepreneurial, and they pushed hard to open new markets for themselves. In 1880, Virginia City moguls William Sharon and Henry Yerington made an offer to the Indians of Walker River Reservation (which had been established by the US government near the river's terminus at Walker Lake in 1859): give us an easement to build a railroad across the reservation, and we will let Indians ride the train for free. But Walker River Numu demanded more and got it: in exchange for the easement across the reservation, they secured not only free passage for themselves but free shipment of fish, game, and produce. Indeed, as one negotiator reported, the Indians were not just amenable to the easement, but "very anxious the road should be built."[39]

By 1881, the Carson & Colorado Railroad line connected Walker Lake and its primary station at the town of Schurz on the reservation not only to the southern mining towns of the eastern Sierra Nevada but to the Virginia & Truckee Railroad and points north. Many of the trains that rumbled up the line from the south carrying ore and other goods all the way to Virginia City and beyond also carried Indian fishermen and their abundant hauls of trout. Railroad company negotiators had assumed that Indians would not have many goods to ship and that the deal would not cost the company very much. But in the first few years Paiutes shipped so many fish that railroad officials tried to renege on the deal, alleging that white men must be secretly running the business. In 1889 alone, Walker River Paiutes sold an estimated 20,000 pounds of fish in Virginia City and surrounding towns, flooding markets and undercutting their Pyramid Lake competitors by a significant margin.[40]

The success of Walker River fishermen in urban markets indicates the growing importance of money in the lives of Paiutes. Here and elsewhere, the relentless environmental change and chaotic mining economy advanced by the American ascendancy forced Paiutes more than ever to look to wages for survival, as observers frequently mentioned. Mining silver and gold was well paid and remained mostly the exclusive work of white men, but across the region Paiutes undertook almost every other kind of day labor, including borax mining, carpentry, construction, road grading, ranch work, and hauling goods. Partly because of the need to pursue work, by the late 1880s only one in every four Paiutes lived on a reservation.[41]

The "Water Utes" had customarily located along the Truckee, the Carson, the Walker, and other rivers and streams that linked the disparate resource zones of their homelands, but the Americans diverted and degraded those watercourses to create a radically new space. Although the geographical location of the Paiute homeland was unchanged—to the uninitiated, it might even have looked the same—within a very short period the resources for survival that Paiutes formerly gathered from the land could be reliably had only from butcher shops, grocers, and dealers in dry goods. In this strange new space, relations between plants, animals, people, and watercourses were almost unimaginably transformed, and to remain connected to the essentials of life—food, clothing, shelter—Paiutes increasingly were forced to relocate along a new kind of river, an abstracted flow that we might call the river of money.

MONEY MADE NEVADA GO. IN VIRGINIA CITY, IN THE settlements along the Walker River, and elsewhere in the state, with the exception of some livestock and hay, practically everything Americans consumed—from pencils to wagons and mining machinery—had to be bought in California or shipped from farther away. As Paiutes adjusted by becoming more market-oriented themselves, they moved from their natal places to join other Paiute outfits and work for money in more cosmopolitan places, not only in Virginia City but in mining camps, ranch outposts, and small towns.[42]

From the 1860s on, Wovoka's family and other Paiutes survived through gathering, hunting, and foraging, engaging in wage labor, selling wild goods, and growing subsistence gardens. Near the head-waters of the Walker River a small colony of Paiutes settled beside the town of Bridgeport, and another colony settled farther along the river at Greenfield (soon to be called Yerington), where Jack Wilson's family lived. Most Paiutes on the Walker River never lived at the Walker River Reservation, which was farther downriver. There several hundred Paiutes began digging their own irrigation system in the 1870s; these were the same people who had pushed hard to secure the Carson & Colorado Railroad line through their land in 1880. Soon the agricultural production of these reservation farmers was substantial. By 1890, they had constructed more than eight miles of primary ditch to water small vegetable patches and hundreds of acres of alfalfa and barley, much of which they transported to market on the railroad. The dependence of Paiutes on modern cash and commerce thus grew. Where one official had estimated that only about 12 percent of Paiutes had been wage workers in 1870, another held that 85 percent of Paiute subsistence at Walker River Reservation came from store-bought goods.[43]

Upriver Numus who lived off the reservation, like Jack Wilson, had less access to fish and no farmland. Their growing reliance on cash made them ever more dependent on wages as the century wore on and rapid environmental changes continued. Their customary activities and means of raising food or money became more difficult. We may surmise that gathering pine nuts and cutting wood became more challenging as the heavy use of wood for stoves, homes, and industry drove the forests into retreat from the American settlements (where Paiutes increasingly gathered). Instead of wintering near pine nut caches, as in the old days, Paiutes now used draft animals and wagons to haul the bounty to their homes near ranches and towns, and in any event, extended trips away would have cost them the chance to work for cash at other employment.[44]

Thus, the new economy of wage labor reoriented the Numu calendar. By 1890, workplace demands kept Paiutes on the ranches where they worked for all but two or three weeks of the year. There was less time to find productive pine groves and not much time to reach and pick the nuts that were available. Pine nutting was (and is) key to Paiute identity, economy, and religion, but by 1890 the nuts were harder to find and gather perhaps than ever before.[45]

The wage economy brought a host of other problems, starting with the sporadic nature of the work. This alone may have made it an inferior replacement for hunting and gathering. The traditional Paiute economy was broad-based, allowing Numus to switch to a new resource if one became scarce. Wage work turned this economy almost upside down. Work itself assumed the status of a resource that everyone needed, all the time—but it could not always be found. There was little work to be had in the winter, a particularly slow time in ranch country, since this was also the hardest time of year to gather and hunt. Numus felt the grip of poverty most keenly during the coldest time of year (which may explain why, in 1889, the Ghost Dance visions and rituals took hold in the winter).[46]

The seasonality of ranch labor, combined with the boom-and-bust cycles that typified extractive industry and Gilded Age capitalism, made wage work a perilously thin reed on which to base community survival. If it failed—and it failed often—there was not much else to fall back on.

All wage workers faced poverty, but Indians were especially vulnerable to it. The federal agents in charge of reservations were under strict orders to compel Indian work and subservience in exchange for assistance. Most of these agents were unreliable political appointees, however, and they frequently resigned, leaving their agencies unattended and assistance undistributed. In addition, most Paiutes could not even claim such support because they did not reside at a reservation.[47]

WAGES THUS BECAME THE PATH TO SURVIVAL, AND LIKE THE starving peasants of Ireland in the 1840s and 1850s or the starving Italians and Poles of the 1880s and 1890s, the Paiutes flocked to the American workplace. Although they remained closer to home than most of the new immigrants, their dispersal for work increasingly strained ties to band and family as the nineteenth century wore on.

In older times, hunting and gathering had dispersed the Numus too, but these economic activities also allowed for periodic reunions of extended family as scattered outfits came together to drive rabbits or antelope. A bountiful harvest of taboose or a good fish run was cause for a multi-outfit celebration. Large gatherings at ritual events like the fall pine nut thanksgiving helped restore community ties after months of dispersal, with the communal prayer and song of the Round Dance helping to bridge divides between people.[48]

But wage work tied men, women, and children to rotating and often far-flung workplaces for all the warm months. By 1890, Paiutes were far more dependent on the river of money than on hunting and gathering. The smaller, non-reservation communities, like Jack Wilson's at Yerington, had no fields of their own and thus no produce to sell. They were especially reliant on wage work and whatever they could scrape together from woodcutting, hunting, and fishing. Moving from workplace to workplace as opportunities arose further restricted their freedom, preventing them from gathering ever-scarcer wild resources that might have gained them at least some autonomy from employers. Bound to a rotation among scattered ranch sites many miles apart and in the towns sprinkled across the Nevada map, and with little time to hunt or gather, Indians found themselves curiously itinerant but no longer nomadic.

Over the course of the 1880s, a series of developments aggravated the difficulties brought on by dispersion. The arrival of the Carson & Colorado Railroad in 1881, with its station on the Walker River Reservation, connected Indians to the transcontinental line at Reno. As we have seen, the new line—which Paiutes rode for free—provided an outlet for cash sales of fish, and by the early 1890s they were shipping barley, wheat, and even some fresh vegetables and chickens to urban markets. But they also shipped their own bodies: Indians sat atop the cars in long rows, bound for hop-picking jobs as far away as Sonoma and Mendocino Counties in California. Walker River Paiutes began to hold annual fetes to honor these migrant workers as they headed off to the fields, not only to honor their economic contribution but to shore up community bonds with them.[49]

The arrival of the railroad thus contributed to the sense of community disintegration among Walker River Paiutes by expanding the range of migration for work. Family networks, already shriveled by disease and violence, now were also more dispersed, sometimes hundreds of miles across a strange, often hostile country. In addition, rail work and travel were extraordinarily dangerous, punctuated as they were by frequent derailures and crashes. In 1890, a sadly typical year, some 300 U.S. railroad passengers died in accidents and thousands of employees were killed and maimed. Journeys by rail were attended by fears that those who went away might not return.[50]

For all its drawbacks, wage work stood alone as the means to raise cash as other options vanished. Beginning in the 1870s, and with increasing force during the 1880s, the state of Nevada imposed conservation laws that restricted Indian fishing in a transparent effort to divert the state's fishing economy to white men. In 1888, the state legislature, hoping to placate the owners of the Carson & Colorado Railroad and abrogate the railroad's agreement with Paiute fishermen, demanded that Congress eliminate the Walker River Reservation. The threat did not materialize, but Walker River Paiutes cannot have remained ignorant of the proposal, which was vigorously opposed by both their own Indian agent and officials at the Office of Indian Affairs. Had it succeeded, it would have left many Paiutes landless, without farms or homes, and therefore even more dependent on wages.[51]

On top of all this, obstacles to ceremonial and social gatherings mounted as the century wore on. The large festivals that drew hundreds or thousands of Indians in urban locations had faced an uncertain future even in their heyday of the 1870s and 1880s. Indians were under constant pressure from employers and authorities to remain near work and abandon their old religion; festivals may not have been suppressed, but they were discouraged. The younger generation of Numu came of age without learning many of the hunting and gathering activities that the old blessing rituals supported, and the fact that many of them spoke more English than Paiute drove a wedge between the generations.[52]

By 1890, many could see that Paiute people were headed for a lonelier future in which ever more of them would be dispersed to far-flung work sites for most of the year. It is small wonder, then, that many would listen to the prophecies of a new era that began to circulate in these days of travail.

CHAPTER 4

THE GHOST DANCE ARRIVES

IT WAS IN THE LATE 1860S AND EARLY 1870S, SOON AFTER Wovoka entered his midteens, that a new ritual emerged—a simple ceremony based on the Paiute Round Dance, motivated by prophecy, and accompanied by all-night preaching and singing. What became known as the 1870 Ghost Dance swept through Indian communities seeking to accommodate themselves to the transformation of their homelands into hinterlands—zones of resource extraction for city markets. Its origins are customarily traced to Walker River where it made a dramatic appearance in 1869 with the prophecies of a Northern Paiute in Mason Valley named Wodziwob, also known as Fish Lake Joe.

We know precious little about the Ghost Dance prophecies of Wodziwob, which began amid the poor trout migration and disease outbreaks of the late 1860s. Sources report that he foretold the return of the Indian dead on a train from the east and the imminent disappearance of white people, who, he said, would be swallowed up by the earth. This is not much to go on; nonetheless, two striking features of these prophecies compel our attention.[1]

First, they appealed to a widely disparate Paiute community as a gesture of unity and healing. Paiutes were a famously local people, with strong kinship networks that wove them into communities oriented to particular river valleys or, more often, sections of river valleys. They recognized no authority higher than the local "talker," or headman (whose power was usually limited to announcing seasonal migrations and exhorting good behavior), and the sense of being related or obligated to their neighbors was perhaps the strongest community bond among them. But the migrations of Paiutes for work and food had dislocated many of the old outfits. Along Walker River, Wodziwob was known as "Fish Lake Joe" precisely because he hailed not from the riverbanks but from the small Paiute community at Fish Lake, Nevada, some 100 miles to the south. In moving to the Walker River sometime before 1870, he joined thousands of other Paiutes of that time who were relocating to places where work and food could be had. To a large degree, the Ghost Dance movement served the needs of Indian communities that had been radically reshuffled and become both more cosmopolitan and often more internally conflicted as strangers arrived from afar in search of work, money, and Indian company. In addition to bringing on the millennium, the Ghost Dance everywhere promised well-being and protection against sickness for those who entered the circle—a ceremonial form that could address the daily challenges of casual laborers who were thrown among strangers.[2]

The second notable feature of these prophecies is how enmeshed they were with the rapidly changing materiality of Paiute life—specifically the arrival of industrialism, as signified by the train carrying Indians back to life in Wodziwob's visions. A train was indeed arriving from the east—the transcontinental railroad was completed in 1869, and trains thus arrived in Nevada from that direction for the first time that year. Moreover, thousands of white people were "disappearing" into the earth every day—working in the mines at Virginia City and elsewhere. These real-world resonances may make the prophecies seem naive, but these fragments of the original visions that come down to us through the record may have had a symbolic meaning: Indians would be saved (the resurrected dead signifying the restored health of Indian community and culture) by engaging modern industry (riding the train), just as so many were attempting to do.

Whatever the prophecies meant, the record is clear that urban life and industrial-era wage work in Nevada were met with a wave of millenarianism that flowed into the Ghost Dance. In 1871 the new Indian agent at Pyramid Lake Reservation arrived to find a large Ghost Dance getting under way. In Virginia City, the all-night millenarian sermons of Paiutes attracted the occasional attention of outsiders. "They have preachers," a Virginia City journalist explained, "who preach very good Methodist doctrine. They sometimes begin preaching early in the evening and preach all night, telling the Indians that if they lie, steal, and murder, they are sure to . . . [end] up in the great desert . . . when they die." The ironic allusion to Methodism was in fact appropriate: Methodism, like Ghost Dancing, flourished in the wake of the advent of wage work and industrial capitalism. Preaching accompanied the central Ghost Dance rite: men, women, and children moving in a clockwise circle, with fingers interlocked. All awaited the transformation of the world into "the fertility and beauty of Eden," as another eyewitness put it.[3]

Paiute enthusiasm for the teachings was evident in a vast gathering in Virginia City in 1871. According to a journalist on the scene, a large number of Paiutes formed themselves into a large circle and with the first notes of the prayers they sang with great solemnity began to revolve "as a solid mass"; "like a huge laboring water wheel," the circle of dancers crept "slowly around for hours." After 1870, Virginia City seems to have become a hub for this kind of ritual expression. Resident Indians set signal fires on hilltops to call dancers from Walker River, Pyramid Lake, Carson Valley, and other communities. The Ghost Dance accompanied—or perhaps heralded—the development of the large urban festivals that came to characterize Paiute life in the 1870s and 1880s. In these periodic congregations in central locations where the most Indians could easily gather, Paiutes sought to compensate for their dispersal by the demands of wage work. For these special occasions, smaller family groups made their way into town from remote ranches and work sites. Thus, at Belmont, Virginia City, and other locations where many Paiutes lived close by, seasonal festivals like the fall pine nut thanksgiving became much larger than they had been in the days before white conquest, and the Paiute hosts of these festivals acquired a great deal of prestige. Over the two decades, then, Paiute dance and religion grew out of this vibrant urban center and the surrounding countryside of resource extraction, especially around the Walker River, where cash markets and wage labor had supplanted hunting and gathering in the short space of a decade.[4]

As a teenager at the time when the 1870 Ghost Dance arose, Wovoka knew Wodziwob. They lived in the same Numu community at Mason Valley. Wovoka's father Numu Taivo was by this time a powerful shaman and a man of great booha who would have known about the movement. (Whether he supported it or not is unclear.) The wave of feeling generated by the ritual no doubt influenced the boy. Although enthusiasm soon diminished among Walker River Paiutes, the 1870 Ghost Dance captivated far-flung Indian communities that similarly depended on wage labor, and the religion thrived not just in Virginia City but in Oregon and in California. It also spread eastward, inspiring Bannocks and Shoshones at Fort Hall, Idaho, where dances to fulfill Wodziwob's vision continued through the 1870s.[5]

WITH ITS BELIEF IN APOCALYPSE, WORLD RENEWAL, AND THE imminent salvation of the virtuous by a benevolent creator, it was easy enough for contemporaries like Nelson Miles and even James Mooney—and some scholars since—to credit some or all of the Ghost Dance religion to missionary teachings, especially those of evangelical Christians and Mormons.[6]

Because they were nearby and because Ghost Dance prophecies in some ways resembled Mormon prophecies, Mormons in particular became prime suspects. The Church of Jesus Christ of Latter-Day Saints was founded in 1830 by a young Joseph Smith in western New York (a region so prone to religious revival as to be called "the burned-over district"). Smith turned against the sectarian discontent of his upbringing to proffer a new gospel that maintained, among other things, that Christ had once walked the Americas and that Indians were descended from the lost tribes of Israel who had fallen away from the true faith. Smith gathered thousands of followers.

Seeking new lands to the west, where they could build a new Zion, and fleeing murderous persecution, Mormons undertook a series of migrations that culminated with their emigration to Salt Lake in the Great Basin in 1847. There Mormon missionaries set about converting Indians, whom they saw as their fallen brethren—upon acceptance of the Book of Mormon, Indian skin would become "white and delightsome"—as they simultaneously made war on them and seized their land.[7]

Mormons probably influenced Paiute cosmology, but evidence for their influence on Wodziwob or Wovoka is slight at best (the accusations of Nelson Miles and others notwithstanding). Salt Lake is 400 sandy miles from Walker River, and the Mormon presence in northern Nevada was limited to a trading post on the Carson River that they founded in 1851 and abandoned in 1857, the year Wovoka was born. To be sure, Mormon ideas may have circulated among the many apostates in the state. Meanwhile, distant church missionary efforts among Indians in Utah did shape Paiute ideas of the spirit world; Paiutes and other Great Basin Indians, including Utes, Shoshones, and Bannocks, became Mormon believers in these years. But there is little evidence that Mormons or their theology had a significant impact along the Walker River until well after 1890.[8]

Aside from Mormons, other Christian missionaries also were thin on the ground in Nevada. While some followers of Wovoka's teachings in 1890 might have interpreted the Ghost Dance as Christian, it seems most likely that both Wodziwob and Wovoka drew at least as much from Numu religious traditions as from Christian ones. A millennial strain had long characterized belief among Paiutes and other Great Basin Indians, all of them peoples "less concerned with how it all began," in the words of one scholar, "than with how it might end."[9]

An imminent apocalypse along with the need to hasten it through dancing had long been characteristic of the so-called Prophet Dance revivals of the Columbia Plateau, the volcanic upland north of the Great Basin. Plateau Indian religions generally featured a remote Creator—often known as Chief, the supreme spirit who created the world and made it perfect—and a subordinate spirit whose relations with people were more intimate. The latter is often cast as Coyote, the trickster who introduced the world's imperfections and thereby made it possible for humans to live in it. Sometimes Chief and Coyote were replaced with spirits, known as Big Brother and Little Brother, that were somewhat like people. The Prophet Dance invoked an end-time in which Little Brother was coming to redeem humanity. Paiutes on the southern fringes of the Columbia Plateau were neighbors to the Walker River and Virginia City Paiutes; it was probably through them that the age-old Prophet Dance tradition echoed in the Ghost Dance promise of prophecy and world renewal.[10]

Thus, even though Mormons and other Christians undoubtedly influenced Ghost Dancers, these relative latecomers were not so much instigators as fellow participants in a confluence of prophecies in the Great Basin through which Ghost Dancers, Mormons, and others exchanged teachings and mutually influenced each other. In Utah and Idaho, the 1870 Ghost Dance prophecies apparently motivated some Shoshones, Bannocks, and Paiutes to seek out Mormons for discussions about sacred matters, and sometimes for baptism. Mormons, meanwhile, extolled such outreach as confirmation of their own beliefs and sometimes incorporated Ghost Dance teachings into their sermons to attract Indian converts.[11]

Mormons and other Christian evangelists, many of them émigrés from the "burned-over district," thus exchanged prophecies with Indians of the Basin-Plateau region, an Indian "burned-over district" that matched any other for its waves of religious upheaval and prophetic visions. Spiritual symbols and ideas moved back and forth, and distinctive new prophecies were woven together among Indians, Protestant missionaries, and Mormons in northern Nevada and along the trail to California—the track of religion, commerce, and emigration bisecting the Northern Paiute world.[12]

Thus, the 1870 Ghost Dance and perhaps the Prophet Dance became key influences on Jack Wilson as he fashioned the next great religious revival to sweep out of the Walker River region—the Ghost Dance of 1890. The new movement was strongly rooted in Numu tradition; Christian influence on Wovoka had been minimal through his young adulthood, and missionary activity in the area had been inconsistent since 1870. Baptists opened a boarding school at Pyramid Lake Reservation in 1882 but, unable to attract any converts, closed the school by the early 1890s. Other denominations fared even worse.[13]

The absence of Christian missionaries among the Indians partly reflected the weakness of Nevada's churches: in 1890 a lower proportion of the state's population attended churches than in any other state. Lacking enough congregants to raise their own churches, Baptists, Presbyterians, Methodists, and others routinely borrowed one another's church buildings, a practice that created a spirit of Christian ecumenism among them. In this religious environment, believers appear to have had access to multiple strains of Christian thinking and to have adopted those teachings that most suited their needs.[14]

But for all its institutional weakness, Christianity may indeed have had some influence on Wovoka. Although Methodists numbered only a few hundred in Nevada, they drew small congregations along the Walker River (with a church at Yerington in 1875) and especially along the Carson River, which some have called the state's "cradle of Methodism." Still closer to home, David Wilson read Bible verses daily at the breakfast table, where young Jack Wilson sat with the rancher's Scottish Presbyterian family nearly every day of his boyhood. There were occasional revival meetings along the Walker River among Presbyterians and Methodists; these "concerts of prayer," led by circuit riders (one of whom married a Wilson daughter), could last for several days. According to one of the Wilson brothers, Jack attended these services and was "impressed" by them, being moved at one point to claim that only he "could save Indians from hellfire."[15]

Jack Wilson was thus mindful of these and perhaps other influences as he worked up a response to a looming crisis in the 1880s. In these years when he was becoming an adult and beginning to prophesy, the sudden onset of economic depression and severe drought threatened to make the refashioned livelihoods of Paiutes impossible. Anthropologists and ethnohistorians have rightly hailed Paiute success in transitioning to the modern workplace; their ability to switch between gathering wild mustard and pine nuts and gathering dollars constitutes a remarkable cultural adaptation. But the boom-and-bust cycles of business in the Gilded Age made wage work an especially precarious way to live. Soon after Paiutes looked away from their decimated landscape and embraced the new economy of wage labor, the Silver State fell on hard times. By 1889, the year Jack Wilson's prophecies began to propagate from the Walker River Valley, few places were more in need of a redeemer.[16]

The first harbinger of the downturn appeared on the Comstock Lode in the late 1870s. Although the bankruptcy of the lode would not be certain for some time, diminishing returns led to corporate contraction and unemployment. By the early 1880s, former miners huddled in caves and camps in the mountains around Virginia City, hoping for a return to fortune. Eventually most of these men left the state, accompanied by assayers, mill workers, hat makers, shop owners, and other business men and women. While the decade between 1880 and 1890 saw 25 percent growth in populations across the United States, Nevada saw its population fall more than 25 percent. By 1890, it was the most poorly inhabited state in the union, with 44,000 residents scattered in small settlements across 110,000 square miles of sagebrush and creosote. San Francisco had more people. "A dying state," the *New York Times* called it in 1889. As a Silver State newspaper editor observed, "Nevada is poor and steadily growing worse year by year."[17]

In other places and times, declining population might imply scarce labor and higher pay. But Nevada wages, which had been among the nation's highest prior to 1880, plummeted as the Comstock went quiet. Although there are few good data for Paiute wages over time, generally speaking we can say that there was strong downward pressure on both jobs and wages in the decade leading up to Jack Wilson's visions.[18]

Even as the Ghost Dance expressed customary Paiute preoccupations with the apocalypse, it also found external affirmation in the millennial anxieties of the conquerors. Nevada's spiraling decline called into question America's perennial optimism about western settlement. From Carson City to the halls of Congress, settler abandonment fueled debates about whether Nevada should even remain a state.[19]

The only economic sector that was improving in Nevada was ranching, an industry most Americans considered so backward as to be practically feudal; it also employed fewer people than ever after a wave of consolidation in the 1880s. Some Paiute men became cowboys, or *pakeada'a*. (The Paiute word is derived from the Spanish *vaquero*.) But prior to 1889, ranching was mostly an open-range enterprise with few fences and few labor needs. Ranchers who expanded their livestock holdings raised at least as many animals as prior settlers had, and probably more, thus decreasing even further Paiute access to traditional bunchgrasses.[20]

To Indians, of course, American "civilization" was not as benevolent as represented in popular culture. But by this time Paiutes depended on American industry to survive. Thus, paradoxically, both the advance of the mining economy through the 1870s and its retreat from 1880 onward had profound and threatening ramifications for them. Paiutes found themselves not only dependent on declining wages but ever less able to supplement them with hunting and gathering. To no small degree, Paiutes had bought into the dream of Progress, because laboring on its ranches and roads and in its mining camps was all that was keeping them alive. The river of money had so supplanted the old rivers that, without wages, Paiutes would perish.

Wage dependency was a frequent topic of Paiute conversation. Jack Wilson himself testified to the necessity of cash for survival, complaining in a rare interview at the height of the Ghost Dance enthusiasm that Nevada settlers would not give Indians "anything to eat unless they pay for it." Another Paiute leader explained how his people made their living in 1891: "We work for the white people and with the money buy our flour, tea, coffee, sugar, and clothing." Such sensibilities had been current for at least a decade. In 1881 a Virginia City settler informed one "Paiute Sam" that the town would soon be abandoned and the Indians could occupy all the buildings for free. According to the *Territorial Enterprise*, Paiute Sam "looked serious" for a time. "S'pose white men all go 'way," he asked. "What Injuns gon' to do?"[21]

In 1882, Sarah Winnemucca, daughter of Chief Winnemucca of the Pyramid Lake Paiutes and a prominent Paiute advocate in the American press, summarized her people's new crisis. They had lost wild game, wild grass, and many of their piñon groves. Now the riches of the Comstock Lode were gone as well. Rumors abounded that settlers would soon abandon the state. "If the white people leave us, to go over the mountains to California," she lamented, "we must go over the mountains with them too, or else starve."[22]

These Paiute testimonies convey a powerful sense of something broken that cannot be put back, of an old world shattered, of a people with no hope but to live in a strange new world and anticipate a new age ahead. From just such sensibilities was the new religion born.

Even as a teenager, the boy stood out. He was first photographed in 1875, when he was about nineteen years old. He is standing on a sidewalk in the town of Mason. To his right a white man sits on a

FIGURE 4.1. The teenage Wovoka, second from left, ca. 1875. Courtesy Mary Ann Cardinal/Nevada Historical Society.

horse, and at his left is a row of white women and men. The photo is grainy, and Wilson appears blurry. Perhaps he moved as the shutter snapped, because we cannot make out his face. But already he wears the broad-brimmed, high-crowned hat that would become a Wovoka trademark. Another lifelong talisman, an eagle feather, appears to dangle from the hat. His appearance is strikingly different from the stolid figures to either side of him, and not just because of the hat, the feather, and his dark skin. His hands in his pockets, his shoulders relaxed, he is jaunty, almost dapper. In a way unusual for an adolescent among adults, and especially for a Paiute teenager among white women and men in 1875, he appears confident and possessed of something like a sense of his own bearing—hints, perhaps, of the charisma for which he would become legendary.[23]

Ten years later that charisma was in full bloom. Wovoka had grown into a tall man, with broad shoulders, piercing eyes, and a deep, resonant voice. He did not speak often, but when he did it was with a solemnity that commanded attention. Wilson never learned to write. He left no personal reflections, and we can piece together only the barest outline of his thoughts or emotions in this period. Like many other Paiute workers, he understood English (although he spoke it reluctantly), and he could not have escaped the sense of political and economic decline in the air. These were years of failing mines, falling population, and anxious talk in settler streets, fields, and kitchens about Nevada's future.[24]

Northern Paiute tradition teaches that spirit power runs in families. Jack Wilson's father was a noted shaman, and the son's own extraordinary gifts appeared when, in the mid or late 1880s, he "began to dream," in the words of one of his white employers. He would fall into trances, his body stiff, insensate. To the Paiutes, these spells suggested communion with the spirits and elevated him as a man of power. Even among whites who dismissed "Indian superstition," the trances inspired something approaching awe. "He wasn't shamming," recalled Ed Dyer, the storekeeper who occasionally translated at Wovoka's meetings with government investigators in the early 1890s. "His body was rigid as a board. His mouth could not be pried open. . . . The whole matter is one to which I still confess considerable puzzlement." Initially friends tried—and failed—to revive him, and some feared he was dead. But in time they became accustomed to his trances. Awakening after a full day or even two, Wilson would describe entering heaven through the Milky Way, wrapped in a blanket. It was a strange story but hard to dismiss, for when he awoke he had ice in his hand.[25]

Accounts of his first full vision diverge on its circumstances. An area rancher reported that Wilson had a vision after falling sick, which Wilson later explained as having died and gone to heaven. A Paiute contemporary put the event near the headwaters of the Walker River, in the Pine Grove Hills, where Wilson was cutting wood. He heard "a great noise which appeared to be above him on the mountain." Laying down his ax, he began to climb toward the sound when he dropped dead. Then God swept down and carried him to heaven.[26]

On this and a subsequent visit, Wovoka saw in heaven "the most beautiful country you could imagine," full of game and fish and populated by Indians and whites who had died but now were all young again. They danced and gamboled. They played ball and "all kinds of sports." During these visitations, God gave him a dance that would make the earth into the heaven he had seen and told him that his people must "meet often and dance five nights in succession and then stop for three months."[27]

These two reports agree that the year of his first vision was 1887, but James Mooney, the only anthropologist ever to interview Wovoka, concluded from additional details provided by the prophet that it must have occurred in 1889. Whenever it was, many more visions followed. Wilson himself would later tell an army scout that God had visited him "many times" since his first vision. By 1889, he had distilled from his heavenly visits a series of key teachings for bringing about the renewal of the earth that God had promised. His people, he said, "must not fight, there must be peace all over the world; the people must not steal from one another, but be good to each other, for they [are] all brothers." In addition, he conveyed the message to the Indians "that they must work all the time and not lie down in idleness."[28]

The prophecies and the instructions for their fulfillment reached Paiute believers at the large Ghost Dances that Wilson began to convene in the late 1880s. In key respects, the Ghost Dance was identical to the traditional, and fairly common, Round Dance of the Northern Paiutes. White observers began to notice an increase in the frequency and size of Round Dances in the late 1880s. As early as December 1888, a local newspaper remarked, "The Mason Valley Piutes [*sic*] are having big dances every night now." These apparently were the first of Wovoka's nighttime Ghost Dances, with the people standing shoulder to shoulder as the circle turned. Unlike Round Dances, these gatherings featured no drum or other instruments, only the beating of thousands of feet upon the valley floor. Over that rhythm rose voices in holy song:

> *Fog! Fog!*
> *Lightning! Lightning!*
> *Whirlwind! Whirlwind!*
>
> *The whirlwind! The whirlwind!*
> *The snowy earth comes gliding,*
>   *the snowy earth comes gliding.*[29]

In the lyrics of the songs (probably composed by Wovoka himself), we see the presence of spirits manifested in the weather. At the same time that he began to convene these dances, Wovoka asserted his power to control the weather, claiming that during his visit to heaven he had been given "control over the elements so that he could make it rain or snow or be dry at will." It was these powers that promised salvation from a new climatic peril: the terrible drought that began in 1888.[30]

Although Nevada rain is always scarce, the state's plants and animals have evolved to survive on the rain and snow that cross the Sierra Nevada, especially in the winter. Already tapering off, that precipitation nearly ceased in 1888–1889, just as the Ghost Dance enthusiasm began to mount. The wild foods that remained were practically obliterated, and the Walker River ceased to flow halfway along its course, withering Paiutes' hay and barley fields at the reservation.[31]

Ghost Dancing addressed this crisis, summoning the redeemer and promising the renewal of the earth. But it also called upon the power of the prophet, the booha he displayed, typically through feats of magic. During the 1880s, the period when he began to go into trances, Jack Wilson gave several public demonstrations of his remarkable spirit power. Of these, white settlers were most preoccupied by the power that may have been most common among Paiutes and, to them at least, less convincing than others: his imperviousness to bullets. Many Northern Paiutes had claimed such power, including Wovoka's father. According to various accounts, after announcing this power to an assembled crowd, Wovoka loaded a shotgun with dust and sand and handed it to his brother. Then he walked away several paces and spread a blanket on the ground. Turning to face his brother, he stepped onto the blanket. Then he ordered his brother to shoot him.[32]

The gun roared. Wilson shook himself. The crowd surged forward. His shirt was riddled with small holes. Balls of shot rolled around his feet. But the man was unhurt.[33]

For all the centrality of magic to Numu life, it was another popular pastime, practical jokes, that may have contributed to Paiutes' pervasive skepticism about claims of extraordinary booha. In the 1880s, emotions were still raw over the trickery of the Ghost Dance prophet Wodziwob, who had been undone (according to some accounts) after being caught using dynamite to create a "magical" explosion.[34]

Wilson, too, had his doubters, and the audacity of his shotgun performance—which suggested that not only was he bulletproof, but he could turn dust and sand into gunpowder and shot—heightened suspicions of trickery. Wilson was not a shaman (as discussed later), but shamans often performed sleight-of-hand tricks as a means of reinforcing the community's sense of their powers. Perhaps, as some alleged, he had blasted an empty shirt full of holes, put it on, loaded the gun with a blank cartridge, and then pretended to load it with dust and sand before handing it to his brother. Then, perhaps, as the gun belched smoke and noise, he dropped a handful of loose shot onto the blanket.[35]

Whites were fascinated by this story (although only Indians appear to have witnessed the event). Eventually officials came to wonder whether the display was an effort to incite an uprising. In the run-up to Wounded Knee, as some of Wilson's followers in South Dakota and Oklahoma donned the allegedly bulletproof ghost shirts, a government agent tracked Wilson down and demanded to know: had the seer staged a demonstration of his own imperviousness to gunfire? "That was a joke," shrugged the visionary.[36]

Regardless of Wilson's intent, the shotgun episode was just one (and perhaps the least impressive) of what came to be known collectively as "Jack Wilson's miracles"—demonstrations that have inspired debate and dissension in the region for over 100 years, and not only among Paiutes. An elderly white informant bemused a local historian in the early 1900s, when Jack Wilson was still alive, by telling the story of a Paiute girl who died in Hawthorn in the 1880s. Some 200 people attended her cremation, went the tale, and watched in awe as Jack Wilson kept a promise to raise her body from the flames up to heaven.[37]

Wilson was even more renowned, however, for another miracle during these same parched, depressed 1880s. On a hot July day, a crowd gathered on the banks of the Walker River, where the big man spread a blanket on the ground and waited. Suddenly a block of ice weighing "25 or 30 pounds" dropped into the center of the blanket. Again there were allegations of trickery. The storekeeper Ed Dyer witnessed this event and later claimed that Wilson had situated the blanket beneath a cottonwood tree "whose dense foliage would serve to hide the object until it sufficiently had melted to release it from whatever ingenious fastening Jack had fashioned to hold it."[38]

There were also Numu among the doubters; indeed, Wilson's displays of booha may have inspired the most contentious argument among his own people. And yet, for our purposes, how he conjured is less important than what he conjured. Whether the ice was miraculous or not, this story and its variations tell us something important about the man and the moment in Mason Valley. In one version, af-ter the ice appeared, somebody produced a washtub and lifted the ice into it. As it melted, the people drank. Afterward the Numus bathed in the river. Recalled Ed Dyer, "It might have been sacramental wine judging from the solemnity."[39]

In another account of the same event, Wilson placed a willow bas-ket under a tree, and into it fell water and ice, which the people drank before praying. In still another report, the ice fell into his hands. And some recalled not ice falling from the sky on that midsummer day, but ice floating down the river.[40]

The most striking feature of these stories is the recurrence of ice—the ice in Jack Wilson's hand after his trance and return from the Milky Way, the ice in the river in the middle of summer. Ice in his hand was a sign of his booha and proof that in his trance he had been to its very source; as such, it reinforced his claim that he could return the rain to this parched land. Making ice appear also hinted at his prodigious weather power (a power that his father and other Numu before him had also possessed). Wilson's booha is said to have come from several spirits, among them Wolf and Eagle. He was a rarity in drawing booha from the elements as well, including two kinds of clouds. "One was a straight high cloud. This was for snow," recalled a contemporary. "The other cloud was dark and close to the ground. It was for rain."[41]

Certain peripheral elements of many Jack Wilson stories resonate with both Paiute and biblical traditions. For example, white horses appear in Numu myths of the spirit who brings rain, called the Man Who Became Thunder, and also in the Old Testament prophecies of the apocalypse. Jack Wilson not only "flew" a white horse but regu-larly rode white horses, and some said these, too, were a source of his booha.[42]

The white horse becomes even more significant in a famous story of a dance near his home, upriver from Yerington. At the gathering—which was attended by "thousands and thousands" of Indians, ac-cording to a witness—Wilson prophesied the arrival of a white horse.

On the fifth day the animal appeared on a nearby mountaintop. "It was beautiful," recalled the witness. "It was the color of snow." As he reassured the anxious people, Wilson beckoned the horse down. Slowly, the animal descended, now and then stopping to neigh and whinny. Its hooves seemed to never touch the earth. When it finally arrived on the dance ground, the horse whirled in place and thick dust rose into the air. A "heavy cloud" then appeared (dark and close to the ground, one of Wilson's sources of booha) and "started to move towards" the awestruck crowd. "It came right on top of the horse." And with the cloud came rain, "for all the people to drink from the cup." The horse departed, trotting up the mountain, water dripping from its sides. Then it vanished. The ground shook.[43]

The bracketing of the entire story with clouds suggests the centrality of the cloud spirit for Ghost Dance acolytes. Like the snow-bearing cloud, the white horse appears on a mountaintop. And like snowmelt, it descends the mountain slowly, floating above the ground (figuratively, flowing). Like a whirlwind—a ghost—the animal spins and raises a cloud of dust, and over its back appears the water-bearing cloud to quench the people's thirst. The centrality of clouds is suggested in another version of the story in which the people do not receive water but take hold of the cloud and eat it, like snow—or manna.[44]

In his own eyes, Jack Wilson's success as a ritual leader stemmed in part from being a cloud-bringer. In 1890 an army scout asked him how he had become so renowned in Nevada. By bringing rain, the ranch hand explained, almost casually, after "I caused a small cloud to appear in the heavens."[45]

The connection between these displays of weather-making booha and the earthly renewal promised by the Ghost Dance is perhaps most obvious in the ice and snow that appear in the Paiute songs of the religion, presumably because snow signals that water will come as the land warms. "The snowy earth comes gliding," proclaim the joyful lyrics, as if the new world being born was mantled in white. Walker River Ghost Dancers were particularly fond of another song whose lyrics connected the snowy mountain peaks to the Milky Way—the

road of the dead along which Jack Wilson had carried the good news
on his return from heaven:

> *The snow lies there*
> *The Milky Way lies there*[46]

Snow and ice figured prominently in Wilson's displays of power
because booha is immanent in frozen water, which promises redemption from thirst; melting ice signifies not only the benevolent spirits
of the high mountain peaks but the emergence from winter and the
beginnings of earthly renewal. Wilson thus appealed to customary
Paiute spiritualism—the booha of the weather maker, harnessed to
the power of water—but also to those who drank from the well of
Christian symbolism, in particular holy water and baptism.

The promise of the dance and its moral code became clear in
that dismal Nevada season of 1889 with Wilson's most miraculous
demonstration of all—the one that garnered him renown near and
far and seems to have validated him not only as a weather maker but
as a prophet.

The sinking fortunes of industry and the declining population
were inscribed in the very earth in the valley of the Walker River.
The booha that flowed with water in the riverbed was gone. By late
summer, as the river approached the Walker River Reservation, it
slowed to a trickle and then vanished completely. John Josephus,
captain of the Indian police at the reservation, had dismissed Jack
Wilson's powers and his prophecy ever since he first heard about
them. Josephus was no fool. He wanted his people to prosper, and he
had aspirations of his own. He dreamed of building a wooden house,
with glass windows, a shingled roof, and a good iron stove to keep it
warm in the winter. But now, with the baking heat and the withering
fields, the policeman was filled with foreboding. If the ranches and
farms failed, where would the Numu work? If their own crops per-
ished, what would they eat?[47]

Putting aside his skepticism, Josephus saddled his horse and rode
a dusty twenty-five miles to the prophet's home. Arriving in the

evening, he implored the weather maker to bring rain lest the people suffer any further. Wovoka sat with his head bowed and never spoke a word. Eventually, he rose and went to bed.

Early the next morning, he told his visitor, "You can go home and on the morning of the third day you and all the people will have plenty of water."

Back at the reservation, the two white employees of the farm office remembered that, upon his return, Josephus announced the promise of rain in three days' time. Two nights later, a storm swept over the Sierra Nevada. On the morning of the third day, Josephus and the other residents of the reservation awoke to find the banks of the Walker River flooded and the irrigation ditches full.[48]

Wovoka was not done. Heavier storms followed through the month of October, and in December seven consecutive days of blizzard conditions heralded the arrival of Nevada's legendary "white winter," a season of epic cold and snow. By New Year's Day, the snow in some places was "belly deep to a horse," in the words of one eyewitness, and tracks on the railroad were so blocked with snow that cattle shipments stalled.[49]

Reports of Jack Wilson's weather making rocked Indian communities, enhancing the reputation of the charismatic young man across the region. In February 1890, hundreds of Paiutes turned out to hear him preach at Walker River Reservation—in the face of a driving snowstorm. "He claims that he alone is responsible for the storms of this season and they all firmly believe it," wrote agency farmer J. O. Gregory.[50]

Long into the twentieth century, stories circulated about Wovoka's weather magic, leaving little doubt as to the mysteries he embodied. He walked through the rain without getting wet. He lit his pipe with the sun. Without burning his flesh, he grasped a hot coal, and when he blew on it, the wind rose.[51]

He protected people from storms. Torrential rains descended on a band of Numu during the annual pine nut harvest in the mountains outside Pine Grove. The rain soaked through tents and drenched firewood. People appealed to Wilson for relief. He ordered them to stack their wet wood, then asked for an eagle feather. He approached the woodpile—"a big, tall man in all that rain," a witness recalled— then raised the eagle feather a full arm's length over his head, directly over the woodpile, and released it into the howling wind.

The feather hovered in place; Wilson knelt, wrapped in sheets of rain.

Suddenly a spark flashed. Then flames roared up through the damp wood, and all began to burn. All but the feather, which turned "the most beautiful color."

Wilson rose and faced the band. "Take from this fire to your tent. . . . Build your fires. The rain will go on but your food will get dry, and everything will be all right."[52]

THE RANCH HAND'S EXTRAORDINARY BOOHA GREW TO SUCH AN extent that white people could not avoid hearing about it. Most scoffed. But in the typescripts of old, unpublished memoirs by Nevada pioneers, in the sheaf or two of scribbled notes from long-ago interviews conducted by diligent historians, and in some surviving voice recordings, in voices barely audible over the hiss of reel-to-reel tape, there hovers something else: a pause in the condescension, a waver in the scorn. As one settler put it, Jack Wilson might have been "an awful fake," but he "wouldn't want to go on record" saying as much.[53]

There remained something about Jack Wilson that the ranchers of Mason Valley, however cocksure in their white superiority, could never quite figure out. Part of it was his charisma. Decades later, long after he died, even those who dismissed his reputed powers remarked not only on his sense of humor, his work ethic, and his kindness but on how he stood out in a crowd. Everyone seemed acutely aware of how much respect he commanded from other Indians. And there was something curious, wasn't there, about Jack and the weather?[54]

As mentioned earlier, some settlers resolved the matter by conceding his ability to forecast the weather—to be a "weathervane"— but not to make it. Others may have tried to buy whatever power the prophet had. Wilson himself claimed that "both the Indians and the whites" had approached him "and asked for rain to make their crops grow." The story has the ring of truth. Whites generally associated Indians with nature and primal forces, and ambivalence about Indian rainmaking cropped up in surprising places. Thus, as late as 1938, one correspondent advised a Kansas newspaper editor to break a drought by consulting Indians, as they were "very close to the forces that govern the natural events of the planets."[55]

Jack Wilson's assertion that whites asked him for rain is supported by at least one story that circulated among settlers. When the rainmaker approached a rancher named Dan Simpson with an offer to make it rain in return for three cattle, the story goes, Simpson refused. Then his cattle began to keel over. Simpson sought out Wilson and struck a deal. One beef steer—if Wilson could make it rain. The relentless downpour that followed allegedly made Simpson a convert. Years later he was still giving Wilson an annual gift of beef.[56]

Perhaps it was the openness of Nevada settlers to Wovoka's rainmaking and their appeals to him for help that inspired Wovoka to make his boldest move yet after he broke the drought of 1889. Flush with his storm-brewing success, Jack Wilson began to articulate a political program. Although it never advanced beyond the most rudimentary proposal, it spelled out the earthly fulfillment of his visions and revealed him to be both in the tradition of Walker River political leaders and a spiritual rebel with much grander designs than predecessors like Wodziwob. With reservation farmer J. O. Gregory as his secretary, Wilson dictated a letter to US President Benjamin Harrison in which he offered a deal. In return for a small monthly stipend and political authority over the West, as well as a plot to farm on the reservation, he could promise regular rain and weekly news from heaven. As he later explained his vision to the ethnologist James Mooney, when God gave him power as a weather maker, he also "appointed him his deputy to take charge of affairs in the west, while 'Governor Harrison' would attend to matters in the east, and he, God, would look after the world above."[57]

White acquaintances laughed at Wovoka's pretensions. Gregory forwarded the letter to his superior, the Indian agent at Pyramid

Lake Reservation. "You will doubtless be amazed at the letter you will have received from Jack Wilson the prophet," he warned. The proposal—money in return for rainmaking and preaching—seemed to prove the naïveté of the simple primitives.

But the settlers themselves remained ambivalent toward Wilson's claims, owing in part to their limited options for managing Nevada's chaotic climate. Some whites felt that his demands for rain payment were clear proof that he was exploiting "superstition" to bilk his people. But in wrestling with questions of rain and climate, American settlers and officials often veered into magic and religion themselves in efforts to make the rain fall in these final decades of the nineteenth century. The Ghost Dance was not an isolated event, but one that emerged from a context of vigorous efforts not only by Indians but by white people to renew the desert West.

CHAPTER 5

INDIAN PROPHECY, AMERICAN MAGIC

F AR BEYOND NEVADA, MAKING RAIN WAS AN AMERICAN PROJECT
of some urgency. The drought and decline in Virginia City and its
hinterlands were symptomatic of a much broader ecological and economic downturn across a wide swath of the trans-Mississippi West.
The first half of the 1880s had been wet over much of the Plains, and
there was seemingly little reason to worry about precipitation. Then
drought clamped down like a vise in 1886; although it loosened its
grip intermittently, the following decade saw severe drought over vast
stretches of the interior West. Blazing summers were punctuated by
devastating winters, with bone-chilling blizzards on the Southern
Plains in 1885–1886, on the Northern Plains in 1886–1887, and, as
we have seen, in the Great Basin with Wovoka's "white winter" in
1889–1890.[1]

Even with these occasional seasons of heavy snow, the climate
proved so searing that sections of Kansas, Nebraska, and South Dakota were depopulated on a par with Nevada during the 1880s; in
fact, through the 1890s residents of the Silver State continued to flee
at only a slightly slower rate than the decade before. When the US
Census Bureau declared the frontier closed in 1890, it based its calcu-
lations on the presence of a minimum of two persons per square mile.

By 1900, some sections of the West—including Nevada and parts of the high plains—had become frontier again.[2]

Even before this time, the science of climatology was as full of quackery as medicine and could be as wishful as dreams. Longing for rain could cause even the ostensibly rational to veer into magical thinking. For instance, various theorists, after confronting the arid western landscape in the 1870s, began to extoll the notion that plowing the soil would release moisture locked in the ground and make the climate wetter. "Rain follows the plow" became the slogan of dryland speculators and settlers. For a time, relatively heavy rainfall seemed to bear out the theory, at least on the Great Plains, and many white Americans came to believe that westward settlement itself was changing the climate and bringing closer to fruition the millennial prophecy of American expansion—that white settlement of the West would perfect the earth.[3]

The drought of the late 1880s was a rude awakening from such fantasies. By 1890, efforts to water the West took on new importance. Making rain, or changing the climate, seemed one of the only ways of making a large quantity of land arable because, in this age before diesel pumps and federally supported irrigation works, moving water to the desert was virtually impossible. The climate "science" that developed in this era looked only slightly less mystical than Wovoka's rainmaking and was more religion or wizardry dressed up like science than actual science.[4]

As Wovoka made his weather, western leaders routinely solicited and were solicited by various self-proclaimed rainmakers who advertised the use of explosives or mirrors (and not uncommonly, prayer) to open the skies in return for money. In 1880s Kansas, Frank Melbourne, "the Rain King," dazzled onlookers with the mysterious fumes he released into the air to make it rain—for $500. By 1888, he had contracted with a group of Kansas entrepreneurs to form the Inter-State Artificial Rain Company, which promised rain for ten cents per cultivated acre as far afield as South Dakota through the use of "chemicles"; at least a half-inch of rain was guaranteed—or no fee. The rise of competing companies and their apparent success in making rain over much of Kansas and other western states led the Rock Island Railroad to finance a rainmaker, who worked his wonders all along the line from Topeka to Colorado Springs until 1894.[5]

To be fair, Americans who laughed at Wovoka also laughed at their own prophets of rain. No rainmaker won universal acclaim among the public. In some quarters, all met with ridicule. But rainmakers also had their supporters, many of them with money and influence. Even skeptics were often prepared to suspend disbelief in hopes that rain might fall. Long into the twentieth century, ranchers in the Southwest routinely invoked magic to explain, predict, or change the weather. In the absence of rain, many also resorted to "water witching"—divining underground water with the use of a forked stick. To this day Christian prayers for rain are part of popular and even official culture across much of the United States. Nevada ranchers like Dan Simpson, who appealed to Jack Wilson for help in 1890, might have been hedging their bets. Why not pay Wilson for his rain magic? The payments were small and had to be made only if the rain came. In that event, there would be plenty of money anyway.[6]

Although Jack Wilson's distinctly premodern-looking rain magic grew out of ancient Paiute traditions, it became woven into the fabric of American efforts to understand and control rain in the 1880s and 1890s. Perhaps inspired by white entrepreneurs, the prophet came to see his rainmaking as a commercial opportunity. "I think that all white men should pay me [for rainmaking]," he told an 1890 investigator. "Some two dollars, others five, ten, twenty-five, and fifty, according to their means." Belief in magic might have been a marker of primitivism, but if white farmers set the standard for modernity in this period, they had little better to offer when it came to making the desert damp. Conjuring rain to save crops marks Wilson and his followers less as primitives than as American moderns.[7]

Another, seemingly very different approach to watering the desert also came to the fore in the 1880s, a decade that saw a decided turn in American life toward the scientific and technocratic in the form of government-supported irrigation projects. In 1888, Nevada leaders announced their support for a US Geological Survey plan to map the public domain to locate and record the best sites for reservoirs, ditches, and irrigation canals. It was an unprecedented program—gathering and analyzing a vast quantity of hydrological data on Nevada and the entire West in order not only to create a series of topographical maps but also to measure the flow of water in every western river across nearly one billion acres of land—in hopes of creating a more standard plan for western development.[8]

Thus, by the fall of 1888 federal surveyors, conducting what we might call a census of reservoir sites, were lugging transits and survey chains into river basins from Montana to New Mexico, including the upper reaches of the Walker River, which turned out to be one of the first locations surveyed. At almost the same moment and in the same place that Jack Wilson heard the "great noise," put down his ax, and was carried into heaven, USGS surveying parties were on the ground assessing the value of the canyons for future reservoirs.[9]

To Nevada's Paiutes, these prospective reservoirs and ditches were not entirely foreign concepts. As we have seen, they knew how to irrigate. Long before whites arrived in Nevada, they had excavated trenches to water pozeeda meadows along the Walker River, and Numu farmers on the Walker River Reservation had created eight miles of ditches to water their farms. The booha that clung to water could be secured not only through magic but through artifice, not just by prayer but by work.

For their part, America's technocrats and engineers could be as spiritual as they were rational. The irrigators' dream mingled plenty of unscientific sentiment—belief—with the science. For all the tabulations of rainfall and stream flow compiled by US surveyors and engineers, none seemed able to think of water apart from its God-given purpose. For them, one belief about water constituted an article of faith, as unquestionable as the Lord's Prayer and the virgin birth: for them, water made farms. Even as they measured the flow of every river and calculated how many acres of soil the water could cover at the appropriate depth and necessary intervals to mature a particular crop, they called this "the duty" of the river—as if God made rivers to water onions.

The duty of the river bore close relation to engineering ideas about the "duty" of a machine: either its measured effectiveness under specified conditions or, more generally, the amount of work it was meant to do. In a sense, irrigation systems were machines for the mass production of farms and all their purported virtues, from yeomen's independence to bodily health.

We look back on the irrigators and their project as the modern, scientific, and secular successor to the old-fashioned prayer-and-hucksterism of the rainmakers, and to a point that is correct. But secularism and rationality do not explain why their irrigation systems had to produce corn, wheat, and beets rather than, say, fish, antelope, and pozeeda. In truth, beneath technocratic secularism lay a deep-seated religious vision. Tightly bound to engineering and politics, this vision is easy to ignore as such, but it flew so presumptuously in the face of material conditions in Nevada, and was so dependent on faith over facts, that it can only be called religious. If the duty of the river was to water crops, the duty of the engineers was to measure, dam, and divert the river to perform this task and thereby fulfill God's injunction to Adam to reclaim the garden from wilderness. As one irrigation engineer pronounced, "Upon us rests the obligation of the Divine mandate—'Subdue the earth.'"[10]

Even more forthrightly religious sentiments animated the exhortations of the era's most famous irrigation promoter, William Ellsworth Smythe, a Nebraska journalist who combined science and the supernatural in grandiose fashion. Elevating irrigation far beyond "a matter of ditches and acres," he lauded it as "a philosophy, a religion, and a programme of practical statesmanship all rolled into one." As Smythe explained, irrigation settlers were men "who keep the lamp of faith burning through the night of corrupt commercialism, and who bear the Ark of the Covenant to the Promised Land." Smythe felt that irrigating the arid West could solve virtually all social problems—the teeming tenements, the expanding dependency on wages and markets, and the widening chasm between rich and poor. For him, irrigation would renew both American society and the American earth.[11]

Over the next decade and beyond, Smythe's vision proved vastly popular, his "irrigation crusade" inspiring a near-religious (or just plain religious) devotion among some followers. In fact, it was partly through this vision that, over the next decade, digging ditches took on a religious tone and the American language of irrigation shifted. In popular parlance, the word "irrigation" began to share space with "reclamation." A term once used to connote the recapture of lapsed believers for the true church, "reclamation" was now used in reference to the redemption of the garden of Eden from the wilderness.[12]

With the support of growing numbers of western boosters and politicians, among them prominent Nevadans, Smythe initiated a broad political campaign whose aim to "make the desert bloom as the rose" was at least as spiritual as it was scientific. Smythe's zeal would one day founder on the hard realities of desert scarcity. Wovoka's rain magic may have been completely unscientific, but Smythe's reclamation project—to transform millions of desert acres into farms for a contented citizenry—represented a wizardry whose relationship to science was equally unclear.

This irrigation program that mixed science and spirit so freely was also profoundly political. Western politicians sought new farmland to lure more settlers to their states, but their efforts had met with limited success. Wovoka's political aspirations—to become "Governor of the West"—were no less ambitious. But these, too, would fail. The prophet's letter to President Harrison apparently never left the office of the Indian agent. After the killings at Wounded Knee, Wovoka would suppress his political goals, which subsequently never became widely known. But his desire for secular power to complement his booha underscores the desire for a new kind of authority expressed in the Ghost Dance movement. Paiutes sought a spiritual and political power that could reorder their relations with heaven, earth, and the American conquerors at the same moment that Americans were elevating engineers to achieve a frankly spiritual objective of earthly salvation.

Partly for this reason, Wovoka retained a great deal of authority among Paiutes, who had always rewarded men with great booha.

Indians along the Walker River took up regular collections for Wilson at his sermons, and throughout his life Indian supplicants gave money in return for his spiritual intervention.[13]

RAINMAKING WAS JUST ONE CLUE TO THE MODERNITY OF THE Ghost Dance prophecies; among Jack Wilson's teachings lie other keys to the usefulness of this religion for Numu and other Indians. For Paiutes, Wilson's weather making underscored the power and relevance of his instruction. The storms he conjured might not have transformed Nevada into the "pleasant land . . . full of game" that he saw in heaven, but his teachings nonetheless promised the restoration of rivers, wild food, and work. If believers wished to secure to themselves the happiness and eternal youth that Wovoka had seen in heaven, their duties were clear. They needed to perform the new dance. As Wovoka himself taught, they were to love one another and "put away all the old practices that savored of war." And of course, they were to work. As Wilson emphasized again and again, God instructed him "that he must tell the Indians that they must work all the time and not lie down in idleness," and that they must not "lie or steal." It was partly to carry out God's exhortation to work that they were to live in peace with the whites.[14]

The teaching about labor would be adapted in various ways among different peoples and prove central to the religion in its early days. In 1891 an Arapaho evangelist named Casper Edson, who had learned to write at Carlisle Indian Industrial School in Pennsylvania, recorded that Wovoka himself instructed his disciples to "work for white men." A Cheyenne account by Black Short Nose similarly dictated, "Do not refuse to work for [the] white man."[15]

Few dimensions of the Ghost Dance of 1890 have been less examined than this commandment to labor—and few are more central to its meaning. Contemporary white observers seem to have either overlooked it or mistakenly believed that the Ghost Dance, being an Indian ritual, was strictly oriented toward the hunting and gathering past. On this point, some army officers and even James Mooney seem to have conflated Wovoka's teachings with those of Smohalla, a Columbia Plateau visionary of the Wanapum people. For decades from his camp on the Columbia River, Smohalla, who was firmly in the Prophet Dance tradition, had been falling into extended trances, recounting visits to heaven, and promising the return of Indian dead. But unlike Wovoka, Smohalla also urged his followers to reject farming, wage work, and other ways of white people.[16]

For Wovoka, in striking contrast, wage work was a holy commandment, an order from God. At the same time, it was a commandment meant only for earthly life. Work was the path to the glorious salvation that awaited Indians in the afterlife, where there would be no more work, only "dancing, gambling, playing ball and having all kinds of sports."[17]

The instruction to work for white people was synonymous with a commandment to work for money; this expressly modern practice seems to have been integrated into other expressions of Indianness, in part through the dance itself. For believers, the Ghost Dance was less about turning away from the modern world than about finding a way to live in it as Indians. Toward that end, the Ghost Dance sanctified wage labor as a proper Indian way of living that Indians could take up without sacrificing Indian identity.

Moreover, in connecting wage work to the well-lived life and holding out the reward of eternal play and natural abundance in the afterlife, Jack Wilson's teachings tried to reconcile Paiutes to the modern workplace in all its brutality, tedium, and uncertainty. Of course, work was not new to Paiutes. Building fish weirs, making yucca twine, weaving rabbit-skin blankets, gathering millions of seeds from wild grass in a single afternoon—all these tasks required intensive labor. But the wage workplace combined tedium in equal measure with danger: rattlesnakes in the hay fields; horses and hay-mows and harrows that ran over workers, breaking and mutilating their bodies; and ranch owners' sexual predations toward Paiute women who laundered their clothes and cooked their meals. Work was uncomfortable, painful, and endless, and it made one vulnerable in unprecedented ways.

The Ghost Dance of 1890 addressed the needs and anxieties of Paiutes in an arduous wage-laboring world, starting with the problems of dispersal and social disintegration. Its greatest attractions may have been its appeal to community sentiment and the way it pushed back against centripetal forces in Paiute life by gathering the people together. Among Jack Wilson's revelations from God was the admonition that the Indians "must have their dances more often, and dance five nights in succession and then stop." The Ghost Dance also prescribed gathering times. Repeated every three months, it functioned not as a seasonal event, like the old dances, but as a marker that drew people together in every season, four times a year.[18]

The dance provided not only a new reason for gathering beyond the usual ritual round but also what was unmistakably an expression of community: men, women, and children holding hands and dancing the circle together. Unlike other ceremonies that were oriented toward local spirits, this ritual spoke of a universal god and welcomed outsiders, evangelizing its core beliefs to all. Among these was its code of behavior—respect the property of others, do not lie, do not fight, "love one another"—which served as insurance against the acrimony and rivalry that often bedeviled Paiute efforts to forge friendly bonds with other Indian peoples, many of whom were traveling to the same workplaces as Paiutes.

Indeed, the importance of the peace teachings should not be underestimated. Tribal hostilities had left a bitter legacy, and Paiute bands were even notoriously, sometimes murderously, competitive with each other. Paiutes refused to gather on reservations in part because of rivalry between outfits. The Ghost Dance was a ritual expressing unity and community solidarity, and in reasserting Indian identity, not only among Numu people but beyond them, across ethnic lines with other Indians, it held out the promise of mutual cooperation and affection.[19]

In encouraging wage work and participation in the cash economy—the only routes to survival for Wovoka's people—the Ghost Dance movement resembled other evangelical revivals across the nineteenth

century. Like other people caught up in rural work—the hobos, cowboys, and lumberjacks who were Paiute contemporaries (and some
were Paiutes)—Indians who worked on even the remotest ranches
and in the most isolated boomtowns served industrial markets: the
hay and wood they cut fueled the draft animals and stamp mills of the
Comstock economy. Besides reconciling the faithful to the industrial
workplace, with all its hazards, by making diligent work a virtue and
a commandment, and besides holding out the promise of a glorious,
work-free afterlife, the Ghost Dance of 1890 also attracted followers
by pointing the way to the river of money and providing religious
authority for spending a life there.

Authorities worried that the dance was a call to rebellion, but
a call to work and harmony suggests anything but violent intent.
At the same time, the new religion offered a religious reform that
threatened the position of religious leaders among the Numu. When
Jack Wilson took aim at authorities after receiving God's word, the
leaders in his sights were not Americans—they were Paiutes. His
goal was not to restore the old ways among Walker River Paiutes
but to overturn them. He sought not purification of the old religion
but advancement of a new one, alongside a new politics to quell a
gathering emergency—the need to heal his people, as the rain healed
the land.

JACK WILSON'S MOVEMENT—HAD IT SUCCEEDED IN ITS ENTIRETY—
would have addressed the crisis of authority bedeviling Paiute society;
this emergency remained largely hidden from whites, but its traces
linger between the lines of the historical record. Authority was always
a contested attribute in Paiute communities. The names of famous
chiefs punctuate the chronicle of Nevada's Indian conflicts from about
1850: Winnemucca at Pyramid Lake, Joaquin and Horseman at the
Walker River community. But in truth, there was little room in Paiute society for chiefs or headmen to exercise authority over anything
larger than an extended family. Paiutes were too dispersed, the outfits
too independent, to compel anything like obedience. The emergence
of powerful chiefs in the middle of the nineteenth century was an

anomaly, a function of war with the Americans, who demanded the elevation of powerful individuals—like Winnemucca—with whom they could negotiate land cessions. After the wars were over, chiefdom of any consequence practically disappeared.[20]

In place of chieftainship, older forms of leadership reemerged. Customarily, the primary leader among Paiute outfits was a sagacious man who announced group decisions about when to move, and where, to gather food or (increasingly in the American age) to get work. Often the announcements included admonitions to behave properly, to look out for one another, and to avoid missteps along the way. Because the central function of leadership took this form of speaking to the community, leading men were often referred to not as chiefs but as "talkers."[21]

It was in these decades after the Paiute War that leadership passed primarily to the "doctors"—the healers who were the gatekeepers between Paiutes and the other world. There was no need for a talker to be a doctor, and certainly many doctors never sought political leadership. But for some reason, as chiefs receded to the point of irrelevance in the 1870s and 1880s, the talkers who emerged in the Walker River country were disproportionately doctors. In the generation after the American conquest, Numus placed their trust in doctors and courted their counsel on community stresses and family crises. They followed their instructions for organizing rabbit hunts and pine nut expeditions. To show goodwill and thank them for their wisdom, Paiutes routinely did work for the doctors and gave them gifts or tokens of appreciation, including food and money. Considering their standing among Indians, it is not surprising that whites routinely mistook doctors for chiefs.[22]

We may surmise that doctors assumed such stature in part because illness was such a threat to community welfare. In contrast to booha, a benevolent energy that emanated from moral order, sickness represented entropy or chaos. Like a sandstorm, it shredded the fragile networks connecting people to one another and to the animals and plants that fed and sheltered them. Each outfit depended so much on the labor of every person that any one individual's departure from full health could become a crisis. A fever or hacking cough cost a family not only the afflicted member's work but also the work and skills of those who nursed that person. Moreover, the age of wage work made it even more challenging to maintain health and well-being. Workplace injuries were a constant danger, epidemics of American ailments to which Paiutes had little resistance continued to reduce their numbers, and in the absence of their traditional food sources, their diets often relied on flour and canned goods bought from the local store.

Paiute doctors cured sickness and certain injuries through ritual intervention because maladies were spiritual events. Many illnesses were believed to come from dreams (one's own or somebody else's), sorcery, or the visits of ghosts. Often illness stemmed from evil deeds that caused the departure of one's soul to the land of the dead, across the Milky Way. The doctor was the primary bulwark against these forces. He or she (women could not be talkers but they could be shamans) deployed their booha to cure the afflicted in rituals that required a gathering of the entire community at the lodge of the sick or injured individual to sing and dance. In orientation and effect, then, Paiute rituals were profoundly social. Doctoring not only required communal participation but helped heal social rifts. A great doctor was a figure whose wisdom and shrewdness made him or her a communal resource.[23]

Given that doctors were leaders of Numu society, perhaps the most striking aspect of the 1890 Ghost Dance is that it was introduced by a figure who was not a doctor. Jack Wilson would become a shaman later, but he had not yet done so in 1889. He seems to have provoked comparisons with them by mimicking their method. Doctors often lay down beside their patients and "died," their bodies remaining "stiff as a board," according to witnesses, for several hours or more. During this time they traveled over the Milky Way to the afterworld—a green and pleasant land like the one Jack Wilson saw in his visions—to seek out the sufferer's errant soul and persuade it to return to the living body it had abandoned.[24]

Jack Wilson not only adopted these traditional shamanic motifs but also behaved like a shaman. He was social but famously reserved,

quiet, and serious, and his ritual pronouncements were major social events. A big, affable man, he also looked the part: like many
shamans, he was handsome and well dressed. The eagle feather he
carried was standard paraphernalia for doctors.[25]

Wilson appropriated the signs of shamanism, however, not so
much to invoke shamanic authority as to stage a symbolic rebellion
against it. The Ghost Dance evoked a heaven that looked in some
ways like a vanished world, but the ritual itself, far from being a return
to tradition, mixed older ceremonial forms with new ones to create a
new ritual. That ritual was accompanied by a new system of beliefs—a
new religion—that invited Paiutes to a peaceful but no less potent
ritual shunning of the old doctors. The Ghost Dance was a means
of circumventing shamanic authority. In contrast to standard rituals,
the Ghost Dance required no shamanic intervention. There was no
need to find the right healer with the proper booha to intervene in
an illness. All one needed to secure health and eternal youth was to
join the circle and live by the code handed down from God to Jack
Wilson. All that was needed was opening one's heart to the message
from heaven.[26]

Why would Jack Wilson promote what was effectively an end run
around the shamans? How could he advocate a belief that undercut
the authority of his own shaman father (still very active in the 1880s)?
Indian religions of the Great Basin and the Columbia Plateau were
characterized by cycles of prophecy and apocalyptic revelation. Nevertheless, why at this moment did so many Paiutes join Wovoka's
circle in a ritual that challenged the authority of their own leaders?

Evidence is thin, but one answer may lie in the tenuous political
order of Walker River Paiutes in 1889. For all the respect accorded
doctors, they seemed unable to heal the social discontent, frictions,
and feuds that roiled Numu society by the time Wilson was a boy.
Moreover, many alleged that doctors aggravated or even initiated a
great deal of social trouble by misusing their extraordinary powers.
This was shamanism's downside. True, a man or woman who could
channel the power of snakes or otters might heal one's ills. But if a
shaman grew jealous or spiteful, that potent booha could become a

weapon for making a person sick, stealing his wife, blinding him, or destroying his children.[27]

In other words, shamanism devolved all too easily into witchcraft, or sorcery. Possessed of such powerful spirit, doctors were among the most dangerous potential sorcerers in any community. Since the primary motivations for this ancient evil were jealousy or resentment, accusations of sorcery generally flowed from feuds in camp. If illness befell somebody involved in a feud or an antagonistic relationship, or if one of that person's family members grew sick, then witchcraft was often suspected.[28]

In the old days, before the American conquest of Nevada, witchcraft accusations had served to modify individual behavior and regulate community mores. Witches were by definition mean, jealous people, and they generally had few kin of repute who would stand up for them when murmurs of "witch" began to circulate. To avoid being accused of witchcraft, Paiutes tried to remain friendly, generous, and cordial with their neighbors. They sought out friends and built kin networks. Selfish behavior that threatened community well-being elicited witchcraft accusations; community-oriented actions fended off any such suspicion and helped the outfits remain strong.[29]

Witches were so dangerous that no Paiute community could tolerate them. Being accused of witchcraft thus put one in a perilous position, and an alleged witch had limited options for responding. Since perceptions of hostility lay at the root of many witchcraft accusations, the accused might make amends. If the gossip about the charges was not too widespread, the accused might modify his or her personal behavior, work harder to avoid giving offense, and hope the allegations went away. In more serious cases, the alleged witch might confess and repent, take a ritual bath to cleanse the bad will, and request forgiveness. If the situation was more dire than that, the accused might flee, for witches were often shunned or even killed.

Perhaps witchcraft allegations had always troubled Paiute society, but fragmentary evidence suggests that the decades leading up to the 1890 Ghost Dance were especially ripe for sorcerers. As Paiutes from distant locations were separated from their close kin and thrown together with other Numus who were only distant relations or none at all, in a context of collapsing resource networks and competition for vanishing work, and as illness ran through the small outfits like fire through the nut grass, it seems to have become harder than ever to avoid witchcraft allegations, and even a number of high-profile doctors were accused. Perhaps the most famous was Horseman.

An Indian hero in the Paiute War of 1860 who led his people in extracting concessions from the Walker River settlers, a man who could make a wall of fire erupt from the desert or a stream of clear water flow from sand, Horseman is said to have stood well over six feet tall. After the war, he was renowned as a powerful doctor, but as the decades passed his power turned bad and his booha soured. Suspicions grew among those who knew him. When one of his patients died, her husband accused Horseman of witchcraft and shot him, but he survived. In 1896 he treated his own daughter for an illness, but she died soon after. Her son-in-law, A-peema'a (also called Pat Hoye), approached Horseman with two companions. While the two men pinned the doctor's arms, the son-in-law shot Horseman in the back of the head and then crushed his skull with the butt of his rifle. Another of Horseman's daughters told authorities that her father had become a witch and that the killer should not be prosecuted.[30]

Perhaps the most notorious witch controversies in the Walker River country were those concerning Tom Mitchell, or Hummingbird, a Paiute from Bridgeport who moved to Mason Valley in the 1890s. Memories of him have diverged sharply over the decades: he has been recalled both as a potent, benevolent doctor and talker and as a jealous, vengeful sorcerer. Born about 1840, Mitchell was something of a prodigy, his power as a doctor on full display by the time he was nine. For all his support in the community, stories circulated among his detractors that he used his powers to harm others, including some of the people who approached him for cures.[31]

Whether or not Mitchell was actually engaged in sorcery is less important than the fact of the allegations and what they suggest about tensions among Walker River Paiutes. Especially intriguing is the entanglement in the lore of Mitchell's dark arts of two particularly famous victims: Wodziwob and Wovoka, the two Ghost Dance prophets. Wodziwob turned away from the Ghost Dance to become a shaman sometime after 1871. He was a very successful shaman, with very powerful booha—until he was witched by Tom Mitchell. After that, it is said that Wodziwob could cure no one.[32]

Jack Wilson ultimately achieved far greater stature among his people even than Wodziwob, and his affability was so renowned that he seems to have had no enemies—except for Tom Mitchell, who, according to some accounts, was Wilson's nemesis. A generation older than Wilson, the shaman seems to have been nonplussed by the younger man's displays of booha. After Wilson became a shaman, he would remain a venerated healer right up until the 1920s, when the prophet of the 1890 Ghost dance is said (by some) to have lost his power after being bewitched—by none other than Tom Mitchell.[33]

There is almost no documentary record of the jealousies, confrontations, and feuds that probably formed the social context of all these witchcraft allegations. For every person in Yerington who has believed the story, there has probably been another to defend Mitchell as a benevolent doctor and never a witch. We cannot even establish whether or not Wilson and Mitchell disliked one another, or whether these stories circulated in their lifetimes or only after the two men died. (Mitchell lived longer, dying in 1945.) But the stories are pervasive and persistent enough to suggest there were deep tensions among shamans, who competed for power and influence, and also between shamans and everyday Paiutes, who feared the jealousies and resentments of their doctors. That tension may partly explain the appeal of the Ghost Dance movement.[34]

Shamanism was nothing less than a brand of specialized power that was prone to abuse, not only through the practice of witchcraft but also through the use of shamanic authority to point out suspected witches. Doctors were central figures in witchcraft allegations even when they were not the alleged sorcerer because no action could be taken without a doctor's confirmation that the suspect had indeed ensorcelled a victim. The effect of this dual role was to up the stakes of shamanic rivalry. Evidence is fragmentary (the census did not count witches), but there are plenty of hints that shootings and killings of doctors plagued Nevada in the decades between 1870 and 1910. In 1891, two witch killings—one at Winnemucca and one at the Western Shoshone reservation at Duck Lake—scandalized authorities. By the early twentieth century, as many of the old doctors died, one Paiute woman in the Walker River country was known to remark that it was "better with all them old timers gone," as there were "too many witches them days."[35]

However much witchcraft anxiety upped the appeal of the Ghost Dance movement among Walker River Paiutes, in its overt teachings—love one another, do not fight, do not steal, do not lie—the new religion also warned against the very behavior that witches were known to exhibit. At the same time, it diminished the need for shamans, the practitioners at the center of witchcraft allegations, by opening a portal to the spirit world that required no shamanic mediation. The circle of dancers came together without recourse to a doctor's prescription or payment for his booha. They could afford to ignore him.

Compared to shamanic magic, the scale of the Ghost Dance remedy was better suited to a post-epidemic world, a time when the ranks of remembered dead so vastly outnumbered the living. The power of a doctor was strictly individuated. It took a very powerful shaman to cross into the afterlife and return even with a single soul. But none recovered more than one soul at a time. Certainly none would hold out hope of conveying all the dead back to life.

The Ghost Dance prophets did just this, thereby raising the possibility that shamans could become unnecessary. Jack Wilson, like Wodziwob before him, promised not just individual health, as the shamans did, but earthly renewal, eternal youth, and freedom from all illness. If the visions were true, shamans were obsolete. If what the prophets promised was genuine, nobody would ever need a shaman again. It was as if Jack Wilson and Wodziwob were saying to their followers, "Come with me, and we will leave these troublesome shamans behind."

Precisely because it threatened to make the office of shaman obsolete, the 1870 Ghost Dance occasioned strong resistance from doctors throughout the Basin-Plateau region. In northern California, the dance took on such healing powers that, in the words of one Tolowa woman, "the old-time doctors were out of business." Not surprisingly, recalled another, "all the doctors said this was the wrong way to worship."[36]

Perhaps it was for this reason that shamans like Tom Mitchell numbered among Wilson's greatest opponents some twenty years later. Who needed a shaman when one could restore youth and health by conducting oneself in the right manner and joining the circle to dance? At least as much as reclaiming lost love, the Ghost Dance drew the old, the sick, and the infirm into the circle at Yerington, Wind River, Pine Ridge, and beyond with the promise of restoring health—often earning the ire of shamans.[37]

In one sense, the Ghost Dance was like a shamanic ritual for the curing of a sick person, if on a bigger scale. It was what anthropologists call "an increase rite"—a ritual prayer for better times, with the larger aim of restoring a fallen people and a broken world. By 1890, the earth had gone dry in drought like a body wracked by illness. The gathering of the people in the circle around the singing prophet reunited the community in ways not unlike the healing ceremonies of the doctor, but without the attendant danger of sorcery. The Ghost Dance offered the hope of brotherhood and love and a world renewed to a fractious, demoralized people.[38]

DRAWN BY THE NEWS OF A RAINMAKER-PROPHET, PERHAPS EVEN a messiah in the land, a dizzying array of Indian peoples sent representatives to Jack Wilson. In January 1889, a visiting party of Bannocks heard the teachings, apparently when he announced his vision after coming down from the Pine Grove Hills, and took them back to their reservation at Fort Hall. Within months, the teachings began moving eastward across the Great Basin as Bannock, Shoshones, Gosiutes, and Utes shared the lessons and performed the dance. When the news reached Wind River Reservation in Wyoming, a Northern Arapaho named Nakash, or Sage, was intrigued by the rumors; with a friend named Yellow Calf, he visited Wilson in the spring of 1889, and the two men subsequently took the prophet's message back to their own people and the Eastern Shoshone. From the valley of the Wind River the word went north and east, to North Dakota with the teachings of a Gros Ventre Indian who had been visiting among the Shoshones when Sage returned from Nevada, and to South Dakota and Montana. Around the same time, the good news arrived in letters written by graduates of boarding schools at the reservation of the Southern Arapaho and Southern Cheyenne in Indian Territory (also called Oklahoma).[39]

Porcupine, the Northern Cheyenne mystic whom Lieutenant Robertson would later interview, picked up the good word, possibly from Nakash, during his sojourn on the rails that fall. There are hints in some sources that a letter "written by an Indian" and inviting delegates to come hear "the Messiah" arrived at reservations in the fall of 1889. Thus, in November and December 1889, Porcupine and some other Cheyennes from Lame Deer—accompanied by still more Shoshones and Bannocks from Fort Hall, the Arapahos Friday and Sitting Bull (not the same as the Hunkpapa Sioux leader), and the Lakotas Good Thunder, Cloud Horse, Yellow Knife, Kicking Bear, and Short Bull—arrived at Jack Wilson's home on the Walker River. In the summer of 1890, twelve Cheyenne and Arapaho, including Black Coyote, Tall Bull, and others who had followed the earlier reports, came to hear the prophet's teachings for themselves.[40]

In the wake of all these visits the word went out. Not everyone was convinced. Omahas and Winnebagoes dismissed the Lakotas who showed up to preach at their Nebraska reservation in April 1890.[41] But there were so many glorious messages in Wilson's prophecy that many of the exhausted folk who gathered in the midst of the shattered desert in that year of trial could only listen in wonder. If the redeemer's return presaged the renewal of the earth and the restoration of plentiful game, then it must be that animal spirits—with their powerful medicine—would also return. Moreover, in the world envisioned by Wilson of reembodiment for dead souls there would be no dangerous ghosts to sicken the living, be they Paiutes or others who feared the angry dead. With its bold blend of beliefs ancient and new, the prophecy promised redemption of the land from the chaos that had engulfed it and the return of Indian people to balance, youth, and health for all eternity. The word had gone forth. In Utah, Idaho, Wyoming, Oklahoma, and South Dakota, among Indians of the high country who were brokenhearted by the loss of loved ones, humiliated, hungry, and sleepless with fear for their children's future, the new vision sang of power and joy and hope.

AS THE DANCES CONTINUED INTO THE FALL OF 1890 AND EVER more seekers came to Wovoka's door, anxiety grew among Nevada settlers. The press coverage of the Ghost Dance ritual in South Dakota, replete with fictional "outbreaks" and killings, was lurid, and fears of an Indian conspiracy in Nevada began to mount. November brought anxious complaints. In the town of Austin, the sheriff wrote to the governor requesting guns after fearful settlers gathered to report the presence among local Paiutes of "many strange fellows"— probably Bannocks. Similar fears gripped the town of Ione. The governor's office, anticipating war, sent arms to these and other locations. But Nevada proved different from South Dakota. In every case, the dances ended before weapons arrived.[42]

Farther afield, a third of the US Army was descending on Pine Ridge, and generals had redoubled their efforts to locate the source of the prophecies. Their staffs pored over reports of the weird rumors from officers in the field. Especially noteworthy was the gospel of Porcupine, a lengthy testament that offered intriguing clues to the identity of the prophet and his location. On November 28, General John Gibbon, commander of the army on the Pacific Coast, sent scout Arthur Chapman to Nevada with orders to confirm what he could of Porcupine's account and, above all, to "find the person who personated Christ."[43]

That very day Chapman boarded a train in San Francisco and traveled over the Sierra Nevada into the Great Basin. From Reno, he followed the track of Porcupine to Walker River Reservation. Chapman was an Oregon settler who had a history with Indians: he was married to an Umatilla woman, spoke Nez Perce, and had seen fierce combat as an army scout in the Nez Perce War of 1877. Stepping down from the train at Walker River on Sunday, November 30, at three in the afternoon, he found small, relaxed groups of Paiutes— men, women, and children—talking and playing cards. Locating the reservation's farm instructor, J. O. Gregory, he began his inquiry. From the farmer the scout discovered the name of the prophet: Jack Wilson.

Gregory told him that Wilson—who "had a good name for being an honest, hard-working Indian"—had been preaching to the Indians for "two or three years." But recently the ceremonies had become more frequent and much larger, and "a great many strange Indians . . . attended these dances who he understood had come from a great way off."[44]

As the farmer and the scout conversed, Paiutes took notice and began to gather around. Gregory introduced Chapman to Captain John Josephus of the Indian police. For white authorities, Josephus was a trusted Paiute subordinate. He was not only a policeman on the reservation but an interpreter for the government. So it was all the more astonishing when Josephus recounted matter-of-factly the story of Jack Wilson's life: his journey to the mountains, his hearing of "a great noise" and putting down of his ax, his ascent to glorious heaven, God's admonition to dance, and the weather-making powers God bestowed on the prophet.

Even more frankly, Josephus confessed that when he first heard these revelations, he did not believe them. But "the country was very much in need of rain" and he was concerned for the "great suffering" of his people, and so he decided to visit Jack Wilson and "try his power over the elements." He told Chapman about riding to Wovoka's house and imploring him to bring the rain; Wovoka promised to do so, and the promise was fulfilled with the storm that filled the Walker River to bursting. "Now," said Josephus, "I am a strong believer in the unnatural powers of the new Christ."[45]

We might imagine that Chapman was doubtful of this gospel according to Josephus. But also listening was another Paiute policeman, Ben Ab-he-gan, who "corroborated every word he spoke."

Even more astonishing, both white employees of the reservation, Gregory and one Mr. Peas, "corroborated his statement in regard to the water." "In fact," Chapman later reported, "all the white people I talked with about the agency, and in Mason and Smith valleys, admitted that the rain did come, but they cannot convince the Indians that Jack Wilson had nothing to do with its coming."[46]

There were also skeptics among the Indians. To allay their doubts, Wilson had invited all to hear his teachings and witness his powers, and so had begun a series of unprecedented gatherings. Not long before, some 1,600 people had participated in a dance at the reservation, among them not only Paiutes but Cheyennes, Sioux, Arapahos, Utes, Shoshones, and Bannocks, as well as a distant people Chapman did not recognize called the Umapaws (perhaps Mojaves).

For Chapman, talking to the prophet himself was going to be more difficult. Wilson had left two days earlier for a distant valley in the mountains. With Ab-he-gan as translator, Chapman boarded the train back up the line to Wabuska, and from there took the stage to Mason, arriving as the sun descended toward the horizon at 5:00 P.M. There they learned that Jack Wilson had gone to the Pine Grove Hills at Desert Creek, some sixty miles farther south and west. The scout and his interpreter hired a wagon and driver. Spending the night in Mason, they set out at dawn the next day to follow the winding course of Desert Creek Road.

After thirty bumpy miles, they met a party of Paiutes heading the other direction. They were coming from the town of Bodie, and some of them had seen Jack Wilson camped near the town of Wellington, which was not along Desert Creek but on a different road, still farther west. Changing direction, Chapman and Ab-he-gan made what haste they could. It took them the rest of the day and part of the evening. Late that night, as snow and rain alternately fell from the sky, they rolled into Wellington and stopped at Pierce's Station, a local inn.

Despite the lateness of the hour, Chapman sent for Wilson, and the prophet appeared almost immediately. He said he was glad to see Chapman and shook the scout's hand. Chapman remarked that he, too, "surely was glad to meet one of such notoriety," and that he "had heard a good deal of him through the newspapers, and would like to ask him a few questions," which he hoped the prophet would be willing to answer.[47]

Wilson agreed. Chapman began with the basics: What is your name? How old are you? What is your tribe?

The answers came quick: Jack Wilson. About thirty. Paiute.

After the preliminaries, Chapman asked him about his preaching, but the prophet's answers were "in substance about the same" as the gospel related to him the day before by Josephus: that Wilson had been to heaven, that he had many visions of God, and that God told him "to send out word to all the Indians to come and hear him." He was to tell the Indians that they must work and remain at peace with whites and each other, and that "we were all brothers." Wilson said that God had given him powers "to cause it to rain or snow at his will" and told him that the world would be destroyed and the good people would be remade as young people. God also urged him, Wilson said, to tell the Indians that "they must have their dances more often."

Wilson recounted for Chapman how he broke the drought after being importuned by Indians and whites—"I caused a small cloud to appear in the heavens, which gave rain for all, and they were satisfied." He expressed his wish that "all white men" pay him for "things of this kind," each "according to their means."

The prophet assured the scout that his teachings were not violent. Indeed, he had told all the visiting delegations that when they returned home they should "say to their people that they must keep the peace; that if they went to fighting that he would help the soldiers to make them stop."

Wilson promised a greener, more benign climate if settlers reformed. It was hard for his people to live in Paiute country now because the whites "do not treat him and his people right; . . . they do not give them anything to eat unless they pay for it." If the settlers would become more respectful, Wilson said, "he would have it rain in the valley and snow on the mountains during the winter, so that the farmers would have good crops."

Chapman warned Wilson that soldiers might be coming. The prophet had heard that rumor already. "I do not care about that; I would like to see them. That is all I care to talk now. We are having a dance next Saturday."

When Chapman left Pierce's Station the next day, it seemed to him that Wilson and his prophecies posed no threat, and that the possibility of an uprising was remote. Most settlers shrugged off the dances. In fact, Chapman encountered only one white man who believed that they could lead to trouble. Wilson's rivals at Pyramid Lake Reservation may have denounced him, but Paiutes generally seemed headed for something other than war. They dressed "as good as the average white man of that country," and the women in particular were "exceedingly well dressed for Indian women." Local whites esteemed the Paiutes "as an industrious and hard-working people" who curiously "preferred to work for the white people" rather than for themselves. Few whites thought there was anything threatening or amiss about Wilson, his visions, or his dances.

In his life among Indians, Arthur Chapman had seen some extraordinary things. In 1877 he was scouting for the US Army as it chased after Chief Joseph, who, with his heroic band of Nez Perce, was headed north from Idaho into Montana, their sights set on Canada. In this epic, 1,500-mile running fight, a supposedly primitive leader and his small contingent of badly outgunned warriors tenaciously defended their women, children, and old people from one of the world's most industrialized and relentless armies. When the Nez Perce fell short and found themselves surrounded within sight of the US-Canada border, Joseph surrendered to General Oliver Otis Howard. It was Chapman who translated those famous words that echo from the Montana prairie down through our own time: "From where the sun now stands I will fight no more forever."[48]

Chapman embodied what historians call "a liminal figure" in that he occupied the edges of more than one culture while not being fully accepted in any. He knew the Nez Perce and had friends among them (indeed, after the war he became Chief Joseph's translator), but he fought with the US Army against them. He could be hotheaded, or maybe he bore a grudge: some blamed him for starting the hostilities in 1877 by firing on a Nez Perce peace delegation early in the conflict. Others said that he was a coward who fled the fight during a critical phase. With his Umatilla wife, his knowledge of the Nez Perce language, and his unpredictability, Arthur Chapman was an ambiguous character in the story of American conquest.[49]

And so he remained in his meeting with the Ghost Dance prophet. Having fulfilled his orders to "find the Indian who personated Christ," he seems to have left his superiors stupefied; there is no record of their response to his interview with the prophet. But the interview clearly satisfied Chapman, who came away from that meeting sounding reassured, certain, and even charmed by the prophet.[50]

And what about the gospel of Porcupine? How much of it could Chapman confirm? Had the Cheyenne actually been to Nevada to meet with Jack Wilson, whom he called "the Messiah"? In his travels, Chapman gathered the facts. When he asked Ben Ab-he-gan about Jack Wilson, he also asked about the Cheyenne mystic. Ab-he-gan confirmed that Porcupine's account as dictated to Lieutenant Robertson in Montana six months earlier, supplemented with details from the reports and speculations of officers, was a true account of the Cheyenne's Nevada journey. Indeed, not only was Porcupine's gospel accurate about his travels, but "I will say," concluded the scout, "that it is wonderfully correct."[51]

PART 2

DISPERSION

CHAPTER 6

SEEKERS FROM A SHATTERED LAND

THE GHOST DANCE WAS KINDLED AS EARLY AS 1888, WHEN rumors of Wovoka's prophecy began to travel along the bands of steel that tied the Great Basin to the Great Plains and the world. By the fall of 1889, the Ghost Dance in Nevada had become a roaring fire, fueled by the joy and exhilaration of widely scattered people who came to hear Wilson's teachings and then dispersed like so many sparks. Where they touched down, new ritual fires often erupted, and from these still more sparks spread to ignite devotions nearby. East of the Rocky Mountains, two such blazes burned so bright as to become beacons of the new religion across the Great Plains. On the Northern Plains, in South Dakota, thousands of Lakota Sioux became enthralled with Jack Wilson's promise of renewal and relief. On the Southern Plains, in Indian Territory—today's Oklahoma— Southern Arapahos took up the religion with at least as much enthusiasm as Lakotas.

By following the religion as it developed among Lakotas and Southern Arapahos after it shifted to the Plains, we can avoid a common mistake. Too many histories of the Ghost Dance focus on Pine Ridge and relentlessly narrow their view of it as the story approaches Wounded Knee, stripping away its complexities and turning to political and military concerns, until the religion is so diminished as to

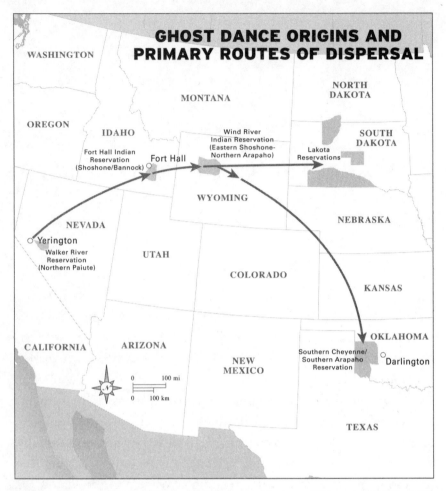

MAP 6.1. Ghost Dance Origins and Primary Routes of Dispersal, 1889–1890

fit in the sights of a Hotchkiss gun. Although Americans forced the Ghost Dance into a cul-de-sac at Wounded Knee, that would prove to be only one chapter in its complicated history. The religion went many places from Nevada and flourished on dozens of Indian reservations. By comparing Lakota and Southern Arapaho responses to the new teachings, we can better understand what the religion meant to Indian believers and why, in spite of the catastrophe at Pine Ridge, it flourished for decades elsewhere.

In the end, the Ghost Dance offered believers, not an immediate and violent rejection of American governance, but an intense spiritual and emotional experience that facilitated their accommodation to American dominance in many areas of Indian life while simultaneously allowing them to seek out health and prosperity on Indian terms. The Ghost Dance, in other words, helped many believers accept conquest while strengthening their resolve to resist assimilation.

IN THE FALL OF 1889, A MAN NAMED SHORT BULL SET OUT FROM the Brule Lakota Reservation at Rosebud, South Dakota, to investigate reports of the new religion. Along the way to Nevada, he would ride trains and wagons with a diverse array of fellow seekers from far-flung places, including a group of fellow Lakota (Western) Sioux, also from South Dakota. From Wyoming came a Northern Arapaho named Singing Grass (who spoke English, a particularly valuable asset to the group); the Northern Cheyenne mystic Porcupine, from Montana; a charismatic Southern Arapaho who would become a major evangelist; and dozens of others who are lost to history.

The hardships endured in the Indian communities these men left behind on the Plains had created fertile soil for the seeds of the new teachings they would bring back. In Oklahoma, a woman named Moki grieved for her children. Her husband, Grant Left Hand, fought back his own sorrow as he worked as a clerk in the traders' store. Nearby, a man named Black Coyote, the chief of police on his reservation, redoubled his efforts to rise from his humble beginnings even though opportunities for wealth and advancement were declining all around him. These Indians and dozens of others would soon be crisscrossing their reservations and the Far West searching out Wovoka's teachings and carrying them to others.

Why did so many from the Great Plains embark on quests to find the new religion at this moment at the close of the 1880s? And why were so many eager to hear its message? East of the Rocky Mountains, the tribes where the religion took hold were scattered along an arc that encompassed most of the Plains and included Southern Cheyennes and Southern Arapahos as well as Kiowas, Kiowa Apaches, Caddos, Pawnees, Lakota Sioux, Northern Arapahos, Northern Shoshones, and Northern Cheyennes. The vast grassland that was their home stretched from northern Texas well into Canada, and east from the Rocky Mountains for 500 miles. Although its very name—the Great Plains—conjures images of unlimited space, for Indian people the 1880s had been a decade of crushing new limits. The disasters that had befallen Paiutes were replicated and sometimes amplified on the Plains, where every single Ghost Dance tribe was confined to a reservation, their old lands stripped away by voracious white settlers and their autonomy smothered in a reeking dependency on federal annuities and rations. With their children dying in waves of illness, their religions under siege by zealous missionaries, and their old economy in ruins—they had even fewer means of making a living than Wovoka's people—they found it nearly impossible to imagine a future for themselves. The appeal of the Ghost Dance was the way it addressed these challenges, offering both a means to survive this harsh era and a hope of ending it in a millennium of earthly renewal.

FOR PLAINS PEOPLES, IT WAS TIME FOR EMBRACING DEFEAT. FROM north to south, Indians of the Plains had seen their autonomy vaporize in a frighteningly brief period. We might begin with Short Bull's people, the Western Sioux, who would provide most of South Dakota's Ghost Dancers. They were nomads who migrated from their earlier homes in Minnesota onto the Plains in the seventeenth century in pursuit of beaver pelts for trade with Europeans; by the eighteenth century, their westward expansion was vigorously fueled by trade in buffalo robes for guns and other goods. As they moved across the Mississippi and Missouri Rivers, the Lakota ascended a high, arid grassland on the western boundary of the Plains at the base of the Rocky Mountains. This grassland sits 6,500 feet above sea level, and the mountains soar up to 14,000 feet, casting a rain shadow eastward for hundreds of miles. In the sheltered river valleys of the Missouri, the Platte, the Republican, the Loupe, and other rivers, early occupants of the region—Mandans, Hidatsa, Arikaras, and Pawnees—had built earth-lodge villages, planted maize, beans, and squash, and hunted the surrounding country for meat and hides. For centuries these horticultural villagers had outnumbered the smaller groups of nomads and dominated the region.

By 1700, the intrusion of horses into this landscape had begun to revolutionize Indian economy and society, allowing them to turn grass and sunlight into speed and mobility. With the expansion of markets for buffalo robes in the United States and Europe, the gun trade increased as well. Meanwhile, new diseases like smallpox and influenza proved deadlier in the dense earth-lodge towns than in far-flung nomad camps. As these forces diminished the horticultural villages and forced them to cede territory, the bison-hunting nomadic villages, notably Lakotas, dramatically expanded in size and power.[1]

These were no aimless wanderers, but mobility was key to their success. They moved across and controlled the high plains by anchoring their lodge-skin villages in river valleys, which provided not only water for people and horses but also meadows for pasture, wood for cooking, and shelter from fierce winter storms. Over the course of two centuries, the Western Sioux spread up the broad gradient of the Great Plains until they reached the Rocky Mountains.[2]

Short Bull was a Brule (or Sicanju) Lakota, and a *wicasa wakan,* or holy man. Slight and small, he was born beside the Niobrara River, in today's western Nebraska, around 1847, when the seven tribes of the Lakotas were at the height of their power. The westernmost of these tribes, the pioneers of the advance onto the Plains, were the Oglalas and Short Bull's own Brule, but close behind and closely related were the Hunkpapas, Sihasapas, Two Kettles, Sans Arcs, and Minneconjous. Fiercely independent, numerous, and well armed, Lakotas pushed aside some enemies in their westward advance and made new pacts with others, until they had carved out a vast realm that covered most of the Northern Plains, including South Dakota, North Dakota, and eastern Montana, and extending southward through most of Wyoming and Nebraska.[3]

It fell to Short Bull's generation to resist the American expansion that followed in the tracks of the Lakotas, who were reluctant to surrender lands or autonomy. Like many of his generation, he had

FIGURE 6.1. Short Bull, ca. 1891. Denver Public
Library, Western History Collection, B-567.

fought in the wars against Pawnees and Crows, and now he returned
to battle, this time against the American troops and settlers in the
campaigns that Americans called the Plains Indian Wars.

Indian resistance, for all its heroism, faced high obstacles. It had
been the environmental revolution of the horse that brought the
Plains nomads to the apex of their power: the speed and power of
their mounts allowed them to cover more territory, hunt more bison,
and carry more provisions than when they moved on foot. However,
a second environmental revolution, the cheap transport across the
region made possible by coal-powered railroads, brought their desolation. During the Civil War, the Union Pacific Railroad extended
its tracks into the southern reaches of Lakota territory, in today's
Nebraska. Now animals and land that had been too remote from

markets to be valuable could be converted to commodities like meat, hides, and grain. Chicago and St. Louis, like Virginia City, began to funnel resources from a vast swath of Indian country to the world market. The rails drew farmers, ranchers, cowboys, buffalo hunters, and others in such numbers that Nebraska became a state by 1866. For Indians, the results were devastating.

The region's wildlife declined so rapidly as to stagger the imagination. In 1790, the Plains probably supported 30 million bison, along with abundant elk, deer, antelope, mountain sheep, and wolves. Trade in bison robes and hides, the expansion of cattle, and the settlement of the eastern prairies all cut deep into the herds. Between 1871 and 1878, some 5 million bison vanished from the Southern Plains. In the same period, millions more disappeared from the north. The last buffalo hunt among Short Bull's people occurred in 1883. In 1889, William Hornaday, an American naturalist, conducted a census of bison over the entire Plains. He found 25 in the Texas Panhandle, 20 in Colorado, and 236 in Wyoming and Yellowstone National Park.[4]

Meanwhile, anticipating and facilitating the flood of settlement, the US government had mostly removed Indians from lands that whites coveted. The 1868 Treaty of Fort Laramie established the Great Sioux Reservation and a series of government agencies to keep the Sioux away from emigrant trails and the railroad along the Platte River in Nebraska. Red Cloud, Spotted Tail, and Man-Whose-Enemies-Are-Afraid-of-His-Horses (who became known in the history books as "Man-Afraid-of-His-Horses"), along with their followers, began making homes on the reservation, a 25-million-acre tract of land that lay west of the Missouri River and encompassed most of the western half of the future South Dakota.[5]

Bands from these reservations would hunt and visit outside reservation boundaries in the early 1870s, but other Sioux bands sought to remain completely independent of the United States and refused to report to agencies or be bound by reservation limits. Led by Sitting Bull, Crazy Horse, and others, these Lakotas stayed free in the north. In 1876, when Custer ventured out to force them to the reservation, the holy man Short Bull was in the crush of horsemen who charged across the Little Big Horn River and drove the bluecoats down. Only when the US Army subsequently closed in on them in 1877 did Crazy Horse lead his followers to the reservation. Sitting Bull and his people ventured to Canada instead, then returned in 1881. Many of these later arrivals to the reservation had never been defeated by US forces and only surrendered because the buffalo were gone and the people were starving.[6]

Short Bull, who aligned with Crazy Horse, surrendered around 1877 and came to live with the other Brules at the Rosebud Agency, part of the Great Sioux Reservation. (Until the Great Sioux Reservation was broken up into smaller reservations in 1889, different tribes of Lakotas lived on the same reservation but were assigned to different administrative centers, or agencies, to secure their rations.) In Short Bull's time, Lakotas lived in *tiyospaye*—small camps organized by extended family—and their acknowledged leader was a tiyospaye chief. When Lakotas gathered on the reservations, they eventually spread out in small settlements across the landscape in their old (and some new) tiyospaye camps. Many of these camps would later become towns.[7]

Meanwhile, Lakotas settled in small clusters of cabins and lodges along streams and rivers across the reservation. They built log cabins because they preferred them in the winter, but in the warm months— and sometimes even year-round—tipis still sprang up beside the cabins as owners entertained visiting guests or took to the old lodges themselves. Those leaders better disposed toward Americans settled nearest the agencies. Other bands settled in the hinterlands; Sitting Bull, for example, finally built a cabin on South Dakota's Grand River, forty miles from the agency at Fort Yates. Along with the rest of the Brule band of Chief Lip, Short Bull built a cabin near Pass Creek, at the western edge of the Rosebud Reservation, keeping as far away as possible from the agent's influence.[8]

SOUTHWARD ON THE PLAINS, THE STORY WAS MUCH THE SAME: nomadic peoples saw their power expand in the first half of the nineteenth century and collapse soon after. Cheyennes and Arapahos preceded Lakotas by at least a century in moving west out of Minnesota and onto the grasslands, where they eventually hunted bison from horseback. By 1850, they had allied with one another and gained control of most of today's Colorado and Kansas. Farther west, groups of Shoshones left their home in the northern Rockies in the sixteenth century and ventured east and south into Texas, where they became Comanches. With the advent of horses and mounted bison hunting, they allied with Kiowas and Kiowa Apaches and attained supremacy over a vast region that stretched from today's Oklahoma southward for hundreds of miles, deep into Mexico.[9]

Violence (US Army attacks began as early as the 1850s) and starvation (from the decline of bison in the 1870s) ultimately pushed all these peoples to reservations. Cheyennes and Arapahos split into northern and southern divisions; Northern Cheyennes and Northern Arapahos took up assigned lands in Montana and Wyoming, respectively, in the late 1870s. Earlier, beginning in 1870, Southern Arapahos and Southern Cheyennes began sharing an Oklahoma reservation of some 4.2 million acres in the western short-grass prairie. By 1875, Kiowas and Kiowa Apaches had accepted lands on the southern edge of the Southern Cheyenne–Southern Arapaho reservation. Their allies, the Comanches, settled there as well the same year.[10]

By this time, Oklahoma was a giant patchwork of Indian reservations. Since the Cherokee Removal in the 1830s, authorities had been assigning Indians to reservations in what was then called Indian Territory to ensure efficient management and more rapid assimilation. Southern Cheyenne and Southern Arapaho occupied the western end of this territory; to the east were more than a dozen other Indian peoples who had been shunted there. In addition to the so-called Five Civilized Tribes—the Cherokee, Chickasaw, Choctaw, Creek, and Seminole—Indian Territory was now occupied by a wide range of prairie, Great Lakes, and other Indians, including Wichitas, Caddos, Tonkawas, Poncas, Otoes, Missouris, Iowas, Sac and Foxes, Kickapoos, Pottawatomies, Kaws, Osages, Shawnees, and Pawnees. Widely divergent in culture and language, and often historically opposed to one another, all Indian peoples in Oklahoma now faced similar conditions of reservation life and economy. New ideas spread easily in such a population, and the Southern Plains would be a particularly fertile seedbed for Indian religious revival, and especially the Ghost Dance.[11]

The desperation that would drive believers to the circle was not yet a foregone conclusion. In and of themselves, reservations did not spell the end of all the old ways. Lakotas ventured away from the Great Sioux Reservation to hunt as late as 1876, and hunting, gathering, and nomadic movement continued even within some reservation boundaries into the 1880s. But the new economy that now characterized the Plains soon strangled whatever was left of Indian autonomy. Farmers broke the short-grass plains with new steel plows to replace the buffalo grass with corn and wheat, and cattle supplanted bison as the region's most populous large animal. Having lost much of their onetime realm to the new state of Nebraska in 1866, Lakotas lost most of the rest of their lands in 1889 when they were incorporated into the states of Montana, Wyoming, North Dakota, and, of course, South Dakota, where most Lakotas were confined to reservations. Reduced to fewer than 25,000 people, they were the most numerous of the Plains tribes, and yet they were a tiny community of Indians in what had become a settler country. In 1890 the census recorded 300,000 non-Indians in South Dakota, and over 1 million in Nebraska. Well over $100 million worth of cattle, horses, pigs, sheep, and mules grazed the old bison range in those two states alone.[12]

On the warmer central and southern plains, in the onetime homelands of the Arapaho, Cheyenne, Kiowa, and Comanche, farm and ranch settlement proceeded even faster than in Nebraska and the Dakotas. By 1890, Colorado, Kansas, and Texas were even more populous and had more farms than South Dakota and Nebraska, and almost all Indians who had resided there had been transported to Oklahoma. Hemmed into their reservations, the best land now firmly in the hands of settlers who grossly outnumbered them, Indians had long since given up armed resistance. The Plains Indian Wars were over.[13]

But settlers were not done taking Indian land. Between 1880 and 1890, Americans responded to drought and the stuttering economy of grain and glut with a renewed, highly energetic white invasion of remaining Indian lands second only to the invasion that had forced them onto reservations in the first place. Plains farmers pumped billions of bushels of wheat and corn into world markets. By the late 1880s, as drought gripped the Plains, crop prices plummeted, leaving many farmers unable to pay their debts. Kansas, South Dakota, and Nebraska farmers flocked to the Farmers' Alliance, a Populist political movement that sought new forms of government intervention to save them from crushing market and climatic forces.[14]

In these conditions, the last thing farmers needed was more farms to produce more grain and drive prices even lower. But the millenarian belief in farm creation as the advancement of civilization inspired angry Populists to demand that still more land be opened to white settlement. Passage of the Dawes Act in 1887 gave Congress and the White House the authority to force Indians to sell most of their reservations (retaining 160 acres for each head of household and smaller amounts for dependent children), and settlers on the Plains urged authorities to do just that. Thus, the Populist movement lent its energies to the destruction of the Great Sioux Reservation and the Indian reservations in Oklahoma, forcing on Indians massive land transfers and renewing settler incursions—"land rushes"—onto reservations that only a few years before had been promised as exclusive Indian land. After the first Oklahoma land rush in 1889, the territory was settled at least as rapidly as had happened in the Dakotas. The 1890 census recorded over 8,800 farms in Oklahoma, comprising over 1.5 million acres, valued at $8.5 million. In 1880, there had been less than 300 miles of railroad in Oklahoma; by 1890, over 1,200 miles of track had been laid.[15]

And still the Americans wanted more. In 1888 Congress sent commissioners west to demand massive land sales by Lakotas, and in 1889 it created the Jerome Commission to arrange the purchase of land from Oklahoma tribes, including the Southern Arapahos. These were one-sided negotiations in which commissioners held all the cards. Indians knew that if they did not agree to sell their land, the Americans could just take it. Rumors of a messiah in the West were thus circulating among Plains Indians at the very moment they were forced to confront new, enormous land grabs.[16]

Across Oklahoma and the entire Plains, new physical boundaries demarcated a radical reorganization of space. In 1874, the Glidden Manufacturing Company of DeKalb, Illinois, became the first producer of barbed wire. Despite the constraints of manufacturing by hand, it sold a remarkable 10,000 pounds of wire that year. As western farmers and ranchers realized the utility of "bob wire" for managing the movements of animals and people on the almost treeless (and therefore woodless and fenceless) plains, sales skyrocketed. In 1879 alone, the now fully mechanized company produced over 50 million pounds of wire.[17]

On their reservations, Lakotas, Cheyennes, Arapahos, and other Indians were isolated in a landscape that was deeply familiar but from which they were also increasingly estranged. Some Indians who traveled between the Northern and Southern Plains remarked that the open prairie they had crossed only fifteen years before was "now thickly settled, covered with wire fences, and has railroads in all directions."[18]

At the same time, across the entire plains, north and south, overstocking of the range had shattered the grassland. Cattle were probably never as numerous there as bison, but they nonetheless exacted a heavy toll, partly because of their grazing habits. Because bison eat almost entirely grass and ignore certain kinds of forbs and sedges, other animals can flourish amid even large bison herds. Cattle, in contrast, graze a wider array of plant species than bison, demolishing grass, forbs, and sedges alike. Bison and cattle both seek river valleys for water and shelter, but bison tend to spread out, away from riverbanks, to graze. Cattle herds congregate in much greater numbers along river bottoms and are reluctant to move away from there even when the grass is gone. In the 1880s, they trampled riparian zones, grazed meadows bare, and stripped riparian forests of their bark until all that remained of many a prairie stream was a mud flat punctuated with dead trees. As cattle replaced bison, they joined a host of other forces reshaping the Great Plains, including relentless hunting by millions of white settlers. In the skies and on the ground, not only buffalo but dozens of species that had cohabited with the great herds all but disappeared. The call of the curlew and the bugling of elk gave way in most places to the lowing of cattle—or silence.[19]

Confined within reservation boundaries, Plains Indian people no longer migrated between river valleys, but to the abstracted river of money: the hunt for game and plants gave way to the hunt for dollars and work. In itself, this was not an insurmountable challenge. Lakotas, Arapahos, and other Plains Indians had a centuries-long tradition not only as independent hunters but as sellers of pemmican and furs to white and Indian merchants. They were no strangers to markets.

But by the 1880s, when Paiutes in Nevada were selling fish, pine nuts, and firewood in settler towns and cities, Plains Indians no longer had much that white buyers wanted—except land. Paiutes could sell their own labor, but almost no wage work was available to the Western Sioux, Southern Arapahos, and other Plains Indians. Their reservations remained remote from the cities, towns, and farms where work might have been available. Even when settlements were not out of reach, the government banned Plains Indians from leaving reservations without permission—which was seldom given.

Lakotas and most other Plains Indians thus had few sources of money. For paid work, they turned to the Indian agency, which employed them in freighting, road building, woodcutting, police service, and the occasional construction of schools, churches, and other buildings. But at best, the reservations generated only a few dozen such jobs. Some Oglala Lakotas, Pawnees, and a few others found employment in Wild West shows. At Pine Ridge, these shows employed far more Lakotas than the agency did: in 1889, 200 Lakota men (and still more women and children in their families) departed the reservation to work with show companies, an industry that paid them tens of thousands of dollars. But only a tiny proportion of all Indians could work in such entertainments.[20]

The scarcity of work led to desperate responses when jobs did become available. By the early 1880s, men flocked to building sites in the Southern Cheyenne camps at Darlington, in Indian Territory, in such numbers that supervisors had to monitor the stone-hauling, brick-making, and lime-burning operations to ensure that all the men on the job had in fact been hired. By the time Jack Wilson's prophecies began to emanate from the Walker River country in 1889, Northern Arapahos at Wind River Reservation were cutting wood and hay, hauling coal, digging irrigation ditches for the government, and scrambling for practically any paying job.[21]

As early as the late 1870s and continuing through the 1890s, Indian men acquired wagons and teams and hauled millions of pounds of goods at Lakota reservations as well as on the Southern Cheyenne–Southern Arapaho reservation in Oklahoma and on the Northern Cheyenne and Crow reservations in Montana. Among the men who undertook the freighting business was Short Bull, who was driving shipments between Valentine, Nebraska, and the Rosebud Agency in South Dakota by 1889. "The Indians make good freighters," observed the agent at Pine Ridge in 1888. "They like the business and apparently never tire of it."[22]

In all these places, Indian entrepreneurs branched out in a variety of ways to make a little money. By 1890, some at Pine Ridge and elsewhere were producing goods for a nascent craft industry, selling moccasins and beadwork to traders who supplied a growing market for Indian curios. Others scrambled to sell other goods. In 1886, as eastern manufacturers bought up buffalo bones and ground them into fertilizer, Brule Lakotas at Rosebud Reservation gathered up 330 tons of buffalo bones and sold them for $8 a ton. Others tried to charge whites for using Indian land. In Oklahoma, Southern Arapahos launched an ultimately unsuccessful effort to tax the aggressive Texas cattle outfits that trespassed on their reservation. Subsequent agreements to lease grassland were also mostly unsuccessful; American cattlemen refused to hire Indians as cowboys and drove small Arapaho herds (from the handful of Indians who acquired cattle in the 1880s) away with their own.[23]

To compensate for the lack of money, some Plains Indians—like their Paiute contemporaries in Nevada—made serious, often enthusiastic efforts at farming, in imitation of the comparatively wealthy and powerful Americans nearby. At Wind River Reservation, Northern Arapahos cut irrigation ditches with a shared plow in the early 1880s. By 1886, Northern Arapaho chiefs in Wyoming and Southern Arapaho chiefs in Oklahoma oversaw large fields and gardens where their families and followers produced hay for market and food for the community. Lakota teamsters pooled their earnings to buy communal farm implements at Rosebud and also at Pine Ridge, where Indian farmers grew 21,000 bushels of corn and 6,000 bushels of potatoes in 1888. Even the Hunkpapa Lakota leader Sitting Bull, who was widely considered a staunch opponent of farming, made at least some of his living on the reservation as most Lakotas did—through a mix of rations, produce from his home garden, and income from raising cattle, hay, and oats. In Oklahoma, aspiring Arapaho and Cheyenne cultivators, in the absence of plows and harrows, chopped through the prairie with hand axes and worked the soil with their fingers.[24]

Across the Plains, as Indian children born in the reservation era matured, Indians grew ever more oriented toward wage work and

FIGURE 6.2. Lakota man and child at home on Rosebud Reservation, ca. 1891. By the time the Ghost Dance arrived, most Lakotas had built log homes, and many were attempting to farm. Note the hoes on the roof. Nebraska State Historical Society, RG2969-PH-2–206.

farming. Compelled by government agents to attend reservation day schools or sent away to government boarding schools like the Carlisle Indian Industrial School in Pennsylvania, Indian children received an education that was overwhelmingly vocational. Boys' instruction emphasized tasks like baking, carpentry, and livestock management, and girls learned laundry, sewing, and cooking. They also learned about agriculture, their education thoroughly imbued with the American veneration of farming as the bulwark of democracy, the guarantor of independence, and the source of wealth and respectability.[25]

But with work scarce and seasonal and farms increasingly unreliable in the drying climate, most Indians on the Plains turned more and more often to rations; that dependency allowed American authorities routinely to deploy their immense power—to withhold rations to compel "progressive" behavior—to starve Indians and crush their resistance. Where once Indians were self-sustaining, now they depended on distant flour mills, canneries, and plantations for their sustenance. Like laborers in distant cities, Indians were among the first people in the world to depend on industrialized food for their survival.

Rations were not welfare, however; they were written into agreements with the US government as payment for land ceded by Indians. However unfair and inadequate, they were the product of a market transaction between Indians and Americans. They were also modern commodities, paid for by the US Congress and delivered to Indian reservations by private contractors. These meager allotments of clothing, flour, beef, corn, beans, coffee, and sugar, together with a few farm implements, were all that kept Indians from freezing and starving to death; after the ration cuts of 1889, they did not even accomplish that much. Lakotas especially could see the impact of poor food on their ailing bodies. "Physically, they are wrecks of what they once were," observed the teacher Elaine Goodale. Southern Arapahos, too, saw their beef ration cut in half in 1889. Forced to create new recipes from poverty rations, Lakotas, Arapahos, and other Plains Indians fried flour in lard to produce what became known as fry bread, a food that fills stomachs but has little nutritional value. It

FIGURE 6.3. Lining up for rations at Pine Ridge, 1891. Denver Public Library, Western History Collection, X-31388.

became a staple of reservations, a potent sign of the transformation of Indian villages into market-dependent communities with little or no money.[26]

In the drought that wracked Nevada in 1888–1889, Jack Wilson awoke from his trance journeys across the Milky Way with ice in his hand. In 1890, Lakotas would testify that some Ghost Dancers returned from heaven clutching buffalo meat.[27]

LIKE ALL PEOPLES, INDIANS SAW THEIR SPIRITUAL CONDITION as one explanation for their economic and political hardships, and many sought religious solutions. Some turned to customary ritual with increased fervor, praying to renew the earth and revive their old autonomy. The Lakota word connoting the sacred or the holy, *wakan*, refers more broadly to spirit power, or the sources of spiritual power, that surrounded all Lakotas at all times. Collectively, these were known as Wakan Tanka, the Great Mysteries. Now holy men like Short Bull led devoted followers in rededicating themselves to ritual observance and the teachings of White Buffalo Calf Woman, a powerful spirit being who had arrived among the people in the distant past and presented them with the Sacred Pipe, which became a key element of Lakota ritual. Along with this gift, White Buffalo Calf Woman had advised the people to learn the seven major Lakota ceremonies that subsequently were given them to ensure growth and prosperity.[28]

The Sun Dance was the most prominent and popular of these ceremonies—and the primary communal religious gathering by the nineteenth century. In the dance, individual dancers made offerings to spirits, most notably Wi, the Sun, the Revered One, also called Our Father, patron of the four great Lakota virtues of bravery, fortitude, generosity, and fidelity. Other spirits manifested during the dance as well, including Grandfather Buffalo, who was essential to virtually every aspect of Lakota life. Grandfather Buffalo was the spirit of the Earth, the force from whom all buffalo came into this world, the patron of domestic affairs, ceremonies, and sexual relations, and as the chief of all animals, the one who controlled the chase. He presided over the Sun Dance and received many prayers and sacrifices.[29]

Lakotas propitiated these and other spirits at summer Sun Dance gatherings through sacrifices made in the space between a circular sacred arbor and a tree cut down and re-erected at the center (the tree marking the center of the world, and its axis). Offerings to the spirits might include only fasting and dancing, but the Sun Dance was famous (or notorious) among Americans for another kind of offering. A holy man would pierce the chests or back muscles of a select group of pledgers, who had specially prepared for the event, using an awl connected by a rawhide thong to the central tree, to a buffalo skull, or even to posts erected near the tree. With skewers in their chests or backs, and blood streaming down in sacrifice to Wi, all of the pledgers stared at the sun and danced until they tore themselves free. Though piercing was restricted to men, women and children could join the devotions by dancing and staring at the sun. With these personal sacrifices, Lakotas implored the spirits to take pity on them and fulfill their requests for success in hunting and war, or offered thanks for the recovery of family members from illness or other misfortune.[30]

Lakotas flocked to the Sun Dance in the 1880s, when they were still new to reservation life and the future seemed hopeless to many. The continuing popularity of the ritual and participants' energy and enthusiasm may partly explain why it attracted so much government hostility. Soon, however, the ceremony and the holy men who led it fell victim to assimilation policy. Missionaries and other ardent Christians tended to see holy men and all ceremonial leaders as competition for Indian souls and as the devil's minions, and Short Bull and others found themselves in confrontations with them almost from the minute they took up reservation life. In 1879, the agent at Rosebud announced a ban on the Sun Dance. Short Bull joined with another man named Two Heart to lead a group of Lakota dissidents north in an effort to reach Sitting Bull's camp in Canada, where they could worship in peace. But the army caught them, and by the fall they were back at Rosebud.[31]

In his campaign against the Sun Dance, the Rosebud agent was operating only on his own authority. But a broader ban soon followed. In 1882, Secretary of the Interior Henry Teller explicitly banned "the old heathenish dances" among all Indians and instructed Indian agents to compel holy men to "discontinue their practices." Teller, like most Indian agents and many other Americans, saw holy men as frauds who kept Indian children from school, manipulated Indian superstitions by employing "various artifices and devices to keep the people under their influence," and persisted in "using their conjurers' arts to prevent the people from abandoning their heathenish rites and customs." Under his new guidelines, agents among the Lakotas initiated a vigorous campaign against holy men, refusing rations to people who participated in the Sun Dance and threatening them with starvation. They ordered the Indian police—handpicked and commanded by the agents—to raid Sun Dance gatherings and harass holy men. When the police met resistance, they assaulted leading holy men and dancers and dragged them to jail. In 1881, the agent at Crow Creek ordered police to put a stop to "a barbarous festival" featuring "an immoral dance"—probably a Sun Dance. The officers shut down the ritual, in the words of the agent, with "a characteristic 'knock down and drag out' of the principal offenders."[32]

Far more than the ritual itself was lost in the Sun Dance ban. The Sun Dance expressed and maintained community well-being in a host of ways, and the ban weakened holy men as a tribal institution. Without property sacrifices—gifts from pledgers who needed holy men to serve as their mentors—their wealth declined.

More broadly, the ban ramped up social friction. A Sun Dance was usually accompanied by a large-scale transfer of goods from richer Lakotas to poorer members of the tribe. Each year's dance was sponsored by a person who had taken a vow to Wi to host the ceremony, often in return for deliverance from danger or illness. As the date for the dance approached, the sponsor sacrificed all of his property by surrendering it to the needy. Other wealthy people also gave generously to the poor as the ceremony progressed. Each gift of horses, buffalo robes, or richly beaded cloth from rich to poor encouraged the spirits to be similarly kind to Lakotas, or as Lakotas put it, "to take pity" on them. Thus, the "vast amount" of wealth that changed hands during the ritual eased tensions among Lakotas and bound them together in reciprocal obligation.[33]

The dance also created a space for other functions that might or might not have been related to spiritual matters. Many holy men and women were among the large, convivial crowd that massed around the sacred arbor, and they took the opportunity to see to the people's spiritual well-being through a wide array of other rituals and ceremonies. Ailments were healed, and seekers took up vision quests—solitary ventures to remote places for fasting, in hopes of an encounter with spirits—with help from holy men. The community also tended to its politics: new chiefs were elevated, new police or camp marshals were selected, and men's societies and ceremonial organizations were convened. In its ritual and social expressions, the Sun Dance regenerated the community.[34]

For Lakotas and others, the Sun Dance—always the most heavily attended of their communal events—was a spiritual request for buffalo and generalized abundance. As bison receded and the old ecology and economy of the Plains collapsed, Indians performed the ritual with ever greater intensity. In the decade before Wovoka's prophecies began circulating, the gatherings were vast. In 1880, the ceremonial circle of the Oglala Sun Dance contained 700 lodges and was six miles in circumference. In 1882, when the Sun Dance convened at Rosebud (probably with Short Bull in attendance), the camp was three-quarters of a mile in diameter as 9,000 people—almost one-third of the Lakotas on earth—assembled for the devotions. After the ban was announced the following year, the next public Sun Dance would not be held until 1951.[35]

Meanwhile, on the Southern Plains the ban on the Sun Dance was less rigorously enforced. The Arapaho Sun Dance, known as the Offerings Lodge, maintained a public face far longer than the Lakota Sun Dance and was performed openly as late as 1902.[36] A number of factors kept religious conflicts from becoming as severe in the south as they already were in the north. Agents watched Lakotas closely because there were 18,000 of them—substantially more than for any other Plains tribe. By contrast, Indian nations in Oklahoma were smaller. There were only 1,100 Southern Arapahos in 1890, and the combined population of the Southern Cheyenne–Southern Arapaho reservation was only about 3,500. There were other Indian tribes in Oklahoma, and eventually, though they would take some time to form, multi-tribal coalitions would emerge to resist ceremonial proscriptions. These differences in population tended to make religious arguments with the government much louder in the north than in the south. Self-conscious, perhaps, about their small numbers, Southern Arapahos became adept negotiators. A large proportion of them acceded to agency demands to send their children to school, for example, perhaps as a strategy to maintain their religious ceremonies. Lakota responses to agency demands tended to be far more variable and, at times, contentious.

For their part, the Southern Arapaho agents in these years appear to have adopted a policy of gradually phasing out the old religion rather than abolishing it all at once. Their relative passivity toward Southern Arapahos probably stemmed in part from their preoccupation with Southern Cheyennes. The two tribes shared one reservation and one agent, whose attention well into the 1880s was focused on confrontations with mostly Southern Cheyenne men who threatened raids and other hostilities off the reservation. The agents seem to have remained almost ambivalent about the Offerings Lodge. When the agent D. B. Dyer attended the ceremony in 1885, he proclaimed the dancers' intense devotion "worthy of a better religion" but also acknowledged the "indomitable heroism" of their sacrifice.[37]

Even such limited tolerance as this was in short supply elsewhere in Oklahoma. In 1887, the Kiowa agent authorized a Sun Dance without piercing and "with a distinct understanding that it should be the last." When Kiowas attempted to hold another Sun Dance in 1890, they were intimidated out of it by their agent's hostility and rumors of an attack by soldiers from nearby Fort Sill. In Darlington, the forebearance of the agent did not last. Although Southern Arapahos were still hosting the Offerings Lodge in 1902, it soon vanished, not to reappear until 2006. In these ways, the reservation period initiated severe persecution of ceremonies across the entire Plains. Like the Offerings Lodge of the Arapaho and the Sun Dance of the Lakota, the religious traditions of other tribes, from the Comanches of Oklahoma to the Blackfeet of Montana, soon became targets for eradication.[38]

Even when a celebration of the Sun Dance or another ceremony occasionally slipped through the wall of religious suppression, the poverty of reservation life militated against the old religions, all of which required property sacrifices that fewer and fewer Indians could muster. For example, among Southern Arapahos, the Offerings Lodge had to be sponsored by a married couple who had achieved seniority in a hierarchical system of sacred societies, or "medicine lodges." Staging the Offerings Lodge required the cooperation of the entire medicine lodge hierarchy, which itself undergirded the social order and depended on chains of property sacrifice. Without a steady supply of horses, hides, and other goods, the stream of property sacrifices proved ever harder to sustain.[39]

EVEN THOUGH SOUTHERN ARAPAHOS PROVED BETTER ABLE THAN many others to withstand the attack on the Sun Dance, the ban on Indian ceremonies and the persecution of the holy men and women who led them demoralized Plains societies everywhere. Among Lakotas, such measures threatened to sever the connections between powerful spirits and the Lakota community. We may assume that Short Bull, like other holy men, was still leading the Sun Dance, or trying to, after the ban was imposed, directing the ritual in secret. It is impossible to tell how successful such events were. However many people the ceremony drew under these conditions, it was no longer a communal festival. For the first time in memory there were compelling reasons not to attend, for doing so earned the ire of officials and police, who confiscated the property and rations of those who danced. The ban on the Sun Dance thus brought fragmentation, alienation, and spiritual isolation.

The proscription on piercing and devotion not only deprived holy men of an important arena for ministering to their people but impoverished them by halting the payments for their mentorship. For all other Indians, the ban was an abject disaster. In old times, a man with sufficient means could pray for the salvation of his loved ones from hunger, sickness, or the hatred of their enemies by vowing to perform the Sun Dance, thus invoking the aid of the Sun and Wakan Tanka. But with the ban on the ritual, such vows could not be fulfilled. Agents were familiar with the problem, but simply— devastatingly—ordered their charges not to make any more vows.[40]

As the desperation of Lakotas mounted at the close of the 1880s, holy men like Short Bull looked for a way to rebalance relationships with Wakan Tanka, to set the world to rights and restore the freedom and well-being of their people. Bison eradication had uprooted and deracinated a religion that honored and requested assistance from Sun, Grandfather Buffalo, and the rest of creation. The spirits still came to seekers; in the Sun Dance circle and on vision quests, Lakotas still encountered Buffalo, Bear, Elk, Badger, and others. But the near-extinction of animals, along with their vanishing autonomy and mounting poverty, left Lakotas asking which ritual measures could restore the balance of forces and regain for them the pity of spirits who not so long ago had made them the most powerful Indians on the Northern Plains.

In this context of a beleaguered old religion and profound economic and social crises, new rites and religions beckoned, and the decades leading up to the Ghost Dance were a period of pronounced religious turbulence. A movement based on a curing ceremony known as the Midewiwin, or Medicine Dance, had burned through the Great Lakes region in the late 1700s, and as the United States pushed Kickapoos, Potowatomis, and Sac and Foxes from the Great Lakes to the Plains, they carried the movement to Iowas, Dakotas, Poncas, and other Plains peoples. Sometime before 1860, another shamanistic movement known as the Grass Dance spread from the Omahas westward across the Plains. The Grass Dance eventually lost most of its religious features, but elements of it were combined with the Medicine Dance to create still another religious movement, the Dream Dance, which first took hold among the Santee Sioux in Minnesota in the late 1870s. Seeking goodwill, health, earthly renewal, and the return of the old ways through prayer and singing, the Dream Dance spread south, reaching tribes in Kansas and Oklahoma by the 1880s.[41]

Oklahoma in particular proved a hotbed of revivalism and millennialism well before Wovoka's prophecies arrived. Spiritual longing arose among its thousands of impoverished Indians, almost all of them relocated from other regions or confined to shattered fragments of former homelands. Ranks of shamans, seers, prophets, and evangelists emerged, heralding new intertribal religious movements. Some of these arose in defense of traditional religions. Others promised to restore bison and the old ways. Still others proposed banishing white people from the earth. As early as 1881, Keeps-His-Name-Always, a young Kiowa, began to prophesy the return of the bison and the destruction of settlers and instructed followers in sacred prayer and ritual to fulfill the prophecy. The prophet died in 1882, but in 1887 another Kiowa, In-the-Middle, claiming to be his heir, revived the prophecy. In-the-Middle promised that the day was fast approaching when white people would be eliminated and the bison would return, and Kiowas flocked to his camp on Elk Creek to await the happy hour. When the prophecy failed, they returned to their homes, deeply disappointed. Two years later, in 1889, In-the-Middle hailed news of the Ghost Dance prophecy as a fulfillment of his own visions.[42]

The Kiowa prophecies no doubt found their way across Oklahoma to the Southern Cheyenne–Southern Arapaho reservation, where the Ghost Dance was soon to blossom, for in spite of agents' attempts to limit intertribal contact, Indians in western Oklahoma frequently socialized and often intermarried. Thus, between the Dream Dance and the Kiowa prophecies, religions that promised the return of the old ways and the renewal of the earth had become a Great Plains tradition well before Wovoka's teachings arrived.

To be sure, not all of the emergent movements were as apocalyptic as the Kiowa prophecies. Another set of practices and beliefs that had a far wider impact emerged about the same time. When authorities became aware of the Peyote Religion a decade or so later, they spoke of peyote as an hallucinogen. Believers, even now, refer to peyote as a sacred herb, a living spirit, even a part of God, who brings enlightenment, teaches righteous living, and ensures well-being.[43]

The Peyote Religion addressed the problem of reservation confinement and surveillance by allowing believers access to spirit power even when they could not move beyond reservation boundaries and remained under the nominal control of the agent. The key element in the Peyote Religion was the flower of the peyote cactus, *Lophophora williamsii,* a plant native to northern Mexico and southern Texas and for millennia widely used as a ritual cure in Mexico. Peyote came to Oklahoma with those Indians who had made raids into Mexico or lived there prior to the reservation period, primarily the Comanche, Kiowa, and Kiowa Apaches, all of whom had become familiar with the powers of peyote to relieve pain and provide powerful visions. Peyote served spiritual needs specifically brought on by the reservation era. Men of Plains societies struggled to pursue vision quests at sacred sites because many of them, now beyond reservation borders and bounded in barbed wire, were off limits to Indians and dangerous to visit. Peyote empowered believers to achieve a visionary state in a short period of time, in a ceremony held inside a lodge and easily hidden from agents, obviating the need to venture far afield or risk injury or arrest for leaving the reservation in a days-long, solitary ordeal.[44]

Peyote use had become institutionalized in Indian Territory by the early 1880s in a standard ritual pioneered by Quanah Parker, the last free war chief of the Comanches and the leading Comanche chief in the reservation period. Central to the Peyote Religion were all-night ceremonies involving small groups of people who gathered in a tipi to sing, eat peyote, and pray, often to Jesus. In the words of one of its preeminent historians, the ceremony had "overtones of Christianity, but [was] so different from all Christian sects that it would provoke them all to do their best to eradicate it."[45]

Given the enthusiasm of evangelists and the proximity of tribes in the increasingly crowded Indian Territory, it did not take long for peyote devotions to spread. Quanah Parker himself led peyote meetings among the Southern Arapaho in 1884. Soon thereafter, a twenty-two-year-old Arapaho and former Carlisle student named Jock Bull Bear began learning the ritual from Parker. Meanwhile, a Southern Arapaho man, Medicine Bird, studied the ritual with Plains Apaches and in 1888 innovated a version that became widely accepted in Arapaho communities.[46]

By the 1880s, then, Plains religious life was infused with a broad range of traditional and new beliefs, from apocalypticism to the more contemplative and ethical teachings of the Peyote Religion.

As Christian missionaries increasingly intruded into this landscape that echoed with teachings old and new, Indian religions certainly grappled with the meanings of Christianity too. In 1869—the very moment when many of the Plains tribes began seriously to consider moving to reservations—President Ulysses S. Grant had articulated his Peace Policy, which placed reservations in the hands of Christian churches. Under the policy, any church that did the work of running a reservation gained exclusive control over it, including the power to select teachers for reservation schools, bar competing churches from the reservation, and appoint agents (who were themselves missionaries). The Peace Policy was applied in Nevada as well, but missionaries there paid little attention to Northern Paiutes, most of whom did not live on reservations anyway.[47]

Indians on the Plains were more systematically confined to reservations than Indians in the Great Basin, and Plains reservations were supervised primarily by Protestant missionaries for over a decade after 1869. Thus, evangelical Christianity had a presence in and near Plains Indian communities that it never had in the Great Basin (except in the few places where Mormon missionaries were present). Under this policy, the first agents appointed for the Southern Cheyenne–Southern Arapaho reservation, in 1870, were two devout Quakers, Brinton Darlington and John D. Miles.

Both men dedicated their missionary efforts primarily to the Southern Cheyenne. Ten years later, in 1880, missionaries from the General Conference of Mennonites began preaching to Southern Arapahos at a mission station at Shelly, on the Washita River, and opened schools for them at Darlington and Cantonment and the Indian Industrial School in Kansas. Among neighboring tribes, Southern Methodists and Baptists had taken up residence by the time Wovoka's prophecies took hold.[48]

All these efforts met mixed results. Mennonites did not achieve their first convert until 1888, and as late as 1900 only about forty Arapahos had declared their faith as Mennonites. Southern Methodists gained a few prominent Kiowa converts in 1888, but had little success in the years following. And yet, even as most Indians proved reluctant to take up Christianity, some seized opportunities to explore it on their own terms. Four Southern Plains warriors, held as prisoners after the Red River War of 1874–1875, volunteered for a year of Christian study in New York, and at least one preached the gospel on his return.[49]

Such stories suggest the powerful ambivalence of Indian communities toward New Testament instruction. On the one hand, many Indians on the Plains were interested in Christian teaching and many experimented with Christian belief and practice. Their reasons were as diverse as the people themselves. Some were genuinely moved by Christian preaching and faith. Some solicited missionaries to serve as allies in their negotiations with the government and provide instruction in English and literacy, key tools for negotiating Indian rights in the reservation era. Many Indians believed that Christianity undergirded the military and economic success of the American people (a belief they shared with most Americans). Since Americans possessed great wealth and ingenuity and defeated one Indian enemy after another, some Cheyennes, Arapahos, Lakotas, and others came to regard the spirit powers of Americans as formidable and potentially worth adopting—or adapting—for their own uses. Partly for such reasons, white and Indian missionaries across the Plains found audiences, however small, of Indian peoples who were often willing to engage and even affiliate with Christian churches, while retaining ties to their old religions.

Thus, even where Christianity did not find ready converts it had influence. And yet, as the growth of the Peyote Religion suggests, even some of those most willing to embrace certain Christian ideals rejected the straitjacket of Victorian Protestantism, preferring new religious forms that combined Indian traditions with new beliefs. In part, such efforts were grounded in the continuing fight against assimilation. All Indians wanted health and prosperity and success in the reservation era, but on terms that were distinctly Indian. In the fight to preserve Indian ways, religion moved to the fore as a furious battleground of ideas and practices, as exemplified in the growing fight over the Peyote Religion and other forms of Indian religiosity.

THIS PHENOMENON OF SIMULTANEOUS ENTHUSIASM FOR RELIGIOUS innovation and resistance to assimilation was also common on the Northern Plains, but with key differences. For one thing, the Peyote Religion did not come north for some time. Also, in the years leading up to the Ghost Dance, Lakotas faced a more concerted advance by missionaries, an onslaught of doctrinaire Christianity that seemed to underscore and backstop the economic and political revolutions sweeping the Plains.

At first, Christianity made slow progress among the Western Sioux. In 1871, Oglalas at the Red Cloud Agency received J. W. Wham, Episcopalian, as their first agent, and Congregationalists established a mission at Cheyenne River the following year. Until later in the decade, however, most Lakotas remained far to the north, well away from agents, missionaries, and even the Great Sioux Reservation, and the churches had limited influence. But once all Indians had been confined to the reservation, Christian missionaries consolidated their authority. Catholics asserted control of Standing Rock in 1876. At Rosebud, Cheyenne River, and Pine Ridge, Episcopalians seized command of preaching, schools, and reservation agencies by the late 1870s.[50]

Although many of the missionaries were forceful in their demands that Indians attend church and receive baptism, conversions and church membership lagged among Lakotas until the early 1880s. At that point, Sitting Bull's people, the last of the Lakotas to refuse to move to reservations, finally returned from Canada. At about the same time, the Peace Policy ended; agencies were returned to government control, with agents appointed by the party that won the White House. With reservations no longer allocated to particular churches, and with churches no longer able to exclude others from the reservations they occupied, the Christian denominations began to compete with one another for Indian converts. The result was a religious free-for-all as Catholics, Episcopalians, Presbyterians, and Congregationalists vied for Indian hearts, urging them not only to abandon "heathenish practices" but also to avoid competing churches. From 1881 to 1890, the number of churches at Lakota agencies mushroomed from six to thirty-one, and the number of missionaries from six to fifty-four.[51]

Significantly, these churches also looked to Indian converts to evangelize Lakotas. Catholics appointed Lakota catechists. Yankton Dakotas, eastern relatives of the Western Sioux, proved particularly influential in spreading the Christian gospels. The Yanktons lost their old homelands in Iowa and eastern Dakota Territory by 1858, when they took up a reservation on the Missouri River at today's Yankton, South Dakota, some 200 miles east of the Lakotas. Congregationalist missionaries among them appointed Dakota preachers—"lay

ministers" like the influential Elias Gilbert—to proselytize among
their Lakota kinsmen. But an even more influential group of Episcopalian Dakotas soon took posts among the Western Sioux.[52]

In 1870, Tipi Sapa, the son of Chief Saswe of the Yankton Dakotas, was converted to Christianity by Episcopalian missionaries and
took the name Philip J. Deloria. Subsequently, he studied for the
ministry at Nebraska College and in Minnesota. By 1885, with the
Peace Policy abandoned and missionaries from competing churches
sharing reservations, Deloria had become the Episcopal minister at
the Standing Rock Agency, where Sitting Bull's people had settled.
The Dakota and Lakota languages are related and mutually intelligi-
ble; though he preached in Dakota, Deloria's message resonated with
his Lakota congregation.

Another mixed-blood Dakota Episcopalian, Charles S. Cook,
studied in Nebraska and at Trinity College in Hartford, Connecti-
cut, before becoming deacon at the Pine Ridge Agency in 1885, and
then priest in 1886.

Finally, a third convert, Ojan, moved to Pine Ridge, where he
became a schoolteacher. The son of a Dakota chief named Medicine
Cow, Ojan had taken the name William T. Selwyn and also studied
in the East. As we shall see, he never rose in the church, but his
closeness to the institution, his powerful backers in the East, and
his education would give him a large and unfortunate influence on
American perceptions of the Ghost Dance.[53]

Meanwhile, whether because so many missionaries were preaching in the Dakota language or for some other reason, in the 1880s
Lakotas suddenly became more willing than most Cheyennes and
Arapahos to join churches. Indeed, an especially salient feature of
this region where the Ghost Dance fervor became pronounced was
that so many Lakotas had joined Christian churches by the time it
arrived that a leading Lakota chief named Big Road would relate to a
journalist, "Most of the Indians here belong to the church." If church
attendance was not quite what he claimed, the numbers suggest that
Christianity did have a strong hold by 1890. Beginning with only a
few hundred Lakota Christians in 1880, church officials claimed by

1889 that 4,757 souls among the 18,000 Western Sioux were Christians. Of the 5,611 Lakotas at Pine Ridge, almost half—2,213—were said to be attending church regularly, and the other Sioux reservations reported similar growth in church attendance.[54]

With good reason, scholars have been cautious with these figures and sometimes dismissed them as unreliable. Indian agents and missionaries often worked in concert, with agents refusing rations to those who did not go to church. Even for those who went voluntarily, baptism and enthusiastic devotion did not always signify conventional conversion. Lakotas, like other Indians, adhered to few orthodoxies in spiritual matters. The central requirement of Lakota religion was (and is) that every individual access the Great Mysteries, Wakan Tanka, by persuading the spirits to take pity on her or him. In this universe, rituals are carefully monitored and guided by holy men, but new beliefs may be incorporated alongside traditional beliefs if found to be helpful and consistent. On the reservation, Lakotas experimented with Christian ideas and practices in an effort to acquire the power of their conquerors without abandoning the old religion. So it was that even seemingly devout church members practiced elements of the old religion, from vision quests to healing rituals, leading missionaries to express frustration at the absence of what they considered "real" Christianity among converts.[55]

Although the number of Sioux converts should not be accepted without question, neither should it be rejected outright. The documentary record contains too many accounts of dedicated Lakota catechists and deacons, late-night meetings of the Brothers of Saint Andrew and the Sisters of Saint Mary, and donations for new churches from Lakotas with no money simply to dismiss their faith as false. Hunts His Enemy, an esteemed warrior and holy man, took the name George Sword and became a deacon in the Episcopalian Church but never ceased to be wary of the old spirit powers. Many, perhaps even most, Lakotas retained at least some of the old beliefs, but to these they added Christian faith. Baptism and church attendance alone may not have been indicative of the kind of conversion idealized by missionaries, but the fact that so many Lakotas could be counted among the faithful provides evidence of the popularity of Christianity among them.[56]

The ubiquity of missionary teachings and Christian precepts on the Plains helps to explain a key aspect of the response to Wovoka's teachings in the region: the widespread association of the Ghost Dance, not just with a messiah, but especially with Jesus. Jack Wilson prophesied a messiah, but he did not mention Christ or Jesus in his meeting with Arthur Chapman, the army scout who sought him out in 1890, or when he met (as we shall see) with James Mooney in 1892. A Paiute contemporary claimed that the prophet never referred to Jesus, not even in later years. It seems possible that Wovoka anticipated some other messiah than the Son of Man.[57]

But Plains believers mentioned Jesus or Christ frequently in their Ghost Dance teachings, perhaps because they gained more exposure to Christianity from missionaries, who were more numerous on the Plains than in Nevada. When word came from the west that a redeemer was on his way to save his Indian children, some Plains believers were quick—much quicker than Paiutes—to call him Christ. Lakota visionaries frequently met Christ in their Ghost Dance visions. According to a white observer among the Northern Cheyenne, they called the religion "the Dance to Christ," and of course Christ appeared regularly in Porcupine's account of his journey to Nevada. He and some others seem to have maintained that Wovoka himself was the savior. The Jesus of Ghost Dance visions differed substantially, however, from the Christ extolled by missionaries, and some Ghost Dancers claimed that their messiah was a different presence altogether. Nevertheless, references to Jesus were so pervasive on the Plains as to lead at least some observers to believe that the religion could be co-opted by authorities. In Oklahoma, Lieutenant Hugh Lenox Scott of the US Seventh Cavalry attended Ghost Dances and spoke often with leading evangelists. Many years later, he recalled the trances of Southern Arapahos who had "gone above in conference with Jesus," and he lamented the failure of missionaries to seize the opportunity when "the name of Jesus was on every tongue." "Had I been a missionary," he maintained, "I could have led every Indian on the Plains into the Church."[58]

IN OTHER CIRCUMSTANCES, HOLY MEN LIKE SHORT BULL OF THE Brule Lakota might have more easily accommodated themselves to the growth of Christianity. It would have been possible to integrate some Christian teachings into Lakota religion, or for the two religions to coexist in ways that would have allowed holy men to retain authority for the many Lakotas who continued to require their guidance. But intolerance of Indian religions by officials and missionaries made such accommodation difficult, if not impossible. Unless Indians found some way to resist, the pressure of assimilation, and especially the ban on the Sun Dance and other rituals, would be a death blow to their religion.

After Wounded Knee, Short Bull would spend several years touring Europe and the East with Buffalo Bill's Wild West show. His colorful, evocative drawings of Lakota dances, enhanced by his notoriety as a leader of the Ghost Dance, made him a favorite of European collectors. Aficionados of Indian art and culture sought him out for

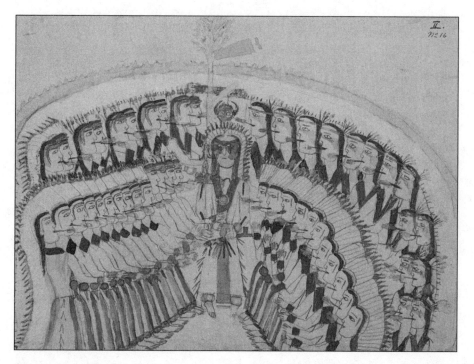

FIGURE 6.4. The Sun Dance, as painted by Short Bull, 1909. Museum Für Völkerkunde zu Leipzig.

years after. The German collector Frederick Weygold visited him at
Rosebud in 1909 and either commissioned or was given a watercolor
image of the Sun Dance. Rendered in vivid red and blue and ac-
cented with inky black, the vibrant painting suggests the energy and
communal bonds of the ritual and the world that took shape around
it. The image is dominated by forty-nine dancers in two ranks, all
clutching eagle bone whistles with eagle plumes at the end that flutter
like smoke as the whistles blow, invoking the voice of Eagle, himself
one of the Wakan Tanka. The balance of the dancers gathered around
the re-erected tree, ornamented with gifts to the Sun, suggests the
power and meaning of the tree: when the tree went up, the world was
made complete. A powerful degree of community is suggested by the
close ranks of dancers, with their similarly painted faces and whistles,
all oriented toward the center and united in ritual devotion. At the
center, staring out at the viewer and holding the sacred pipe, is the
holy man and intercessor in charge of the ritual, perhaps Short Bull
himself. The image conveys a powerful sense of longing and sorrow,
not only for the ritual, but for the world it once called into being.[59]

So with many other people on the Plains. The Ghost Dance
flowered in the empty space that remained when the Sun Dance
receded.[60] From this radically transformed landscape, desiccated by
drought and poverty, Lakotas sent their emissaries west in search of
the new religion. Short Bull's quest was in many ways a continuation
of the religious struggle that had overtaken the reservations as the
bison vanished and poverty mounted. Wovoka's prophecy promised
a restoration of the ceremonial circle shattered by the ban on customary religion and a new balance between people and spiritual forces
to ensure abundance, peace, and freedom. This hope drew Short
Bull and other Brules and Oglalas westward to Nevada, along with
Cheyennes, Arapahos, Shoshones, and others, in search of a way not
only to save their own authority but to bridge the looming abyss that
had opened in the spiritual and communal lives of America's Plains
Indians.

CHAPTER 7

PLAINS PASSAGE

His quest to find the prophet turned Short Bull into one of the most influential Ghost Dance evangelists. Determined to see the prophecy through to fulfillment, he was widely blamed later for much of what went wrong. In the fall of 1890, after he returned from Nevada, the enthusiasm of his many Lakota followers helped to attract the baleful gaze of officials. Efforts to crush the new faith would culminate with an army invasion, the killing of dozens of Minneconjou and Hunkpapa Sioux believers, and a shooting war. How did the teachings of Wovoka, as relayed by Short Bull and others, provoke such a hostile response from the United States? How could the prophet's exhortations to work and make peace have set in motion the chain of events that led to the ravine at Wounded Knee and the tangled, shattered bodies of so many Ghost Dancers?

Two explanations have predominated. The first was deployed by army officers as troops began to march. "At first, the teaching of the new religion was one of peace, " related General Nelson Miles, but "false prophets, medicine men, and disaffected leaders" had altered it to inspire the "savage spirits" of their followers. The only remedy was to put the Sioux "entirely under military control, and at once."[1]

Ever since then, the militancy of Short Bull and a few other Lakota leaders has offered many people a seemingly simple explanation for the complex and confusing developments in South Dakota in 1890. How else to reconcile Wovoka's teachings with the renowned bulletproof "ghost shirts" worn by the Lakota faithful? How else to explain the deadly shoot-out that erupted during the government's attempted arrest of Sitting Bull, a defender of the new religion? What else could account for the inexplicable refusal of Indians to stop dancing when the army arrived? It was Short Bull, after all, who led hundreds of Ghost Dancers onto a defensive high plateau in the Badlands known as "the Stronghold." Successive Lakota delegations enjoined him and his holdouts to come into the agency. His defiant speeches ring out from the history books. "We prefer to stay here and die, if necessary, to loss of liberty," he reportedly thundered to Sioux diplomats in January 1891. "We are free now and have plenty of beef, can dance all the time in obedience to the command of Great Wakantanka. We tell you to return to your agent and say to him that the Dakotas in the Bad Lands are not going to come in." Some followers actually fired shots over the heads of the peace envoys. How could any religion that urged Indians to "work for the white man" become entangled in such violence unless Short Bull and other leaders had somehow twisted it into a siren song of militancy? Long after 1890, scholars continued to follow the lead of General Miles and, without quite blaming the victims of Wounded Knee for their own destruction, attributed the violence to secret Lakota plans for an uprising.[2]

But even the specter of Lakota militancy is subordinate to the second, often implicit explanation for the religion's failure. Once historians and others embraced the narrative of the Ghost Dance as a religion that sought to restore the old ways, it became almost impossible to imagine it having a future, whether its believers were violent or not. How could people so naive as to expect a return to a primordial past of buffalo and a fully restored earth possibly escape a reckoning with the modern world? The question is no longer how a faith trying to throw off the shackles of history could have ended in tragedy, but how it could have ended otherwise. The religion's failure, in this telling, was inevitable. Naïveté had to give way to modernity.

Make no mistake: something did go wrong after the Ghost Dance reached Pine Ridge and Rosebud. But the Ghost Dance, as received on the Plains, was oriented not solely to the past but also toward Indian survival in both the reservation era and the future. Many millenarian religions, including Christianity and Islam, seek restoration of a prelapsarian earth while offering believers a path through the challenges confronting them. They encourage the faithful to advance the end of history by upholding a code for living that allows adherents to succeed, or at least survive, in the present. So it was with the Ghost Dance.

Appreciating the pragmatic appeal of Ghost Dance teachings sheds new light on how Lakotas understood them and on Short Bull's role in the trouble that arose. To be sure, Lakotas changed Wovoka's religion to suit their own traditions and help them address their own unique challenges. Even so, the original Nevada teachings had a great deal of relevance and appeal for South Dakota Indians, and in eschewing war and authorizing Indians to take up life beside the river of money, the Paiute and Lakota Ghost Dances were more similar than different. The cause for war, as we shall see, came from other quarters.

Our new understanding of the Ghost Dance on the Plains starts with Short Bull on his westward quest. The story of his journey to Nevada and the teachings he brought back illuminate facets of the religion's appeal that have long eluded scholars and, taken in context, can unravel the mystery of how a religion of peace that attracted so many Indians of widely varying backgrounds could meet with such violence at Pine Ridge. Despite his image as a provocateur and a militant, the real story of Short Bull suggests a complex, thoughtful man whose goals have been largely misunderstood for over a century—just like his religion.

BEFORE THE RESERVATION ERA, SHORT BULL FOUGHT MANY skirmishes and battles, but he was no war leader. Among Lakotas, a holy man did not generally assume the role of chief. Moreover, when news of Wovoka's prophecy first reached him in 1889, he was about forty-two—too old for war parties, which were in any case a thing of the past. Indeed, the man was so nonconfrontational that his stature in the Ghost Dance movement perplexed the official who knew him best. "Short Bull is not an aggressive Indian and has not in any way been considered a Chief or leading man and is but slightly known," the puzzled agent J. George Wright wrote to superiors in Washington. Long after the Ghost Dance troubles passed, others described Short Bull as a mild-mannered, thoughtful man. A decade after Wounded Knee, he assisted the physician James R. Walker in his research on Lakota medicine at Pine Ridge. Not long after that, he helped a visiting judge, Eli Ricker, in his research into the Wounded Knee massacre. Ricker found Short Bull to be "an open, generous and kind-hearted man . . . gentle and benevolent," and always wearing a smile.[3]

Short Bull is central to our story, not only because he became the unlikely alleged leader of the "hostile" faction at Pine Ridge and Rosebud, but also because he was the only Lakota emissary to leave a detailed account of his pilgrimage to Nevada and its aftermath. The scarcity of such documents has compelled Ghost Dance scholars to rely mostly on the testimony of nonbelievers. Few Ghost Dancers produced written accounts; most could not write, and the crushing of the religion at Pine Ridge effectively silenced them. Thus, James Mooney's foundational study of the Ghost Dance, *The Ghost Dance Religion and Sioux Outbreak of 1890*, is still widely regarded as the authoritative text on Lakotas' experience of the religion—despite its lack of testimony by Sioux Ghost Dancers, apart from a sample of their songs. By the time Mooney arrived at Pine Ridge, most leaders of the new religion, including Short Bull, had been sent away. Those who remained refused to speak to him. When he visited Short Bull and other evangelists at the military fort where they were confined, they apparently did not trust him and told him little. Consequently, Mooney's sources were mostly self-proclaimed nonbelievers who had denounced the religion as false and some who even helped to suppress it.[4]

For decades after Wounded Knee, Lakota believers continued their public silence on the subject of the Ghost Dance, and no memoir of a Lakota Ghost Dancer appeared in print. It was not until 1931 that Black Elk, the Oglala holy man who became a Ghost Dance leader (and eventually a Catholic catechist), recounted his experience to John Niehardt, the poet laureate of Nebraska. Although the book *Black Elk Speaks*, published in 1932, was written from memory many years after the events in question, it remains the most comprehensive account of the religion from the perspective of a contemporary believer.[5]

All of which makes Short Bull even more critical to our investigation, because not long after Wounded Knee, with the help of an amanuensis, he produced a memoir of the Ghost Dance. The document slipped past government investigators, including James Mooney, and remained almost unknown for the next century. Only in recent decades has it been rediscovered. When the sheaf of handwritten pages labeled "As Narrated by Short Bull" finally emerged in the 1990s, it showed no author, date, or any record of provenance. It was found in the archives of the Buffalo Bill Museum in Golden, Colorado, where it had been filed away and forgotten decades before. The fact that it turned up in a museum devoted to a great show business entrepreneur and entertainer only seemed to detract from its credibility.[6]

But in fact, the location is the first clue to the authenticity of the manuscript. Along with two dozen other supposed militants, Short Bull was detained by the US Army in early 1891. Initially imprisoned at Fort Sheridan near Chicago, he and most of the other prisoners were invited to join Buffalo Bill's Wild West show for a season in Europe. Short Bull and the others who joined toured with the company for several years. Noticing the connection around the year 2000, Sam Maddra, then a graduate student at the University of Glasgow, pointed out that the handwriting of the document appears to match that of George Craeger, the Lakota translator with Buffalo Bill's Wild West show in the early 1890s—precisely the time when Short Bull was with the company.[7]

As with any source, we must beware of accepting the narrative uncritically. But along with its provenance, its style and content help to establish its credibility. The memoir lacks the romantic trappings that would betray a white author masquerading as Short Bull. Many of its claims can be corroborated from other sources, and it bristles with details only Short Bull could have known.

In the end, Short Bull's memoir opens a window into how Wovoka's teachings were received by Plains seekers, including not only Lakotas but also the Northern Cheyenne and Southern Arapaho emissaries who accompanied the holy man on his journey. But most of all, the account gives us key insights into the meaning of the religion for its primary evangelist—and the man who also became known as the leader of the "hostiles" in South Dakota.

Establishing Short Bull as the real author of the document only enhances the mystery surrounding it. For it tells a peculiar story, one that stands sharply at odds with the conventional history of the Ghost Dance. Indeed, for those who explain Wounded Knee via the well-beaten path of Lakota militancy, Short Bull's narrative is perplexing and profoundly troubling.

By 1889, with buffalo hunting and other old ways long faded away, Short Bull had become a wage-earning teamster, driving freight wagons between Valentine, Nebraska, and the Rosebud Reservation in South Dakota. In the fall of that year, during a stop in Valentine, a messenger handed him a letter and said, "Take it to the council house." Short Bull carried this message back to the reservation and left it at Rosebud's council circle, where a crowd had gathered to celebrate ration day with vigorous, social "Omaha" dancing.[8]

When he returned that evening, he was abruptly confronted by two men who stripped him of his blanket and walked him to the center of the council circle. The council presented him with a new blanket and new leggings and told him that he had been selected for "a great mission," on which he would be accompanied by Scatter, an age-mate and friend. "We have a letter from the West saying the Father has come and we want you to go and see him. . . . You must try and get there, see him, recognize him, and tell us what he says and we will do it. Be there with a big heart. Do not fail."[9]

Why Short Bull was selected is not clear, but we do know that Sioux leaders usually appointed trusted individuals with wide respect in the community for critical missions. For his part, Short Bull found himself confused and doubtful that night. The next morning he returned to the council house for further instructions, joining a crowd of people inside. The wind that day was filling the council house with dust, but "as soon as the reading of the letter began" after it was unfolded, "the wind ceased." Short Bull felt his spirits lift. The letter—which Short Bull would later discover was written by an Indian—announced a great gathering of Indians from all over the United States, in the distant west, to hear the good news brought by the Father. As Short Bull later recalled, "I had no belief in it before but now my mind was made up." He rose. "If I have to stay two years," he announced, "I will try and see him myself and bring you his words."[10]

As a former "hostile" who had fought at Little Big Horn and a holy man who defended the old religion, Short Bull was always a figure of suspicion in agency circles. So were many of the men who accompanied him to Nevada. Scatter and Short Bull were Brule Sioux, from the Wazhazha band, who closely identified with Oglalas. The others were all Oglalas and veterans of Little Big Horn or other fights against the Americans in the 1870s: also setting out for Nevada were He Dog, Flat Iron, Yellow Knife, Brave Bear, Twist Back, Yellow Breast, and Broken Arm. They were joined by Kicking Bear, who lived on the Minneconjou Reservation at Cheyenne River but was born Oglala. Both Kicking Bear and He Dog had ridden beside Crazy Horse in the horseback charge that shattered the US Seventh Cavalry line in 1876; after Crazy Horse surrendered, Kicking Bear had gone with Sitting Bull to Canada.

All of these men were relative newcomers to the reservations, having arrived only in the late 1870s or early 1880s. Authorities regarded such "wild Indians" with suspicion and contrasted their renowned hostility to reservation life—their "nonprogressivism"—with the more accommodating "progressivism" of chiefs like American Horse and Young-Man-Afraid-of-His-Horses (the son of Man-Afraid-of-His-Horses, who had succeeded his father as chief). Their people had come to the reservation in the early 1870s and were generally more amenable to assimilation projects like schools and farming.[11]

But for all his "nonprogressive" reputation, Short Bull's journey was as modern as any taken by his white contemporaries. He and Scatter drove a borrowed buggy to Wyoming. With the other Lakotas, they caught a Union Pacific train, probably at Rawlins, and rode it to the Wind River Reservation of the Eastern Shoshones and Northern Arapahos. Here the Lakotas were joined by Porcupine of the Northern Cheyenne and a number of Northern and Southern Arapahos, including Sage, the emissary who had visited with Wovoka earlier that year, and the Arapaho Sitting Bull. This growing band of seekers pressed on to Fort Hall, Idaho, the home of the Northern Shoshone and Bannock tribes, who welcomed them and told them more about the messiah. The excitement was contagious, and the delegation continued to grow. By the time Short Bull and the others left Idaho for Nevada, probably in early 1890, their party numbered around 100.

Upon reaching the Northern Paiute reservation near the main rail line at Pyramid Lake, Short Bull and the others encountered an Indian community that seemed to have found a footing in the reservation era. Short Bull remarked on how self-sufficient these Paiutes were. The women "were dressed like white women." The villagers barely needed their small rations because they were not poor like Lakotas. "They are rich—they fish continually and sell it." If the Paiute people were so well-to-do, surely the teachings of the Paiute prophet must be powerful.[12]

The fellowship shrank over this final leg of the route, but many persisted on the journey. In addition to Porcupine, Sage, and the Arapaho Sitting Bull, some thirty other Indians from this party made it to Walker River Reservation. This group camped in a vast circle that included Western Sioux, Cheyennes, Arapahos, Gros Ventres, Paiutes, Bannocks, and others Short Bull did not know, "with every train bringing more and more people." The crowd grew to some 1,600 Indians, who subsisted on pine nuts and fish for several days, until word came that the Messiah was approaching. A wagon appeared, driven by an Indian "in white man's clothing" and carrying one passenger, a man wearing a striped blanket and "a broad brimmed brown hat with two eagle feathers in it"—Jack Wilson himself.[13]

The prophet entered a small lodge that had been erected for him, with the covering rolled up so he could be seen. He turned to face the south. He took off his hat and laid it on the ground upside down, so that the crown opened to the sky. Two old men, his interpreters, seated themselves on the ground, cross-legged, one before and one behind the prophet, with their hands extended to grasp their knees.

Short Bull was sitting directly in front of Jack Wilson "and looked him all over from head to foot." Wilson began to speak. The interpreter in front of the prophet translated into English; Singing Grass, the Northern Arapaho who understood English, signed the words to Short Bull and the other plainsmen. Wovoka's words so moved the holy man and teamster that even two years later, when recounting this moment, he fell into a trance.

"I have sent for you and you came to see me," said the prophet. "I will talk with you tomorrow. Today I will talk with these people who have been here so long." He then turned to the west, and the whole crowd turned with him. He began to pray. Immediately after the prayers, the dance began, and the prophet joined Short Bull and all the men and women, who were singing and dancing "with hands joined in a peculiar way, knuckle to knuckle going round and round, keeping it up for a long time." The next morning a crier called an assembly, and all gathered to sit in a vast circle.[14]

As we have already seen, in the newspaper panic over the Ghost Dance, Short Bull was depicted as a combative recalcitrant, and sometimes he was depicted as a warmongering menace. In one account, when the mixed-blood Louis Shangreau approached the holy man's Ghost Dance camp in the Badlands with a peace offering from officials, Short Bull allegedly denounced Shangreau as an instigator of Sioux destruction. "I know he is a traitor. Kill him! Kill him!"[15]

These representations make Short Bull's account of Jack Wilson's sermon even more remarkable. As the holy man told it in 1891, Wovoka had never told him or anyone to fight. Rather, he instructed them to take up a new way of life: "Have your people work the ground so they do not get idle, help your agents, and get farms to live on." Just as important, "educate your children. Send them to schools."

And in keeping with the ecumenical spirit of the Ghost Dance and Nevada Christianity, he told them to go to church, but to avoid denominational disputes. "When you get back, go to church. All these churches are mine." He warned them to keep the peace: "I want no more fighting," he said, "and whenever you do anything that is bad something will happen to you. I mean fights between Indians and whites." Before very long, Wovoka promised, "all nations will talk one tongue," and until then "all over the world one should be like the other and no distinction made."[16]

But what of the end-times prophecy? What about the vision of destruction raining down on white people? According to Short Bull, it was only later, on the fifth day, that the prophet spoke of the world to come. Even then, Short Bull did not receive this teaching until he was shaking hands with the prophet to say good-bye. "Soon there would be no world," the memoir records the prophet saying to Short Bull, almost as a personal aside. "After the end of the world those who went to church would see all of their relatives that had died." The judgment would be global—all people would face it. "This will be the same all over the world even across the big water."[17]

The gospel according to Short Bull was so peaceful that when he repeated parts of it later, some critics accused him of making it up to exonerate himself from his Badlands militancy. And in truth, the gospel appears to address contemporary Lakota concerns so directly that it is hard not to speculate that Short Bull misheard or misconstrued it. Farms, churches, and schools seemed more appropriate to the circumstances of Lakotas and other Plains peoples—who were urged to accept allotments for cultivation, pressured to choose between Catholic, Episcopal, and other missions, and forced to send their children to boarding schools and reservation day schools—than those of Walker River Paiutes, who had little arable land, almost no missionaries, and, prior to 1890, only one reservation day school.[18]

The evidence for the authenticity of these teachings, however, weighs heavily in Short Bull's favor. For one thing, the key exhortations of his version of the teachings—to farm, go to church, send their children to school, remain at peace, and love one another—closely approximate what we already know Jack Wilson preached. If the injunction to work seems to have been absorbed as "work the ground" and "get yourself farms to live on," it may be that Wovoka actually did include farming as a category of virtuous work. The sermon Short Bull heard took place, after all, at Walker River Reservation, where Wovoka's audience included the very Northern Paiutes who had excavated eight miles of irrigation ditch and turned themselves into commercial farmers. So, too, would his call to education have resonated among Paiutes: a boarding school in Carson City had been authorized since 1888; after it opened in 1890, Wovoka sent his own children there and urged others to do the same.[19]

All this points to the likelihood that the prophet himself, not Short Bull or some other evangelist, introduced these teachings, perhaps in part to address the needs of his Plains followers. His religious movement had become pan-Indian, and by 1890 Wovoka was overtly seeking power as a political leader beyond the Numu community. Only weeks before his sermon at Walker River he had dictated his letter to President Harrison in which he offered regular rain and weekly news from heaven in return for a stipend, some farm land, and political authority over the West. It is hardly surprising that a man of such ambition would meet with Plains seekers to hear their challenges and fears, and it seems likely that he tailored his teachings to address the needs of both Paiutes and Lakotas, as well as others.[20]

However the teachings came about, in the spring of 1890 Short Bull and the others took away from Nevada a set of instructions that addressed head on the seemingly insurmountable challenges facing Lakotas and other Plains peoples. But even assuming that Short Bull knew the true message of Jack Wilson, when he returned to Pine Ridge, did he twist and pervert Wovoka's teachings into a warrior creed? Arguments that he did generally rely on a sermon he allegedly delivered at the end of October 1890. By that time, Indian police were constantly intruding on the camps with orders from agents to stop the dancing. The account of the sermon—the only one attributed to Short Bull—comes to us via the *Chicago Tribune* and is said to have originated in a telegram from an army officer to General Miles. "I

will soon start this thing in running order," Short Bull is reported to
have announced. Because "the whites are interfering so much," he
told the assembled crowd, "I will advance the time" and bring an end
to the world sooner than previously promised. Calling for the dances
to continue, he advised his followers:

> If the soldiers surround you four deep, three of you, on whom I have
> put holy shirts, will sing a song, which I have taught you, around
> them, when some of them will drop dead. Then the rest will start
> to run, but their horses will sink into the earth. The riders will jump
> from their horses, but they will sink into the earth also. Then you can
> do as you desire with them.[21]

This sermon makes no mention of farming, education, or Christian churchgoing. On the contrary, "do as you desire with them"
evokes a chilling, take-no-prisoners militancy that was so useful for
making the case about Lakota violence that it was reprinted in military documents and in books about Wounded Knee ever after.[22]

And yet, we can be almost certain that Short Bull never said many
of the things alleged by the *Chicago Tribune*. A few lines farther on
he is reported to have announced that "men must take off all their
clothing and the women must do the same," instructions that, in
radically violating Lakota notions of ritual propriety, would have subverted his authority as a holy man. (In any case, they appear never to
have been followed: there were no naked dances.) The inclusion of
these fictional instructions in the so-called sermon casts doubt on
its authenticity and raises the question of its source, which has never
been discovered. The archive of official communications regarding
the Ghost Dance is comprehensive. Letters and telegrams in the fall
of 1890 were copied and forwarded to multiple officials, so that orig-
inals and copies proliferate throughout. And yet, neither the original
telegram nor any copy of Short Bull's sermon has ever materialized
in the official record. Whoever first related this story about a sermon
by Short Bull—most likely a paid interpreter or a policeman currying favor—seems to have been telling the *Tribune* reporter what

he wanted to hear. And even though it was probably fictional, the account provided cover to officials for suppressing the religion by invoking the ultimate specter of savagery: Indians dancing naked with blood in their eyes.[23]

Of course, if there was any part of this sermon allegedly delivered by Short Bull that he did in fact deliver, it might have been the vision of the millennium coming early. The evangelist might even have told his people that soldiers would sink defenseless into the earth. As we shall see, when peace unraveled and the army began to shoot Indians in December, Short Bull did threaten to take up arms.

But whatever he did or did not say at that gathering in October, there is much more compelling evidence that war was not on Short Bull's mind, nor on the minds, for that matter, of the other ritual leaders who were enjoining Lakotas to take up farming, churchgoing, and education, as Wovoka instructed. In late January 1891, a month after the Wounded Knee Massacre and only two weeks after Short Bull and his followers had ceased to dance and returned home from the Badlands, an Oglala named Big Road explained the teachings to a newspaper reporter. Big Road was no novice. He had been a war leader in the troubles of 1876, and in 1890 he was a camp chief, a holy man, and a leader of the Ghost Dances at Wounded Knee Creek. In the fall of that year he is alleged to have told his followers that he "intended to keep up the dance all winter, or fight."[24]

In his talk with the reporter, Big Road proved a vigorous advocate for the new religion. Short Bull was not present, but Big Road's exposition so impressed other Ghost Dancers in the room that they could not help saying how truthful it was. Little Wound—according to his agent the "high priest over all the ghost dances" and "the most stubborn, headstrong, self-willed, unruly Indian on the reservation"—prefaced his own remarks to the journalist: "I want to say that Big Road has talked straight about the dance." According to Crow Dog, a Brule and another Stronghold militant, "Big Road told the truth about the dance. . . . Big Road talked straight."[25]

And what did Big Road say? His account of the teachings in that January of 1891 is as astonishing as Short Bull's, and too similar to the evangelist's to leave any doubt about what was taught in the Bad-lands and across the Lakota reservations:

> I want to say something about the ghost dance. Many people do not understand it because the truth has not been told them. Most of the Indians here belong to the [Christian] church; we have many church houses. This dance was like religion; it was religion. Those who brought the dance here from the west said that to dance was the same as going to church. White people pray because they want to go to heaven. Indians want to go to heaven, too, so they prayed, and they also prayed for food enough to keep them out of heaven until it was time to go. . . . We danced and prayed that we might live forever; that everything we planted might grow up to give us plenty and happiness. There was no harm in the dance. *The Messiah told us to send our children to school, to work on our farms all the time and to do the best we could. He also told us not to drop our church. We and our children could dance and go to church, too; that would be like going to two churches.* I never heard that the Messiah had promised that the Indians should be supreme or that the white men should be destroyed. We never prayed for anything but happiness. We did not pray that all white people should be killed. The shirts we wore were made for us to go to heaven. The dance was not a war dance, for none who went in it was allowed to have one scrap of metal on his body.[26]

If this remarkable testimony is not enough, there is further evi-dence that such teachings circulated among the emissaries who made the journey to Nevada with Short Bull. According to an account by George Sword, chief of the Indian police at Pine Ridge, the prophet told the emissary Good Thunder, "My grandchildren, when you get home, go to farming and send all your children to school."[27]

The Lakotas were not the only Plains people receiving such mes-sages. Porcupine, who gave the army an account of his journey to the prophet in June 1890, met with another army officer a little more than a month before Wounded Knee, on November 19, 1890. Porcu-pine spoke in support of Cheyenne efforts to build fences and homes along the Tongue River. Then, in explaining the Ghost Dance, he mentioned Cheyenne gardens—an uncharacteristic reference for a traditionally nomadic people, and seemingly an allusion to Wovoka's instructions to begin farming.

> If we dance, our gardens will grow nice and we will never get sick or crazy. We must not quarrel or scold each other. We must not hate each other. Must love each other. We must love all the world. . . . I must not tell lies. . . . We must work; if the white man asks us to work we must say yes and not no. . . . [We] must not quarrel with the whites or kill them. We must dance. If we don't dance we will get crazy and poor.[28]

It seems impossible that Big Road, Porcupine, and other evangelists could have urged believers to farm, send their children to government schools, and attend church while also exhorting them to go to war with the government. To be sure, some Ghost Dancers would take up arms after the army cracked down on the religion and began killing believers late in the fall. But the evidence seems clear that when Short Bull and the other emissaries left Nevada in the early spring of 1890, they bore a message that extolled hard work, farming, education, humility, and hope. The question is not: how did Lakotas twist the religion? Rather, the question is this: why did officials construe it as hostile from the beginning?

Part of the answer lies in officials' preconceptions about the dancers. In the run-up to Wounded Knee, it was a widely held assumption by Indian agents, the press, and the public that the Ghost Dance appealed primarily to "nonprogressive" Indians—those who rejected assimilation and clung tenaciously to the old ways—and that so-called progressives—those who went to school, learned English, and took up farming and Christianity—rejected Wovoka's prophecy. Observers routinely made these assumptions everywhere the Ghost Dance appeared, and particularly in South Dakota.

But Short Bull's memoir and the evidence that corroborates it suggest that the Ghost Dance was not oriented only to the past, but rather looked ahead to the future and back to the past at the same time. The religion urged believers to engage in wage work, education, and farming while instructing them to maintain customs of dance and ceremony and to pray for the restoration of the earth and Indian autonomy. In other words, the religion was both "nonprogressive" and "progressive."

Indeed, the meaning of the religion becomes clear only when we cease to evaluate it on that mythical spectrum of human advancement holding that all Indians could be found in either the nonprogressive or progressive camp. The categories themselves assumed the disappearance of Indians: nonprogressives, in abjectly refusing all change, were purportedly destined to be swept aside, and progressives willing to assimilate to the American order would "progress" toward whiteness. In reality, Indians regularly confounded these expectations by combining old and new in novel formulations and mapping out alternative strategies to remain Indians while accomplishing other goals—and nowhere more so than in the Ghost Dance.[29]

Grasping the complexity of Indian responses to the reservation era is key to seeing the troubles in South Dakota for what they were. If we turn away from the Northern Plains and follow the Ghost Dance south to Oklahoma, we can see how believers there combined old and new, tradition and innovation, and averted crisis. In the Dakotas, officials regarded the religion as a bastion of nonprogressivism. In Oklahoma, too, the religion took on many "nonprogressive" characteristics, including huge dances, ecstatic visions of the old life restored, belief in an Indian redeemer and the imminent arrival of the millennium, and the reprisal of older dances and ceremonies. At the same time, the prominence among the Oklahoma ritual leadership of educated, literate, English-speaking Indians, including some who were government employees, suggests that the religion was powerfully appealing to the very people whom agents most valued for their "progressivism." As a result, some officials held back from condemning the religion outright.

Seeing the dance unfold on the Southern Plains helps us to appreciate how wide its appeal and effect might have been on the Northern

Plains had it not been so brutally suppressed. With its simultaneous in-vocation of the Indian past and promise of an Indian future, the Ghost Dance attracted believers from a wide swath of reservation society. The documentary record of teachings on the Southern Plains is woe-fully slight. Thus, we cannot know if Indians there heard all the teach-ings as articulated in Short Bull's memoir, but something very much like them seems to have guided Oklahoma believers. On the Southern Plains the Ghost Dance met a different fate than at Wounded Knee, growing into a religious movement that lasted decades.

THE GHOST DANCE IN OKLAHOMA GREW PRIMARILY FROM THE efforts of two Southern Arapahos, Sitting Bull and Black Coyote. Sitting Bull was the emissary who accompanied Short Bull to Ne-vada. A soft-spoken, humble man with a winning smile, Sitting Bull had considerable influence on the Southern Plains, leading one ob-server to compare him to John the Baptist. He was born about 1854 in Wyoming. Although his family was Southern Arapaho, he grew up on the Northern Arapaho reservation at Wind River in Wyoming and lived there until the fall of 1890.[30]

Thus, Sitting Bull partook of the excitement about the Ghost Dance that seized Wind River early in 1889 when Sage and Yellow Calf, the Northern Arapaho elders who had visited with Wovoka, brought the teachings to their people and the Eastern Shoshones. Through word of mouth and letters written by school graduates, Wind River became a central point of diffusion for the rumors of prophecy that swirled thick on the Plains that fall, and this was pre-sumably one reason that Short Bull and his company stopped there on their westward quest. When the Lakotas left Wind River to jour-ney on to Nevada, Sitting Bull, determined to seek the prophet him-self, went with them.

While they were away, Black Coyote, also a Southern Arapaho, arrived at Wind River to consult relatives and investigate rumors of the new religion. An ambitious, gregarious man in his thirties, Black Coyote was chief of police at the Southern Cheyenne–Southern Arapaho reservation. He joined in the welcome for Short Bull, Sitting

FIGURE 7.1. Sitting Bull, Southern Arapaho evangelist of the Ghost Dance, 1891. Photo by James Mooney, National Anthropological Archives, Smithsonian Institution, 91–20209.

Bull, and the other emissaries when they returned from Nevada. He danced in the Ghost Dances that followed and learned the songs and the prophecy. In April 1890, Black Coyote became the first Southern Arapaho to carry the teachings to Oklahoma.[31]

In keys ways, both Sitting Bull and Black Coyote were keepers of old ways for Southern Arapahos. Neither man was educated, and at the time neither was Christian. Both were senior members of medicine lodges, with responsibility for upholding ceremonial tradition. But at the same time, neither one could realistically be considered "nonprogressive." In fact, Sitting Bull had scouted for the US Army in the Sioux War of 1876. As police chief at Darlington, Black Coyote occupied a position that was created by the government to undermine the tribal elders who normally kept the peace. He held the post at the pleasure of the agent, who consistently praised him for his work on the government's behalf.

After Black Coyote arrived from the north and began to teach the Ghost Dance, it swept western Oklahoma like a prairie fire. It went first from the Southern Arapaho to the Southern Cheyenne. Both tribes held Ghost Dances several times a week, beginning at dusk and continuing until dawn. Soon the circle began to turn among the Kiowa, Wichita, Caddo, and Pawnee. In September 1890, following in Black Coyote's wake, Sitting Bull returned with his family to the Southern Arapaho and began to teach. His preaching, at least some of it in Plains sign language, at which he excelled (he spoke no English), inspired an intertribal ferment of religious feeling. That month some 3,000 Indians—Arapahos, Cheyennes, Caddos, Wichitas, Kiowas, and Plains Apaches—gathered at a great camp on the South Canadian River and danced until dawn every night for two weeks straight.[32]

The dancers' enthusiasm reached even greater heights when Sitting Bull announced, several days into the revival, that he would perform a "great wonder." The next day practically every Southern Cheyenne and Southern Arapaho was present; there may have been 800 people in the dance circle alone. After they had danced for several hours in anticipation of Sitting Bull's miracle, the apostle stepped into the circle, wearing a broad-brimmed hat with a single eagle feather (much like Jack Wilson himself). He approached a young Arapaho woman. Before her eyes, he began to pass the eagle feather back and forth. Within moments, she fainted.

Sitting Bull repeated this procedure again and again, until nearly 100 Ghost Dancers had fallen prostrate within the circle. The evangelist calmed the astonished crowd, reassuring them that the sleeping people were visiting the spirits. At the next dance, those who had been unconscious recounted stunning visions of their time in the spirit land, where they met and spoke with old friends and played old games. With Sitting Bull's encouragement, they worked these visions into songs that rose from the Plains like spirit itself. Thus were born a raft of new Ghost Dance devotionals and a host of new seers and prophets on the Plains.[33]

The new songs and accounts of Southern Arapaho visions natural-
ized the Ghost Dance on the Southern Plains, lighting a fire that sent
sparks of religious excitement across a vast region. The wide appeal
of the dance had several sources. The most obvious was the return to
dance itself—to the ceremonial circle that had been suppressed by
agents and missionaries over the previous decade. Although there
had been other dances during that time, joining hands and turning
the circle to the rhythm of song restored a sense of community and
reinforced Indian identity while fulfilling the ritual instructions of
the prophet.

The songs, too, suggest the expressive appeal of the new ceremony. Many of the most poignant Southern Arapaho songs evoke a
profound sense of despair and the alienation of reservation life amid
the convergence of drought, emotional desolation, and poverty as the
people grappled with US demands for ever more land.

> *Father have pity on me,*
> *Father have pity on me,*
> *I am crying for thirst,*
> *I am crying for thirst,*
> *All is gone—I have nothing to eat,*
> *All is gone—I have nothing to eat.*[34]

Just as appealing were the trances, which marked a transformation
of the Ghost Dance on the Plains. Back in Nevada, Wovoka fell
into trances, but dancers apparently did not. On the Plains, visions
became a common experience for everyone—spectacularly so among
Lakotas. While thousands of Western Sioux joined the circle on various reservations, dozens of people at a time not only fell into trances
but had ecstatic fits. North and south, then, visions became key to the
ritual's appeal. Many joined the circle hoping to meet with the spirits
or visit heaven, which appeared as the earth restored to paradisiacal
beauty. Most dramatically, perhaps, they hoped to meet their kin,
especially departed children. Children died in large numbers from
starvation and sickness in the early reservation era, and the religion's

promise of resurrection and trance meetings with them was central to its enthusiastic embrace by bereaved parents, especially mothers.[35]

After receiving the teachings of Black Coyote and Sitting Bull, those with the most compelling and consistent trance experiences often emerged as ritual leaders of the Ghost Dance. So it was for Moki, or "Little Woman," a Southern Cheyenne woman whose story illustrates how the Ghost Dance offered trance experience, visionary achievement, and ritual authority all at once—a combination that may have been particularly attractive to Indian women.

Moki was married to Grant Left Hand, the son of Left Hand, a leading chief of the Southern Arapahos. By 1890, she had borne two children. Her first child died as an infant, and Moki's grief nearly overwhelmed her. But before too long she was pregnant again, and the sky seemed to lift when she brought a boy into the world. He grew into a bright and energetic toddler, and Grant and Moki orbited him like adoring planets. But when he was four years old, he awoke one night, ailing. Almost before his mother and father could reach his side, he died.

The desolation of his parents was nearly total. When time did nothing to assuage Moki's grief, her husband and family and all her friends grew concerned, for none seemed able to reach her in the unending night of her sorrow.

Then came the Ghost Dance. Grant Left Hand dismissed the teachings at first. But Moki, hearing the promises of loved ones returned to life, went to the circle. Falling into a trance, she reunited with her children and played with her little boy.

When she told her husband, he at first could not believe what he was hearing. But he was soon persuaded to try. Announcing, "I want to see my little boy," he, too, went to the dance. As he explained long after to all who would listen, he fell into a trance. When he awoke, he found himself astride a horse, with his departed son. Together the father and son rode across the green prairies of heaven.

Drawing on her visions for inspiration, Moki composed some of the most moving Ghost Dance songs. Among Arapahos and other Plains peoples, the spirit of the crow was both the Creator itself and a messenger to the heavens. Thus, her songs, like many others, featured the crow as a benevolent spirit.

> *The crow*
> *The crow*
> *I saw him when he flew down,*
> *I saw him when he flew down,*
> *To the earth, to the earth.*
> *He has renewed our life,*
> *He has renewed our life.*
> *He has taken pity on us,*
> *He has taken pity on us.*

Inspired by his own visions, Grant Left Hand created the Crow Dance, a separate ritual that accompanied the Ghost Dance among the Southern Arapaho and eventually among other tribes as well. Together Grant Left Hand and Moki became leading evangelists for the Ghost Dance movement.[36]

Just as it did for Moki, the Ghost Dance provided other women with the means to envision their restored children and reunited families. Thus, one Lakota woman memorialized her trance meeting with her deceased child in a two-line song, all the more poignant for its brevity:

> *It is my own child!*
> *It is my own child!*[37]

Other Lakota mothers made gifts for the spirits of lost children they saw in visions. So many people carried traditional toys, games, or children's clothing into the Ghost Dance circle as gifts for the children they embraced in trances that the dance came to resemble, in Mooney's words, "an exhibition of Indian curios on a small scale."[38]

Visionaries saw not only children but deceased parents, and their songs convey a sense of longing for family reunion across the divide that separated the worlds of the living and the dead, the present and the past. A young woman of the Western Sioux recounted seeing the spirit of her departed mother and imploring her to return to the living and assuage the grief of her little brother:

> *Mother, come home; Mother, come home,*
> *My little brother goes about always crying,*
> *My little brother goes about always crying,*
> *Mother, come home; Mother, come home.*[39]

The frequency of visions like these kept the promise of restored family at the heart of Ghost Dance devotions and gave women a central place, with new ritual status, in the Ghost Dance movement. Women were present in the circle along with men among the Lakotas of the Northern Plains, and on the Southern Plains women became ritual leaders and teachers of the new religion among the Southern Cheyenne, the Kiowa, the Pawnee, and others. Galvanized by women like Moki, Plains women assumed a stature that customarily had been reserved for men.[40]

As MUCH AS PROSPECTS FOR FAMILY REUNION DREW DANCERS TO the circle, so, too, did the restoration of old-time ceremonies and rituals that long preceded the Ghost Dance. In the circle, visionaries encountered not only immediate family but spirits of old friends and ancestors, many of them joyfully engaged in customary dances and rituals that had been suppressed on the reservation. Some encountered ceremonial leaders who had died years before. Returning to consciousness, they announced that spirits had given them instructions to revive old customs, including long-vanished religious rites. Thus, the Ghost Dance revival restored other, older dances—key attributes of Indian practice and history—to the community.[41]

The past, then, was a powerful presence in the Ghost Dance circle, but so, too, was the present. In addition to reunion with lost loved ones, the Ghost Dance also spoke to the desire for good health among the living, for keeping their souls in this world until they were old. The dance was always, even in its most millennial moment, a prayer for the health and well-being desperately sought by Plains Indians in the face of the high mortality rates of the early reservation era. From the Great Basin to the Plains, the ailments of Ghost Dancers were said to vanish as they joined the circle and opened their hearts.[42]

Thus, Ghost Dance songs express visions of numerous, happy, and eternally youthful Indians as well as the resurrection of ancestors who, in returning to life, will restore customs and ceremonies now forgotten. Often the songs call to mind abundant food, particularly buffalo meat. In the words of a Lakota song:

> *The whole world is coming*
> *A nation is coming, a nation is coming.*
> *The Eagle has brought the message to the tribe,*
> *The father says so, the father says so.*
> *Over the whole earth they are coming.*
> *The buffalo are coming, the buffalo are coming.*[43]

The vast gatherings of Black Coyote and Sitting Bull initiated a dramatic wave of Ghost Dance enthusiasm that not only carried on through the Wounded Knee Massacre but deepened and broadened in the aftermath. The Ghost Dance called to the past and to tradition, but its widespread adoption also called into being new ritual forms and new ritual leadership in a new era—the age of the reservation.

Among other tribes, the Arapahos had a reputation as particularly religious people. Other peoples often asked for their assistance in spiritual matters, and now they turned to Arapaho evangelists for instruction in the new religion. Southern Cheyennes, Wichitas, Caddos, and others learned the dance from Southern Arapahos and borrowed Southern Arapaho songs. With so many people from different tribes experiencing trance visions under his guidance, Sitting Bull's status as a priest of the new religion was bolstered, and he was given authority to appoint ritual leaders not only among his own people but among neighboring tribes as well. During the fall of 1890 and winter of 1891, he visited the Caddo and Kiowa and appointed seven ritual priests for each tribe to become its Ghost Dance leaders. In "giving the feather" (the tail feather of an eagle), he conferred on these priests the talisman they would wear as a kind of badge during the dances. After these ritual appointments, each tribe began to compose its own Ghost Dance songs.[44]

Within Southern Arapaho society, young ritual leaders would soon emerge to support—and at times supplant—the leadership of Sitting Bull and Black Coyote. Leaders like Grant Left Hand, Caspar Edson, and Paul Boynton would take charge of devotions across the reservation and beyond. Many of the new leaders had been educated in government boarding schools, and many held jobs at the agency or the reservation store. So prevalent were educated Arapahos among the ritual leadership that the conclusion is unavoidable that something in the new religion held special appeal for them.

Indeed, part of the attraction of the Ghost Dance was its amelioration of a growing institutional crisis. Reservation poverty and the end of war parties had severely constricted the passage of young men and women through the medicine lodges—the system of ceremonial organizations that undergirded the entire social order. In offering a profound way of closing the chasm opened between younger and older generations by the decline of the lodges, the rise of the Ghost Dance was so timely that many could not help but see it as providential.

Traditionally, Arapahos tracked their progression from infancy to old age through the sequence of medicine lodges. An Arapaho boy could hope to move alongside his age-mates from the Kit Fox Lodge as a young boy to the Star Lodge as a teenager, and then usually by his twenties to the first of the sacred lodges—the Tomahawk or Clubboard Lodge—signifying that he had become a mature man. Thereafter, if he lived to old age, and if he prospered enough to make the requisite offerings of property to his ceremonial sponsors, he might proceed through the Spear Lodge, the Lime Crazy Lodge (named for Lime-Crazy, a cultural hero who acted in contrary ways, a feature of ceremony in this lodge), the Dog Lodge, and the lodge known simply as Old Men. If he was very accomplished, wise, and a ceremonial leader, he might become one of the Seven Old Men, the priests who presided over all ceremonial life.[45]

In signifying the acquisition of knowledge and wisdom from older generations and spirits, lodge advancement provided a key identity within Arapaho society. Each adult lodge had governmental functions. For men who advanced, as well as for the women who married them, the lodges marked the ideal progression of a well-lived life. Wives' work and generosity were essential to their husbands' progress through the lodge system. Just as the Seven Old Men watched over men, the Seven Old Women guided all Arapaho women in their ceremonial obligations and duties, including quillwork, lodge ornamentation, and cradleboard making, all of which required adherence to ritual conventions to gain the assistance of spirits.[46]

Key to the entire system were the gifts, in the form of property sacrifices, that were required of anyone seeking advancement. Dozens of horses, bundles of arrows, large quantities of meat, and vast amounts of high-quality quillwork, moccasins, and expensive goods of all kinds regularly made their way from junior men to the senior lodge members who guided the younger acolytes into successive lodges. Senior lodge members reciprocated: as ceremonial "grandfathers," they presented gifts to their protégés and to the junior lodges. At a material level, the lodge system wove Arapahos together into a social fabric.[47]

The social and economic changes of the reservation era taxed the lodge system. Endemic poverty curtailed property sacrifices, and peace made it impossible for young men to perform war deeds, which had to be recited in lodge ceremonies to animate ceremonial regalia. Young men, especially those who were born on the reservation or came there as children, found it increasingly impossible to rise through the system.[48]

Although both Sitting Bull and Black Coyote had war experience and lodge standing before the Ghost Dance arrived, one of the most striking characteristics of the new religion among Southern Arapahos was the lack of wealth and war experience and the low rank in the lodge system of its most ardent disciples and leaders. These younger men (and sometimes women) were the cohort of Grant Left Hand and Moki, born in the 1850s and 1860s. In addition to its many spiritual benefits, the Ghost Dance allowed these young evangelists to garner status and wealth. As neighboring Cheyennes, Caddos, Wichitas, Kiowas, Plains Apaches, and Pawnees sought out the new religion, they welcomed Arapaho evangelists with gifts. One army officer who watched Sitting Bull "give the feather" to the Caddos reported that the evangelist received in turn "12 horses, a bunch of cattle, a pile of blankets, 2 good saddles, 2 good rifles, and an un-known sum of money."[49]

It takes nothing away from the sincerity of Grant Left Hand's trance reunion with his son to point out that he had met with much frustration in the older lodge system, but the new religion seemed to reward him. In 1890, the year he first turned Wovoka's circle, he was already in his early thirties but in the ceremonial lodge system he was only a Star—that is, not yet advanced to the Tomahawk Lodge and not properly a man. In the Ghost Dance, however, he would be admired and honored as a visionary and as the creator of the Crow Dance, a key auxiliary ritual to the Ghost Dance that eventually took on a life and popularity of its own.[50]

So it was with other young leaders of the new religion. By the late 1890s, some evangelists, distinguished by the authenticity of their visions and by their safe return from long journeys to see the prophet, had qualified for the ceremonial duties of piercing the ears of children and cutting their hair, duties normally carried out by senior lodge men with war exploits. Rendering such service brought the young evangelists, now men of reckoning, property sacrifices from the chil-dren's parents.[51]

Still another attribute of this generation of ritual leaders, though even more counterintuitive than their youth, might explain some of the religion's hold on them. Grant Left Hand was typical of a subset of leaders in having attended Carlisle Indian Industrial School. He could read and write.[52]

Although Wovoka was a great supporter of education, the re-cord is unclear on whether or not the Arapahos knew that. Never-theless, something about the new religion attracted educated men and women, who proved instrumental in its propagation and were particularly well represented among ceremonial leaders. Caspar Edson and Arnold Woolworth, both Carlisle graduates and literate English speakers, translated newspaper coverage of the Ghost Dance to followers. Joining them was Red Feather, a Cheyenne/Arapaho who also attended the Carlisle school, where he acquired the name Paul Boynton. After finishing school, he served as interpreter at the agency. Boynton led Ghost Dances and became a noted composer of Ghost Dance songs after being drawn to the ritual out of longing for reunion with his departed brother. Some older, uneducated Arapahos seem to have depended on educated assistants; for instance, the Arapaho Sitting Bull had no schooling, but Smith Curley, his primary assistant, reportedly did. James Mooney concluded, after several years of interviewing believers, that "the Ghost dance could never have become so widespread, and would probably have died out within a year of its inception, had it not been for the efficient aid it received from the returned pupils of various eastern government schools." These graduates "conducted the sacred correspondence for their friends at the different agencies, acted as interpreters for the delegates to the messiah, and in various ways assumed the leadership and conduct of the dance."[53]

Wovoka's insistence on the importance of education might have helped recruit these leaders by sanctioning their sacrifice—their years of loneliness and alienation in faraway schools—as spiritually significant. The religion certainly seems to have salved the profound disenchantment that troubled so many on their return. Grant Left Hand, for example, trained at school as a cobbler, but back home could find no work in the trade. Since 1882, he had clerked in the traders' store at Darlington. At least he had a job. Many others found none, despite their literacy, fluency in English, and vocational training in carpentry, sewing, and other "civilized" pursuits.[54]

On top of its economic failings, education often imposed a social burden by separating graduates from the mostly uneducated "camp" Indians and making them objects of concern, suspicion, or even contempt. A prime source of this alienation was skepticism about their new skills. To the non-schooled Indians, educated kin and neighbors seemed peculiar in their ignorance of old ways and knowledge of trades like baking and harness making. Were these new ways even properly Indian? Consequently, many graduates were left with no way to make a living, little prestige, and weakened bonds to neighbors and kin, and they were often ignorant about tribal customs and traditional ceremonies. Ultimately, they faced the challenge of proving their Indian identities.[55]

In this regard, the Ghost Dance validated graduates by extolling the wage work and farming in which they had been trained. A white observer of Sitting Bull's Ghost Dance in the fall of 1890 reported that the evangelist urged his followers "to work and plant corn and to live at peace with the white man because Jesus wants it—these things are generally believed and continually talked about together with the coming of the buffalo." As we have seen, Black Short Nose, the Southern Cheyenne elder, returned from meeting Wovoka in 1891 with the instruction to believers, "Do not refuse to work for the white man." Similarly, Caspar Edson, a Southern Arapaho Carlisle graduate who accompanied Black Short Nose, instructed Ghost Dancers to "work for white men." The prophet's exhortations to labor seemed to sanctify and naturalize all of the modern occupations in which students at Carlisle and other schools were educated, but which lacked any traditional status among Indian peoples.[56]

Although the new religion required no particular skills of its believers, propagating it did require linguistic talent and literacy in English, which, along with Plains sign language, would become its lingua franca. Starting with the letters from boarding school students that first brought word of the teachings to Southern Arapahos, and including Jack Wilson's own letters to followers (a method of communication that might explain his enthusiasm for education), the boarding school graduates were key to the new religion and empowered by it. To be sure, not all educated Indians on the Plains endorsed the new teachings. Luther Standing Bear, a Brule Lakota of the Rosebud Agency who attended Carlisle, eschewed the Ghost Dance, as did Yellow Eagle, a Northern Arapaho graduate from Wind River Reservation. But other school graduates on their reservations took up the religion, including Circle Elk, a nephew of Short Bull, who joined the Lakota circle.[57]

At the same time, Arapaho elders also endorsed the Ghost Dance, apparently seeing it not as a threat to the lodge system but as confirmation of its power. Senior lodge members Sage and Yellow Calf, the Northern Arapahos who traveled to Mason Valley early in 1889, would later be said to have foreseen the arrival of new teachings in visions and then gone to seek them out. In other words, the Ghost Dance prophecy came to men of standing in the old lodge system and was therefore an expression of it. Perhaps the rise of younger, often educated Arapahos to ritual leadership seemed foreordained as well.[58]

The spread of the Ghost Dance in some ways mimicked the propagation of the Peyote Religion, which also took hold among young and educated people on Indian reservations and would be labeled "demoralizing" and antiprogressive by officials. The eruption of the peyote ritual immediately preceded the Ghost Dance among the Southern Arapaho and served, as we have seen, as a vital context for the propagation of Jack Wilson's teachings. There were key differences between the two religions. Because the effects of peyote superficially mimicked drunkenness, some Arapahos who supported the Ghost Dance, particularly elders, condemned peyote as degeneracy (as Jack Wilson himself would do in Nevada some years later).[59]

But like the Ghost Dance, the Peyote Religion not only helped heal a generational divide but gave rise to a new body of young ritual leaders: Young Bear, Heap of Crows, Cleaver Warden, and Paul Boynton each led either Ghost Dances or peyote ceremonies, and Boynton led both. All of these leaders were young, and Warden and Boynton, like many other Peyotists, were school graduates. In fact, over 100 Peyotists are known to have attended Carlisle, whose students constituted a vital network for dispersing the Peyote Religion across the nation, just as Carlisle students did for the Ghost Dance. Most of these young men who led peyote devotions and the Ghost Dance continued to participate in the old medicine lodge system, but peyote and Ghost Dancing were central to their lives. The ceremonial lodges would continue into the twentieth century, but within two decades they had atrophied for lack of advancement by younger people. The Peyote Religion and the Ghost Dance, meanwhile, had grown, if anything, more vibrant.[60]

WHEREAS THE GHOST DANCE WOULD MEET BRUTAL SUPPRESSION on the Northern Plains, Southern Plains officials were more temperate in their response, perhaps in part because so many trusted agency employees had become Ghost Dancers. Black Coyote's dual roles as chief of police and movement evangelist may help explain how the agency remained calm as the new religion gathered enthusiasm. The fact that many educated Ghost Dance leaders were employed as translators and clerks probably helped as well. In contrast to the full-blown white panic that met the emergence of the Ghost Dance among Lakotas, authorities observed its advent at the Southern Cheyenne–Southern Arapaho reservation with comparative calm. Agent Charles Ashley adopted a wait-and-see approach. After Black Coyote returned from the north with the new religion, Ashley allowed the large and fervent gatherings to continue and did not intervene. He was disconcerted that the Arapahos seemed to stop tending their fields during the dances, and in the summer of 1890 he warned against a rumored mass departure in quest of Christ. But even after Sitting Bull returned and the revival entered its new, more enthusiastic phase, Ashley maintained his composure. Commissioner of Indian Affairs Thomas J. Morgan himself visited the Cheyenne and Arapaho reservation in late November. Meanwhile, in lurid, largely fictional accounts, newspapers in the north were already reporting that the enthusiastic reception for the new religion on Lakota reservations signaled an imminent "outbreak" by the Sioux. Despite similarly hysterical press reports from Oklahoma, Morgan reassured his office that he had had a "good meeting" with tribal leaders and had received "no indication of trouble at Darlington."[61]

For all the focus here on the educated leaders and aspiring wage workers and farmers drawn to the Ghost Dance, it would be wrong to characterize the religion as specifically and exclusively for them. Had that been the case, it could never have achieved popularity in Oklahoma, where most Indians did not go to boarding schools and many struggled to reconcile jobs and farming with traditional Arapaho culture and with Indianness more generally. It seems more correct to describe the Ghost Dance as a religion that could reconcile those Indians who were more hopeful about the new economy and saw their future in innovating new ways with those who were less hopeful and sought to preserve more of the old life. Not all Indians joined the Ghost Dance, of course. Some did not experience elation or have visions, and so decided it was not for them. But those who did join were drawn in part to its unifying spirit, which brought together those who had found their way to the river of cash and those who had been less able or more reluctant to approach that riverbank.

And finally, the Ghost Dance also offered a bridge between believers in the old religion and believers in Christ. Indeed, people from both groups claimed the Ghost Dance as their own. Heinrich R. Voth, a Mennonite missionary at Darlington who worked closely with Arapaho students and studied the dance intently in 1890 and 1891, commented that it represented a "compound" of Indian and Christian belief. He hoped that it would lead believers to a more refined Christianity, but in the meantime, he observed, it served as a meeting place between traditional believers and those more inclined toward Christianity. Among the Southern Arapaho and Cheyenne, Voth noted, many Indians made "the accusation that they have given up too much" of the old ways. Others maintained that if they wanted to keep young people invested in tribal affairs, "they have to make concessions to civilization and Christianity, which has more or less gained an influence over the rising generation." In Voth's view, this divide was not so much expressed by the Ghost Dance as resolved by it; "hence the desperate effort in the ghost dances, on the one side, to revive many old customs, and on the other side to give due consideration to the ways of the whites and mix into the old religious customs as much as possible some of the customs of the whites and even of the truths and methods of the Christian religion."[62]

FROM ITS ORIGINS IN THE REVIVAL OF 1890, WHEN IT HELPED to bridge the religious, economic, and cultural fissures that coursed through Indian communities, the Ghost Dance went on to exert a long-term influence on the Southern Plains. For years to come, it rejuvenated customary rituals and renewed devotion to Indian dance and ceremony.

The peaceful reception of the Ghost Dance in Oklahoma stands in stark contrast to the cataclysm that erupted in the Dakotas. And yet, the religion that spread onto the Northern Plains with Short Bull and other Lakota emissaries to Pine Ridge, Rosebud, Standing Rock, and Cheyenne River was the same religion, with the same strengths and broad appeal, that had spread on the Southern Plains. For such a disaster to descend on a peaceful, unifying religion, another set of interests and influences had to be at play.

Short Bull's party returned to South Dakota, the holy man later recalled, "by the same route [on which] we came, only one accident occurring, the train was overturned and fell over an embankment but no one was hurt." In the months ahead, the tragedy they avoided in that train wreck would be multiplied many times over, and the casualties would include not only members of Short Bull's own family but, for a time at least, the joyful promise of redemption itself.[63]

CHAPTER 8

LAKOTA ORDEAL

T HE REMARKABLE WELCOME THE GHOST DANCE RECEIVED IN Indian Territory was mirrored in at least one way in South Dakota: soon after Short Bull and the others returned, they ministered to growing crowds of rapt and devoted believers, buoyed by a current of exhilaration and joy.

But there were also critical differences. In South Dakota, the Ghost Dance was given a much more hostile reception by officials than had occurred in Oklahoma. The agent at the Southern Arapaho–Southern Cheyenne reservation seems to have been unaware of the new religion until after it arrived, at which point, as we have seen, he reacted with caution. In contrast, authorities on the Sioux reservations were militantly opposed to the Ghost Dance, as Short Bull quickly discovered.

The day after he returned to Rosebud, the holy man set out for the council house, eager to "tell them all about what I had seen and heard" in Nevada. He never made it: on his way he was apprehended by the Indian police, who took him to the agent J. George Wright. The evangelist told the agent about his meeting with the prophet, and he would later recall Wright's warning: if he conveyed his story to the Indians, "I would be a dead man." For the moment, Short Bull was intimidated into silence. He might have expected the agent's hostility. Over at Pine Ridge, Good Thunder and two other emissaries also had been arrested and detained by the Indian police immediately upon their return from Nevada. Under orders from the agent Hugh Gallagher, they had remained in custody until they promised to not even discuss the Ghost Dance in a council.[1]

Of course, these crude attempts to suppress the Ghost Dance gospel would fail once the good news began to spread by word of mouth across the reservations. Ghost Dances began in out-of-the-way locations and might have seemed too small to attract official attention, but they grew in size and prominence as the summer of 1890 faded. As the new faith advanced, so did official alarm. By the fall, officials and the press were trafficking in stories of "Indian trouble"—a dark power looming on the border of the settlements involving a fanatic, a conspiracy, and a bloodletting to come, either in the next season or at the next moon.

Why were authorities in South Dakota waiting for the emissaries to return? And why did they so quickly order them arrested? Rumors of "outbreaks" had swirled often among white settlers and officials near Indian reservations. Agency reports from virtually every Indian reservation mentioned such rumors periodically, and Oklahoma was rife with them in 1890. But agents usually dismissed them as the product of ignorant fantasy (which they almost always were). There was plenty of incompetence and ungrounded fear among reservation superintendents in South Dakota, and some of the Ghost Dance trouble can be attributed to it. But Gallagher and Wright were seasoned agents with years of experience. Why would both men succumb to the powerful sense of foreboding around South Dakota reservations that was mostly absent from other reservations where the Ghost Dance appeared? Although initially these two agents claimed to have the new religion under control, as summer gave way to fall they, too, joined the chorus of voices clamoring for action. What changed their minds?[2]

The clues to this mystery are embedded in the broader context, like telltale footprints in the sandy reservation soil. In a season of political upheaval, many feared that the government was losing control;

specifically, the two agents and many others grew concerned about the rising power of the "nonprogressive element"—those Lakotas who refused (or were said to refuse) assimilation. Partly because of the identity of Ghost Dance evangelists and many followers as former "hostiles" who had fought the United States in the war of 1876, and partly because the new religion promised a return of Indian autonomy and the old ways, officials interpreted it as a rejection of the government's civilization program. Like wearing "Indian" clothes, practicing plural marriage, and showing hostility to schooling, farming, land sales, and allotment (breaking up the reservation to assign separate lots of land to individuals), the Ghost Dance became associated with nonprogressive Indians. Agent Daniel F. Royer at Pine Ridge, for instance, reported in November 1890 that the dancers were exclusively nonprogressives "who refused to sign the late Sioux Bill and have in the past fought every measure that tended towards the civilization of Indians."[3]

With some notable exceptions in recent years, historians have often followed the lead of officials and labeled Ghost Dancers as "nonprogressive" and their Indian opponents as "progressive." But just as we saw among Northern Paiutes and Southern Arapahos, these labels do little to explain the religion's appeal and development, or the violence that ultimately engulfed it.[4]

For one thing, it proved impossible to predict who would join the Ghost Dance based on individuals' supposed inclination to assimilate or not. Red Cloud, reviled by the agents as a bitter nonprogressive, defended the right of other Lakotas to join Ghost Dances but remained throughout a doubter and a critic, predicting at the height of the movement that "the enthusiasm of the men in it will melt away like a spring snow." On the other hand, Agent Royer considered Young-Man-Afraid-of-His-Horses to be a stalwart progressive and was therefore perturbed when the chief joined the dancing at Pine Ridge. By October, Young-Man-Afraid-of-His-Horses was "persuaded to give the dance up," according to the agent, but others were much harder to convince. Agent James McLaughlin wrote in mid-October that at Standing Rock the religion "now includes some of the Indians who were formerly numbered with the progressive and more intelligent," and that instead of denouncing the faith, "many of our very best Indians appear 'dazed' and undecided when talking of it." At Pine Ridge, farmers who owned modern machinery joined the Ghost Dance, and "some of our best Indians are nearly crazy over it," marveled Philip Wells, the mixed-blood interpreter working for the government. Another observer would lament the "converted and educated Indians who have become infected with the craze, and have been swept by it back into pristine barbarism."[5]

In fact, the Ghost Dance did not sort progressives from nonprogressives so much as it threatened to dissolve the boundaries between them, drawing them into alliances around a religious revival that authorities interpreted as atavistic savagery. There may be few moments more dangerous to a colonial order than the collapse of a system for classifying the loyalties of subject peoples. Categorizing Indians into camps that were "for" or "against" the government's civilization program was the key instrument by which authorities understood, managed, and manipulated Indians; they used this system to decide who would receive rations and perquisites like farm equipment and employment, and who would be shunned and deprived of administrative favors. Through it they identified those Indians who needed to be compelled to follow the road to assimilation and those who could be counted on to serve as (and rewarded for being) models of "right behavior." The new religion was terrifying to officials—and troubling to not a few Lakotas—precisely because it confounded labels that had become an important tool for administering reservations and simplifying the complex politics of Lakota people.

The disintegration of these categories explains their increasingly reckless use by agents and officials during the Ghost Dance crisis. Authorities frequently labeled the same individuals one way and then the other, as conditions on the ground shifted. In reality, almost no Lakota was, or ever could be, wholly in favor of assimilation, and at the same time, few if any could reject all the practices identified with it. Real life required mixing old and new, often in surprising ways: many Indians who went to school rejected farming because it proved impossible in the arid ravines of western South Dakota, and those who took up work as clerks or teamsters often longed for at least some traditional dances and rituals. But by 1890, the badge of "nonprogressive" could at any moment be hung on any Lakota who disagreed with the agent and the federal government. Once agents made known their opposition, they perceived Indians who abstained from the Ghost Dance—for whatever reason—as progressive. Dancers, on the other hand, showed themselves as nonprogressive simply for defying their agents. Some began dancing, showing their nonprogressive colors, and then stopped, becoming progressive, only to become nonprogressive and take it up again as the crisis worsened. The categories became circular and practically useless for understanding the appeal or meaning of the religion.

Even at its height, the Ghost Dance was a minority religion; at most, about one in three Lakotas joined the circle in 1890. The problem was less the size of the dances than the way they congregated Indians whom authorities hoped to divide. Among the minority who believed were both Indians who farmed and Indians who did not, both avid supporters of the new government schools and their harshest critics. The Ghost Dance offered simultaneously a route to the past of buffalo and horses and a near-term future of wage work, farming, and churchgoing (although white authorities in South Dakota remained blind to these instructions to accommodate reservation life). In this sense, the religion offered a potential bridge between Lakota rivals, just as it did among Southern Arapahos: Indians who had clashed with one another over divergent responses to US policy prior to 1890 might join hands in the Ghost Dance circle.[6]

Tragically, the American response to the Ghost Dance only aggravated preexisting divides, in some cases turning the religion into a wedge between the very groups that many Lakotas had hoped to reconcile. One result was the weakening of the authority of Indian agents and other officials, and that in turn made administration of the reservations even more contentious. When they became frustrated enough, these officials would turn to the army to enforce their will.

IF HOSTILITY TO FARMING AND OTHER ASPECTS OF THE assimilation program cannot explain why some Lakotas took up the religion, what does? There is no single solution to this puzzle, but believers' devotion was often affected by events that were less about the Ghost Dance than about other issues to which the ritual became attached. The uproar that accompanied the spread of the Ghost Dance among the Western Sioux had many causes, each with a long history of its own, but the foremost of these concerned land and subsistence, especially rations. The forced cession of lands and breakup of the Great Sioux Reservation had occurred over much of the previous decade, reaching an awful climax in 1889. With Lakotas pulled into disputes with the government and with one another before the Ghost Dance even arrived, the new religion's call for peace and Indian unity was all the more appealing.

Hoping to wrest more land from the Sioux, the government tried, and failed, to break apart the reservation as early as 1882. Lakota opposition proved insurmountable. The government tried again in 1888, when Congress sent Captain Richard Henry Pratt, director of the Carlisle Indian Industrial School, to negotiate a land purchase that would shatter the reservation. Prior treaties had stipulated that three-quarters of all Lakota men had to sign any agreement for it to be valid. But in 1888, opposition was so entrenched that at some agencies no effort was even made to gather signatures. Pratt left a failure.[7]

In 1889, Congress approved statehood for North and South Dakota. Determined to pry more land away from Indians in the mistaken conviction that South Dakota settlers would soon flock westward and needed a railroad, Congress sent General George Crook, as the head of a new commission, to negotiate with Lakotas. Crook demanded that they sell 9 million acres—almost half the Great Sioux Reservation, including much of the most arable land. The Indians would be left with six smaller reservations on which they were expected to take up individual parcels of 320 acres each.[8]

Toward this end, Crook called Lakotas to the agencies. Few declined the invitation. When negotiations began, nearly all expressed outright opposition to the land sale. Smiling, Crook nodded. He lifted the ban on dancing for the duration of the negotiations, and his commission bought large amounts of food for the Indians encamped about the agencies. Festivities commenced, but still the men refused to sign.

So Crook applied pressure. When any of the men requested permission to return home to tend to their farms, Crook said no. In essence, the government took Indians hostage until they signed away their reservation.[9]

Captivity is an intimidating condition, and Crook was an intimidating man. Opposing him was no child's game. To the Indians, he was a known quantity: a three-star general (thus his Lakota name, Three Stars), Crook had done battle against them, and they had surrendered to him in 1876. To Lakotas, he was the US Army, and they knew well what the army had done to them. Knowing that he could call down an invasion at any moment, many quailed when he loudly questioned the "loyalty" of Lakotas who refused to sign. They needed no one to tell them that "disloyal" Indians were "hostiles."

Congress had awarded the Crook Commission an enormous (for its day) budget to buy off opponents among the Sioux. Negotiations dragged on for weeks as the commission browbeat and bribed opponents, one by one, man by man. Even then, there were not enough signatures. To reach the necessary three-quarter threshold, the commission had to include the signatures of white husbands of Lakota women and mixed-bloods. The commission also had to leave the papers, along with a large amount of money to pay out more bribes, with the agencies, which would forward the expanded lists of signatures to Washington later. And finally, when the commission still failed to get enough signatures, it undercounted Lakotas so that it could claim that three-quarters of the adult men had signed. Congress threw the ceded lands open to settlement even before ratifying the agreement. By then, Lakotas knew that they had been defrauded. This was no agreement. It was theft.[10]

The initial result was a series of deep fissures between those who had signed and those who had not. At Pine Ridge, leaders who

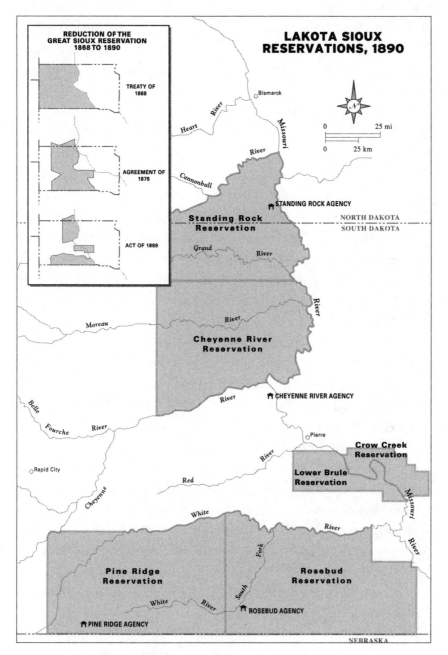

MAP 8.1. Lakota Sioux Reservations, 1890

endorsed the agreement, notably American Horse, were promptly reviled by those who had not, such as Red Cloud and Little Wound. But feuding soon broke out even between leaders who shared opposition to the land sale (and especially between Red Cloud and Little Wound).

Contributing to the souring of relations among many different factions was another development almost immediately after the deal had been concluded. The land that comprised Lakota reservations had been held in common. The agreement forced on Lakotas by the Crook Commission included provisions that not only sold off 9 million acres of the reservation but applied pressure to change the nature of property holding on the part that remained. Specifically, the agreement committed signers to allotment—acceptance by each male head of household of individual title to 320 acres (less for younger people) to start them on the road to farming and its mythical correlate, self-sufficiency.

Because self-support was central to the discourse of allotment, accepting individual title implied the loss of rations. Lakota opponents of the cession had warned that signing the paper meant surrendering rations, the mere idea of which could raise a panic. Americans saw rations as gratuitous support for Indians unwilling to work, but to Lakotas, the stream of food, clothing, and blankets was payment for land already ceded in prior treaties and agreements. Moreover, rations were sometimes all that was keeping them alive.

Throughout the 1889 negotiations, Crook had assured the Indians that there was no threat to rations. Despite allotment, all rations stipulated in previous treaties would continue. But Congress, oblivious to Crook's promises or Lakota needs, imposed "economies" in the Indian budget soon after the negotiations concluded, compelling the head of the Office of Indian Affairs to strip 1 million pounds of beef from Pine Ridge's annual rations and another 2 million from Rosebud. This announcement, coming close on the heels of the land sale, brought supporters of the cession like American Horse and others who signed the agreement into widespread disrepute. "They were made the targets for derision by the non-signers," reported the agent, "who called them fools and dupes and told them they were now getting their pay in the same coin they had received before whenever they were so foolish as to make contracts with whites."[11]

The starving winter that followed brought many to the brink of despair and did nothing to diminish these divisions. Sioux bodies weakened by malnutrition succumbed easily to repeated epidemics. Measles had taken a toll in 1888–1889, and influenza descended in 1889–1890, killing many more people, especially children. In 1890 the reservations heaved with such discontent that rumors of uprisings or "outbreaks" were already rife well before the Ghost Dance made its appearance.[12]

For officials, these conditions made the task of managing the reservations ever more difficult. Governance was already impeded by other obstacles, which, combined with the recent problems, made it hard for authorities to discern the course of events (and at least as hard for historians to interpret the documentary record). For one thing, the sheer size of the Lakota population made the agents' jobs harder than at other reservations. Even after decades of war and epidemics, Lakotas were the most numerous of all Plains Indians. There were over 4,500 Lakotas at Pine Ridge alone, and across all six Western Sioux reservations the combined population stood close to 18,000. This was a tiny minority compared to the state's settler population of 300,000 and the 1 million settlers in neighboring Nebraska. But even if only one in three Lakotas—somewhere between 5,000 and 6,000 people—joined the Ghost Dance, that number well exceeded the combined total population of 3,500 Southern Arapahos and Southern Cheyennes in Oklahoma.[13]

Even when they were operating relatively smoothly, reservations were exercises in control that continually failed. The sheer number of Lakotas, combined with their refusal to be cajoled or intimidated into giving up all mobility, made Western Sioux reservations even harder to police than most. Indians were not supposed to venture beyond reservation boundaries without permission, and agents kept watch on the most prominent leaders to make sure they stayed in place. But others came and went, visiting friends and relatives, comparing notes about reservation life, and relaying messages. Agents were often dimly aware, at best, of their movements. With reservation populations this big, complicated, and mobile, agents were constantly on guard against challenges to their authority. In this context, even a minority religious movement could cause consternation.

Unfortunately for agents—and for Indians too—Congress's decision to reduce rations in 1890 undermined their power to placate or intimidate Lakotas into going along with government demands. Rations represented the primary benefit that agents could use to reward "progressive" behavior. With rations reduced, agents had even less to offer than usual. Thus, the front line of government authority at the reservations was diminished even as political and social friction among Indians increased.

In a context this complicated, no single issue—and certainly not positions on allotment—could foreshadow which Lakotas would support the new religion. Red Cloud, for example, never joined the Ghost Dance despite his unbending opposition to the land sale. But as Wovoka's teachings spread, a sizable number of land sale opponents did enter the circle, notably Little Wound and Big Road, both of whom became ritual leaders. Their earlier warning that selling land would lead to a ration cut now seemed prescient. With their opposition to the government thus esteemed as wisdom, their leadership of the Ghost Dance enhanced its appeal.

As events at Pine Ridge and Rosebud attached the faith to an increasingly broad stream of dissent from assimilation policy, particularly land cessions, in Lakota society, the weave between opposing land sales and performing the Ghost Dance became so tight that authorities had difficulty telling them apart. Rumors about one were often mistaken for rumors about the other. To the chagrin of authorities, the so-called nonprogressives persisted in their opposition to the land cession even after Congress passed it into law with the Sioux Act. In the late winter and early spring of 1890, around the time the emissaries returned from Nevada, opponents of the cession began organizing to discuss their options. Letters went back and forth among them, and soon a meeting was proposed for the spring at Cheyenne River Reservation, among the Minneconjous.

Authorities and members of the public soon got wind of the plan and began circulating rumors of an imminent "Sioux outbreak." In May a land speculator from Pierre, South Dakota, named Charles Hyde sent a note to the Secretary of the Interior advising him that "the Sioux Indians or a portion of them are secretly planning and arranging for an outbreak in the near future." Officials investigated. Hyde's source turned out to be "a mixed-blood Sioux" enrolled at the Presbyterian College in Pierre, who claimed to have received similar messages in correspondence from "relatives or friends at Pine Ridge Agency advising him to look out for himself as the Indians might break out."[14]

The government would file this correspondence and documents of the subsequent investigation in its massive compendium of letters and reports dedicated to the Ghost Dance, known in the archive of the Bureau of Indian Affairs as Special Case 188. Many researchers ever since have assumed that the "outbreak" referred to excitement about the Ghost Dance. But the rumor had nothing to do with the Ghost Dance, which in May was a very small affair. Agents assured Washington that no trouble was likely, and their reports make it clear that the warnings sent to Pierre, and forwarded by Hyde, were referring to the discontent and plans for a meeting (so much for the "outbreak") of the leading Lakota opponents of the land cession. Agents (to their credit) were particularly dubious about Hyde's warning. All announced that the Indians showed no inclination to fight and that they could control matters without intervention from Washington. Hugh Gallagher at Pine Ridge was the only agent who so much as mentioned the Ghost Dance, which he did by way of dismissing it, almost as an afterthought: "The excitement caused by the reported appearance of the 'Great Medicine Man' in the North will I am sure soon die out without causing trouble."[15]

Meanwhile, over at Rosebud, yet another special census added to the discontent. With the national decennial census already under

way, authorities ordered an additional special count of Brule Lakotas on the grounds that Indians had been inflating their numbers to
gain more rations. Some Brules allegedly fooled census takers into
increasing the number of dependents in each family. There was some
truth to the charges: some families had done exactly this to compensate for the continual shrinkage of rations allotted by the government
to each person. As subjects in the state's ongoing experiment in social
control through counting people, Brules were fully aware that the
government would use the census to tighten its grip.[16]

Some set out to subvert the project. It was at this point that Brule
chief White Horse refused to let his followers be counted. At the
same moment, spies and the Indian police fed information about
the proposed council at Cheyenne River to the agent at Rosebud,
J. George Wright. He threw White Horse and others in the guard-
house, told them they had to let the census proceed, and warned
them that if they tried to attend any meetings off reservation they
would face more time in jail.[17]

ALMOST SIMULTANEOUSLY, THE ROSEBUD AGENCY SAW THE
eruption of yet another land dispute. Separate from the bitter residue
left by the Crook Commission, it would have profound implications
for the Ghost Dance revival. After 1877, the Wazhazha band of the
Brules had settled along Pass Creek, a verdant stream lined with
cottonwoods and box elders that coursed through broad meadows
along the northwest edge of the lands served by the Rosebud Agency,
where Brules were to draw rations. To the west, across the creek, lay
the Pine Ridge Agency, where Oglalas were assigned.

To administrators, Pass Creek was a nest of nonprogressivism.
Reaching the settlements of the Wazhazhas—who were overwhelmingly opposed to the land cession of 1889—took a full day of travel
or more from the Rosebud Agency. That Wazhazhas secreted themselves from the prying eyes of the government made agents all the
more suspicious of them.

Even so, Wazhazhas harbored few illusions that they could live by
the old ways alone. After settling at Pass Creek in 1878, they spent

the next twelve years putting up cabins and, with the help of the agency staff, opening up land to plant small fields of corn. Protestant Episcopalian missionaries built them a school. These "nonprogressives" had made their way into the reservation world.

Then, in 1889, the Sioux Act delineated the boundaries of the six new reservations. For reasons that remain obscure, those who drafted the law moved the border of Rosebud Reservation. On the map, the shift was small—the boundary moved from Pass Creek to the next creek to the east, Black Pipe Creek—but it essentially delivered the Pass Creek lands to Pine Ridge Reservation. During the 1889 negotiations, the issue went unnoticed. But in the aftermath, the confusion placed at issue a wedge of land sixteen miles wide by sixty-seven miles long, occupied by some 400 Wazhazhas who had, according to their agent, "broken considerable land and built fair houses." Now these villagers of Pass Creek suddenly found themselves illegally occupying a remote part of Pine Ridge Reservation.[18]

The government ordered the Wazhazhas to move to Rosebud. Not surprisingly, they refused to go. Instead, they demanded that they be transferred to the Pine Ridge Agency, with the Oglalas, so that they could remain at Pass Creek and keep their property. In August, the agent at Rosebud, J. George Wright, attempted to force the Wazhazhas out by cutting their rations—the same rations that had already been reduced by Congress.[19]

The many confrontations between officials and Ghost Dancers at Pine Ridge have long contributed to an assumption that belief in the new religion was peculiarly fervent among Oglalas. That perception partly stemmed from the arrival during this time of crisis at Pine Ridge of other, particularly devoted believers, including the Minneconjous and Hunkpapas who traveled there from reservations in the north and ultimately were killed at Wounded Knee.

But the most voluble and persistent Ghost Dance believers were found among the western Brules of Rosebud—who also fled to Pine Ridge during the troubles. The Pass Creek question was perhaps their most consistent complaint. Ghost Dances began on Lakota reservations in the spring of 1890, but only in September did the agent at

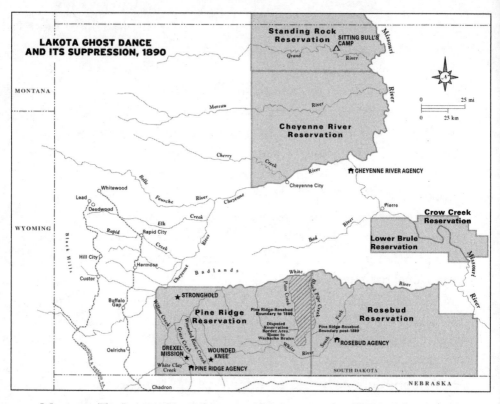

MAP 8.2. The Lakota Ghost Dance and Its Suppression, 1890

Rosebud begin to hear of the ritual, and by that time its grip was strongest in the Pass Creek settlements. In repeated demands to the government, Pass Creek Wazhazhas—the largest contingent of "hostiles" in the Badlands—made it abundantly clear that the land issue was as much on their minds as the religion. They would be among the last to surrender to the army, insisting to the end that they be allowed to become official residents of Pine Ridge Reservation after the boundary change. In their devotions and their demands, they were led by another Pass Creek Wazhazha: Short Bull himself. His determination was partly millennial, inspired by prophecy and belief, and partly political, driven by a refusal to accept the loss of the homes his people had made. Indeed, the commitment and energy of his many followers at Pass Creek helped to catapult the holy man into a leadership position in the movement across the Western Sioux reservations.[20]

Land sales and allotment were such contentious issues at Pine Ridge, Rosebud, and other Lakota reservations that contemporary observers concluded, and influential scholars have long agreed, that Lakotas were driven to the promise of millenarian deliverance in no small measure by the threat of allotment itself. There is truth in this claim: Lakota discontent over allotment did indeed energize the Ghost Dances.[21]

But that discontent resulted from the particular historical conditions of Sioux reservations, where furious arguments about land had been inspired only partly by allotment. Just as important was that the land cession had been carried out even more aggressively than elsewhere. Then, after the cession—a de facto theft—was passed into law, what appears to have been bureaucratic bungling changed reservation boundaries and stripped Brule Lakotas of still more property, without compensation. Not surprisingly, the result was multiple layers of antigovernment sentiment concerning land.

The land issue at Pass Creek should remind us that for Indians, being opposed to allotment and land cession did not necessarily imply opposition to farming or home building. Cabins and cornfields sprouted just as well on communal as on allotted land. The Pass Creek Brules took up a religion that promised millennial deliverance and the restoration of the old ways, but their aspirations for this earth were to keep both the communal holding of the reservation and the homes and small farms they had built up over the previous decade. If there was a sense of hopelessness and rage in their religious fervor, it stemmed less from a "nonprogressive" opposition to farming and labor than from the government's attempt to strip them of the farms they had worked so hard to build.

Indeed, had there been no land cession and no boundary change in South Dakota, the Lakota Ghost Dance might have taken on a very different meaning. Nothing in the Ghost Dance teachings necessarily predisposed it to becoming an anti-allotment religion. Jack Wilson himself requested farmland as part of his compensation for serving as "Governor of the West," and he would spend much of his life pressing government officials to allot farms for himself and his people.[22] His exhortations to take up land—"get farms to live on"—could even have been construed by some believers as an embrace of allotment. In fact, just as Lakotas were receiving the Ghost Dance teachings from Short Bull and the other emissaries and infusing it with their heartfelt opposition to allotment and the new reservation boundaries, the Ghost Dance was giving Arapahos in Oklahoma considerable help in accepting allotment. A brief look at the Arapaho experience suggests that the tension in South Dakota arose primarily from other, contemporary conflicts, not from the Ghost Dance.

IN THE SUMMER OF 1890, WHILE SOUTH DAKOTA AGENTS TRIED to head off the meeting of allotment opponents and rumors of the Ghost Dance began to circulate, Indians in Oklahoma faced a crisis of their own. Congress, determined to break up the Southern Cheyenne–Southern Arapaho reservation just as it had the Great Sioux Reservation the year before, sent the Jerome Commission to Oklahoma. Meetings with this commission did not start out much better for Southern Arapahos and Cheyennes than meetings with the Crook Commission had for Lakotas. Demanding more land than Indians wanted to sell, the government also offered a poor price, warning that if the Indians did not accede, Congress could take all the land it wanted without paying a cent. Southern Arapahos feared the loss of grazing land for their cattle and horses, and many doubted that they could make a living on 160-acre farms. Although the agent believed that Arapaho leaders favored conciliation, resistance was pervasive among their followers.

In the midst of these difficult negotiations, Left Hand and other chiefs consulted Sitting Bull, the Ghost Dance leader, for guidance. They probably did so in deference to his religious standing and his many followers. In the fall of 1890, the evangelist's influence was at its peak. Not only was he receiving many gifts from eager acolytes, but he was trailed by crowds of people who often approached him, according to one observer, to "rub their hands on him, and cry, which demonstration he received with patient fortitude."[23]

So it might seem incongruous at first that this charismatic preacher, whose followers thrilled to the promise of a coming millennium that would restore Indians to a renewed earth, told Left Hand and the other leaders that he approved of selling the land. His reasoning was at least partly millennial: soon the Messiah would come and restore the earth to Indians. Meanwhile, he said, cash from the sale would allow believers to buy gifts for the resurrected souls of loved ones who would shortly be returning.[24]

These reasons concerned the millennium, but publicly he also spoke of the premillennial times ahead. In announcing to the commission his support for the agreement, he embraced education and farming, saying that he would send his children to school, and expressed eagerness to "have something to call my own and have everything on my farm." Others followed in his footsteps, and in the end the Indians accepted the government price—$2 million for about 3 million acres, with $500,000 to be paid in cash and the rest to earn interest that would be paid annually to individual Arapahos.[25]

In addition to Sitting Bull, other Ghost Dancers also played a prominent role in negotiating the final settlement. Paul Boynton, the Carlisle-educated Ghost Dance visionary and leader, helped persuade the government to pay more interest than originally proposed. Black Coyote, too, voiced support for the land cession and urged the commission to ensure that rations continued to flow.[26]

By mid-November, as events on Lakota reservations in the north spiraled toward disaster, Arapaho men had voted overwhelmingly to accept allotment. In the short term, the sale of the land brought piles of silver dollars to Arapaho households. In the words of one Arapaho eyewitness, some people spent at least some of the money on "bundles of shawls and dress goods—enough to give to their folks when the resurrection came."[27]

It is impossible to say for certain how essential Sitting Bull's endorsement was to the acceptance of allotment among Southern Arapahos. But in promising salvation to those who took up farms and ultimately deliverance from earthly tribulation, the Ghost Dance seems to have aided some of its leaders in accepting land sales and earning cash as economic strategies. Although the Ghost Dance has long been presented as a strictly traditionalist ritual that expressed only rejection of government policy, in practice it empowered some followers to accept harsh new realities and move toward the river of cash without fear of abandoning their Indianness. By allowing them to accept allotment while also anticipating millenarian renewal of the old ways, the new religion enabled them, in their hearts, to reject assimilation.

The religion could have worked in similar ways among Lakotas. One can easily envision a scenario in which the Ghost Dance allowed disparate groups to join hands in the circle and find their way through a period fraught with land cession, drought, and diminishing rations. Short Bull and other Ghost Dancers might even have helped their people negotiate with the commissioners, as their counterparts in Oklahoma did.

But by the time the Ghost Dance arrived at Pine Ridge and Rosebud, the Crook Commission had completed its aggressive, manipulative work. Southern Arapahos could turn to the promise of the Ghost Dance to remain united during negotiations and help them bear the loss of land as another sign of the broken world that was about to be renewed. Lakotas, on the other hand, could turn to the Ghost Dance only as a people already divided. In Oklahoma, matters were helped by the agent's decision not to ban the Ghost Dance: the Arapaho Sitting Bull led some of the largest Ghost Dances of the period during the Jerome Commission proceedings. In contrast, when Lakotas took up the new religion, the government set out to crush it; labeling all dancers as "hostile," officials denied them rations and threatened force.

Such measures inevitably widened internal divisions among Lakotas, and the contentiousness of intra-Lakota politics would play a role in the Ghost Dance troubles. Even before the reservation period, Lakotas were known for their disputes; the careful consensus building typical of Arapahos was harder to achieve among the dispersed Lakota bands and tribes. Southern Arapaho institutions to negotiate agreements among tribal members were still in place in 1890, and most young Arapahos accepted the lodge system, a ceremonially sanctioned, age-based hierarchy. While this system, too, would eventually fail, it endured well into the twentieth century, allowing Arapaho peoples, north and south, to avoid the kinds of factions that troubled other Indian peoples, including Lakotas.[28]

In contrast, the Lakota men's societies, which elected members from far-flung bands and provided a forum for police, judicial, and other governmental matters, had diminished with the demise of buffalo hunting and the Sun Dance. With the US government replacing tribal institutions on the reservation, almost all of these societies ceased to function. Structural shifts like this simply aggravated the factionalism that had always troubled Lakotas. When confronted with threats like the land cession and the mounting poverty of the reservation, divisions widened further still. The suppression of the Ghost Dance would drive a painful, dangerous wedge into those fissures.[29]

Although Lakotas were certainly afflicted by internal division, the divisions among Americans also bore much responsibility for the course of events in South Dakota. In 1890 the government that supervised the reservations was itself badly divided. The US Army command was angling to seize control of the reservations from the Office of Indian Affairs, and both were confronting the powerful lobbying of humanitarian reformers and church missionaries, who were themselves fiercely divided between Protestant and Catholic.[30]

The divisions among Indians, mixed-bloods, and whites, between the US Army and the Office of Indian Affairs, between Ghost Dance believers and nonbelievers, and among competing Christian missionaries and their followers inflated so many preexisting disputes into arguments about the Ghost Dance that questions of devotion or opposition are necessarily complicated, even contradictory. In this fractured landscape, American fear of the Ghost Dance provided openings for many of its opponents, including white missionaries and even some Indians who were feuding with Ghost Dance supporters for other reasons or currying favor with officials, even to the extent of misinforming them. In the end, it was the American fixation on subduing and assimilating "the warlike Sioux" that created the gravest tensions surrounding the Ghost Dance and opened the door to the manipulations and misrepresentations that led to army violence and the killing of so many believers.

FOR ALL INDIANS, IT WAS A SUMMER OF LOOMING DESPAIR. Drought pummeled their potato and corn fields and withered the already scarce chokecherries, grapes, and other wild foods, along with the grass that fed deer and cattle. Without an increase in rations, another deadly winter was certain. Under these circumstances, with so many eager for deliverance, some Lakota hearts opened to the religion.

Agents would have opposed the Ghost Dance simply because it was a dance and they routinely condemned all Indian dancing. Their opposition was also stoked, however, by the fact that the holy men, priests, and healers who presented the teachings to Lakotas were, in their estimation, leading "nonprogressives," retrograde troublemakers, and the devil's own emissaries.

Hardening the agents' opposition was the receipt of secret information from a seemingly knowledgeable source. The key context for this confidential tip was the formidable language barrier that bedeviled relations between agents and Indians. The language gap between agents and Southern Arapahos and Cheyennes in Oklahoma was less troubling. Agent Ashley estimated that of the 3,500 Arapahos under his charge, 500 could read and some 600 could speak English "sufficient for ordinary intercourse." As we have seen, some educated Arapahos became Ghost Dance leaders.[31]

In South Dakota, on the other hand, relatively few Lakotas had been to school. Many had been on the reservation less than fifteen years, and some for only a decade or even less. In 1879 the Brule chief Spotted Tail had engaged Captain Richard Henry Pratt in a fierce argument over the militarized education for boys at Carlisle Indian School. Spotted Tail settled the dispute by withdrawing a large group of Lakota children from the school, an act that made Lakotas even more reluctant than other Indian parents to send their children there. Reservation day schools would eventually fill the gap, but in 1890 they were new enough that those Lakotas with some education were still young and their English often marginal.[32]

To serve as translators, agents typically hired mixed-bloods, most of whom were the adult children of Lakota mothers and French-speaking fathers (often traders of French Canadian ancestry). Because many of these mixed-bloods had scouted for the US Army in the wars against the Sioux, and because not all of them had been raised alongside other Lakotas, many Lakotas did not trust them. How much agents could rely on these translators was another matter: their Lakota was not always strong, and their French was often better than their English.[33]

This mutual skepticism of interpreters cast almost all Indian-white communications into doubt. Later in the fall, the agent at Cheyenne River, Perain Palmer, would note Indian distrust of the interpreters and wonder who he himself could rely on: "It is very difficult to tell what Indian can be trusted. The friendly Indians apprehend trouble and are suspicious of the interpreters, say Indians all lie & Interpreters all lie [and] when they talk on important matters they want several Interpreters present." Given the miasma of mistrust and translators' many competing agendas, Palmer had little sense of what was actually happening in his own jurisdiction. "It is impossible to tell at this time what the dancing Indians intend to do." Unable to accept guarantees from anybody, Palmer (like most other officials) assumed the worst—that the Ghost Dancers were "no doubt preparing for an outbreak in some direction."[34]

The language barrier and the spiraling discontent on the reservations predisposed authorities to accept almost without question anything said to them by the handful of Indians who spoke English. This dependence conveyed extraordinary power to one particularly unscrupulous Ghost Dance opponent and provocateur. In April 1890, immediately after the emissaries had returned from Nevada, and with discontent among Lakotas reaching new heights and agents struggling to head off the planned meeting of land cession opponents, a key informant approached Pine Ridge agent Hugh Gallagher with an ominous warning. William Selwyn, the Yankton Sioux who received an Episcopalian education in the East, had arrived at the reservation as a schoolmaster several years before and was now serving as postmaster at Pine Ridge. Claiming to have interviewed Good Thunder, Short Bull, and others who had recently returned from Nevada, Selwyn shared with the agent the alarming discovery that, as the believers told him, they were following a supposed redeemer who was "the son of the great spirit who has been killed by civilized people once" and who now "had come down to kill all the white people."[35]

This extreme interpretation of the prophecies, in which the Messiah did not rapture Indians to a new earth but instead secured the old one by slaughtering whites, was precisely the kind of bellicose vision that agents and the public feared. It implied a plan for an uprising. Ever since, many have viewed Selwyn's message as tantalizing confirmation that Short Bull and other emissaries twisted Jack Wilson's teachings to start a war.

But there are reasons to doubt that the evangelists told Selwyn anything like what he claimed—if indeed they told him anything at all. To begin, why would Short Bull and the others have trusted the postmaster with sensitive information? Admittedly, Selwyn's connections among Lakotas were strong: he was a nephew of Sitting Bull and had four children with an Oglala wife (they divorced in 1886). But even so, he was no confidant to people at Pine Ridge. His upbringing ensured that many Lakotas would see him almost as foreign. In the early 1870s, Selwyn had become a ward of William Welsh, an Episcopalian missionary, who educated the boy by sending him first to Nebraska College in Omaha and subsequently to a public school in Brooklyn and then Andalusia Hall in Pennsylvania. Selwyn spent three years in the East and came to move easily in the white world, in part because he could write the English language better than many settlers. On his return, he developed close connections to agents and other powerful officials. He served as census taker at Standing Rock in 1881; in 1887 he was assigned to teach school at Pine Ridge, and he was the translator for Richard Henry Pratt and the Sioux Commission in 1888. He seems to have been trusted by Gallagher and other Americans—his appointment as postmaster (and he may have been the nation's first Indian postmaster) required the backing of Senator Richard Pettigrew.[36]

Selwyn's opposition to the Ghost Dance shows the wide range of responses to the religion by boarding school graduates who felt alienated from their home communities. Southern Arapahos who had been at Carlisle and other schools became leaders of the Ghost Dances, and educated Lakotas also joined. Selwyn seems never to have felt the religion's appeal, but beyond that, the question of his motivation hangs over every word of his alarming tip. Exactly what the postmaster hoped to gain by telling his stories about the Ghost Dance in 1890 is not clear, but we know enough to guess. Selwyn had made a career out of currying favor with powerful white interests, gaining their trust, and claiming his reward. His Episcopalian sponsors had hoped that, like his fellow Dakota converts Philip Deloria and Charles S. Cook, he would become a missionary to Lakotas, but he disappointed them. The closest he came to the ministry was his appointment as schoolteacher. Soon after taking up that post, he began working his eastern connections and gained a more lucrative position with the US Postal Service. Then, in 1890, shortly after his alarming report to Gallagher, he returned home to Yankton, perhaps fleeing the ire of Oglalas who knew he was plotting with the agent.

Once home, his means of pursuing personal wealth would make him a particularly divisive figure. Within three years of the Ghost Dance troubles, he had instigated a deep schism by championing the sale of Yankton Dakota land to the government. Fighting him every step of the way were a good many Yanktons, including his own father, Chief Medicine Cow. Allegations followed these disputes that he had lined his own pockets at the expense of other Dakotas—a charge that is said to have contributed to his brutal, untimely death in 1905.[37]

In the fifteen years between the Ghost Dance trouble and his demise, Selwyn was markedly adept at telling white officials what they wanted to hear. When South Dakota politicians began to clamor that the Yankton people had too much land, he made himself into the politicians' Indian friend—a literate, Dakota-speaking "progressive" who confirmed for them that other Indians could become "civilized" only if they were relieved of their "excess lands." Playing this role was typical of how Selwyn gained the trust of powerful interests, who then cut him into their game. He made a great deal of money.[38]

Selwyn seems to have previewed his modus operandi at Pine Ridge in 1890. As Little Wound, an Oglala chief, would later explain, a great deal of misinformation about the Ghost Dance came from Indians who "hoped to get to be chiefs and head men by making trouble and talking with the agent." It seems highly unlikely that evangelists of the new religion told Selwyn the things he claimed they did. Short Bull and the other emissaries knew that he worked for the government and was close to the agent. Even if they had been planning an uprising, why would they have told him?[39]

Nevertheless, neither Gallagher nor any other agent appears to have questioned the tale of William Selwyn. He was, in the words of another agent, a "full-blooded Indian," and his report was enough for Gallagher to arrest Good Thunder and the other emissaries who had just returned from Nevada and to ban any Ghost Dances.[40]

One wonders who else received Selwyn's warnings, and how many of the rumors of an uprising actually originated with him. For the effect of Selwyn's warning seems to have compounded over time, shaping official accounts in surprising ways. Consider the nervousness of another well-regarded Indian informant who helped convince officials to shut the religion down over the next few months. In early September, Charles S. Cook, the mixed-blood Dakota priest at Pine Ridge, warned Bishop William Hare of the Protestant Episcopal Church about the "wild fanaticism" of the new religion. Whether or not Cook meant for his message to get to Washington, Bishop Hare passed the communication to officials there. They appear to have received it as another "inside" message from an Indian closely acquainted with the Ghost Dance. But on close inspection, Cook's information looks like a recycled version of Selwyn's. Cook was also from Yankton and, in fact, a close associate of Selwyn's. Like Selwyn, Cook had been educated in the East—he had degrees from Trinity College and a divinity school in Minnesota—and he spoke

Dakota. In spite of his credentials and connections, Cook appears to have gathered all his information about the Ghost Dance, not from Indian believers, but from Agent Hugh Gallagher, who in turn received much of what he knew—or thought he knew—from William Selwyn.[41]

We shall return to Selwyn, whose allegations in the run-up to Wounded Knee became even more incendiary—and more questionable. For now, the story of Selwyn's warning alerts us to the danger of relying too much on agency sources in interpreting the Ghost Dance or the intentions of its leaders and supporters. Agents who lived in close proximity to Indians did not always have reliable information about them, and, as we shall see, agency denunciations of the religion were often informed by sources with their own motives for opposing the new faith. The Ghost Dance crisis became a primary arena in which men and women who hoped to gain influence with the government, secure privileges or better treatment, or build their own networks of followers joined the Indian police or took other measures against the Ghost Dance, thus marking themselves as forthright "progressives." Religious rivalries among Indians and their jockeying for influence played a very large role in shaping rhetoric around the Ghost Dance. At key moments "inside" informants relayed news or information that agents accepted without question, largely because it suited the timbre of the times—marked by language divides and political unrest—and corroborated their own prejudices regarding Indian religion.

Pine Ridge agent Hugh Gallagher seems to have passed the information in Selwyn's warning to the Rosebud agent, J. George Wright, who then arrested Short Bull. Another key confrontation was taking place simultaneously, however, one that had profound impacts on the developing crisis. Neither Gallagher nor Wright made any arrests themselves; both sent Indian police to apprehend the emissaries. The army would not arrive at the reservations until late November. Until that time, the primary arm of the state for suppressing the Ghost Dance would be the Indian police, whose attempts to shatter the Ghost Dance circle would aggravate another simmering dispute in Lakota camps.

CHAPTER 9

TIN STARS AND HOLY POWER

IVISIONS BETWEEN THE INDIAN POLICE AND THE HOLY
men and traditional chiefs long preceded the Ghost Dance and
made police efforts to suppress the religion all the more difficult.
The scene at the Brule council meeting in the fall of 1889, when
Short Bull received his mission to seek the prophet, gives us a hint
of the unrest. The wind was blowing and dust was in the air, and the
mysterious letter telling of a messiah in the West had not yet been
read aloud. As they awaited the joyous news of a religion of peace,
Short Bull later recalled, every man in the council house was carrying a gun because earlier that evening a son of a chief named Two
Strike "had choked one of the Indian Police, and a fight was going
on outside."[1]

What kind of fight was it? His memoir does not say. Perhaps
there were angry words, with fists. Perhaps knives or clubs. Maybe
guns were drawn. Whatever happened that night, Short Bull's narrative suggests that his mission to Nevada took place against a back-
drop of continuing troubles with the police. The day he accepted the
mission and announced he would go, he also requested that, in his
absence, council members uphold the peaceful promise of the new
religion. "My brothers, you are all sitting here with your guns, this is
not what the messiah wants us to do, and when I leave here I ask you

to drop your arms, follow my trail, watch my movements and have no trouble with the whites or police."[2]

In the Lakota camps, the Indian police was less the arm of the law than of the agents. The people who took up the Ghost Dance (and many who did not) were engaged before 1890 in an ongoing series of contests over the meaning and limits of police power, which was a new force in Lakota life. These confrontations had not only divided Indians from Americans but divided Indians from other Indians. In particular, Indian police carried the authority of agents in trying to marginalize the chiefs. Although Lakota chiefs had scarcely more authority than Paiute talkers, officials believed that they were autocrats whose dictatorial powers kept their people in bondage and that together with holy men they were the primary forces of "nonprogressivism" and savagery. Agents hoped that diminishing the power of these traditional leaders would enhance their own authority—even if they accomplished this by essentially elevating new chiefs to replace the old ones. They challenged the authority of the chiefs through a host of measures, from distributing rations solely to heads of nuclear families (rather than following the customary practice of awarding goods to chiefs for conveyance to followers) to appointing policemen answerable solely to themselves.[3]

As part of the reform movement that removed Indian reservations from the control of the army, the Indian police were created in the late 1870s, primarily as a tool that agents could use to enforce their will without having to rely on troops. With power to arrest white people as well as Indians, the constables promised a new degree of order within reservation boundaries, where unscrupulous settlers often stole Indian livestock and sold whiskey in violation of the law. Just as importantly, agents hoped that selecting men from among the tribes to serve as officers would put an Indian face on US law, making it more acceptable to other Indians and swaying at least some Indian loyalties toward the agent. The blue-uniformed, tin star–wearing, revolver-packing Indian constables, whom Lakotas called the *ceska maza,* or "metal breasts," would carry the authority of the agent

FIGURE 9.1. Indian Police, Rosebud Reservation, ca. 1890. The reservation police force was a new institution that strained the tribal political order to the breaking point during the Ghost Dance revival. Nebraska State Historical Society, RG2969–02–051.

into Indian camps and cabins and prove a force—it was hoped—for assimilation.

Lakotas were hardly the only Indian people to have a new police force thrust upon them. In other places, older tribal institutions helped the constables adapt to Indian needs at least enough to ameliorate the worst frictions. In some tribes, police appear to have successfully brokered some conflicts between Indians and the government. Some even retained their authority as the agent's enforcers while becoming leaders of the Ghost Dance. There seems to have been little tension surrounding the police at Walker River Reservation, where the chief of police, Josephus, became a leading apostle of Wovoka. In Oklahoma, Black Coyote, a leading Ghost Dance evangelist and ritual leader among Southern Arapahos, was also chief of the reservation police force. He and several other police officers were senior lodge men, and their police work benefited from the continuing strength of the lodge system, which preserved a high degree of consensus among senior men and allowed for considerable behind-the-scenes negotiation to smooth over controversies. In addition to being police chief, Black Coyote was also a ranking member in the Lime Crazy Lodge, whose members bore responsibility for controlling community behavior through spiritual means.[4]

The police on Oklahoma reservations remained open, even committed, to customary religion, for police work and traditional spirit obligations were both viewed as ways to protect people from harm. This attitude helps to explain why the government's ban on dances and other ceremonies in 1882 was enforced less consistently among Arapahos, and with less intimidation, than among Lakotas. The documentary record also shows that Black Coyote and other police routinely consulted with tribal leaders before agreeing to the agent's commands (a practice that seems to have worked for all parties, despite the agent's irritation).[5]

By contrast, among Lakotas, whatever order the police achieved came with an equal amount of friction and resentment, partly because the police exacerbated preexisting divisions among Lakotas. Oglala society, as we have seen, was organized into tiyospaye, and the numbers of these bands rose and fell with the fortunes of leaders and their followers. In 1879 there were seven bands: Kiyuksa, Payabsa, Itesica, Waglukhe, Tapisleca, Oyukhpe, and Wazhazha (not the same as the Brule band of the same name, who were Short Bull's people). Feuds and disputes between these bands could arise when their chiefs competed for influence at the annual summer gatherings. There was no formal office of "head chief," but some gained much more power through their wealth and the number of their followers. Although Lakota civil conventions forbade killing other Lakotas, with enough friction, bonds of kinship and alliance could fray. Disputes among the tiyospaye could have violent, sometimes fatal, results. In 1841 a furious brawl erupted between followers of rival chiefs in an Oglala camp, culminating with the killing of Bull Bear, the chief of the Kiyuksas who had emerged as the most powerful member of the Oglala council of chiefs, allegedly by Red Cloud, an Itesica, who subsequently claimed Bull Bear's position of influence. Red Cloud's primacy never sat well with some other chiefs, including Little Wound, who was Bull Bear's son. Little Wound became head of the Kiyuksa band after his father's death and eventually moved with his followers to Pine Ridge—the reservation where Red Cloud continued to act as head chief of all Oglalas. Little Wound himself never relinquished his claim to this position: "I am the head chief of the Oglalas and my father was the head chief."[6]

In the old days, when Oglalas dispersed into separate river valleys during the winter and there was space enough to put between jealous rivals, passions cooled more easily and peace was more easily maintained. Now, on the reservations, any number of chiefs and aspiring chiefs with competing agendas had been jumbled together. Agents' elevation of some men as new chiefs and willingness to bestow on them extra rations, farm equipment, property, and other perquisites drove tensions even higher. Having Indian police forces upped the ante in these struggles: the agencies now appointed friends and relatives of their favored "progressives" to the Indian police, who were seen as partisan enforcers not only for the agent but also sometimes for other chiefs.[7]

The idea of a police force was not completely alien to Lakotas. In the large summer camps of the pre-reservation era, order was maintained by camp marshals called *akicita* (pronounced ah-KI-chi-ta), who were selected through a complex process originating with the council of chiefs; they were drawn from the ranks of celebrated warriors, and often from one of the men's societies. Their power was temporary; they held the office only until the summer communal gathering disbanded and the people dispersed to the river valleys for the winter. But during the summer encampment their authority was great, and they resorted to intimidation and physical force without hesitation, even against tribal leaders. At the height of his powers in the mid-1860s, Red Cloud himself would submit to an akicita whipping for refusing to break camp at the appointed hour.[8]

Red Cloud carried his respect for the office of akicita onto the reservation, where he opposed the creation of the police force and insisted that the traditional marshals (answerable to himself and other chiefs) could enforce the law. Only two of Red Cloud's Itesica men joined the new force. Little Wound, on the other hand, seems to have endorsed the police force by 1879, perhaps to gain influence with the agent and strengthen his hand against Red Cloud. Eighteen of Little Wound's Kiyuksas soon wore the metal star—the largest contingent of Oglalas serving on the force. A half-century of feuding between Red Cloud and Little Wound had now become institutionalized in the police force.[9]

The large number of Little Wound's followers serving on the Indian police force would become a problem, however, not just for Red Cloud but for all chiefs, including Little Wound himself. For the long-term effect of the police force was to undermine the authority of every traditional chief. Whereas akicita were appointed to a temporary office by a council of chiefs, Indian police served at the pleasure of a white agent, potentially for life, and carried out his orders. Those orders often involved confronting the chiefs in ways that violated Lakota tradition and were seen by other Lakotas as profoundly disrespectful. This was often the purpose of agents' orders: to strip authority away from chiefs and empower the agents. In joining the police force, the new officers created or deepened divisions between themselves and the chiefs and could even use their new position to exert authority over chiefs with whom they were feuding.[10]

The agent's orders often compelled officers to countermand the authority of the chiefs, even when the police thought it unwise. Little Wound would become a Ghost Dance leader, and the Indian police who would soon descend on his camp to shut down the ritual presumably included some of the men he had encouraged to join the force in the first place. The Indian police walked a fine line between pleasing their agents and courting ostracism by other Lakotas, including their own kin, for violating norms of deference to chiefs. Many refused to serve on the force for this reason, and the agencies often had trouble recruiting men who were widely respected. Pine Ridge agent Valentine McGillycuddy achieved perhaps the greatest success in this regard when he appointed George Sword, who was not only a renowned warrior and holy man–turned–Episcopal deacon but the son of a chief and a nephew of Red Cloud. Sword's dedication to the police, however, earned him the enduring enmity of his uncle.

Despite Sword's presence in their ranks, the police generally were held in low regard. "The police are looked upon as a common foe, and the multitude are bitterly opposed to them," remarked one frustrated agent. Another observed frankly in 1890 that "many of the best Indians will not serve." The upheaval of the late 1880s seems to have further lowered popular regard for the police, until the fabric of the force began to tear. By October 1890, only five of the original fifty officers recruited at Pine Ridge in 1879 were still on the payroll. Most of the others had quit and been replaced by less experienced officers. Although some blamed the lack of better recruits on the low salary of $5 per month for privates and $8 per month for officers, the friction caused by the intrusion of this force into Lakota life probably discouraged just as many.[11]

These were the men to whom agents first turned to suppress the Ghost Dance.

DESPITE THE UNPOPULARITY OF THE POLICE, AT LEAST FOR A TIME after his arrest Short Bull appears to have kept his word to them and abstained from dancing. During that spring of 1890, enthusiasm for the religion seems to have been contained. Kicking Bear attempted to hold a dance at Cheyenne River, but few joined in. He went back to Wind River for the summer to stay with the Northern Arapahos. Other dances took place over the summer, but agents either did not hear about them or paid little attention.[12]

Kicking Bear returned in late summer. Whether through him or some other influence, the Ghost Dance began to grow at Pine Ridge in August, at Rosebud and Cheyenne River in September, and at Standing Rock in October.[13]

In September at the Rosebud Agency, hundreds of Brules moved to the camp of White Horse (who had resisted the census the previous year) and began Ghost Dancing. Others moved to Pass Creek and the Wazhazha camps, where Short Bull led the devotions. Agent J. George Wright reported that, "although no violence of any kind was contemplated nor arms carried" in the dance, he told the Indians that "it must be abolished, causing as it did, excitement and physical prostration and attracting the Indians from other camps, abandoning their stock and homes, taking their children from school and having a demoralizing effect generally." He barred participants from receiving rations, and the dances declined in number.[14]

Short Bull was leading dances again by October, however, with dancers who supported themselves by breaking another agency regulation. In an effort to encourage animal husbandry and plowing, the Office of Indian Affairs had distributed cattle "breeding stock" and draft oxen to Lakota men. Although prohibited from slaughtering these animals, the dancers felt that the agent's refusal to provide rations left them no choice. Illegal cattle killing began to accompany Ghost Dances and quickly emerged as a sign of the new religion almost on a par with the dance itself. It also provided primary proof—in the eyes of agents and much of the public—that the dancers were nonprogressive and uncontrollable. Lakotas drawn to the Ghost Dance saw it differently: asserting property rights to the animals, they demanded the same right that white farmers had to kill the cattle they owned. Famished seekers who joined the circle found immediate gratification of their hunger, as if the promise of the teachings was already starting to come true. At the same time, the popular appeal of the feasts presented a major challenge to those chiefs who allied with the agencies. The near-starving conditions of agency life tempted their followers to join the joyous feasting of Ghost Dancers, undermining the followings that these agency chiefs needed to maintain their own authority. American Horse, a self-identified "progressive" chief, explained the political calculus of Ghost Dance leaders to his own agent: "The non-progressives started the ghost dance to draw [followers] from us."[15]

FIGURE 9.2. Lakota men butchering a steer, Rosebud Reservation, 1891. During the Ghost Dance revival, officials viewed the mundane act of butchering Indian cattle as a sign of antigovernment hostility. Nebraska State Historical Society, RG2969–02–073.

In the middle of September, dancing also took on greater enthusiasm at Cheyenne River. It carried on through much of the fall as some 400 Minneconjous attended the dances under the leadership of Hump, a leading Minneconjou chief. Refusing orders to cease their devotions, Ghost Dancers earned the label of "hostiles" in the correspondence of the new agent, Perain Palmer, who warned that "there is no doubt now that the Hostile Indians at all the dancing camps are preparing to defy the authority of the Department."[16]

At Standing Rock, Agent James McLaughlin kept a close watch on the venerated Hunkpapa leader Sitting Bull and refused to let him leave the reservation. So instead, the chief and holy man invited Kicking Bear to visit. After the evangelist arrived at Grand River on October 9, he initiated large and enthusiastic Ghost Dances of some 450 people. The agent sent the Indian police to stop the dances and escort Kicking Bear off the reservation. After some discussion, Kicking Bear went peacefully, but the dances continued. Here as elsewhere, the new ritual appeared to threaten the program of assimilation. Attendance at the agency school dropped from forty students to fewer than ten in the space of two months. Although leaving school contradicted Wovoka's teachings, it appears that the excitement about the coming millennium persuaded many parents to follow another of the prophet's commandments by bringing their children to the dances: when the schoolteacher, John Carignan, remonstrated with parents, they explained that the children had to leave school to attend "church" every day.[17]

Nevertheless, McLaughlin remained calm. By mid-November, he was reporting that the "excitement" among the dancers had subsided, and he warned against military intervention. "I feel quite confident the interference of the military at this time will result in resistance and probably precipitate a fight and consequent bloodshed." Instead, McLaughlin hoped to use the Ghost Dance excitement to achieve a personal ambition: the arrest of Sitting Bull and his removal from the reservation, a goal toward which he worked for several more weeks.[18]

Meanwhile, the worst confrontations involving the Ghost Dance erupted at Pine Ridge, in part because of the incompetence and volatility of the new agent. Daniel Royer was a minor functionary in the Republican Party of South Dakota who wrangled himself a job as superintendent of the Pine Ridge Reservation at the very moment in October when the Ghost Dance took on renewed strength. Within four days of assuming his new duties, he warned superiors that troops would be required to suppress the Ghost Dance. In subsequent weeks, he ordered all dances to cease and all Indians to move to agency headquarters. But his mix of pleading and threats failed to quell the new religion. By the first week of November, Ghost Dancers had assembled in four large camps on White Clay Creek, Wounded Knee Creek, Porcupine Creek, and Medicine Root Creek. Prominent among them were chiefs like Big Road, Torn Belly, and Little Wound, as well as close relatives of other chiefs, such as Jack Red Cloud. Some 1,500 Lakotas turned the sacred circle at Pine

Ridge. All refused to come into the agency. All subsisted by butchering agency cattle.[19]

The wave of Ghost Dancing would have been hard enough for officials to accept had it only swept up those Indians known as habitual troublemakers—the "nonprogressives" who often resisted agency initiatives. But between the lines of agency reports one discerns a rapidly eroding sense of order, not least because many Indians who had been reliable advocates of farms, churches, and schools were suddenly becoming Ghost Dancers.

Among the most prominent of these was Little Wound, chief of the Kiyuksas. A Christian who led a farm settlement of Episcopalian converts, many of whom worshiped at their own Saint Barnabas Episcopal Chapel (built and equipped with funds from the estate of Mrs. John Jacob Astor), Little Wound had been a prized "progressive" in the eyes of the former agent, Valentine McGillycuddy. But events of the prior year had opened the chief's heart to the Ghost Dance. He had held the line and refused to sign on to the land cession in 1889. Then, in 1890, his young daughter died, her illness aggravated by hunger, for which he understandably blamed the government.

Early in the fall, Porcupine visited from Montana, preaching about his vision of the Messiah, whose return was imminent. Little Wound's approach to the religion seems always to have been tentative. "Now whether Porcupine really saw the Messiah, or only had a pleasant dream, I do not know," Little Wound confessed to his former agent. But nonetheless, he gathered his followers. "My friends, if this is a good thing we should have it," he announced, "if it is not it will fall to the earth itself. So you better learn this dance, so if the Messiah does come he will not pass us by, but will help us to get back our hunting grounds and buffalo." By the fall of 1890, Little Wound had become the leading chief among Ghost Dancers at Pine Ridge. Confronted by the fact that even reliable Christian farmers like Little Wound had turned to the new religion, Royer frothed in panic. "The only remedy for this matter," he warned, "is the use of the military."[20]

Ghost Dancers were indeed refusing agency commands to stop dancing. While numerous commentators saw this as a sign of impending "outbreak," the documentary record makes clear that, until well after the army arrived, no Ghost Dancer or any other Lakota drew a weapon against any official, or indeed against any white person. Even in the thick of the crisis, until the army arrived, white observers reported being well received and even welcomed in the dancing camps.

But if the presence of white observers did not incite Ghost Dancers to violence, the Indian police did. In every incident in which dancers pulled guns, the presence of Indian police was the precipitating factor and the constables were the object of their anger. In early September, for example, Agent Gallagher ordered twenty-five Indian police to accompany him to a Ghost Dance on Pine Ridge Reservation, in the camp of the band chief Torn Belly. They were intercepted by eleven armed dance defenders who told them that they would fight rather than allow the police to interfere. Gallagher wisely withdrew.[21]

That the police were the target of their hostility is clear, for Ghost Dancers seem to have had no hesitation about dancing in the presence of government observers—so long as they came without police. Several weeks later, Special Agent E. B. Reynolds approached the same dance circle. He brought employees from his office, but no Indian police. His party was gladly received and accepted an invitation to watch the dance. They stayed for hours.[22]

By October, the band of the Minneconjou chief Bigfoot, which would be decimated by the Seventh Cavalry in December, was "becoming very much excited about the coming of a Messiah," according to Agent Perain Palmer. Palmer knew this because his police had told him so. He sent them to stop the dances, but the dancers persisted. "These Indians are becoming very hostile to the police," reported Palmer. "Some of the police have resigned."[23]

At Pine Ridge, confrontations with police reached crisis levels. On November 11, a ration day, Royer ordered the Indian police to apprehend a man called Little, whose alleged offense was cattle killing. When confronted by the officers, Little pulled a weapon (appropriately, a butcher knife). Royer reported that at this point a "mob of the Ghost Dance[r]s" some 200 strong surrounded the police and refused to let them take Little away. Witnessing the scene was the reservation physician Charles Eastman, a Santee Sioux who had been educated in Boston and who understood Lakota. Years later he recounted that at least one person in the crowd was brandishing a tomahawk over the heads of the police, threatening their lives. Some were shouting for blood. At this point American Horse stepped out from a council meeting in the agency offices and called to the crowd "in a clear, steady, almost sarcastic voice":

> Stop! Think! What are you going to do? Kill these men of our own race? Then what? Kill all these helpless white men, women, and children? And what then? What will these brave words, brave deeds lead to in the end? How long can you hold out? Your country is surrounded with a network of railroads; thousands of white soldiers will be here within three days. What ammunition have you? What provisions? What will become of your families? Think, think, my brothers! This is a child's madness.

Eastman recalled that the words of American Horse "had almost magic power," and the crowd quieted. At this point, Jack Red Cloud, the son of Red Cloud, stepped up to American Horse. Leveling a cocked revolver in the face of the chief, he shouted, "It is you and your kind who have brought us to this pass!" Illustrating the traditional self-restraint of a Lakota leader, American Horse said nothing. In silence, he turned his back on Jack Red Cloud and his angry people and slowly climbed the stairs to the council room.

The crowd dispersed, taking Little with them and, according to Royer, "making all kinds of fun over the attempted arrest and the inefficiency of the police force."[24]

This incident helped precipitate Royer's notorious telegram sent several days later—"The Indians are dancing in the snow and are wild and crazy"—and initiate the tragic events culminating at Wounded Knee. But in an important sense, these events were only tangentially related to the Ghost Dance. Little's defiance had less to do with dancing and more to do with the attempt to arrest him for killing cattle. This confrontation can be viewed as a fight over the absence of rations, the right of Lakotas to feed themselves from beeves that were issued to them, and the treachery of the police for trying to stop them.

But what of Jack Red Cloud's denunciation of American Horse? It could have meant many things. The most judicious interpretation of his claim that "it is you and your kind who have brought us to this pass!" is that he had in mind, not the Ghost Dance, but the Sioux Act of 1889 and the subsequent decline in rations, for which American Horse and the other treaty chiefs ("your kind") were by this time being roundly blamed. Although the excitable Royer wrote that Little was surrounded by a mob of "Ghost Dancers," the agent routinely conflated Ghost Dancing with any kind of resistance to his wishes. There is no evidence that Little's supporters were exclusively Ghost Dancers. The crowd that surrounded Little was primarily challenging the authority of the Indian police to arrest an Oglala for feeding his people from Indian cattle, and all available evidence suggests that the question of dancing remained in the background.[25]

And yet, the way in which the Ghost Dance hovers over this confrontation suggests that dancing had become not only a religious ritual but a political act. By this time, as already discussed, killing cattle in defiance of the government was practically synonymous with Ghost Dancing. Jack Red Cloud, who had presided over dances at his camp and who opposed the land cession, confronted American Horse, who condemned Ghost Dancing and signed the land cession. If on one level the confrontation had little to do with the Ghost Dance, on another level the dance had come to represent the right of Lakotas to land and food—rights that the police routinely tried to deny.

For the police, the strength of the Ghost Dance was astonishing because it marked a dramatic reversal. For the better part of a decade, they had suppressed the old religion, targeting holy men with violence and intimidation. Now the waxing of the Ghost Dance had restored the holy men to influence.

When Short Bull returned from Nevada with the new teachings, he and other holy men who took up the new religion were able to make themselves its leaders and define its practice, shaping it to fit

Lakota culture and traditional ceremony. There had been little time for leaders outside the fraternity of the wicasa wakan to emerge, and apparently there were no prospective challenges to their authority as there were with Numu doctors and leaders of Southern Arapaho medicine lodges. Thus, in the hands of the holy men, the new ritual in South Dakota developed a strong resemblance to the Lakota Sun Dance.[26]

As in the Sun Dance, the Ghost Dance circle turned around a central tree that had been felled and re-erected, its trunk bristling with lengths of ribbon, plugs of tobacco, bits of calico, and other property sacrifices, the limbs festooned with banners of red, white, and blue (or the American flag, which neatly combined all three sacred colors). Holy men painted the dancers and attended them in the sweat lodge and in the dance, much as in the Sun Dance. We may interpret the Lakotas' enthusiasm for the new religion, and their willingness to defend it, partly as a response to the crushing of the Sun Dance, a ritual destruction that had impoverished their spiritual lives. Similarities between the two ceremonies were so strong that despite the absence of piercing in the new religion, Mary Collins, a Congregationalist missionary at Sitting Bull's settlement, proclaimed that the Ghost Dance was "nothing more than the old Sun Dance revived."[27]

To a degree, the Ghost Dance reassured with its familiarity. It arrived as the reservation was reeling not just from economic collapse and political conflict but from physical and ritual hunger and a longing for communal gathering and a way to appeal to spirits. Feasting on cattle eased the hunger of believers, and the sense of Indian identity expressed in the Ghost Dance circle restored a powerful sense of belonging.

And yet, despite its familiarity, there were unfamiliar parts of the Ghost Dance ritual that urgently required adaptation. In the old religion, visions were mostly private. In the Sun Dance, for example, pledgers did not seek visions, and though they turned to holy men for help with interpreting the signs they received from spirits, pledgers did not announce those visions publicly. Normally, visions were sought only through a solitary vision quest. The Ghost Dance made visionary experience much more public and revelatory. The crowds massed, the circle turned, and dozens of people might collapse into trances as they met their ancestors, their recently deceased children, God, Jesus, Crow, or Eagle. The behavior of those in the grip of a vision—high-stepping, pawing at the air, shaking, prostrating themselves, pounding and kicking the ground, and fainting—might well have alarmed the holy men at first, suggesting that some vast power had indeed manifested itself in the bodies of believers. But the visionaries were so energized and voluble about their experience that family, friends, and neighbors were often persuaded to join the circle to seek visions of their own.[28]

Besides its ability to generate crowds of visionaries, the Ghost Dance also turned visions into a community resource. As dancers collapsed and then awoke from their trances, they explained what they had seen to the wicasa wakan who waited in the middle of the dance circle. These men then related the visions to the crowd. Unlike the traditional rituals, the new ritual, in publicly revealing individual visions, provided a dramatic, inclusive means of expanding visionary elation and thus creating community out of shared spiritual experience. At Sitting Bull's camp in November, a woman who fainted was carried to his lodge. As she lay unconscious on the ground, Sitting Bull "interpreted" for the crowd her experience with deceased family members in the afterworld.[29]

While it made visions into subjects of discussion that inspired and reassured believers, the Ghost Dance also vastly increased visionary ranks. The Sun Dance drew pledgers only from men who could afford its stiff economic obligations. The economic costs of participating in the Ghost Dance were lower, and participants came from a much wider swath of Lakota society. With the circle open to all, including any number of children and women as well as men, visions came thick and fast.[30]

Other attributes of the ritual gave everyday Lakotas, even the poor, a path to status in the community of believers. Visionaries gained prestige for their spiritual authenticity, journeys to the afterworld, and conversations with the deceased or with God or the Messiah.

Such visionaries might join the holy men at the center of the Ghost Dance circle. There was no need for expensive regalia: no metal- or beadwork was permitted in the dance, and even the so-called ghost shirts and ghost dresses were optional. Not seen among Lakotas until October, ghost shirts were made for particular dancers by holy men (including Black Elk and Short Bull) and by women visionaries. It seems likely that the presentation of a ghost shirt obliged the recipient to reciprocate with a gift; if so, this would be one reason why only a minority seem to have worn them.[31]

Thus, the Ghost Dance emerged as a more democratic, less hierarchical ritual, and one that required less economic outlay from aspiring visionaries. Compared to the Sun Dance, the Ghost Dance was a ceremony for a people not only spiritually yearning but radically impoverished.

In the summer and fall of 1890, the Ghost Dance inspired dramatic, visceral, and often overwhelming elation among an unusually large group of participants; as women and children as well as men, and everyone from the poorest to the most well to do, were swept up in the visionary wave, the visionary base of Lakota ceremony dramatically expanded. Lakotas' excitement about Ghost Dance visions registers in their song lyrics, as does a new spiritual presence, referred to as "the father." Athough the Sun and other spirit presences were sometimes called "father" in specific ritual contexts, the Ghost Dance marked a new use of the term as a gesture to a singular creator spirit who had sent the new teachings—thus the ubiquitous refrain, "the father says so."[32]

Besides the references to "the father," many Lakota songs tell of longing to see departed children and parents:

> *Who think you comes there?*
> *Who think you comes there?*
> *Is it someone looking for his mother?*
> *Is it someone looking for his mother?*
> *Says the father*
> *Says the father*

Others saw the future, with Lakotas united, their dead restored to life, and all returned to their former wealth and power on a new earth:

> *My child, come this way,*
> *My child, come this way,*
> *You will take home with you a good country,*
> *Says the father, says the father.*[33]

As one missionary reported from a Ghost Dance on White River, the ecstasy of the dancers was visible and palpable. The visionaries "staggered either into the circle or outside of the circle, flailing their arms around, falling to the ground, rolling in the dust, scraping the ground, raising themselves again, falling back down, now on their backs, then on their faces, until they remained lying down dead tired and completely exhausted."[34]

In the face of such passions, the police were understandably hesitant to attack the Ghost Dance circles with the same brazen force they deployed against the Sun Dance. They were also afraid. Holy men on the Plains, like doctors in the Great Basin, could veer into witchcraft. "The wakan man is feared by all the people," said George Sword, himself a wakan man. The first time James McLaughlin sent thirteen Indian policemen to arrest Kicking Bear at Sitting Bull's camp, they returned without him. The two officers in charge were "in a 'dazed' condition," reported McLaughlin, "and fearing the powers of Kicking Bear's medicine."[35]

Now the formidable powers of the wicasa wakan were all the more intimidating for being augmented by the spirit that gripped the dancers. The crowds were big, and dancers were in the throes of some spiritual power; whether one believed in the new religion or not, something was happening to these people. When the dance circle was threatened, Ghost Dancers—ecstatic, numerous, and devoted—made it very clear that they would meet violence from the police with violence of their own.

CHAPTER 10

SPIRIT OF THE GHOST DANCE

FIGHTING BACK AGAINST THE RESURGENT HOLY MEN AND THEIR followers, the Indian police who remained on the force, with the new recruits who joined, sought to manipulate agents into reinforcing their ranks. Perhaps they had in mind that the government would fund more police positions. Perhaps some wanted the army to intervene. Whatever their reasons, many Indian police continued to inform the agencies throughout the fall about the meaning of the dances and their purpose, and much of what they conveyed was false. During this time, the agents reported many times that dancers were planning a war, but tellingly they reported only threats communicated through unnamed sources—who, we can assume, included the Indian police—not threats issued by Ghost Dancers themselves.

The diversity among the police officers precludes any broad generalizations about their motives. Some were warriors of renown. Others appear to have been ambitious, violent, and more feared than respected. Walter Campbell, who interviewed many Lakotas for his 1932 biography of Sitting Bull, summarized the composition of the 1890 reservation police as "the fiercest and most hard-boiled scrappers on the reservation."[1]

There had always been such men among Lakotas. But in the past, their ability to gain a following had been limited by social conventions that required leaders to show not only fearlessness but also generosity, kindness, and humility. Now, with agents willing to steer perquisites like farm equipment, money, and extra rations their way, even violent, antisocial men could gain small followings and expand their influence.

Lakotas were fearful of this new regime and often denounced the police for their calumnies and ruthlessness. In an interview between an *Evening Star* journalist and Lakota leaders in 1891, Little Wound, Big Road, and others claimed that Indian policemen "lied a great deal" about the Ghost Dance. Such complaints might be expected from Ghost Dance leaders, but condemnation of police meddling also came from some less likely quarters. Throughout the fall, American Horse's opposition to the Ghost Dance put him on the side of the police (some of whom he helped save from the angry crowd during the attempted arrest of Little that November). But when it was over, even he sought to have the entire force abolished: "We do not want any more Indian police here; they always make trouble." Josephine Waggoner was an educated Hunkpapa and an Episcopalian convert who never took up the Ghost Dance and indeed thought it misguided. She had family friends on the police force, and she retained great admiration for Bull Head and Gray Eagle, two of the officers who arrested (and then killed) Sitting Bull. But in relating events she witnessed at Standing Rock Reservation in 1890, she would recall, "The police had the law back of them and although there were some very good men among them, there were others that were mean and treacherous, who were always reporting stories to the authorities— some of which were utterly untrue. . . . A great deal of injustice was practiced under the blanket of the law."[2]

Whether or not police provocateurs were angling for army intervention, the inability of the agents' handpicked enforcers to suppress the religion brought about just this result. With Ghost Dances increasing in popularity in late October, President Benjamin Harrison ordered the Secretary of War to investigate the religion. Brigadier General Thomas H. Ruger, commander of the Department of

Dakota, toured the Standing Rock and Cheyenne River Reservations. He saw no cause to send troops, but his meeting with Agent James McLaughlin at Standing Rock persuaded him that the Hunkpapa chief Sitting Bull should be removed from the reservation by Indian police, acting with military support, at some point in the near future.[3]

A week later, from his embattled office at Pine Ridge, the over-wrought Daniel Royer was begging to be allowed to go to Washington to explain the crisis in person. His superiors refused, but the Secretary of the Interior requested help from the president. Two days later, on November 13, President Harrison ordered the Secretary of War to assume responsibility for "the suppression of any threatened outbreak, and to take such steps as may be necessary to that end."[4]

WITH POLICE GIVING FALSE REPORTS TO AGENTS, AGENTS RELAYING at least as much hearsay, innuendo, and rumor as eyewitness testimony, and press accounts purveying bloody, ludicrous fiction, officials in distant places had by November come to see the Ghost Dance as a rite that whipped Indians into frenzy and spun the reservations toward chaos.

But unlike the fantasies of agents and police, actual accounts from Ghost Dance camps reveal a dramatically different picture. It is a testament to the placidity of both the religion and Lakota communities that at the very moment the army was authorized to crush the Ghost Dance—as rumors of soldier battalions raced through Indian camps and authorities clamored for help—two Christian missionaries set out, apparently unarmed, on a journey through the camps of Short Bull's followers on the Rosebud Reservation. We might dismiss such a journey as the rank foolishness of Christian idealists, but these were no greenhorns. The Reverend Edward Ashley had spent years among the Eastern Sioux at the Sisseton Agency, where he learned to speak Dakota. Now rural dean for the Episcopal Church of South Dakota, he was in charge of missionary work at Rosebud and Cheyenne River. In mid-November, he traveled from the Rosebud Agency north to Cheyenne River with A. B. Clark, the Episcopal missionary to the Rosebud Reservation. At this point, Short Bull and his followers

were gathered in camps along creeks at the western edge of the Rosebud Reservation, and these camps, in the heart of the Ghost Dance
ferment, were Ashley and Clark's destination.[5]

Episcopalian leaders saw the Ghost Dance and Christianity as spiritual enemies, as mutually opposed in a cosmic struggle for dominance
in Lakota hearts. According to Bishop William Hare, for example,
Wovoka's religion was "the effort of heathenism grown desperate to
restore its vigor and reinstate itself." At Rosebud, the missionaries had
opened at least two schools and proselytized extensively among the
Brules by 1890, and the purpose of Ashley and Clark's journey was
to denounce the new religion and call Lakotas back to the true faith.
An excerpt from Ashley's report was published in a South Dakota
newspaper, where it reads as a "pilgrim's progress"—the story of a
faithful Christian journey through a dark valley of unbelief. There are
potentially ominous signs throughout: a club-wielding man lurking
outside a sermon, young men with painted faces staring at the reverends as they stop to speak with a catechist, and telltale marks of Ghost
Dances and cattle killing all along their route. Readers, at least the
doctrinaire Christians among them, might have had little doubt about
how far the strange religion had insinuated itself into Lakota lives.[6]

And yet, even if these Christian missionaries reviled the Ghost
Dance, it is far from clear that Ghost Dancers rejected Christians.
What stands out in the account is a curious openness to Christianity and education that persisted—even percolated—alongside camps
that were allegedly possessed by the Ghost Dance "craze." At Black
Pipe Creek, where Short Bull had recently led a series of Ghost
Dances, the churchmen held services in the schoolhouse. Although
Ashley claimed that a herald had warned people to stay away from
them, children filled the building and adults listened to the service on
the porch. Driving on to Corn Creek, the missionaries held a service
that met with as much enthusiasm as the one at Black Pipe Creek,
and two adults even came forward for baptism. Among those turning
out for another well-attended service—this one at Pass Creek, the
heart of Ghost Dance fervor—were schoolchildren, all of them well
groomed by their parents, "their hands and faces clean, hair combed,

and neat in dress." For their final service, Ashley and Clark moved on to White Elk's camp. Attendance was sparse, but those who came seemed "very much interested" in the sermon, and the churchmen baptized two infants. The churchmen then left Rosebud and returned to their homes.[7]

To Ashley and Clark, the stalwart Christians of Rosebud were the beating heart of progressivism itself. Ashley summed up his report by attesting to their ability to overcome the nonprogressive Ghost Dancers in their midst. "I could not help thinking how much courage it must have taken to stand up and vow allegiance to the true Messiah when the false prophet seemed so strong."[8]

Indeed, the courage of the Lakotas who prayed with Ashley and Clark was considerable. After all, the army might have descended at any time. But if the missionaries made their journey to challenge the Ghost Dance, was that also what their Lakota congregants intended in attending their services? Or is it possible that Lakotas saw the new religion as benign? And were some of these eager congregants—to pose a question that Ashley and Clark undoubtedly asked themselves, even if they did not report it—in fact themselves Ghost Dancers who attended church?

The evidence is hardly conclusive, but the complete absence of hostilities throughout the missionaries' journey suggests that relations between Lakota Christians and Ghost Dancers were characterized by something other than boiling resentment. Ashley worried about a man with a war club standing outside the service at Black Pipe Creek, but the weapon appears to have been the badge of office for an akicita, the camp marshal standing by to keep order. The man listened to the sermon through a window and shook hands with the missionaries afterward. The missionaries also shook hands with two painted Ghost Dancers whom they met at the house of their catechist, a man named Frank.

And if Ghost Dancers were at odds with Christians, what explains the eagerness of some Brules, in the midst of the Ghost Dance revival, for baptism? Would so many Lakotas have attended Christian services in the schoolhouse, with their children, if Ghost Dancers were a threat to them? As we saw at Sitting Bull's camp, Ghost Dancers often withdrew children from school "to attend church" at the dances. Whether this expressed hostility to education is unclear, but if there was such hostility, why was it that at this moment, on the brink of crisis and tragedy, all schoolteachers remained at their posts on Rosebud Reservation? Indeed, at Pass Creek the missionaries found the day school still open and the teachers, Mr. and Mrs. Garrett, still in residence. In reality, teachers did not leave their schools until later—after agent E. B. Reynolds ordered them closed because he feared hostility from Ghost Dancers.[9]

Far from seeing the Christian missionaries as spiritual opponents, some Wazhazhas hoped to enlist them as allies in the struggle that preoccupied the camps at that moment: the political fight over the reservation boundary. After the service at Pass Creek, the Episcopalians were approached by a number of men, including Lip, chief of the Wazhazha band in which Short Bull made his home. It is not clear from the account whether Lip attended the service or merely met Ashley and Clark afterward, but he seemed glad to see them and sought to recruit them to the Wazhazhas' struggle to remain in the Pass Creek country. He pointed out to the Episcopalians that his people had settled at Pass Creek in accordance with the government's prior boundary, had built farms, homes, and schools, and were loath to abandon them. Lip requested that Wazhazhas be officially placed under the authority of the Pine Ridge Agency, with the Oglalas, so that they might "stay on Pass Creek where he and his people have put up houses and opened up farms," reported Ashley.[10]

On the way to Corn Creek, Ashley and Clark had passed Short Bull's lodge. The evangelist was not at home, but his tipi sat at the center of a scene with telltale signs of dances, sweat lodges, and the "stealing" of tribal cattle: red, white, and blue streamers fluttered from trees that had been cut down and re-erected at the center of dance circles; visitors from other camps had pitched their tipis along the creek, with many of them clustered near Short Bull's lodge; a group of men prepared for a sweat bath; and another man drove cattle into camp for the feast that evening.[11]

To Ashley and Clark, the paradox of their journey through a landscape where both the Ghost Dance and Christianity seemed to have
strong followings could be resolved only by portraying the situation
as hostile and unstable and by alleging (and praying) that Christians
would prove the stronger force. Dancing Indians violated every notion of Christian decorum and signified the return of the old religion. The only desirable outcome, to their minds, was Christianity
driving the Ghost Dance back into the darkness whence it came and
converting—or reclaiming—all the dancers.

For the historian, however, it is hard to interpret the scenes Ashley
described as anything other than peaceful, even bucolic. Wazhazhas
appear to have been living by Ghost Dance precepts that, with the
exception of dancing, were not that different from Christian ideals.
They abided by the primary commandment of the prophet by keeping the peace. Wovoka's instructions to farm, send their children to
school, and go to church had become Lip's mission; in his conversation with Ashley and Clark, the chief related an army officer's observation that the Wazhazhas were already "located where there were
schools and churches," and that they "should remain there, as these
could not be moved." If Wazhazhas were having some trouble following Jack Wilson's instructions to cooperate with the agent, that was
only because the government seemed to change its mind arbitrarily
about such fundamental things as reservation boundaries. In every
other way, they were doing precisely as the prophet commanded.[12]

The parallels between Christian and Ghost Dance practice made
it hard to separate one from the other in the Pass Creek country, and
to many Lakotas the distinctions between them were often insignif-
icant. As we have seen, a Lakota could attend mass and embark on a
vision quest in the same week, without necessarily feeling conflicted.
Missionaries and officials hoped that Christian Lakotas, paragons of
progressivism, would enforce a doctrinaire proscription against the
old ways and serve as self-selected opponents of the Ghost Dance.
Thus, Agent Perain Palmer at Cheyenne River had recruited many
of them to approach Ghost Dancers to persuade them to cease their

devotions. We have no record of these conversations or their content. Palmer was certainly convinced that they helped cool the movement.[13]

Christians and Ghost Dancers certainly could take opposite positions on the usefulness and meaning of the dance, and as the threat of violence grew during the fall some Ghost Dancers took issue with some self-identified Christians. Earlier that November, Ashley reported to Agent Palmer that he had been barred from a Ghost Dance on Cherry Creek. But his account of this confrontation includes a detail that casts the Pass Creek journey in a different light. It was a sight that chilled him to the marrow and probably inspired that journey of preaching and baptism through the Ghost Dance camps. Peering into the distance at the Ghost Dance circle on the banks of Cherry Creek, the reverend had glimpsed "quite a number of Christian Indians among the dancers." This sight was more disturbing even than being barred from Cherry Creek, and neither he nor Palmer seems to have wanted to consider or discuss it at any length, at least not in writing.[14]

The sight of a dance circle that brought Episcopalian and traditional religionists together was alarming for several reasons, not least because it was led by traditional holy men, who, in the eyes of missionaries, were the very incarnation of paganism and savagery. And yet holy men and their followers, those who kept to the old religion and avoided church services, seemed to be recruiting Indian Christians. And the sacred circle turned with a remarkable lack of friction between the Christians and "pagans." Even after weeks of vocal opposition to the dance from Palmer's Lakota Christian messengers, only one small Ghost Dance camp on the Moreau River allegedly banned Christians from attending—and the context raises the question of whether the ban applied to all Christians or merely those who were working for Agent Palmer.

There are signs throughout the documentary record of similar slippage along the boundary line between Ghost Dancers and Christians. Little Wound's Episcopalians took up the Ghost Dance on Medicine Root Creek, and not far to the west, at Holy Rosary Mission, all converts had gone "off to the ghost dance" by the end of September, according to the disappointed Jesuit, Father Emil Perrig. At Rosebud, even Palmer conceded that some of his anti–Ghost Dance Christians had actually joined the dances "out of curiosity." He alleged that they found it "a delusion" and subsequently denounced it, but his admission points to what Ghost Dancers and Christians shared: an openness to religious experience and an ongoing search for spiritual authority. Ashley and Palmer undoubtedly knew and refused to admit that both Ghost Dance enthusiasm and Christian devotion resided in the hearts of many individuals, and that even in the midst of the unfolding crisis—or perhaps because of it—those who had widely divergent responses to the new religion and Christianity continued to share religious ideas.[15]

What did the Ghost Dance mean to Christian Lakotas who took it up? Although missionaries viewed them as "backsliders" who succumbed to the temptations of paganism, it seems likely that some Indians who attended church services with Ashley and Clark saw the Ghost Dance as a form of Christianity. For some Lakotas, much as for Porcupine, the Ghost Dance evangelist to the Northern Cheyenne, the new religion seemed to fulfill the prophecy extolled by the Americans that Christ would return to redeem the poor and the dispossessed—meaning Indians. At the same time, the Ghost Dance offered a sense of fulfillment to more traditional believers, who appear to have seen it in much the same way as Southern Arapahos—as a "new pipe" or new instruction from Wakan Tanka that fulfilled the old religion.[16]

What emerges from between the lines of the hushed correspondence between Ashley and Palmer is that the old, reliable line between Christian and pagan—the basis for distinguishing "progressive" from "nonprogressive" Indians—was becoming uncertain. The Ghost Dance bewildered the missionaries who confronted it, for it upended all of their assumptions about the progress of Christ in Indian country. To be sure, Christ was everywhere in Ghost Dance visions as Christian teachings became embedded in or engulfed by the new religion. A Lakota woman observed by Special Agent E. B. Reynolds claimed that in the throes of her Ghost Dance vision she "saw Christ and shook hand[s] with him." Black Elk recalled many years later having "seen the son of the Great Spirit himself" in his Ghost Dance visions. So, too, did Kicking Bear. Some Lakotas, like peoples of the Southern Plains, even reserved Ghost Dances for Sunday.[17]

Missionaries might have expressed joy that these Indians were communing with Jesus. In fact, back in the summer, Ashley himself had speculated (as Lieutenant Hugh Lenox Scott would speculate in Oklahoma somewhat later) that the Ghost Dance was Christianity— or at least close enough to be co-opted by it. Upon first hearing about the Ghost Dance teachings of Kicking Bear, he mused that the evangelist "has mixed his idea of heathen customs with the Christian idea of the second advent." This, to him, presented "a great opportunity for the gospel to be preached as St. Paul did on Mars Hill," and he hoped that Dakota clergymen like the Reverend Charles S. Cook would sermonize outdoors and bring Indians literally and figuratively inside the church.[18]

But Ashley soon became less excited about the Ghost Dance, and by November he was preaching against it in the camps of the Wazhazhas. Although his diary does not indicate the reason for his disillusionment, it probably stemmed in part from the disapprobation of the religion among the Episcopalian hierarchy, especially his superior, Bishop Willam Hare. Church rejection of the Ghost Dance might have stemmed in part from the distinction that some Ghost Dancers appear to have drawn between the Christian Jesus and the Messiah of their visions: dancers informed one Jesuit missionary that they had been instructed by the Messiah himself not to call him Jesus. There is a hint here that at least some Lakotas did not see the new religion as Christian, but as the vision and teachings of an Indian prophet who had encountered a distinctly Indian redeemer. To missionaries, the emergence of the Ghost Dance raised another possibility: perhaps the religion was "deviltry," in the words of Father Perrig. Was this figure in Indian visions Satan himself?[19]

But even if followers of the non-Jesus messiah were in the minority, and even if most Ghost Dancers believed that they were seeing the same spirit presence evoked in the New Testament, the Christ of Ghost Dance visions was very different from the one missionaries had been expecting. Episcopalians and other Christians taught their Lakota charges that they must accept only Christ and reject all other spirit powers as false. Ashley himself had sermonized in mid-September that "no man can serve two masters"—Indians must reject their old religion and its Great Mysteries because Christ alone could lead Lakotas to civilization.[20]

But in the Ghost Dance, Lakotas seemed less inclined to forsake the old spirits for Jesus than to add Jesus to their ranks. The Christ of Ghost Dance visions seemed to represent a friendly, protective, and encouraging figure who greeted believers, not with the solemnity befitting the Son of Man, but with the warmth and intimacy of a personal friend in heaven, much like the old spirit protectors who functioned as personal friends and guardians for individual Lakotas. In September, Agent Reynolds recorded an account of a young woman who fell into her trance and was carried to Christ by Eagle:

> A young woman said when she fell an eagle hovered over her and picked her up carrying her to a house, the door being open the eagle went in first and she followed, and saw Christ and shook hand [*sic*] with him three times and said He was glad to see her as she had been there before.

This Christ could also remonstrate with visionaries, but even this sterner Jesus alarmed missionaries, not least for being strangely indifferent to assimilation; he even encouraged Lakotas to forsake English. Reynolds noted that another visionary he observed in September "said that Christ would not see him because he spoke the English language."[21]

Lakota Christians who joined the Ghost Dance probably understood themselves not to be rejecting Christianity but rather combining the teachings of missionaries with those of Short Bull and other leaders of the old religion who, as evangelists of the Ghost Dance, were marshaling what was effectively a new religion that incorporated a Messiah figure—for some, Christ himself—alongside older spirit powers. By custom, Lakotas were nominally free to adopt spiritual beliefs in accordance with their own visions and experience. In the Ghost Dance circle, these combinations of old spirits and new wheeled and spun in dazzling new formations, potentially as numerous and diverse as the believers themselves.[22]

By 1890, missionaries counted nearly 5,000 Lakotas as Christian; thus, they were taken aback that growing church attendance in an "Indian country dotted over with chapels and schools" was followed by a surge in Ghost Dancers. Their only explanation was that many of their Christian converts had not yet understood Christian teachings. But the simultaneous enthusiasm for church attendance and the Ghost Dance was a paradox only if believers had to choose one or the other—Christianity or the old spirits. The Ghost Dance expressed not only the belief of many that the two religions could be combined but also their longing to do just that.[23]

LAKOTAS, OF COURSE, KNEW THAT AMERICANS SAW THINGS differently, but part of the attraction of the Ghost Dance may have been that it allowed them to heal sectarian divisions that emerged in the wake of the church missions. Infighting among missionaries was often bitter: they viewed their counterparts from different churches as religious rivals and spiritual seducers who could carry away the souls of the ignorant. By 1889, Indians had grown familiar with their doctrinal disputes. Episcopalians, for example, warned Indians about "praying to statues" with Catholics, and Catholics with equal fervor warned their charges away from Protestant heresies. Religious conflict created trouble even in the federal bureaucracy. When a Baptist preacher, Thomas J. Morgan, became Superintendent of Indian Affairs in 1889, he immediately took issue with Catholics in the Indian Service (which was one reason Gallagher left the agency at Pine Ridge in 1890).[24]

These mutual jealousies did not go unnoticed, and missionaries feared that Indians, witnessing such discord, might become "confounded" or "distrustful and indifferent." But whatever else they learned, Indians quickly recognized that there were different ways to worship Christ, and that many of them were not only tolerated but advanced by the American state. By the 1880s, and probably before, Christian pluralism had become key to Lakota understanding of Christian religion and American politics. Despite Episcopalian dominance at Pine Ridge, Red Cloud elected to become a Catholic. He and Chief Spotted Tail at Rosebud invited rival denominations to their reservations, in part to balance the missionaries' influence against one another. It was the responsibility of a traditional chief to lead his people to abundant food, and it may have been a factor in their decisions that missionaries often recruited new followers with large feasts. (Upon being told that there were some 400 Christian denominations in the United States, Sitting Bull joked that if each of these would send a missionary to recruit new believers, at least there would be plenty to eat.)[25]

Listening to the importuning of the priests and reverends over many meals and in religious services, Indians picked up on key facts of America's religious politics, including the need to demand their own rights of worship; this realization disappointed missionaries and officials, who had hoped that Christian teaching would make Indians more tractable. When officials tried to crush the Ghost Dance, some Indians responded by insisting on their freedom of conscience, which they had learned from watching disputes between missionaries. Thus, when Father Florentine Digman, a Jesuit missionary, journeyed to camps on the south fork of the White River in the fall of 1890 to warn believers of "deviltry" in the Ghost Dance, he was rebuked with demands for the same rights of worship as non-Indians enjoyed. "You are a Blackrobe," said one Ghost Dancer, using the Lakota term for Catholics. "We know you speak the truth. For this reason chief Spotted Tail had asked the Great Father to send Blackrobes as teachers for his people. But instead he sent us White Robes [Episcopalians], saying they are alike." The evangelist then schooled the priest on his obligation to abide the Ghost Dance in deference to American traditions of religious pluralism. "Now you white folks have different prayers[,] [t]he Blackrobes prayers and that of the White Robes[,] and you quarrel [with] each [other] [and] say the other is not right. We Indians do not want that strife. Let us alon[e] then, and let us worship the Great Spirit in our own way."[26]

The unnamed Lakota in this exchange may have seen the dance not only as an Indian religion that deserved respect but as Christian; his insistence that the dance be understood within a US tradition that tolerated disparate Christian beliefs certainly suggests as much. In another sense, however, his defense of the Ghost Dance would be echoed in Big Road's explanation to the visiting journalist in January: "This dance was like religion; it was religion." Big Road probably said that the dance was *wochekiye* ("prayer or way of praying"), which was glossed as "religion" in the English translation. In claiming religious standing for the Ghost Dance, Big Road threw a cloak of state protection around it in the minds of American readers, and he underscored that idea by comparing the dance to "church" (for which he probably used the Lakota term *owachekiye*, "place of prayer," or *tipi wakan*, "holy house"). The fact that another Ghost Dancer could make similar arguments to Father Digman in the remote areas of Rosebud Reservation months before Big Road met with the writer from the *Washington Evening Star* suggests just how widespread such ideas had become among Lakota believers, and just how far they had traveled toward invoking American legal traditions to defend the dance.[27]

The dancer who confronted Father Digman expressed another primary concern that appears to have made the Ghost Dance attractive to both followers of the old religion and self-identified Christians: a pervasive Lakota desire to be at peace with other Lakotas over religious matters and avoid "that strife": the denominational disputes that so divided White Robes and Black Robes, Protestants from one another and from Catholics, and all Christians from followers of the old Lakota religion.

In time, Lakotas would accommodate rival Christian teachings in part by adopting one church or another within their own band, thus minimizing the potential for internal religious conflict. Thus, the old tiyospaye camps became either Episcopalian or Catholic towns.

Virtually all people in these towns, however, would continue to some degree to adhere to the old religion, a key marker of Lakota identity.[28]

During the 1880s, however, these strategies had not yet been developed, and sectarianism troubled a great many Lakotas. In an effort to ameliorate that problem, the Yankton Dakota Episcopalian Philip Deloria, from his pulpit at Standing Rock Reservation, helped introduce to Lakota camps the Brotherhood of Christian Unity, an organization dedicated to building Christian amity across sectarian lines. In the fall of 1890, as the Ghost Dance gathered adherents, BCU meetings ran until the small hours of the morning.[29]

The Ghost Dance also appears to have held out the promise of easing sectarian divisions and, at least until the army invaded the reservations, reducing the friction between Christian and traditional religions. It was, among other things, a unity dance, and its call to one circle reminded dancers of their Indianness and their subordination before the Great Mysteries (wakan tanka). The circle welcomed everyone whether or not they held a place in their hearts for Christ. Serving this function among Lakotas would have been in keeping with its role among Southern Arapahos, who found the Ghost Dance appealing as a bridge between disparate religious believers. In the words of the missionary Heinrich R. Voth, the Ghost Dance united young Christian Arapahos with those who felt that they had "given up too much of the old ways." Even as the sight of Christian Lakotas in the Ghost Dance on Cherry Creek put fear in the heart of Reverend Ashley, who saw their participation as "backsliding" into paganism, for some Lakotas it appears to have been a place where traditional believers could unite with Christians.[30]

To be sure, there were at least as many Christian Lakotas who opposed the Ghost Dance as those who supported it, and we must keep in mind that most Lakotas never took up the Ghost Dance at all. But for officials, the most alarming feature of the Ghost Dance was not the number of dancers but the way the new religion revealed the porosity of their categories pagan/Christian and nonprogressive/progressive, thus subverting the narrative of progress and calling assimilation into question. Across the Lakota reservations, officials, priests, and reverends watched in shock as many Indians who had shown strong commitment to learning the ways of American civilization now turned out to be believers in the new faith.

Ghost Dancers probably took heart from a few voices in the press and in the church that rose in support of Indian freedoms. Father Francis Craft, a Catholic priest who had been withdrawn from his mission at Rosebud for his outspoken condemnation of Protestant missions, returned to see the Ghost Dance and said that he found it "to be all right, quite catholic and even edifying." Among those who, unlike most officials, showed an openness to Indian revival practices was one white observer who described the movement in a newspaper article (which may have been read and shared by literate Lakotas) as "a genuine, old-fashioned camp-meeting like those held in the south by our colored brethren." Others who were similarly inclined urged that Indians be allowed to worship in whatever manner they saw fit. One John Gray of Chicago, with apparently no more information than he was able to glean from newspapers, expressed humanitarian concerns for Indian freedom to worship Christ and urged official restraint. "This dance is to Indians what a 'Camp Meeting' is to white men. . . . We should not act the part of the 'Spanish Inquisitors' with them but let them worship God as they please."[31]

But these were distinctly minority voices. To most missionaries and officials, the map of expanding Ghost Dance devotions across the reservations seemed to signify the complete reversal of the assimilation program. Much as it has done throughout American history, from Millerites to Mormons, millenarian excitement at this moment drove a temporary abandonment of institutions, which seemed to contradict Wovoka's instructions. Schools emptied, congregations and parishes saw their memberships melt mostly or entirely into the Ghost Dance, and the sacred circle now gathered even those Lakotas whom officials had counted on to crush such heresy. The rhythmic song and dance of the new religion filled the air, creating a call to Indian unity that many Lakotas found alluring but whites viewed as a threat.

To authorities, the Ghost Dance had become a de-assimilating force, a rotating wheel that turned Indians who had embarked on the road to "civilization" back toward their origins and created something unrecognizable: a new "church"—for that is what believers called the new religion—that elevated Eagle, Buffalo, and Bear to the same plane as Christ and made him a "friend" to Indians, like one of the guardian spirits of old. All of this occurred under the care and direction of the traditional holy men. For believers, the leadership of the wicasa wakan gave the innovative and synthetic new religion a strong sense of continuity with the old. The Ghost Dance combined old spirits and a new redeemer, old traditions and new ways, and where it would lead, none could tell. To believers, it was exhilarating. To Lakota nonbelievers, it seemed strange and likely to fail, and they grew ever more worried about the government's determination to shut it down. To authorities and most missionaries, it was terrifying.

CHAPTER 11

INVASION AND ATROCITY

DESPITE THE PLACIDITY AND OPENNESS THAT GHOST DANCERS showed toward the visiting Episcopalians at Pass Creek, authorities and other opponents of the Ghost Dance remained hell-bent on ending it. By the time Reverend Ashley and the missionary Clark returned to their homes, events had taken a sudden turn. Since receiving the president's orders to suppress the Ghost Dance, the army command had waited for a chance to make a move. On November 15, about the time Ashley and Clark began their tour, Agent Royer at Pine Ridge sent the telegram that triggered the invasion of the Lakota reservations: "Indians are dancing in the snow and are wild and crazy. . . . *We need protection and we need it now.*"[1]

General Nelson Miles issued his orders, and troops under Brigadier General John R. Brooke marched forth. On November 20, nearly 400 soldiers, including three troops of the African American Ninth Cavalry, marched into Pine Ridge and set up camp. Over at Rosebud, 230 infantry and cavalry thundered up to the agency.[2]

Even before the troops arrived, Indian teamsters driving wagons north from Valentine had told Short Bull that the army was coming to arrest him and that if he did not surrender, they would attack. The news "made me angry," he recalled later. "I called my people together on Pass Creek and told them to move forward [to Pine Ridge], and

I would stay here alone as I did not want them to have any trouble on my account." The holy man then announced, "If they want to kill me they are welcome." Short Bull's family and most of his people fled west to escape the troops, accompanied by about 1,100 other Brules, including Chief Two Strike and hundreds of Pass Creek settlers who abandoned their homes. On November 21, they arrived at Wounded Knee Creek on Pine Ridge, where they joined other Wazhazas who had made their way there back in July.[3]

The air was thick with rumor. While Two Strike went to Wounded Knee, other Ghost Dancing Brules under Crow Dog and White Horse went to Pass Creek to join Short Bull and the followers who remained with him. On November 25, Short Bull and this large group moved away from the army, up the White River, to camp at White Clay Creek, where they joined Little Wound's Oglalas and weighed their options.[4]

Meanwhile, various actors, particularly among the Indian police, kept the agents agitated with warnings about an "outbreak." The day after the army occupied the reservations, Indian police at the Yankton Agency arrested a Ghost Dancer from Rosebud named Kuwapi, or One They Chased After, who was allegedly evangelizing among Yankton Dakotas. He denied this charge but confirmed, when asked, that "there will be a trouble in the west by next spring."[5]

By "trouble" did he mean war? Or just discontent? There is cause to ask this question because the interpreter in this encounter—who also provided a transcript of the interview with Kuwapi—was none other than William Selwyn, the Dakota postmaster and Episcopalian convert who had told agents J. George Wright and Hugh Gallagher back in the spring that Short Bull and the other evangelists were planning an insurrection. Having resigned his position as postmaster at Pine Ridge, Selwyn had moved back to Yankton Reservation and taken a position as agency farmer in July. At some point he had conveyed the same warning to his agent at Yankton, E. W. Foster. On November 21, Foster, who valued Selwyn's "considerable influence with the Indians" at Yankton, sent him with the police in pursuit of Kuwapi and requested a written summary of his report on the Ghost Dance.

Selwyn helped make the arrest, and he reported to Foster as instructed. But he did more than merely repeat his earlier warning. He now claimed that the mysterious prophet of the new religion had ordered the evangelists to keep their real plans secret, and that since warning Gallagher and Wright in the spring he had read letters from Sioux and Cheyenne Indians relaying "secret plans" for "a general Indian war in the spring."[6]

These new allegations only underscore the many unanswered questions about Selwyn's earlier claims. It is probably true that many Indians brought letters to him for reading, as few Lakotas were literate. It may be that some letters did mention a possible rising in the spring. In two letters intercepted by Agent James McLaughlin, two Indian correspondents warned Sitting Bull about the army's arrival at Pine Ridge and advised him that they were planning to fight when the weather turned warm.[7]

Neither of the letters to Sitting Bull was from a tribal leader; both might be construed as excited messages from angry men without real influence. Were these letters proof of an actual plan? Or did they reflect a decision *not* to fight the army, at least not until the spring? Indeed, if there was any plan for "a general Indian war," would its leaders circulate news of that plan through the mail? Even if they thought their correspondents could find a trustworthy, literate friend or relative to read the message, what Indian actually believed that officials could not open the mail if they wanted?

Whatever the concerns of the letter writers, the Ghost Dance does not seem to have been among them. Neither of the letters intercepted by McLaughlin mentioned anything about the Messiah or the religion. Across the Plains, Ghost Dancers circulated predictions that the Messiah would return in the spring, so authorities seem to have believed Selwyn's allegation that the religion itself was the cause of the prospective violence. The real causes, however, were the army invasion, the confiscation of Indian property, and the continuing threat of starvation.

Lurking behind all of Selwyn's charges are unanswered questions about his actions. If he had damning information from letters, why was he relaying it only now, months after he quit his job as postmaster? If he had read incriminating letters, why did he never produce them? Why did he keep them from the agent?

Eager for confirmation of their prejudices and presuppositions, officials did not ask these questions. Selwyn's report was filed in Washington, where it served as yet more proof of the Ghost Dance threat, a suspiciously well-timed confirmation of the need for the army occupation that, more than any other single factor, had radicalized Lakotas and turned them against the government.

At this point, General Brooke ordered all Indians—both believers in the Ghost Dance and nonbelievers—to gather at the agencies. Nonbelievers—or more correctly, those who were willing to forgo dancing for the time being—were then designated as "progressives," or "friendlies," and they streamed into the Pine Ridge Agency grounds and erected lodges. Dancing Indians—"nonprogressives" and "hostiles"—were divided. Some thought it best to go to the agency and cease dancing for the immediate future. But many Oglala dancers refused to come in, and as the army demands were circulated, a gathering of the faithful was announced in the camp of Little Wound on White River. Short Bull, Big Road, and other dance leaders congregated there as well and considered their next move.

At about this time, Little Wound received a message from the agent at Pine Ridge asking him to bring Short Bull and his people to the agency. He and Short Bull attempted to comply. Short Bull recounted that he and ten men reached the lodge of Twist Back, another emissary, at the Oglala camps at the agency. There he was warned that the "Indian soldiers"—either scouts or the Indian police—were moving to surround him. Quickly, he made his escape back to friendlier environs.[8]

In this chaotic reshuffling of camps, the army occupation had abruptly changed the politics of dancing, and not always in ways that officials had intended. Paradoxically, the arrival of troops only convinced many believers that Wovoka's prophecy of the Messiah was about to come true. Down in Oklahoma, Arapahos, Cheyennes, and others who received letters from Lakotas warned nearby army officers about the futility of sending troops to stop the religion, a move that had only increased the fervor of Lakota believers.

If the new religion was false, why were the Americans so worried about it? Why were they trying to stop the circle from turning? Did they actually believe that it would bring the Messiah? Were white people frightened of an Indian Messiah? On the scene, Lieutenant Colonel Guy Carlton was concerned enough to explain the views of Indian believers to superiors in Washington.

> They believe that the "Messiah" dance is a prayer to the "Messiah" to come and bless them, and they want to know why the whites object to their dance (prayer), and will naturally soon think that they (the whites) are afraid of his coming, and are trying to prevent it by preventing the Indians dancing, i.e. praying for him to come.[9]

But as the occupation galvanized believers, it also hardened non-believers in their opposition (one effect, at least, that army leaders intended). Many Lakotas came to resent the faithful for causing the army to come to the reservation. They were innocent, these Lakotas protested. It was because of the Ghost Dancers that they had to leave their warm cabins and wait out the frigid fall in thin canvas tipis at the agency. Dancers, on the other hand, continued to maintain that the government had no right to stop a prayer for peace. They resented the willingness of nonbelievers to abide the crushing of an Indian ritual and the new religion. But even with the reservation divided and the sides so entrenched, it seemed clear that the standoff could not long continue. Without rations, the challenge of feeding the faithful was certain to overwhelm the movement.

Before long, signs appeared that the Ghost Dance might be winding down under the pressure. The dancing camps began to fracture; by November 27, Little Wound and Big Road had come into the Pine Ridge Agency, and followers streamed in behind them.[10]

Although determination to uphold the religion may have played a role in the next move of the remaining Ghost Dancers, the prevailing emotions among the Lakotas seem instead to have been confusion, fear, and a deep unwillingness to accept the uncertain land tenure and diminished rations that had so undermined their well-being. On top of all that, they were terrified by the army invasion. Such concerns led the remaining Ghost Dance leaders to make a move of their own, even as Little Wound and Big Road gave in and moved to the agency. It is at this point that Short Bull's memoir for the first time mentions plans for the armed defense of his people. Red Cloud and Little Wound let it be known that they would join him if there was trouble; a messenger from the Oglala camp at the agency informed the holy man, "Red Cloud says if they do anything we will fight them, and Little Wound says the same."[11]

Launching a plan to survive without government aid while they awaited the millennium—or some other resolution, perhaps even a war—the dispersed camps of Ghost Dancers gathered together. On November 30, Two Strike and some 700 followers moved down Wounded Knee Creek, along the way foraging provisions from the empty cabins of the nonbelievers who had gone to the agency. They seized untended cattle. Some gave vent to their anger at those Indians who had taken sides against them, ransacking their vacant homes and burning haystacks.

Short Bull and Kicking Bear, meanwhile, moved down White River to the mouth of Grass Creek, taking cattle from the agency herd near the mouth of Willow Creek. Here the two remaining camps of Ghost Dancers met. Together with their cattle they moved down the White River a little farther, then turned north and headed for the Badlands. There they ascended an elevated plateau between the White River and the Cheyenne River. Today it is known as Cuny Table, and from this vantage they moved onto another geological formation known as the Stronghold, a small table about three miles long and two miles wide, connected to Cuny Table by a slender finger of land barely wider than a wagon chassis. It was an eminently defensible position for a terrified, faithful people.[12]

General Miles, commanding forces in the field, decided to encircle the Stronghold and wait the believers out. Meanwhile, using the press as his weapon, he ginned up fear of a giant Indian war as a means to guarantee more congressional funding and, he hoped, acquire complete military control of the Sioux reservations. He made harsh demands of the Commissioner of Indian Affairs, who soon acceded, ordering all Indian agents to "obey the orders of the military officer commanding on the reservation in your charge." The army had taken over a civilian agency in the field. Lakotas were now under martial law.[13]

WITH THE STANDOFF IN THE BADLANDS, MOST OF THE TENSIONS now concentrated at Pine Ridge. Other agencies seemed to be quieting. At Lower Brule Reservation and the Crow Creek Agency, the agent arrested several dozen Ghost Dancers and confined them. The movement thereafter never gained a foothold there.[14]

At Cheyenne River, among the Minneconjous, the prominent Ghost Dance leader Hump acceded to army requests to cease dancing. On December 9, he broke camp on Cherry Creek and came into the agency. Thereafter he worked to persuade other dancers to come in. The only remaining Ghost Dance leader at Cheyenne River was Big Foot, who led his people away from Cherry Creek and back to their cabins at Deep Creek on the Cheyenne River.[15]

Soon things seemed stable even at Pine Ridge, and possibly headed toward resolution. Between late November and late December, Ghost Dancers continued to file into the Pine Ridge Agency, where they were separated out from the Lakota population for special observation in "hostile" camps that stretched out from the agency. With Short Bull, Two Strike, Crow Dog, and their followers surrounded in the Badlands, the odds of peace seemed good. Eventually cold weather would come. Either the holdouts in the Badlands would be swept to a new earth, or they would come into the agency.

Meanwhile, isolated and desperate in the Badlands, the followers of Short Bull, Two Strike, and the others were fractious and more of a threat to one another than anyone else. Short Bull's memoir corroborates other accounts of camp leaders, all of whom struggled mightily to contain the fear, anger, desperation, and fearsome arguments of their followers. "You must stop, you should do right, have no fighting," Short Bull implored. Warning that stealing cattle and other goods was only making their situation worse, he proposed a return to the agency to "sell our ponies, pay for these cattle and have no more trouble." But none would follow, and when he pushed the matter, "telling them to go to the agency and that as soon as I got over being mad I would come in too," they cocked their guns and threatened to kill him.[16]

On December 3, Father John Jutz, a Jesuit missionary at Pine Ridge, ventured to the Badlands to try to bring the remaining Ghost Dancers into the agency. He was met by a deputation that included Two Strike, Kicking Bear, and Short Bull. In complaints that underscore how much the Ghost Dance had become entwined with the politics of food and land, these Lakota negotiators did not mention the new religion at all, but focused their new protests on two betrayals by the US government. The first was the ongoing special census at the Brule reservation, the one White Horse had been jailed for resisting. In indexing rations to population, officials had turned the modern wonder of the census into a weapon of impoverishment and subjugation. An unnamed Lakota explained that the census reported "many less for each tepee than the tepee contains. We are to receive food according to that enumeration. We shall starve." Before they allowed that to happen, he vowed, the Sioux would fight, "and the whites shall see more blood and more dead killed by our guns than ever before." The same man then complained that the president had "put a new boundary line between Rosebud and Pine Ridge Agency that makes many of us leave our homes and give them to others." Again, the speaker averred that fighting was inevitable if the new border remained.[17]

Nonetheless, Jutz assured them that they could have all the rations they needed and they would not be harmed if they surrendered, and some in the deputation agreed to come down to Pine Ridge and meet with General Brooke. The council with Jutz ended with a feast and dancing.[18]

When the delegation to General Brooke returned to camp, there was a Ghost Dance that spun dozens of people into trances, some for as long as twelve hours. The mixed-blood scout Louis Shangreau was present and said that afterward, as the dancers recovered, Short Bull addressed his people and reminded them of the Messiah's instruction: "He tells me to send my children to school, to make large farms, and not to fight anymore." On December 12, Two Strike and Crow Dog announced that they would leave the Stronghold and head to Pine Ridge, and by December 15 they were camped near the agency. Only Short Bull and a few hundred followers held out. Short Bull sent a note to one of the negotiators who had come to talk him out of the Stronghold, saying he would come in but wanted no trouble with the army: "We don't want to fight. You told us to quit the ghost dance and we will quit my friend."[19]

Suppressing a religion without bloodshed has never been easy; indeed, it may never have been done. As was perhaps inevitable, zealous authorities shattered the fragile process in South Dakota. Standing Rock Reservation seemed very calm: the dances were small, and contained near Sitting Bull's cabin at Grand River. It was at this point that Agent James McLaughlin decided to arrest Sitting Bull.

The new religion was at best a pretext for this decision. McLaughlin's move, like the land cession and the flight of the Brules from Pass Creek, had almost nothing to do with the Ghost Dance. Although Sitting Bull allowed Ghost Dances to take place at his camp and turned the police away when they tried to stop it, he was also rumored to be a skeptic. Upon hearing the resurrection prophecy, he allegedly said, "It is impossible for a dead man to return and live again." One Indian police officer reported that when he and his fellow policemen confronted Sitting Bull about the dances, the chief replied, "The education of my children is uppermost. I have a school in my locality. This dance is not the most important undertaking. They will, eventually, stop."[20]

In November, McLaughlin came to Sitting Bull's camp on Grand River to demand that he stop the Ghost Dances. The holy man offered to go with him to Nevada to assess Jack Wilson's prophecy and his powers; he promised that if they found no prophet, he would come back and tell the Lakotas they were on the wrong path. McLaughlin brushed him off and reiterated his demands.[21]

Much more than the religion, McLaughlin was motivated by deep personal animus toward the chief. Agents and chiefs were typically jealous of each other, and as we have seen, it was government policy for agents to undermine the authority of chiefs. But even in this context, McLaughlin's campaign against Sitting Bull was unusual in how far it veered into outright hatred. The agent was otherwise renowned for his even-keeled command of the Standing Rock Agency, but the subject of Sitting Bull seemed to agitate some internal drama in him. "Sitting Bull is a man of low cunning, devoid of a single manly principle," wrote McLaughlin to his superiors that October. "He is a coward and lacks moral courage. . . . He is an Indian unworthy of notice except as a disaffected intriguer. . . . He is opposed to everything of an elevating nature and is the most vain, pompous, and untruthful Indian that I ever knew."[22]

The record is devoid of events that could have transpired between the two men to explain such venom. The agent had baldly reviled Sitting Bull for years, and now the Ghost Dance provided him with the pretext he needed to dispose of the chief. With the permission of Washington, McLaughlin planned to have Sitting Bull confined at some distant prison until his influence among the Hunkpapas diminished.

So it was that well before dawn, on the icy morning of December 15, several dozen Indian police thundered toward Grand River. A supporting detachment of the Eighth Cavalry moved into position near Sitting Bull's cabin, hiding to avoid being noticed by any Indians who caught advance word of the police invasion. If there was trouble, went the thinking, the cavalry would rescue the police.

As the Indian constables rode into Sitting Bull's camp, the dogs began to bark, but nobody was awake to see their arrival. The policemen dismounted, fingering their weapons and nervously watching the surrounding cabins and lodges. Light was beginning to gather on the horizon when Lieutenant Bull Head stepped up to the old chief's cabin and rapped on the door.

Among Lakotas, holy men were not often chiefs, and chiefs were not necessarily holy men, but occasionally a man emerged who was both. Such a man was Sitting Bull. In a very real sense, the knock at the door that morning was the sound of a new authority, the police, announcing its challenge to the old authority, the chief and holy man. Although the Ghost Dance was secondary in all this, the calamity that resulted would profoundly affect its future.

TRADITIONALLY, LAKOTA CAMP MARSHALS HAD NO AUTHORITY over religious ceremonies. But there was an important exception to this rule, one that, in extreme circumstances, gave them some say in religious life. The akicita could, by tradition, punish or kill a holy man for misleading the people.[23]

By the account of at least one policeman, the officers seem to have believed they were enforcing this traditional prerogative. "We were called to take a final action to suppress the ghost dance," recalled one officer, Private John Lone Man, "which was becoming a menace to the Tribe." The tragedy that resulted illustrates all too well the yawning divide between new authorities and old.[24]

To be an Indian policeman was to cast your lot with the agent and uphold his authority, in hopes that by doing so you could gain wealth and standing and ensure the well-being of your family and perhaps gain followers yourself. As the agents tried to unseat chiefs who opposed them, such efforts became the policeman's own. Because the chiefs so often dismissed or discounted police authority, and because they still commanded so much loyalty among their tiyospaye, the police were already apprehensive of them. Police were especially leery of Sitting Bull, whose reputation for courage, generosity, kindness, and humility, combined with his long record of opposition to the US government, had earned him a devoted following that protected him to the point that his authority was almost unassailable. When police had arrived at his camp in October with orders to take Kicking Bear and his party to the agent, Sitting Bull intimidated them into abandoning their mission, telling them that his visitors would leave the following day. McLaughlin claimed that the chief "was very insolent to the officers and made threats against certain members of the force."[25]

Whether or not he made any threats, Sitting Bull was a holy man of considerable power. In 1856, when he was about twenty-five, he had pledged himself at the Sun Dance on the Little Missouri River, where he hung suspended from skewers through both his pectoral and back muscles. Struggling to break free, he stared into the sun and prayed for health and food for his people. In 1876, at a Sun Dance on the Rosebud River, he had danced for four days and had a vision of soldiers falling upside down into camp, foretelling the defeat of Custer. By 1890, heavy scars on his arms, back, and breast testified to his numerous Sun Dance devotions. It was said that he could understand the speech of wolves and birds and that, possessing unswerving powers of divination, he could foretell the future with remarkable accuracy. Small wonder, then, that the policemen who confronted him in December 1890 were so intimidated.[26]

After banging on the door, the officers entered Sitting Bull's cabin. Lighting a match in the predawn dark, they found the old chief sitting up in bed with one of his wives and a child. Bull Head told Sitting Bull he was under arrest. "This is a great way to do things," the chief said, with some sarcasm. "All right. I will go with you. I will put on my clothes." But when the officers attempted to walk him out the door to the horse they had saddled for him, his wives set up a wail and his followers gathered around demanding his release.

Meanwhile, in the cabin, Catches-the-Bear, a close friend of Sitting Bull's and one of his senior counselors, glowered at Bull Head. A feud between them had begun years before, in the pre-reservation era. In a seemingly trivial fight over a bag of rations, Bull Head had struck Catches-the-Bear. Bad feeling between them escalated with continued insults, and Sitting Bull increasingly took the side of Catches-the-Bear. Bull Head, by then an enemy of Sitting Bull, joined the police force and ultimately became the ranking officer in charge of police.

Now, abruptly, as the police tried to lead Sitting Bull away, Catches-the-Bear culminated the years-long feud: he opened fire on Bull Head, blasting a hole in the policeman's side and knocking him to the ground. The single blast was followed by a roar as others among the chief's followers also opened fire.

At this moment, as he lay mortally wounded on the floor, Bull Head responded in a way that boldly signaled the real issue in this fight: the ongoing struggle for power between the new police force and the old chiefs and holy men. From where he fell on the floor, Bull Head raised his gun and instead of attempting to shoot Catches-the-Bear—his assailant and the man with whom he had long feuded—he blasted a hole through the sternum of Sitting Bull, who was unarmed. The bullet exited through the back of Sitting Bull's neck, snapping his spine. At the same instant, as Sitting Bull's people poured a fusillade of fire into the police, another officer, Red Tomahawk, fired his pistol into the back of Sitting Bull's head. The lifeless body of Sitting Bull, legendary chief and holy man, crumpled to the floor.

The point-blank shoot-out went on for several more seconds, taking the lives of six policemen and even more of Sitting Bull's followers. When it was over, the police found Sitting Bull's teenage son, Crow Foot, hiding in the cabin. They dragged the unarmed boy from hiding as he begged them not to kill him. Some say they killed him in the cabin and threw his body out the door. Others say a blow across the mouth sent him staggering outside, where he sprawled on the ground. All of his potential defenders had fled, and the boy, stunned and prostrate, posed no threat. But it made no difference. Two policemen stepped up, lowered their weapons, and shot him.[27]

The police victory at Sitting Bull's home would be a Pyrrhic one. They killed the old leader, his son, and some of his followers. They scattered his people. But they could not keep order. As the fight in the cabin erupted one policeman sped to the Eighth Cavalry to alert them that the arrest had gone wrong. The army immediately began lobbing shells from a Hotchkiss gun into Sitting Bull's camp. By this time, Sitting Bull's followers had retreated to the cover of the woods across the Grand River, and the shells threatened to kill only the policemen. Eventually, the troops arrived and for at least thirty minutes exchanged fire with Sitting Bull's followers, who then withdrew.[28]

AT CHEYENNE RIVER, THE GHOST DANCE LEADER BIG FOOT WAS contemplating a move to Pine Ridge, where Red Cloud and others had invited him to visit. Red Cloud had defended the right of Indians to dance as they saw fit, but he had not been a Ghost Dancer himself. It seems likely that he and other Oglalas were trying to secure Big Foot's renowned skills as a negotiator to help them defuse troubles in the Badlands, in the northern part of Pine Ridge Reservation. Big Foot was not only a famed mediator for feuding Lakotas but also known for urging peace with whites.

But while Big Foot was on his way to the agency at Cheyenne River in mid-December to pick up ration goods, a number of grieving refugees from Sitting Bull's camp found their way to his followers. Sitting Bull's band had dispersed across Standing Rock and some made their way to Cheyenne River, the nearest neighboring reservation, spreading panic and a tale of treachery along the way. On hearing the news of Sitting Bull's killing, Big Foot grew nervous. The fight with Indian police was bad enough, but now the army had also exchanged fire with Lakotas. What did the violence portend?

Elsewhere, Indian desperation was finally culminating in sporadic violence. On December 18, some Indians, perhaps from the Badlands, engaged settlers and soldiers in a skirmish on Spring Creek. Most of the fighting, however, was between Indians. Some of Short Bull's followers fired shots over the heads of a delegation of Lakotas from the agency. On Christmas Day, the camp of Cheyenne scouts monitoring the Badlands was attacked by a party of the holdouts, some said by Kicking Bear himself, and both sides suffered casualties.[29]

Army commanders in the field grew increasingly wary. On hearing that Big Foot, who was still en route to pick up rations, was on the move, officers feared he was bound for the Stronghold and sent out patrols to place him under arrest. When a cavalry group caught up with him, Big Foot agreed to return with them to camp. But subsequently, fearing the prospect of his own arrest and the isolation of his people amid the troops said to be bearing down on them, he led his Minneconjous on an escape path out of Deep Creek and toward the Badlands at Pine Ridge.[30]

In Short Bull's camp, a new consensus was emerging that it was time to surrender. A day or two before the Minneconjous reached the Badlands, on or around Christmas Day, a delegation arrived in the Badlands from the Pine Ridge Agency to persuade Short Bull and his followers to come in. The delegation was a mixed group of Lakotas that included both consistent opponents of the new religion, like Fast Thunder and No Neck, and once-ardent Ghost Dancers who had gone into the agency, among them Jack Red Cloud and Crow Dog.[31]

"They brought us presents, we killed one of the stolen cattle and made a feast," remembered Short Bull. He then demanded resolution of the Pass Creek question—the right of the Wazhazhas to claim Pine Ridge, not Rosebud, as their agency—before he would surrender. "I told these chiefs that if my people would be allowed to go to Pine Ridge to live and draw rations there they would all be satisfied to go in."[32]

For weeks, the camp of Short Bull and the other holdouts in the Badlands had been torn by strife between Ghost Dancers and negotiators, as well as between factions of believers. In mid-December, when Crow Dog and Two Strike announced that they were leaving for the agency, Short Bull's followers attempted to stop them and a brawl erupted. (It failed to keep Crow Dog, Two Strike, and their followers from departing.)[33]

Tension also threatened to overwhelm this meeting with the Pine Ridge delegation when Fast Thunder, who ostensibly came to negotiate Short Bull's surrender, denounced him for believing in the new prophecy. The next morning, however, the Ghost Dancers convened a council at which bad feeling seemed to erode from the high bluffs like sand in the wind. They decided that everyone should leave the Badlands at once and move to the agency. Some set out immediately. On December 27, the rest of the camp, all except Short Bull and an uncle, Come-Away-From-the-Crows, set out for Pine Ridge. Finally, a day after the others had left, the holy man and his uncle set out for the agency. Nightfall caught them before they could reach the rest of the party, who had camped at Drexel Mission, north of the Pine Ridge Agency. It was December 28.[34]

At almost the same moment, Big Foot, who had fled Cheyenne River Reservation with his Minneconjou followers and headed for the Badlands, became sick with pneumonia. He had been desperate to stay out of the hands of the army. It is not clear whether he had wanted to camp with Short Bull and the others in the Stronghold, but in any event, he had not taken his people there but to a separate location. When a group of messengers arrived announcing that Short Bull and his people were going to the Pine Ridge Agency to surrender and asking Big Foot to join in so that all could make peace, he agreed to move to the agency too. No doubt hoping for safety in numbers, and eager not to be left out of peace negotiations, Big Foot and his people moved south.[35]

So Big Foot, some 400 Minneconjous, and a few dozen Hunkpapas, steering clear of the army patrols that now scoured the country, zigzagged their way toward Pine Ridge Agency through the Dakota winter, with no intention of turning back. Eventually, Big Foot grew so ill that he abandoned efforts to avoid the army. Better, he decided, to get a military escort to Pine Ridge. On December 28, the Minneconjous met troops of the Seventh Cavalry. That afternoon, as demanded by Major Samuel M. Whitside, they settled into camp along a dry ravine that emptied into Wounded Knee Creek.[36]

Big Foot's band had been among the last to refuse to come to the agencies. Once before, the army had tried to escort him into captivity, but he and his people had slipped away. Now the Minneconjou chief and his people were headed for Pine Ridge essentially as captives. Short Bull and his followers, too, were headed for the agency. That night at Wounded Knee, most soldiers, thinking the trouble was all but over, spent hours celebrating with kegs of whiskey brought to them by a nearby trader. The Indians, on the other hand, spent a sleepless night, their fear mounting as the revelry grew louder and soldier reinforcements arrived from Pine Ridge.

The next morning the sun rose on a gathering of about 350 impoverished Indians surrounded by 470 soldiers—equipped with rifles, many sidearms, and four rapid-fire Hotchkiss cannons—who had been drinking all night. It was a sunny day, unseasonably warm, without a breeze. The army distributed rations to the Indians, who ate quickly, anxious to be on the road to Pine Ridge and safety.

Colonel James Forsyth had assumed command from Whitside, his junior officer. Bearing orders to disarm Big Foot's band before he brought them in, he called a council in his encampment. Almost all the men in the village attended, as did a group of boys in school uniforms. A line of soldiers stretched out between the council circle and the Sioux lodges, and during the meeting Forsyth reinforced it. Thus, as the meeting progressed, a wall of troops stood between the men in the council circle and the women and children, who stayed among the lodges along the ravine. Forsyth demanded that the Lakotas surrender their guns. Big Foot sent men to retrieve the weapons from the lodges, and they soon produced several dozen guns, mostly old and some broken. Forsyth was convinced that there were more. Now angry and by some accounts still drunk from the previous night's festivities, he ordered a search of Lakota lodges for more weapons.

This was a violation of his orders: General Miles had told Forsyth explicitly to keep Indians and soldiers separate. The troops detailed for the search went into the Indian camp and did not stint in their efforts. They entered lodges, tossed the bedding around, even searched the skirts of women. They turned up war clubs, knives, and some arrows, and here and there indeed a new gun, for some of the Indians had hidden new guns out of fear the army would take them. But even with these efforts, the soldiers turned up a total of only thirty-eight guns, most of which were so old as to be almost worthless.

Forsyth, now incensed, ordered a search of the men, who were mostly wearing blankets. Big Foot, weak from pneumonia, barely able to speak, and bleeding from the nose, urged the men to cooperate. The older men complied readily, but some of the younger men dragged their feet. Soldiers turned up two guns on the first three young men they searched.

In this way, Whitside and a soldier named Varnum were disarming the men, one at a time, when they reached a man who had the same name as the Ghost Dance evangelist in Oklahoma, Black Coyote. This Black Coyote was deaf, and as yet no one had had the chance to sign to him why the guns were being surrendered. Now he shouted, in Lakota, that he did not want to surrender his gun. It was expensive, and he would give it up only after he was paid for it.

Two soldiers leapt at Black Coyote and began to wrestle for his gun, which was pointed at the sky. Suddenly, it went off.

Nobody was hurt. But Forsyth, enraged, screamed, "Fire! Fire on them!"

"It sounded much like the tearing of canvas," recalled Rough Feather. "The smoke was so dense," said White Lance, "I couldn't see anything."

The massed firepower of the troops shredded the council circle. Most of the men were killed or wounded in the first volley, but those who could grabbed guns and fought. The rest headed south toward the lodges, trying to provide defensive cover as women, children, and old people stumbled and ran for the ravine to the south. There a few men and even some women fought back with guns taken from their own dead or from fallen soldiers. And there the army opened up with its dreaded Hotchkiss guns, slaughtering groups of huddled Lakotas, most of them women and children. When soldiers on the high ground to the north unleashed another Hotchkiss gun, exploding shells destroyed a great many Lakotas fleeing along the road, including nine women trying to escape in a wagon. Back in the ravine, a few survivors managed to straggle out of the fight and flee, escaping the soldiers who stood watch and shot anything that moved, any body that breathed, twitched, or raised a hand to surrender.

Back at the council circle, Philip Wells, the mixed-blood interpreter for the army, called out that it was safe now for any survivors to surrender. Big Foot, still prone in front of his tent at the council circle, began to sit up. A soldier shot him through the back. His daughter rushed to his side. A soldier gunned her down.

Forty minutes after the shooting began at the council circle, the guns there and near the village fell silent. But the killing was not done. Those who had managed to escape to the hills or ravines of the surrounding country now became prey for the cavalry. Unarmed children and women were shot at point-blank range. For hours the horse soldiers took no prisoners at Wounded Knee. The bloodletting did not end until noon.[37]

EVER AFTER, THE SEVENTH CAVALRY AND ITS DEFENDERS INSISTED that Big Foot and his people were militants, that the young men were inflamed with passion and draped in ghost shirts, convinced of their own invulnerability. Such was the justification for the Wounded Knee Massacre.

Those sympathetic to the victims (who include some defenders of the Seventh Cavalry) would often characterize the fallen as noble savages—primitive people who, unable to understand or cope with the modern world, were drawn to a religion that promised to turn the clock back. In this telling, the clash between Indians and modernity was inevitable, and even writers who denounced the actions of the Seventh Cavalry presented the killing of Indians as tragically unavoidable.[38]

Both of these positions—the advocacy of slaughter to impose modern order and the defense of Indians as premodern innocents—rest on the idea that Indians at Wounded Knee were primitives, trapped like wild animals in the cage of modernity.

The truth was far more complicated. The shooting began, not because Indians imagined that their redeemer would help them vanquish the Seventh Cavalry that morning, but because an Indian man insisted on being paid for the gun he was about to surrender. Black Coyote may have been foolish to argue with the soldiers, but he was hardly resisting the modern age: he wanted cash. The Minneconjous had worked hard to make themselves part of post-conquest America. When they left their village on Deep Creek to begin their trek to Pine Ridge, they had been fearful of losing their property during their absence. When the news came that soldiers were coming for them, they had been haying in the meadows to provide winter fodder for their cattle and horses. The people had voted to go to Pine Ridge and attend the peace efforts under way. Before they left, they closed up their "houses, fences, and gates to make things solid and secure," remembered Joseph Horned Cloud. As they made their way south their wagons proved too wide for the narrow trails through the Badlands, so the men took out axes and spades and cut a road that subsequently became known as Big Foot Pass. To this day, cars drive past it on the scenic loop through Badlands National Park.[39]

Also among the Minneconjous were the boys from the reservation day school, still in their uniforms. And there were others who had already gone to school, who could read and write. Joseph Horn Cloud was in his midtwenties that sunny morning at Wounded Knee when he grabbed a gun and fought before fleeing amid a thick fog of gunsmoke up the ravine away from Forsyth's killers. He had spent two and a half years at the day school at Cheyenne River. When he was eight, he had attended a school for a year with white students and Indians away from the reservation, in a settlement north of Pierre. He had gone to this small country school after his grandfather and two uncles, at the invitation of a Congregationalist missionary, left the reservation, abandoned their rations, and tried to homestead like white people. For a time, these families succeeded; these Minneconjous turned into homesteaders. But like many other Great Plains farmers in the 1880s, they struggled to make grain grow in the arid soil and to live off the declining prices they received for their produce. After five years, unable to pay the property taxes, they returned to the reservation at Cheyenne River. There, by 1890, the family of Joseph Horned Cloud had assembled a small estate: a log house with dishes and cups as well as guns, bridles, a wagon, a harness, four saddles, nine quilts, and a tipi. Joseph kept a stack of schoolbooks and translated for the family at Congregationalist services.[40]

Big Foot's band included its holy men and warriors, its buffalo hunters and quillworkers. But it also included its fence makers, gate hangers, hay gatherers, stock raisers, road builders, farmers, churchgoers, and students. These were the victims at Wounded Knee: people who sallied forth courageously into the future to do the things that white people demanded without becoming who they demanded—that is, without becoming white. The people lost at Wounded Knee were not merely bodies to be counted, and they were not naïfs clinging to a vanished past. They were people trying to leave a familiar past and move toward a strange, hostile future.

On that journey, the spirits had come to them and validated Wovoka's prophecies, promising a glorious new earth and the return of their autonomy and many of the old ways, the life and games and loved ones they missed. What they had heard of Wovoka's other teachings—that they must farm, attend church, and send their children to school—we cannot know. But had they needed spiritual encouragement to take the road they were forced to take—a road they had at times so arduously built for themselves—they could not have found better than the Ghost Dance.

To the west of the slaughter at Wounded Knee, Short Bull and his uncle were still making their way to Pine Ridge. It was soon after sunrise, he recalled, when "we heard the firing of guns and cannon." Setting out to investigate, the two Lakotas met a white man loading a wagon with firewood. He told them the gunfire was from soldiers "practicing at targets, and they shoot all the time." Whether they believed him or not is unclear, but Short Bull and Come-Away-From-the-Crows continued in the direction of the shooting. They scaled a nearby hill. From the top, they looked down on the slaughter happening by Wounded Knee Creek. "Everything was in a fearful state," remembered Short Bull. In the distance they could see other Indians heading toward the sound of the firing, "and it looked as if trouble was near."[41]

Trouble indeed. When the roar from that first volley reached the Pine Ridge Agency, about ten miles away, the Indians suspected what had happened. Over 100 Brule and Oglala men leapt to their horses and raced to the sound, weapons at the ready, intent on rescuing their fellow Lakotas. These were the men Short Bull now saw heading into the teeth of the massacre. Among them were some who had been with him in the Badlands and had left for the agency only the day before he did, and who had camped there only for a night or two. By the time they reached the massacre site, the slaughter was over. The Seventh Cavalry had dispersed to hunt down and kill those who survived the initial onslaught. The Lakotas thundered into a pitched battle with several dozen Seventh Cavalry men from C Company. They rescued a party of Minneconjous captured by the troopers, and then retreated. But few of them would stay at the agency now. Back at Pine Ridge, most of the Indians who had accepted army promises of peace and security were now fearful and angry. They bolted for the hills.[42]

Short Bull and his uncle descended the hill to the ravine. He encountered a cousin, Many Wounds, whose parents had both been cut down. In the end, Short Bull would count twenty-three relatives among the dead. What he did for the rest of the day he does not say, but the next morning Short Bull and four others hitched up four wagons they found at the site and gathered as many wounded as they could find, including one of Short Bull's uncles, until they had loaded over forty people into the wagons.

Wounded Knee Creek was the home of Big Road's band, and like other Lakotas, many of them had put up cabins. Big Road had led his people into the agency late the previous month, and now their cabins were empty. Short Bull took those among the wounded who seemed likely to die to the deserted houses and left them there; "with the rest we started for our camp." He returned to the cabins the next day, but they were empty; another rescue party of Indians had taken the wounded to the agency. The killing field was covered in snow.[43]

In the massacre's chaotic aftermath, many Lakotas feared that they, too, would be killed. So even as some wounded went into the agency, most of the Indians who had surrendered before the killings now raced for the hinterlands. Two Strike, Little Wound, Big Road, and their followers had only just come into the Pine Ridge Agency from their camps, but now they fled. At Drexel Mission, the teacher Elaine Goodale watched from the chapel window as the tipi village quickly came down and "a long line of loaded wagons disappeared in the distance." Brules camped at Pine Ridge also retreated into the countryside, along the way forcing Red Cloud—who had remained neutral—to join them. That night they camped in the valley of White Clay Creek, fifteen miles north of the agency. This was the camp Short Bull now found himself in. Survivors of Big Foot's band arrived the same night, many of them wounded. Camp numbers swelled to about 4,000 people.[44]

With the army having fired on Lakotas at Sitting Bull's camp and at Wounded Knee, skirmishing now spread. Some retreating Brules fired shots at the Pine Ridge Agency. General Brooke, who was in command there, ordered his troops not to return fire, and the attack, such as it was, ceased. On the day after the massacre, real fighting erupted as the army pursued fleeing Lakotas. Forsyth led his Seventh Cavalry troopers into a cul-de-sac north of Drexel Mission and was soon pinned down in a hot crossfire until he and his command were rescued by the African American Ninth Cavalry. A party of Lakota warriors attacked a wagon train of the Sixth Cavalry on January 1, but was driven off. General Nelson Miles arrived and threw a cordon around the "hostile camp" of refugees in White Clay Valley, then sent out emissaries to request that the Indians come in.[45]

In the refugee camp, division was rife. With the arrival of Miles at the agency, Red Cloud, Little Wound, Big Road, and other Oglalas announced that they should trust the general to protect them and go in. But Short Bull and other Brules were not ready to capitulate. For the next ten days, factional disputes roiled the camp as Oglalas leaned toward surrendering and Brules, many of them still impassioned not only by the many killings but also by the confiscation of their property at Pass Creek, held out hope for some other resolution.

"During all this time my heart was bad, yet I did not want my people to fight the government," Short Bull later claimed. "I might have done much harm but always kept my people from it, I wanted no fighting, I wanted to do as the Messiah bid me." Eventually Short Bull relented and instructed his people to go in. "We will surrender our guns and have peace," he announced. The next morning Short Bull and his band set out for the agency.[46]

When the "hostiles" at last arrived on January 15, they walked into the agency in two columns of 4,000 people, with 7,000 horses, 500 wagons, and 250 travoises. The army marched close behind. Kicking Bear laid his gun at the feet of General Miles. "I had a good Winchester rifle which I surrendered freely," recounted Short Bull. "General Miles asked me if I had any more guns, and I told him I had an old patched up gun—the stock and barrel being wrapped with buckskin and not worth anything. He asked me to turn it in, which I done."[47]

So ended the "Ghost Dance War."

PART 3

PERSISTENCE AND RENEWAL

CHAPTER 12

THE ROAD FROM WOUNDED KNEE

WHAT WAS THE FATE OF THE GHOST DANCE AFTER THE Wounded Knee Massacre? Practically from the moment gunfire erupted that day, faith in Jack Wilson's teachings was said to have evaporated, helping to turn 1890 into what seemed a providential year for American conquest. Just as the census results that year led analysts to conclude that the frontier was closed and the West was finally settled, so, too, the massacre of Ghost Dancers seemed to ring down a curtain on the Old West. With its ending came many others: the end of free land, the end of some purported "American innocence," and the end of Indian spirituality.

Supporting this narrative was the rise of a story that back in Nevada the mass killing of his followers brought upon the prophet an insurmountable crisis of faith. Early in 1891, Wilson received a visit from a Kiowa seeker, Wooden Lance, or Apiatan, who had journeyed from Indian Territory in hopes of a vision. As Apiatan later recounted, he found Wilson lying on his back, singing to himself, with a blanket over his face. The prophet stirred, removed the blanket, and asked the seeker what he wanted. Apiatan asked that he be allowed to see his departed young child. Wovoka replied that this was impossible, because "there were no spirits there to be seen."

Apiatan was devastated. Noting that Wilson had no scars, he questioned aloud whether he was the messiah about whom the Kiowa had heard. Wilson told him he need go no further. There was no other messiah. He was the one who had preached to the others. But the Sioux, Apiatan reported Wilson as saying, "had twisted things and made trouble, and now Apiatan had better go home and tell his people to quit the whole business." Disgusted and demoralized, Apiatan left. Soon after, Apiatan returned to the Southern Plains and, before an assembly of Kiowas and other Indians, denounced Wovoka as a fraud.[1]

At this point, however morally contemptible the massacre was, it seemed to have accomplished what many Americans desired: it terminated the Ghost Dance.[2]

But events in Nevada suggest something amiss in Apiatan's story. The prophet, in fact, continued to teach the new religion after Apiatan departed. Seekers still trekked to his door. "Many Indians from distant tribes have been here and are now visiting him," reported agent C. C. Warner late in 1891, "and from eighty to a hundred have been to see him during the past six months." If the Ghost Dance died at Wounded Knee Creek, how was it that the earnest devotions of these far-flung pilgrims continued so long after Apiatan's visit?[3]

For that matter, if Jack Wilson lost his faith after Wounded Knee, how was it that a delegation of Caddos ventured out from their Indian Territory reservation to Nevada in the fall of 1891 and returned with their belief so renewed that they danced for at least the next two years?[4]

When Short Bull and Kicking Bear went to Nevada in 1890, among the Lakotas accompanying them was a man known as Cloud Horse. If Jack Wilson blamed Lakotas like these for destroying his teachings, why did he meet with Kicking Bear again when he made a return visit to Nevada in 1902? And why did he meet with Cloud Horse and two other Lakotas, Chasing Hawk and Bear Comes Out, when they came back to Mason Valley in 1906? He was still exchanging letters with Cloud Horse, advising him about matters of spirit and health, as late as 1911. Would he have so counseled those he blamed for destroying his movement?[5]

Mass murder is a powerful force, but there is great power, too, in stories. They can reveal the truth, or they can seduce us into convenient falsehoods. Sometimes they do both. And there are few better examples of the dark side of the narrative art than this hoary tale of a new religion murdered in its cradle. The story of Wounded Knee, that tangled knot of narrative seductions and bloody verities, has proved so useful to writers and filmmakers seeking a poetic ending to an era that it has come to stand for the entire history of the Ghost Dance. In doing so, these storytellers have inadvertently closed off a great deal of inquiry into the meaning of the religion, its appeal for Indians, and its larger place in American history. Thus, for over 100 years, this telling of the Ghost Dance's end has maintained its grip on scholars and the public alike, transfixing us with the horror of the killing ground, compelling us to mourn the Indians, their primitive religion, and the frontier as part of a vanished past, and constraining us from looking too closely at the facts that point to a dramatically different outcome. Lifting our eyes from the bloody ravine, we can see that, across the land, the good news yet traveled in 1890. Indians still danced, from Nevada to Utah, across the Southern Plains; by 1897, they were dancing north, into Canada.[6]

If we follow the Ghost Dance on its journey, we can begin to appreciate the religion's strength and deeper meaning. Key developments in the ritual in the aftermath of Wounded Knee allowed it to flourish so well, in fact, that in some places it became a tribal institution. As such, it was a force not only for cultural and ethnic persistence but also for a broader democratization of Indian religion that expanded the corps of believers, reformed older shamanistic and priestly hierarchies, and opened up new paths to spirit and feeling for Indians in the post-conquest world.

As we follow the real story of the Ghost Dance on the Plains, we will learn why so much has remained hidden from all but a handful of scholars (and many more Indians, who have known all along).

This is a story, not of a religion's demise, but of spiritual articulation and persistence, of believers working with spirits to craft new forms of ritual observance to suit their needs, and of a new religion that thrived for decades, often hidden from public view in the shadows of Wounded Knee.

In most places—perhaps everywhere—the persistence of the Ghost Dance was a contested development, and there were many Indian dissenters. Among these was Apiatan. Whatever his actual experience in Nevada, his story about the false messiah served his personal ambitions, as we shall see. But even among his people, who carefully listened to his warnings, the Ghost Dance would not die.

Paradoxically, the Ghost Dance religion after Wounded Knee owed its continuance and further development in part to the exertions of the social scientist who appears to have believed it would soon vanish. About the time Short Bull and his followers were negotiating their final surrender at Pine Ridge, James Mooney arrived in Darlington, Oklahoma. In venturing to the Plains to study the Ghost Dance in the immediate aftermath of Wounded Knee, Mooney became not only a scholar of the religion but a participant, at times unwittingly, in the shaping of its future.

Its enduring influence notwithstanding, Mooney's study, *The Ghost Dance Religion and Sioux Outbreak of 1890,* has its interpretive shortcomings. Among them is one seeming contradiction in the narrative. Deep in the text, Mooney asserts that the Ghost Dance movement was "already extinct" among most of the tribes where it had taken hold, having been killed by the army among Lakotas and died "a natural death" elsewhere. But he seems to distinguish between the early, ecstatic phase of the religion's development, which he calls the "movement," and the religion itself. As if hastily rewriting the introduction and overlooking the later claim, he announces on the first page of the book that the Ghost Dance "still exists" and "is developing new features at every performance." This inconsistency has only reinforced the long-standing desire of writers and other storytellers to overlook the survival and development of the religion in favor of a story about its tragic demise.[7]

The internal contradiction in Mooney's Ghost Dance writing may reflect his intellectual struggle as he broke with dominant theories of religion and its development: he was writing a report on the Ghost Dance that attacked the foundations of the very religious intolerance that had given rise to official panic in the first place. Indeed, and ironically, in articulating the beginnings of an intellectual shift in American religious and social thought, James Mooney, scholar and skeptic, came to the aid of Indians in search of a new religion and ultimately served the cause of the prophet. In ways that he never acknowledged but that could not have avoided his notice entirely, he became a force in the development and expansion of the religion in the communities where he worked.

As we follow the religion on its journey through the heartland beyond South Dakota, it becomes hard to disagree with Ghost Dancers who testified to its power. Despite formidable opposition, it seemed unstoppable, its propagation abetted in ways both intentional and not, by a broad range of people, including a great many Indians, a few benign officials, and even the rebel social scientist who sought to write its postmortem.

In mid-January 1891, less than a month after the massacre at Wounded Knee, James Mooney, not quite thirty years old, stood on the edge of a dance circle on the Southern Plains, transfixed by the enthusiasm of Cheyenne and Arapaho who were "dancing the ghost dance day and night." As some Indians donned old regalia for the dance, he scribbled urgent requests to Washington for photographic glass plates so he could take pictures.[8]

Mooney was astonished by the commitment of the Arapaho and Cheyenne to the new faith. The dancers included, in his words, "all the older ones, all the middle-aged, down to the boys and girls, even little children who were not much more than able to stand upon their feet."[9]

To some readers, Mooney's account related a typical Victorian adventure. Like the explorer Richard Burton, who disguised himself as a Muslim and became the most famous non-Muslim European to enter Mecca, Mooney's book tells a gripping tale of a lone white man penetrating a closed community of dark-skinned believers to unearth the mysteries of an exotic religion. Although the Indians banned white gawkers, they took to Mooney. "I am so far in with the medicine men that they have invited me to take part in the dance," he bragged to his superiors at the Bureau of Ethnology, at the time the world's leading institution for the study of ethnology, or cultural anthropology.[10]

Like other ethnologists in the bureau, Mooney spent much of his time in far-flung corners of the United States, investigating Indian languages, religion, and material culture in an effort to record as much as possible before the old ways of native peoples disappeared. Beginning in 1887 and proceeding for the next three years, he lived for months at a time among the Eastern Cherokee in Appalachia, working closely with Cherokee consultants and interpreters to gather and translate key texts in Cherokee medicine and healing. He had made the important discovery of sacred—and secret—medicine books compiled by Cherokee healers. After persuading them that their influence would be honored by preserving their writings, he was able to trade with them for the books, which he spent long hours translating before he archived them in Washington.[11]

The Eastern Cherokees were a remnant community of the much larger Cherokee people. After most Cherokees were forced west on the Trail of Tears in the 1830s, those who became known as Eastern Cherokees had remained near their old homelands by hiding in the mountains. Mooney wondered if the Cherokees who went to Oklahoma had changed their healing practices and began to plan a journey west to find out. While preparing for that journey, he read the newspaper coverage of the Ghost Dance on the Plains. Deciding to research both Cherokee medicine and the new religion, Mooney embarked on a study of Wovoka's teachings that would dominate the next four years of his life.[12]

For all Mooney's energy, initiative, curiosity, and intelligence, his revelations about the Ghost Dance testified to the openness and initiative of Ghost Dancers themselves. If he had not been welcomed by ritual leaders, his participation in the religion, and the analysis that flowed from it, would have been impossible. Not only would the study Mooney finally produced convey his own insights about the Ghost Dance, but it would also reflect the contributions and some of the ambitions of these believers, who created the context for his study and shaped its message. The ethnologist blazed a path into the dance circle, but its members made it possible by reaching out to him, for reasons of their own, and bringing him inside.

The task before them was an urgent one. Oklahoma newspapers were "full of stories," as Lieutenant Hugh L. Scott observed that month, about frantic settlers arming themselves against an impending Indian "outbreak." These same stories were "read by the Eastern graduates" of the boarding schools, who "do not know what to expect." The Ghost Dance carried on under the dark cloud of threatened attacks by mobs of settlers or the US Army.[13]

While the suppression of the faith ramped up the fears of believers, it also hardened the devotion of some. As we have seen already, Oklahoma Indians remonstrated with the commander of the Seventh Cavalry at Fort Sill, Lieutenant Colonel Guy Carlton, pointing out to him that there had to be some truth to the religion; otherwise, why would the Americans be attempting to crush it? If it was false, wouldn't the Americans just ignore it? According to Hugh Scott, the massacre in the north at Wounded Knee "caused the excitement in the South to be greatly intensified."[14]

It was in this moment, amid the fervent anxiety that followed on the massacre, that Mooney stepped off the train in Oklahoma. With the dreadful news from South Dakota still so fresh, he might have been met with a great deal of suspicion. Instead, believers turned him into an important federal ally and protector.

Two groups of Arapahos seem to have taken a particular interest in Mooney because of his connection to the federal government and to have worked together to assist him and steer his interpretations. The first of these groups was the Indian police. As we have seen, policing at the Southern Arapaho–Southern Cheyenne reservation had created fewer of the tensions so prevalent on Lakota reservations, in

part because policemen like Black Coyote interpreted law enforcement in ceremonial terms. Lodge members and police made joint
decisions in law enforcement matters because everyone saw policing
as part of the ritual obligation of lodge members.

Just as important was Black Coyote's view of himself as an agent
of the national government; as Mooney put it, "the Arapaho police
considered themselves a part of Washington." This self-perception
explains why Black Coyote and several other policemen approached
the ethnologist from Washington and "invited me to their tipis at
night where they would explain the religion and give me the songs."[15]

The success of these meetings depended on the participation of
the second group—the boarding school graduates. Cleaver Warden,
Paul Boynton, Robert Burns, and Grant Left Hand all served as interpreters for Mooney, and Boynton and Left Hand (and perhaps
Warden and Burns) were avid believers in the new religion. Aware
that hostile public perceptions could lead to disaster in Oklahoma
just as at Pine Ridge, these believers approached Mooney upon his
arrival "very anxious to explain conditions," as he put it, "so that
Washington might know why they were dancing and that they were
not going to hurt anybody." As Mooney later recounted, "I did not
have to ask them. They said, 'We will help you. We are glad you
are interested and we want the white people to understand.'" When
Mooney offered to pay the police for their work, the constables de-
murred. "They said they did not want anything, that they were glad
Washington had sent somebody out there to go back and tell the
truth about their dance."[16]

Thus, Mooney's book took the shape it did in part because young
Arapahos found it to their advantage to provide the man from Washington with information and to offer him housing, food, and com-
panionship in hopes of educating Washington authorities about the
religion and shaping Indian policy. As the anthropologist reinterpreted the dance for Americans, then, Indians sought to shape that
interpretation to suit their own needs. Admittedly, because Mooney's
police sources could not read his account and it is not clear if the
boarding school graduates ever did, his Indian consultants were

forced to trust him. But because they did, *The Ghost Dance Religion* became a kind of intellectual collaboration between Indians and their interlocutor. This partnership was asymmetrical and unequal, to be sure, but the Indians' role in it was still powerful.[17]

From the beginning, Mooney's work in Oklahoma was arduous. Learning the Ghost Dance songs took weeks, but there was no rush. Deep snow covered the ground upon his arrival, and until it melted there could be no dances. While they waited, Black Coyote convened rehearsals of Ghost Dance songs in his tipi, where Mooney would join up to twelve believers at a time around the fire. Passing a pipe, each participant would make offerings to the cardinal directions, and Black Coyote would stand, facing the northwest, eyes closed and arms outstretched. While the others bowed their heads, Black Coyote would offer "a fervent prayer for help and prosperity to his tribe, closing with an earnest petition to the messiah to hasten his coming." Then, after choosing a song to begin, Black Coyote would start "in a clear musical bass," and the others would join in. Mooney meticulously wrote down every word. "They invited me to call for whatever songs I wished to hear, and these songs were repeated over and over again to give me the opportunity to write them down." So it went for three hours every night. After the singing ended, the work continued: Black Coyote and the others would explain the meaning of lyrics and answer Mooney's probing questions.[18]

When the snow had melted enough for dances to begin again, rehearsals ended and Black Coyote and the others invited Mooney to join the ritual. Standing shoulder to shoulder with the other dancers, turning clockwise with well over 100 believers, and singing the songs he had learned by heart, Mooney partook of the new spirit. Twice he felt the telltale twitch in the hands of the dancers beside him and watched as they and dozens of other women and men broke from the circle and fell into the center in spasms, collapsing into unconsciousness. The ethnologist was awed by the "maniac frenzy" of the dance, its explosive power, and the strength of the trances it induced. "They lie where they fall, like dead men, sometimes for an hour or longer, while the dance goes on."[19]

FIGURE 12.1. Southern Arapaho Ghost Dance, 1891. Photo by James Mooney, National Anthropological Archives, Smithsonian Institution, GN-00044d.

Mooney took photographs only in the daylight because he worried that the flash would alarm the Indians, who were already fearful of an army attack. The photos show Arapahos stretched out unconscious, or standing with eyes closed and holding hands to the sky, or in prayer with two hands stretched out to the northwest. The circles of dancers in Mooney's photos, hands clasped together, moving shoulder to shoulder, are reminiscent of the Virginia City gatherings two decades before of Nevada Paiutes—the "solid mass" of dancers that "like a huge laboring water wheel" crept "slowly around for hours."[20]

In early February, Mooney moved to Anadarko, Oklahoma, and the Kiowa Agency, where he embarked on gathering materials for an exhibit of Plains Indian life at the upcoming World's Columbian Exposition in Chicago. He continued his research into the Ghost Dance, which was soon in turmoil because of the denunciations of Apiatan. A well-regarded man of about thirty who had recently lost his son, Apiatan later said that his interest in finding the prophet was driven by a desire to see his child again. In spite of this heartfelt motivation, something seems to have raised doubts in him. He proposed taking a journey in search of the Messiah, in hopes of advising his people regarding the truthfulness of the religion. With money raised by Kiowa leaders for the purpose, and with blessings by holy men and a send-off by practically the entire tribe, Apiatan set out in September 1890.[21]

After Sitting Bull, the Arapaho evangelist, arrived among the Kiowa the following month, the Ghost Dance flourished in Apiatan's absence. The first intimation of disillusionment came in February, when a letter arrived from Apiatan, who was then at the Northern Arapaho reservation in Wyoming. Mooney was at the Kiowa Agency by this time, and he heard the letter (which may have been a telegram) read aloud by Apiatan's sister, a Carlisle graduate named Laura Dunmoi. Apiatan briefly related that he had seen the messiah, and that he was a fraud.[22]

On February 19, Apiatan himself returned to Anadarko and appeared before a large intertribal gathering, with James Mooney and Agent Charles Adams among them. The Arapaho Sitting Bull arrived with many followers to hear the Kiowa's challenge.

Apiatan rose and described his meeting with Wovoka, how he found the prophet singing with a blanket over his face, how saddened he was to learn that Wovoka was not omniscient but an ordinary man, how he instructed Apiatan to go back and tell his people to "quit the whole business," and how, "discouraged and sick at heart," he had left Nevada and journeyed home. The crowd of listeners was large and diverse, with members from many neighboring tribes. Every word Apiatan spoke was translated not only into English but also into Comanche, Caddo, Wichita, and Arapaho, with frequent repetitions. The meeting took an entire day. Apiatan took questions from Adams and Indian leaders, and then Sitting Bull was asked to respond.

"The scene was dramatic in the highest degree," wrote Mooney. In a sense, Sitting Bull himself was on trial, but there was more than that at stake. Hanging in the balance were the ecstatic visions, the social standing of believers and visionaries, and the new religion's promise of deliverance from the poverty and social erosion of reservation life.

Sitting Bull rose. He "insisted on the truth of his own representations." He reminded his listeners that he had visited Jack Wilson the year before and explained again what the Messiah had said. But Apiatan did not back down. Kiowas had shown gratitude for the teachings; they had made Sitting Bull generous gifts of money and horses. Now Apiatan accused the evangelist of "deceiving the Indians in order to obtain their property." Sitting Bull remained calm. Speaking "in a low musical voice," the evangelist pointed out that he had never asked anyone for ponies, and he announced that those who "did not believe what he had told them . . . could come and take their ponies again." Apiatan replied that that was "not the Kiowa road; what had once been given was not taken back." Sitting Bull did not relent. At the conclusion of the meeting, he rose, drew his blanket around his shoulders, and crossed the river to the camp of the Caddos, where the dances continued. His Arapaho followers went with him.[23]

Kiowas were persuaded to follow Apiatan—for a time. But others were not, and their continuing enthusiasm may have drawn strength from whispered rumors about the Kiowa doubter. Some said his wife's dedication to the Ghost Dance made him jealous of either the religion or its leaders; another story circulated that he had never actually visited Wovoka but "had been hired by white men to lie to the Indians."[24]

In addition to the Caddos, the neighboring Wichita soon took up the dance as well. Indeed, Sitting Bull "gave the feather"—appointed ritual leaders—among both Caddos and Wichitas that same month. "From this time [almost two months after Wounded Knee] all these tribes went into the dance heart and soul, on some occasions dancing for days and nights together from the middle of the afternoon until the sun was well up in the morning," reported Mooney. Expectation of earthly renewal was pervasive and profound, with all anticipating "that the great change would occur in the spring." Winter cold failed to diminish their devotions, wrote Mooney, "the trance subjects sometimes lying unconscious in the snow for half an hour at a time."[25]

Mooney watched as devotion to the religion expanded throughout the first half of 1891, despite the Wounded Knee massacre and Apiatan's denunciation. He noted that in February, around the time of Apiatan's return, the Southern Arapaho and Southern Cheyenne sent another delegation to Wovoka; its members included Caspar Edson and Tall Bull, the captain of the Cheyenne police. They stayed for months, danced near Mason Valley, and met the prophet, from whom they received sacred red paint, which they duly carried back to the devotions in Oklahoma.[26]

When the prophecy was not fulfilled that spring, devotions nevertheless continued. In August 1891, more Arapahos and Cheyennes traveled to Nevada; one senses a desire to reconnect with the prophet about when the end might come. The travelers included Mooney's closest consultants, Black Coyote, Grant Left Hand, and Caspar Edson, as well as the Arapahos Little Raven and Red Wolf and the Cheyennes Black Short Nose and Standing Bull. Left Hand and Edson served as interpreters, and they also wrote down Jack Wilson's teachings in a message that became known as "the Messiah Letter," which they carried back to Oklahoma.[27]

Not until several months later would Mooney see this letter for himself. Meanwhile, its teachings reshaped Ghost Dance practice and made a profound impression on believers around him. The text of the Messiah Letter indeed suggests that Wovoka adapted his teachings to address new realities in the aftermath of Wounded Knee, and it illuminates the ways in which believers were changing the ritual as Mooney watched.

Implicit in the prophet's new instructions was one key for minimizing confrontation with authorities. Wovoka opened the letter with new rules governing the form of the dance. No longer would there be dancing for days on end, as on the Plains; now he imposed a limit. "When you get home you must make a dance to continue five days." Dance four nights in a row, he instructed, then dance into the morning of the fifth day, "when all must bathe in the river and then disperse to their homes." This sequence was to be repeated once every six weeks, and there was to be no departure from it: "You must all do in the same way."[28]

This was the same form that Wovoka had taught in Nevada from the beginning, but now he reiterated it with urgency, as suggested by its placement at the opening of the letter. In his meetings with visitors, he was equally firm about the six-week cycle of the ritual. At about the same time that Black Coyote and the others left for Nevada, Mooney noted, a combined delegation of Caddos, Wichitas, and Delawares also set out. They returned with the same instructions and quickly put them into effect: They danced for five consecutive days, into the next morning on the last day. Then all bathed in the river before dispersing to their homes to wait for six weeks before dancing again. Southern Arapahos even inscribed the instructions into their Ghost Dance songs. "Five and you must stop," says the closing song of the ritual. Says another, "Once you have done it five times you must stop, our Father says to us."[29]

Why Wovoka felt compelled to impose a strict schedule for the dance is impossible to know, but one of its effects was to head off further conflict with the US government. As we have seen, Ghost Dancing in Nevada tended to cease anytime authorities moved against it, in part because Wovoka and his followers had learned to suspend dances and rotate them to remote locations to avoid causing alarm. Whatever the inspiration for the prophet's instructions, they seem to have diminished the weeks-long dances that riled authorities and inflamed the press in Oklahoma. In allowing Indians only five days for dancing followed by a six-week pause, the schedule provided ample time for anxious white officials and observers to calm themselves and for rumors of "Indian outbreaks" to subside.

The Messiah Letter included not only instructions in dance form but promises of rain and renewal. Immediately after the dance instructions that opened the letter, the prophet thanked believers for their gifts and assured them of his affection—"I, Jack Wilson, love you all"—and sent them rain. "When you get home I shall give you a good cloud. . . . There will be a good deal of snow this year and some rain. In the fall there will be such a rain as I have never given you before."[30]

He then issued instructions governing behavior. When loved ones died, "you must not cry," he informed his believers, an injunction against the mourning rituals in which people generally destroyed their own property. They "must not hurt anybody or do harm to anyone.

You must not fight. Do right always." There was to be no lying. "Do not refuse to work for the whites and do not make any trouble with them until you leave them," he warned.[31]

Then he gave them even more good news: "Jesus is now upon the earth. He appears like a cloud." The letter is the only instance in the documentary record in which he invoked the name of Jesus, and it came with general resurrection. The dead were all alive again. "I do not know when they will be here; maybe this fall or in the spring." He closed by reiterating the form of the dance: every six weeks, to be conducted with feasting and concluded with bathing. He asked the emissaries who carried the letter to return in three months' time.[32]

The promise of the letter was echoed in the songs of the dancers. On the Southern Plains, the prophecy of rain and renewal was as powerful as it had been in Nevada.

> *There is our Father*
> *The ground is all damp,*
> *Whenever he makes me dance,*
> *Because that is what I have been given by our Father.*[33]

As with so many messianic movements, believers tempered their zeal when the Messiah did not appear at the expected hour. In Mooney's words, when the Messiah failed to arrive in the spring, "the wild excitement gradually cooled and crystallized into a fixed but tranquil expectation of ultimate happiness under the old conditions in another world."[34]

BY SUMMER'S END IN 1891, MOONEY HAD RETURNED TO Washington to spend days poring over the voluminous correspondence about the Ghost Dance in government files.

Mooney's work often displayed a reporter's flair for investigation and story. In fact, he had been a newspaperman. His first job, starting at the age of twelve, had been as copyboy at the *Richmond Daily Palladium,* and as he grew older he occasionally reported for the paper, honing his craft as a storyteller. He left journalism after he finished high school, but as an ethnologist, he continued to pay attention to newspapers. Newspaper stories about the Ghost Dance had led him to Oklahoma, and on at least one occasion he would report on his own research in the *Daily Palladium*. At this point in his investigation, he became almost a kind of foreign correspondent, reporting from Indian country. In the fall of 1891, he once again set out from Washington, this time in a focused search for the Ghost Dance and its origins.

He disembarked first in Nebraska, at the Omaha and Winnebago reservation, primarily because it was on his route and he wanted to see if the Ghost Dance had had an impact there. Indeed, he reported, several Lakota Sioux from Pine Ridge had visited the reservation in April 1890 to share the teachings of the prophet. Another group of Dakota visitors from the Yankton Agency had relayed the same teachings. The Omaha and Winnebago, however, "put no faith in the story," Mooney reported.[35]

Aboard the train again, he journeyed northwest to Pine Ridge, intent on understanding the meaning of the religion among Lakotas. He had little luck. "I found the Sioux very difficult to approach on the subject," Mooney wrote. Where Southern Arapahos had reached out to the federal man in hopes of inscribing their understanding of the religion into the official record, Lakota believers had neither the ability nor the desire to speak with him.

Although the religion still had Lakota followers and secret Ghost Dances continued into 1892, Mooney could not discover the activity because no one dared speak about it. The army was still camped at Pine Ridge, the massacre was only a year old, and most of the religion's leaders—Short Bull, Kicking Bear, and twenty-one other Lakotas—remained in effective exile. Having been sent to an army fort after Wounded Knee as "hostages," most of them had now journeyed to Europe with Buffalo Bill's Wild West show. The Indian police were newly entrenched and supported by federal troops ringing the agency, and public talk about the religion remained taboo. For all anyone knew, the young man from Washington might be laying a trap for those foolish enough to answer his questions.[36]

Mooney characterized the most common response: "The dance was our religion, but the government sent soldiers to kill us on account of it. We will not talk any more about it." He told one Lakota believer that Arapahos had shared information and even invited him to join the dance. "Then don't you find that the religion of the Ghost dance is better than the religion of the churches?" rejoined the Ghost Dancer. When Mooney hesitated, the believer shut him down: "Well, then, if you have not learned that you have not learned anything about it." He refused to speak any longer.[37]

Those few Lakotas who agreed to talk with him had motivations that were the opposite of the Arapahos': most of them were opponents of the religion, and some presumably were eager to justify their role in suppressing it. American Horse was helpful, as was Ellis Standing Bear, a Brule Lakota who had been at Carlisle Indian Industrial School. Others were attached to either the Indian police or the army. One of Mooney's primary sources was George Sword, the police captain at Pine Ridge. His interpreters there included mixed-bloods Louis Menard, from the agency at Rosebud, and Philip Wells, the notorious translator for the army at Wounded Knee. Others included Santee Dakotas, who "looked with contempt on the beliefs and customs of their more primitive western brethren, between whom and themselves there was in consequence but little friendly feeling." The absence of testimony from actual Lakota Ghost Dancers would force Mooney to rely on these and other, even more problematic, sources in writing his book.[38]

Meanwhile, the silence at Pine Ridge was a wall that his inquiries could not surmount. With so few willing to speak with him, Mooney took photos at Wounded Knee—of the killing field and the mass grave with its four corner posts smeared in red paint.[39]

Mooney had noticed already a curious gap in the public narrative of the Ghost Dance troubles: for all the hysterical press coverage, not a single journalist had tracked down Wovoka, to whom he now referred—as Plains believers did—as the messiah. As Mooney later recalled, "The messiah was regarded as a myth, something intangible, to be talked about but not to be seen." It was time to find the prophet.[40]

Mooney had already written to C. C. Warner, the agent in charge of the main Paiute reservation at Pyramid Lake, to ask if he could photograph Wovoka. Warner discouraged him. He preferred to ignore the prophet for fear of lending him credibility, Warner wrote, and had in fact never seen the man. "I do not know as it will be possible to get a photo of him," the agent advised. Furthermore, he warned, there were no "ghost dances, songs, nor ceremonials" on any of the reservations he supervised. Warner's willful ignorance infuriated Mooney, who promptly made plans to go to Nevada.[41]

Another days-long, rattling transcontinental rail journey brought Mooney to Walker River Reservation, where officials informed him that Wovoka lived forty miles away in the settlement of Mason Valley. But the prophet's uncle, Charley Sheep, lived nearby. "He spoke tolerable—or rather intolerable—English," Mooney later recalled, so they did without a translator. But Sheep was suspicious. What was Mooney doing in Nevada? Keeping his Ghost Dance assignment quiet for the moment, Mooney explained that he was "sent out by the government to the various tribes to learn their stories and songs." He had gathered much from other tribes, and "now wanted to learn some songs and stories of the Paiute, in order to write them down so that white people could read them."[42]

Then he showed Sheep some photographs of "my Indian friends from across the mountains"—Black Coyote and other Arapahos and Cheyenne he had worked with in Oklahoma. Some of these men, Mooney knew, had recently visited Wovoka as disciples. Examining the photographs and recognizing the men, Sheep was quickly put at ease. For the next week, Mooney stayed in Sheep's lodge at Walker River. He and Sheep sang Paiute songs, Mooney collected Paiute stories, and they talked while the household bustled with the preparation of pine nut mush, the tending of children, and a visit from a Numu doctor who tended an ailing child.[43]

After a few days, Mooney cautiously broached the subject of the Ghost Dance. Sheep readily offered several songs and a description of the ritual. Mooney explained that as a Ghost Dancer himself, he hoped to meet the Messiah "and get from him some medicine-paint to bring back to his friends" among the Arapaho and Cheyenne. Sheep happily agreed to take him to see Wovoka.[44]

IT WAS ON A BRIGHT NEW YEAR'S DAY IN 1892 THAT MOONEY and Charley Sheep took the train and coach upriver to Mason Valley. In Greenfield (soon to be renamed Yerington), they met with storekeeper Ed Dyer, who knew Jack Wilson and who also spoke fluent Paiute. Dyer informed them that they could find Wovoka twelve miles away, near the mining town of Pine Grove, and agreed to go with them.[45]

After hiring a team and a buggy, Mooney headed into the Pine Grove Hills with Dyer and Sheep. The road was almost empty. Deep snow covered the ground (proof of the weather maker's magic, claimed Sheep from the driver's seat). The desert stretched around them vast and white and silent. Not long after setting out, they drove past a dance ground, the brush shelters heaped with new-fallen snow. After several miles, they saw a man off to one side of the road, standing with a gun over his shoulder. "I believe that's Jack now!" exclaimed Dyer. Sheep reined up and shouted to the man in Paiute. The man shouted back. It was Wovoka, hunting jackrabbits.[46]

As Wovoka approached, Mooney saw a young man with his hair trimmed square on a line below his ears. He was dark-skinned and "compactly built," but nearly six feet tall. He was also well dressed, wearing a broad-brimmed felt hat with a beaded ribbon under his chin and a good pair of boots. His face was open, dignified. "With a strong, hearty grasp," the prophet took the scientist's hand and asked what they needed.

Sheep explained Mooney's visit: He was sent by the government. He knew the Arapaho and Cheyenne disciples and would be seeing them again soon. He wanted an interview.

The prophet weighed the matter. He was loath to speak to non-Indians about the religion, but Mooney's standing as a federal agent appears to have given him pause. He spoke thoughtfully. He did not like to talk to the whites. Some of them had lied about him. At the same time, some of the Indians had disobeyed his instructions, "and trouble had come of it." Still, "as I was sent by Washington and was a friend of his friends, he would talk with me," Mooney later related. Just now, however, Wovoka was hunting. Mooney's party agreed to find the prophet at his camp that evening.

After shaking hands all around, the prophet returned to the chase. The party drove on to a nearby ranch, arriving at dusk. They ate a meal, then started through the dark desert, beneath a moonless sky, for Wovoka's camp.

A proud social scientist, Mooney was driven throughout his career by rational thinking and empirical evidence. He retained a high degree of respect for the beliefs of others, however, even when he found them naive or preposterous. He may not have believed in the religions of Indians, but he recognized in them a deep longing and a universal human pursuit of ancient mysteries. He was an ethnologist out to gather data, but he was also searching for an eminence—a mysterious person who had inspired the devotions of thousands of people. Thus, during his travels Mooney sometimes looked more like a disciple seeking the prophet than an objective social scientist in search of an interview.[47]

At no time did the journey seem more mysterious than that evening. After leaving the ranch house, the ethnologist and his party rattled through the sagebrush for an hour before Charley Sheep confessed that he was lost. With only a single lantern and the pale reflection from the mantle of snow, they had little hope of finding their way back to the ranch in the vast darkness. Unable to find the Indian trails amid the cattle tracks that crisscrossed the snow, they circled and doubled back again and again. Numerous times they thought they spotted lodges only to discover that they were snow-covered clumps of sagebrush, which loomed as big as houses in the night. The cold was bitter, and those in the party were approaching the limits of their endurance. They shouted repeatedly, and in the silence they listened in vain for an answering cry.[48]

Fending off panic, they formulated a new plan. Leaving Charley Sheep with the wagon, Dyer and Mooney fanned out along the cattle trails, shouting frequently to keep in touch with one another and avoid becoming lost. After traveling far enough to know that neither had hit the right trail, they returned to the wagon, moved it forward a short distance, and repeated the effort.

After some time, Sheep called out and the party regrouped in front of the wagon. Sheep said that he had heard something ahead of them. The party waited in silent suspense, peering into the darkness. A burst of sparks flew up into the starry sky. They had found the prophet.[49]

They entered the low doorway of Wovoka's lodge. This small home—ten feet wide and about eight feet high—was made from bundles of tules laid over a wooden frame, with the top open to the stars. In the center blazed a fire of sagebrush, and every now and then somebody threw a fresh piece of sage onto the fire and a shower of sparks rushed upward into the sky.

About half a dozen people sat or lay around the fire, including Wovoka, his wife, a boy who seemed to be about four—and of whom Wovoka seemed very fond—and a baby. Except for a few baskets, there was no furniture. All the Paiutes wore Western dress, but there were no pots or pans, nor any other sign that outside the lodge was a rapidly industrializing nation.

Mooney had only one night with Wovoka and had not had time to familiarize himself with the history of Paiute wage labor, or with their struggles amid drought and the collapse of the Nevada economy. Thus, he fitted them into a narrative of Indian decline. He described the tule lodge and its absence of modern implements as a sign of Paiutes "accept[ing] the inevitable while resisting innovation"— an interpretation that ran counter to the history of Numus generally and the Ghost Dance in particular. The "lodge" or *kana* was a temporary accommodation for the family while Wovoka worked and hunted nearby ranches. In reality, as we have seen, Paiutes were innovative and ambitious, and so especially was Wovoka, who would be one of the first in his community to move into a wooden frame house.[50]

Wovoka was friendly and asked Mooney again why he wanted an interview. Charley Sheep answered, but the conversation took a long while; Wovoka repeated everything his uncle said before answering, as if making sure he understood everything correctly. Knowing that this man was from the government, Wovoka knew that he had to choose his words carefully. The wrong communication could cause trouble. It helped, no doubt, that the prophet could trust his translator. Mooney observed that Wovoka and Dyer "seemed to be on intimate terms," and in fact the prophet and the storekeeper had known each other for years. Dyer had attended the miracle of the ice and many of Wovoka's gatherings, including at least one Ghost Dance. For Wovoka, if the right words, translated into English, found their way into print, actually preserving something of the gospel, the government might stop harassing him, his people, and his many believers.[51]

Prompted by Mooney, Wovoka recounted briefly the story of his life, and then they began to discuss his prophecy. Wovoka made it clear that he had had more than one revelation. The dance had appeared to him four years before, in 1887, and the visit to heaven came in 1889.

The prophet was adamant about what he had and had not seen in his trances. He was not responsible for the ghost shirts of the Sioux. When his people danced, they did not fall into trances, as Plains dancers did. And the prophet "earnestly repudiated any idea of hostility toward the whites, asserting that his religion was one of universal peace." In fact, he urged his people to "follow the white man's road and adopt the habits of civilization."[52]

And no, he was not Christ, no matter what any of his followers may have believed. Yes, he was a prophet who had received a divine revelation. He had been with God, a claim he made "as though the statement no more admitted of controversy than the proposition that 2 and 2 are 4." And indeed, God had given him complete control over the elements.[53]

At Mooney's prompting, Wovoka recounted his visit to heaven "when the sun died," which Mooney later fixed as the eclipse of January 1, 1889. The prophet asked after his disciples on the Plains, "particularly of the large delegation—about twelve in number—from the

Cheyenne and Arapaho, who had visited him the preceding summer and taken part in the dance with his people." When Mooney pulled out his photographs of the disciples, Wovoka relaxed considerably.[54]

Gesturing to his camera, Mooney requested a photograph of Wovoka. The prophet hesitated. No one had taken his picture before, he said, and he had even turned down an offer of $5 to allow himself to be photographed. (Perhaps he did not recall being photographed when he was a teenager.) But, he continued, he could see that Mooney was different. He came all the way from Washington to learn about the religion. Mooney's friendship with Ghost Dancers to the east satisfied Wovoka that he was a good man. He would sit for a picture—in return for $2.50 for himself and a like amount for each member of his family.

Wilson's eagerness to earn money from his image suggests just how modern and innovative he was, even if it did not change the ethnologist's view of the Paiutes as people who "accepted the inevitable while resisting innovation." Mooney balked at the price, offering Wovoka instead his standard per diem, "for his services as informant," and promising to send him a copy of the picture when it was finished. The prophet agreed.[55]

Mooney later claimed to have spent only part of that evening at the lodge, and then to have departed. But Ed Dyer later recalled multiple interviews over "many all day sessions, " and the party must have remained at least one night in or near Wovoka's lodge, because the photograph shows a daylight scene. In the back stands Charley Sheep, in a winter coat and a broad hat. Wovoka sits in the foreground, on a wooden chair of a kind that might have been found in a comfortable dining room (and seems to have come from the nearby Morgan ranch). He dressed carefully for his portrait, as if trying to send a message through the photograph. An eagle feather is lashed to his right upper arm with a bandana, and his right hand rests on his knee; with his left hand, he holds a broad-brimmed hat, also perched on his knee. (Mooney learned later that "the feather and the sombrero were important parts of his spiritual stock in trade.") Although they are outdoors, with snow piled around their feet, Wovoka wears what

FIGURE 12.2. Jack Wilson (seated) and Charley Sheep, January 2, 1892. Photo by James Mooney, National Anthropological Archives, Smithsonian Institution, GN-01659a.

appears to be a good suit of clothes, but without the jacket. His white shirt is covered only with a vest, and on his lower arms he wears calico sleeve covers, of the kind worn by workmen in his time. He sits at an oblique angle to the camera, staring straight ahead, into the distance. Except for the eagle feather inserted into his armband, he looks less like a dreamy prophet than an ambitious laborer, perhaps a store clerk just finished with his prayers, about to rise and go to work.[56]

After taking the photograph, Mooney prepared to leave. Wovoka gave him articles to show to his followers in Oklahoma: a rabbit-skin blanket, pine nuts, magpie tail feathers, and "some of the sacred red paint, endowed with the most miraculous powers, which plays so important a part in the ritual of the Ghost-dance religion." Then, "with mutual expressions of good will," the men parted ways. Charley Sheep went back to his reservation, and Mooney boarded the train for Indian Territory.[57]

MOONEY WAS UNPREPARED FOR WHAT HAPPENED NEXT. ON arriving back in Oklahoma, he was greeted as an emissary from the prophet. Cheyenne and Arapaho believers sought him out, "anxious to hear the report of my journey and see the sacred things that I had brought back from the messiah." Reports of his meeting with Jack Wilson circulated quickly. In groups and alone, men and women came to the ethnologist. One at a time, they took him by his right hand—the hand that had touched the prophet's hand—and intoned long prayers. Sometimes with lips moving silently and sometimes aloud, they implored the father to bring the new world soon, "with a petition that, as the speaker himself was unable to make the long journey, he might, by grasping the hand of one who had seen and talked with the messiah face to face, be enabled in his trance visions to catch a glimpse of the coming glory."[58]

They trembled while they prayed, and some wept. Often, before finishing, wrote Mooney, "the condition of the devotee bordered on the hysterical, very little less than in the Ghost Dance itself." All the while, others waited in quiet reverence for their turn. Standing amid small crowds of devoted Indians and at the front of a long line of supplicants, each waiting to grasp his hand and pray in hushed tones, Mooney soon became embarrassed. But as he put it, "until the story had been told over and over again there was no way of escape without wounding their feelings."[59]

To the faithful, the objects that Wovoka gave Mooney were also of special interest, and they asked to see them, especially the sacred red paint. The paint was in fact clay that Wovoka collected from Pine Grove. Grinding it and mixing it with water, Paiutes made it into elliptical cakes about six inches long. Paiute Ghost Dancers wore it in the ritual, and Wovoka gave it to all the disciples who visited. They in turn carried it back to their home reservations, where they mixed it with red paints of their own before sharing it with the dancers, for whom it facilitated health, long life, and better visions during the trance.[60]

For these reasons, Mooney was inundated with requests for small amounts of the paint, but he wanted to keep it for scientific sampling, so he was parsimonious. Eventually, however, his rationing failed. "My friends were very anxious to touch it," and each man who did rubbed it on his palms, "afterward smearing this dust on the faces of himself and his family." Mooney put the paint away.[61]

Even though the pine nuts he carried with him from Nevada were "not esteemed so sacred" as the red paint, they had a similar attraction. One evening the ethnologist visited the lodge of the Arapaho chief Left Hand to speak about "the Messiah and his country." In the circle around the tipi hearth, each of the adults took Mooney's hand and prayed. Afterward, Mooney gave them nuts, explaining that these were food among the Paiutes in Nevada. Left Hand shared his small portion of pine nuts with his wife, and the couple stood. Stretching out their hands to the northwest, "the country of the Messiah," they prayed long and earnestly to Hesunanin, "Our Father," asking that he bless them and their children through the "sacred food." They asked him to send the Messiah soon. The other men and women bowed their heads and listened, breaking in occasionally with appeals of their own to Hesunanin. Afterward, they divided the pine nuts and shared them among all present, even babies, "that all might taste of what to them was the veritable bread of life."[62]

Mooney had become more than a scientist or an interested white observer. He was now a powerful intermediary between the prophet and the faithful, with standing in some ways similar to that of a priest. Indeed, when he visited among the Northern Arapaho at Wind River the following year, many believers responded to him just as their Southern Arapaho kin had done. One man, enacting a ritual meant to bring on a trance immediately, approached with hands held out, "with short exclamations of hu!hu!hu!hu! as is sometimes done by the devotees about a priest in the Ghost Dance."[63]

Of course, Mooney was not a priest. He did not lead devotions. Still, if he was not a teacher of Wovoka's lessons, he discussed the prophet's words and their meaning with his Arapaho and Cheyenne friends, conveying a residue of the holiness with which Wovoka and his teachings were imbued. To the faithful, Mooney had shown himself to be at least as much a seeker as a scientist. By dancing with them, he had shared in their quest for renewal. But more than that, he had contributed to it. He had borne gifts from Wovoka himself.

In a sense, he had become an avatar of the prophet, and his very presence brought on shows of greater devotion and faith. Other delegates who returned from meetings with Jack Wilson may have met similar receptions, but in key ways the reaction to Mooney was different. He was an emissary not only to Wovoka but from Washington; it seems possible, even likely, that his status as a government man made his gifts from Wovoka all the more powerful. The Ghost Dance religion expanded as rapidly as it did in the aftermath of Wounded Knee in part because of the presence of a government agent who, at least as far as other believers could tell, embraced it. If a man from Washington could be so bold as to Ghost Dance in the aftermath of Wounded Knee, then perhaps they could feel safe in doing the same.

In the end, Mooney's dual standing as co-religionist and government agent led Indian believers to make him a kind of delegate for the religion in Washington. Soon after his return to Oklahoma from Nevada, he received a visit from several men who had gone out to meet Jack Wilson the previous summer. Black Short Nose, a Cheyenne evangelist, explained that the Cheyenne and Arapaho "were now convinced that I would tell the truth about their religion, and as they loved their religion and were anxious to have the whites know that it was all good and contained nothing bad or hostile they would now give me the message which the messiah himself had given to them, that I might take it back to show to Washington." Black Short Nose then drew "from a beaded pouch" the Messiah Letter, written in English by Caspar Edson, containing the message from Jack Wilson. On the back of the letter was another account of the same message, dictated after Edson's return by Black Short Nose to his daughter, a student at one of the government schools. When he returned to Washington that fall, Mooney took the letter to the Commissioner of Indian Affairs, Thomas Morgan, who thereby learned the words of the prophet from the Arapaho and Cheyenne evangelists: that Indians must not lie or steal, must keep the peace, and must work; that rain would come, and that Jesus was on earth. He presented Morgan with a copy, had another copy made for himself, and returned the original to Black Short Nose.[64]

Mooney journeyed to Oklahoma one last time before completing *The Ghost Dance Religion* in the fall of 1893. This time he brought with him a graphophone, a recording device, for the collection of Ghost Dance songs. The Caddos were still dancing.[65]

CHAPTER 13

WRITING *THE GHOST DANCE RELIGION AND SIOUX OUTBREAK OF 1890*

B<small>Y THE SUMMER OF</small> 1893, M<small>OONEY HAD BEGUN TO COMPOSE</small> his report in earnest. He finished it a year later, in 1894. *The Ghost Dance Religion and Sioux Outbreak of 1890* ultimately achieved vast influence, and today virtually every study of the religion (including this one) depends on it.

It was a book that came close to never being published. The manuscript sat on his employer's shelf for nearly two years before it went to press. The director of the Smithsonian Institution—in which the Bureau of Ethnology was housed—even asked to have it suppressed. The book would eventually be well received in many quarters, but its core arguments so offended powerful assimilationists that they would later seek revenge by derailing Mooney's career.

The controversy surrounding Mooney's Ghost Dance research would prove in keeping with his overall record. During his thirty-six years at the Bureau of Ethnology, James Mooney brought more unwanted attention to the institution than any other employee. He claimed always to be an objective scientist, but some authorities became increasingly uneasy about his apparent sympathies with "pagan" Indians, which, in their view, subverted the cause of assimilation. What first put his superiors on edge was his study of the Ghost Dance, in which he challenged the dominant anthropological theories of the day.[1]

Here we briefly turn away from the Ghost Dance to consider how white contemporaries interpreted it. Mooney's study—which I shall call *Ghost Dance Religion* for brevity's sake—did more than any other book and more even than the ongoing dances to shape how white America understood and remembered not only the Ghost Dance but also Wounded Knee and American conquest more broadly. This was both good and bad: Mooney got a great deal right, but he also got critical things wrong. To understand why, we need to learn how Mooney's relationship with official Washington became so troubled, because in the tensions between him and his superiors were born some of his key insights—and some of his errors.

In Washington, DC, the concern about Mooney's sympathies with Indians was symptomatic of the social distance between himself and the leaders of the agency where he worked. The Bureau of Ethnology bore more responsibility than any other institution of the time for turning anthropology into a professional discipline, but key investigators perpetuated a sense of the field as a gentlemanly avocation. The result was a workplace atmosphere that never quite suited Mooney, whose origins were decidedly humble.

Bureau staff included a considerable number who began their careers as amateurs and hobbyists of the sort who dominated Victorian science. Foremost among them was the director, John Wesley Powell. He loomed especially large in Mooney's career as a powerful father figure: he not only hired and mentored the younger man but had created the bureau in which they both worked. Ultimately, it was Powell's theories that Mooney rejected on the way to writing *Ghost Dance Religion*.

Raised in rural New York and Ohio, Powell lost an arm battling for the Union at Shiloh, but returned to combat. After the war, he briefly became a professor of biology in Illinois. In 1869, using his wartime connections to gain federal sponsorship and a great deal of newspaper attention, he set out on an expedition into the bone-jarring, gunwale-smashing rapids and mysterious chasms of the Grand Canyon. This expedition made him a darling of the mass press, who loudly proclaimed his leadership and daring, and other expeditions would follow. Powell's fame was such that Mooney had probably been hearing about him since boyhood, and his survey reports made major contributions to American geology and geography.[2]

It was anthropology that most attracted Powell, who devoted himself to researching Indians during his travels in the Colorado River country. Afterward, he assumed a leading position in the intellectual movement to advance the field. In 1879 he persuaded Congress to found the Bureau of Ethnology as a center for anthropological research. He argued the need to coordinate anthropological research with the assimilation of Indians, but his ambitions were larger still, extending to broad social reform.[3]

Powell exemplified an intellectual elite who had grown increasingly troubled by a world in which effects seemed ever more remote from their causes and doubts were mounting regarding the ability of Providence alone to guarantee national success. One could extol the "Progress" that had brought into being the globalized, industrialized, and networked world, but its harsh realities included sequential financial emergencies that had combined with the tenuous condition of the new laboring classes and the rising curve of immigration to bring social strife to dangerous levels.

Amid these crises, the nation's leaders found themselves mostly unable to explain what was happening or predict what would happen next. Like Indian religious and political leaders in the Far West, they were afflicted by a crisis of authority, although of a very different kind. Powell, like many others of his class, hoped that an increasingly chaotic world could be controlled by apprehending and analyzing social organization and human development. The decades after the Civil War had seen the development not only of modern anthropology but also psychology, economics, sociology, and political science, as well as the modern professional field of history. The insights of these disparate but related fields of inquiry would radically remake how

Americans talked and thought about their country and the world. Indeed, their emergence marked a divide between nineteenth-century thought and the social analysis that would characterize the twentieth century.[4]

Powell was at the vanguard of this intellectual revolution. Under his direction, the Bureau of Ethnology soon emerged as the world's leading center for anthropology, helping to transform the field from a hobby of leisured adventurers into a salaried and meritocratic profession with standards enforced by peer review. It was the possibility of earning a regular wage in the conduct of anthropological research that first brought James Mooney to the door of Powell's Washington office.[5]

For all its professionalism, Mooney was never an easy fit in that office. Socially, it must have been intimidating to him: if the bureau was not a gentlemen's club, to Mooney at times it felt like one. The members of Powell's inner circle and his own standing as the revealer of Colorado River mysteries retained for the agency something of the romance of the era's great explorers. Among the founding ethnologists whom Mooney worked with were old friends of Powell's such as Colonel Garrick Mallery. A descendant of Puritan colonists, Mallery graduated from Yale and became a Philadelphia lawyer before joining the Union Army in 1861. He was wounded, captured, exchanged, and returned to the front during the war, and afterward he served in the army in Dakota Territory. There he took up what became a remarkable study of Indian pictographic writing and sign language. Forced out of military service by his aching wounds, he joined his old comrade Powell at the Bureau of Ethnology and labored at his landmark sign language study until his death in 1894.[6]

Mallery was Powell's good friend, but the director's favorite subordinate was Frank Hamilton Cushing. Born sickly in 1857, Cushing showed a childhood devotion to Indian studies. But Cushing also had a well-to-do father who financed his research in hopes that it would improve his health. Having published his first paper on Indian artifacts at the age of seventeen, by the time he was twenty Cushing had dropped out of Cornell University to become a curator at the

Smithsonian Institution, where he lived in the castle towers like some brilliant madman in the attic. Vain and eccentric, he came to the attention of Powell, who brought Cushing into his bureau. Eventually becoming almost like an adopted son to the old soldier, Cushing even "summered" with Powell in Maine, where they paddled the inlets and surveyed shell middens together.[7]

At the bureau, Cushing made his name by going out to western New Mexico and pioneering a form of research that became known as "participant-observation." He submerged himself for years in the culture of the Zuni, ascended to membership in the highly secretive Bow Society, and, by some accounts, lost touch with reality. By the end of his research, he considered himself a "full-blown Indian," and the story is told that he once showed up at an anthropological meeting wearing Zuni regalia. (Powell told him to go home and get dressed.)[8]

Powell, Cushing, and Mallery all hailed from the same social class, what one historian has called "American gentry": while not necessarily wealthy, they were well off, they attended college, they were mostly northeastern by birth, and their religious views were liberal or even eccentric. This was the class that dominated the push for social science and pioneered most of its innovations.[9]

They were also, in the parlance of our own time, "connected." They came from the same places and went to the same schools as many Gilded Age industrialists and financiers. Even if the gentry often disapproved of corporate excesses and sought to ameliorate their effects through new social policies (undergirded by the new social sciences), their own friends and associates included these financiers, railroad presidents, and factory owners, who bankrolled expeditions and endowed colleges, universities, and museums.[10]

These men of means were also on the make, out to advance their own standing. In 1878 Powell led this cohort in founding the Cosmos Club, the capital's first elite society devoted to literature and the arts. The next year, in 1879, he led the creation of the Anthropological Society of Washington (which eventually became the American Ethnological Society), and from these two associations many joined him in founding the National Geographic Society in 1888. Together

Powell and his circle played a not inconsequential role in transforming muddy, malarial Washington into a cosmopolitan city renowned not only as the nation's capital but also as an important center of intellectual life.[11]

Mooney arrived in the spring of 1885, seeking a position by walking into the bureau offices in the Hooe Iron Building on F Street. By then, the same address was home to the US Geological Survey, and John Wesley Powell had become director of both the bureau and the survey. From his corner office, he commanded the nation's most vigorous and influential scientific center, one that was bigger, better funded, and more active than any university science program of the time.[12]

PERHAPS IT WAS IN THAT CORNER OFFICE THAT POWELL MET with Mooney. Wherever they met, the two men who faced one another that spring day shared a fascination with Indians, but they had arrived at that interest from radically different starting points that could never be reconciled completely.

Part of the difference was generational: Mooney was almost three decades younger than Powell. Although he was undoubtedly attracted by the romance of Victorian anthropology embodied by Powell himself, Mooney was drawn to Washington primarily by the systematic study that the old explorer had helped launch, and by the nexus of budding professional associations and clubs he had founded.

But James Mooney could never quite join the intellectual constellations that orbited Powell. He was never close to the old man in the way Mallery was. He was younger than Cushing, but never benefited from Powell's fatherly interest. He was not invited to Maine, and he did not join the Cosmos Club. Mooney was never connected. At the bureau where he worked for more than three decades, he remained a perpetual outsider.

It would be easy enough to blame all this on Mooney's personal bearing. Compared to the larger-than-life personalities of Powell and the other gentry, Mooney seems reserved, both in his correspondence, which was occasionally dyspeptic, and in photographs. As a

FIGURE 13.1. James Mooney, ca. 1900. National Anthropological Archives, Smithsonian Institution, 02862900.

younger man, he wore his hair long, like Byron, but in later photographs he looks severe. He was a less public figure than his colleagues at the bureau, perhaps because he could afford to be: the newfound professional standing of his field allowed him to trade less in personal connections to make his way in the capital, as Powell and especially Cushing did, and to rely more on publication of his findings. Mooney was also a fiercely private man. He left no collection of papers in any archive beyond the reports and official correspondence that remained the property of his employer. We know little about his decades-long marriage or his views on anything except anthropology. In the most famous photograph of him, he looks almost businesslike, his eyes burning with an intensity hinting at some inner struggle.

That struggle may well have arisen from Mooney's intellectual positions, especially his apparent disregard for Powell's own social theories, which unsettled his superiors. Powell was a dedicated patrician, with enlightened views for his day. He abhorred social Darwinism. Like other intellectuals after the Civil War, he hoped for a society that would transcend racial division. To his mind, the key to understanding modern society hinged on older theories of social evolution, which held that certain stages of social development were universal and that all peoples, no matter how "savage," could reach the advanced stage of civilization that white Americans and Europeans enjoyed. Powell believed that anthropology was a tool toward this end: it could inform those developmental processes, showing elites how to understand and guide unruly, colonized peoples and working classes from savagery and barbarism into benevolent civilization. He was particularly interested in religion and myth, which he saw as providing keys to "the primitive mind" that would allow the assimilation of exotic peoples into the single, benevolent world civilization that he believed would one day emerge. "To study men," Powell once wrote, "we have to study mind, and to study human evolution we are compelled to study the development of the mind."[13]

More than anything else, in Powell's view, assimilation required a revolution in thought for which Indians could be prepared only through long tutelage by white benefactors—especially in matters of religion. Adapting older ideas of social evolution to the study of religion, he maintained that all religions advanced in stages from primitive, animistic beliefs—"the lowest and earliest stage" when "everything is a god"—to civilized, monotheistic faith, which developed only with a strong dose of the morality that was assumed to evolve with civilization. To him, religions at the earlier stages of development were clearly inferior—if they were religion at all. "Religion, in this stage of theism, is sorcery," Powell maintained. Moreover, for religions moving from lower stages to higher ones, "the way is long, for evolution is slow." To Powell, true monotheism featured "a god whose essential characteristics were moral qualities" and emerged only when "the moral qualities are held in highest regard in the minds of the men."[14]

This theory of religious development as a kind of upward ladder guided the ethnologists at Powell's bureau, and similar ideas would exert a powerful hold on anthropology into the early decades of the twentieth century, when they finally began to fade. The decline of social evolutionary thought was long attributed primarily to the work of Franz Boas, the "Father of American Anthropology," the scholar who, after his appointment at Columbia in 1896, trained graduate students to think less in terms of race and civilization than of co-existing "cultures" to be evaluated on their own terms rather than in terms of comparative "advancement." The push against cultural evolution, however, had begun earlier, and a key locus was the Bureau of Ethnology, where Mooney's anthropological work was instrumental. Mooney had tried to use Powell's model from time to time, but in truth he had little use for rigid ideas of stages in human development. It was partly his rejection of conventional thought that allowed his work on the Ghost Dance to stand out—and attracted to himself considerable controversy.

Mooney's ambivalence toward theories of social evolution stemmed not merely from brash impatience or a personality quirk, but in part from differences in biography. Unlike his colleagues, most of them relatively educated, well-heeled insiders, Mooney was a son of poor Irish immigrants, and he had never been to college. Self-conscious about his descent from a people who were uprooted by colonialism and widely derided in the United States and England as "savages," Mooney cultivated an identity, a politics, and an anthropology that can best be understood as neither strictly Irish nor "American," but Irish-American. Not surprisingly, he would soon enter into a problematic relationship with the "progress of civilization" in whose service Powell professed to labor and for which he had created the bureau.

For if the social sciences in this period were largely the invention of a gentry class, the members of this class were not simply Americans but primarily Anglo-Americans. The science of assimilation was a highly colonial program, and the social models on which it depended emanated from colonizing powers, especially the United States and England. In this milieu, Mooney was something of a gate-crasher. He was one of the first anthropologists whose worldview was shaped by a family that had been at least as colonized in the Old World as it was colonizer in the New.

JAMES MOONEY WAS BORN IN 1861. HIS FATHER, JAMES Mooney Sr., hailed from County Meath, north of Dublin. According to family legend, in Ireland the senior Mooney traipsed the byways as an itinerant teacher of Irish history, poetry, music, and language. It was an outlaw occupation, banned by the British Crown, which sought to Anglicize the Irish by forcing upon them, along with political subservience, the English language, English history, and the Anglican Church.

James Mooney Sr., met his wife Ellen Devlin, in County Meath. The couple immigrated to the United States in 1852, after surviving nearly a decade of suffering and upheaval in the Potato Famine. They lived briefly in New York, then moved to Richmond, Indiana, where the scholar of Eire spent his remaining days as a ditch digger. The Mooneys had two daughters, and then their first son, James Jr., was born in 1861. But James Sr. sickened and died within months of the boy's arrival.[15]

Although their skin may have been the same color as that of other northern Europeans, cultural prejudice and a history of colonization kept Irish people from ever quite becoming white in the nineteenth-century United States. To the English and most Americans, the Irish Celts were like Indians: indolent, unclean, licentious pagans incapable of civilization or real Christianity. When the Potato Famine brought catastrophic rates of death and migration that cut the Irish population by half, some English anticipated that their colonists would replace the Irish in Ireland just as Americans had supplanted Indians. "In a few more years, a Celtic Irishman will be as rare in Connemara as is the Red Indian on the shores of Manhattan," crowed *The Times* of London. Consequently, most Irish who emigrated, including James

Mooney's parents, saw themselves as exiles from the country of their birth, which was being effectively recolonized by a regime that aimed for their extermination.[16]

In its time, the famine migration was the largest pulse of non-English humanity ever to reach the United States, dwarfing even the slave trade. Between 1845 and 1855, over 1.5 million Irish arrived, announcing the birth of the mass immigration and global migration that would define the modern era.[17]

Anti-Irish hostility grew with this influx of impoverished, starving migrants. Americans mixed critiques of the "Celtic" race with anti-Catholicism and racialized the newcomers as "savages" and "white Negroes." Nativist anti-Irish riots convulsed Philadelphia in the 1840s, and anti-Irish sentiment abounded as the Civil War approached. "The great majority of the American people are, in heart and soul anti-Catholic, but more especially anti-Irish," wrote one emigrant in 1860. "Everything Irish is repugnant to them." Thus, far from being dissipated by the experience of migration, Irish identities were galvanized as their claims to white privilege were, at best, grudgingly acknowledged by a society that defined them as "ambiguously white."[18]

Barely four decades after his parents arrived in the United States, James Mooney's scholarship would push the boundaries of acceptance for the nation's growing religious diversity. His classic book on the Ghost Dance, along with his subsequent forays into Peyote scholarship, effectively urged a reversal of assimilation policy and acceptance of disparate ways of believing. His work might be read as a response to anxieties about the growing non-Protestant populations in the United States, particularly the Catholic and Jewish communities that grew in the age of mass migration. While the nation cried out for rapid assimilation of these immigrants, James Mooney's own family history and his scholarship on Indian religions would make him deeply suspicious of that social model.

But as much as culture contributed to Mooney's development into an intellectual outsider, another important influence was his childhood experience of poverty; his ideas grew from his experience not only of ethnicity or race but also of class. His contemporaries at the bureau included Jeremiah Curtin, an Irish American Catholic who shared with Mooney a dedication to Irish lore but very little else. Curtin's family migrated before the famine. Wealthy enough to attend Harvard and travel the world, Curtin was part anthropologist and part cultural gadfly, and a much better fit with the gentry adventurers who surrounded Powell than Mooney, who grew up under much more trying circumstances.[19]

Reared as an Irish nationalist, Mooney became skeptical early on about "civilizing" projects. Ellen Mooney raised her children in a kind of dual nationality—as patriotic Americans, to be sure, but with a profound devotion to Irish history, literature, and music. Young James Mooney proved a bookish child who read the volumes in the small family library and became a rapt listener to his mother's tales of the distant homeland and its glories, now sullied by English oppression. He learned the meaning of "the wearin' of the green" and heard the saga of the long Irish struggle to escape the English boot. Born to exiles who did not retreat from their culture in a new land so much as try to salvage it, Mooney rose to fame, fittingly enough, as what today is called a "salvage ethnologist." He was a scholar who sought to record authentic Indian lore in texts and procure genuine artifacts for museums against the eventual development that almost all white people expected: the disappearance of Indians themselves.[20]

Becoming an ethnologist was no easy feat. In the heartland of an anti-Irish nation, and in the wake of the death of its patriarch, the Mooney family struggled. Ellen Mooney supported her three children as a domestic worker, keeping house and taking in laundry. Her son, slight and sickly, had a congenital heart condition that would weaken him all his life.[21]

In these boyhood years, James Mooney was an inveterate compiler of lists. He kept a list of all the sewing machines ever made, and perhaps drawn to the colorful advertisements featuring firefighters and flaming buildings, he began a list of all the insurance companies in existence. At the age of eight, he began compiling what he intended to be a list of all the books ever published.

His next list would change his life. By Mooney's own account, when he was twelve, in 1873, after the Modoc War broke out in California, he heard somebody remark that "every little Indian war brought to light another tribe that no one had ever heard of before." This comment inspired him to begin compiling a list of every Indian tribe.[22]

This explanation of his Indian list is simple and unaffected, but it suggests an important connection between his Irish origins and his later interests. When it erupted, the Modoc War was a media sensation, and it occasioned a great deal of blood-curdling commentary in the nation's press, demanding revenge and extermination, after the Modocs' Captain Jack shot and killed General Edward Canby during a peace negotiation. Some Irish Americans joined this dreadful chorus for, as Fintan O'Toole has observed, "the wounded pride of the Irish dispossessed often found a salve in the joy of dominating others." Many embraced their Celtic racial distinctiveness essentially by claiming not so much to be as white as the English as to be more white—and therefore more entitled to subjugate blacks, Indians, and Chinese. In 1863, in response to the Union Army draft, the Irish of New York City rose up in a vast lynch mob threatening anyone of color and murdering many African Americans as well as Chinese and even some Indians. In California in the 1870s, the demagoguery of the Irish immigrant Denis Kearney energized lynch mobs of the anti-Chinese movement. Many Irish joined the US Army in the West, where they waged war on Indians. In 1863—the same year as the draft riots—an Irish immigrant officer named Patrick Connor led US troops in a massacre of a Shoshone village at Bear River, Idaho. Others flocked to the brutal militia outfits that slaughtered Indians by the score—and were less frequently slaughtered in turn. When Numu warriors bloodied Nevada militias in the Paiute War of 1860, the bodies of Irish immigrants lay among the dead.[23]

But among Irish American intellectuals, there was also a contrary opinion, one given voice by a prominent Irish immigrant and newspaperman, John Boyle O'Reilly. As editor of the *Boston Pilot*,

O'Reilly held forth against the Modoc War as an American parallel
to the English subjugation of Ireland. "We have too much and too
old a sympathy with people badly governed, to join in this shame-
ful cry for Modoc blood," wrote O'Reilly. "We grant that they have
committed murder, and that they are unstable, treacherous, and dangerous. Who would not be so, with the robberies and outrages of
generations boiling in their blood?"[24]

Young James Mooney may have read Boyle's column. The *Pilot* was the nation's most widely read Irish immigrant newspaper; a
beacon of Irish nationalism, it was a standard community resource
in scattered Irish ghettos and gathering places. But whether or not
he read the *Pilot* (indeed, it may not have been available in Richmond's small Irish community of fewer than 1,000 immigrants) is
less important than its bright line of dissent in matters of race and
conquest from the fiercely anti-black, anti-Chinese sentiments that
had become something of an Irish American tradition. Dissenters
like O'Reilly identified the Irish as a people who had a history too
much like that of Indians to happily abide their extermination. Indeed, O'Reilly's position turned sympathy for Indians into an expression of Irish liberty and nationalism.[25]

Such sentiments reflected a persistent strain in Irish thought
that ran against the era's mania for progress. The startling economic
growth of western Europe and the United States in the nineteenth
century inspired a pervasive triumphalism about the course of industrialism and human advancement. But the sentiment had less purchase in Ireland, where fortunes tumbled. Alone among the nations
and former nations of western Europe, Ireland, afflicted by the famine and impoverished by Britain's trade policy, saw its population
decline precipitously in the second half of the nineteenth century.
(Indeed, to this day Ireland has not recovered its pre-famine population levels.) This bitter experience made Irish people deeply and
abidingly skeptical not only about empire but about the "progress"
claimed by its supporters. From the Irish perspective, the wonders
of industrialism, mechanization, and colonialism often seemed more
destructive than benevolent.[26]

Thus, in the very years that Mooney's career as an anthropologist unfolded, a tradition of Irish and Irish American opposition to US empire would mature, even if only among a few commentators. Irish nationalists in the United States such as Patrick Ford, editor of *The Irish World,* and James Jeffrey Roche, who assumed the helm of the *Boston Pilot* after O'Reilly's death, became prominent opponents of US overseas expansion in the Philippines and Puerto Rico. To the jingoists who took up President William McKinley's call for "benevolent assimilation" of Filipinos and Puerto Ricans, Roche answered, "The 'White Man's Burden' . . . is never so heavy that he cannot carry it out the door or window of the house he has just burglarized." On these questions, leading Irish nationalists not only extolled the cause of a free Irish nation but expressed deep doubts about the continuing expansion of American territory, which mimicked too much, in their view, the British Empire. For all the participation of Irish immigrants in the Indian Wars, the US dispossession of Indians allowed Mooney to craft a critique of conquest and colonization that spoke partly to his own nationalism and also underscored a broader cultural skepticism toward progress and its blandishments that had long percolated among Irish people.[27]

We may say that Mooney developed what the African American intellectual W. E. B. Du Bois in 1897 called a "double-consciousness": a sense that he was both an American and something else, the product of a very different history and a different identity. How early Mooney developed this consciousness is hard to say, but it seems likely that it first arose in his boyhood, when his sense of his own Irishness shaped his emerging appreciation of Indians.[28]

MOONEY CULTIVATED HIS INTEREST IN INDIANS NOT ONLY WITH a skeptical sensibility about the supremacy of white civilization but despite a complete absence of teachers or encouragement—or even time to read. With his family in financial straits, he moved through a series of jobs, and his education ended with high school. For a brief period he taught school, and then, at the age of twenty-one, he became a reporter and editorial writer for the *Richmond Independent.*[29]

Outside of work, he took up a rigorous study of Indian history that would profoundly affect the course of his life and that developed—in its orientation to questions of Irish history and politics—in creative tension with dominant trends in anthropology. Mooney would be preoccupied with Ireland's struggle for independence throughout his life, and the final decades of that fight were taking place just as he began working in anthropology. At the age of eighteen, he began a lifelong advocacy of Irish home rule and also founded a chapter of the Irish Land League to raise money for the struggling tenants who still comprised half the population of Ireland. By that time, he had for two years been constructing a map of North America on which he located each Indian tribe in its historic homeland. He hoped eventually to expand this into a map of the hemisphere, showing the lands of every Indian people with the boundaries of their original territories and the treaty cessions made by each. Although this larger goal was never realized, by his early twenties the map took up six square feet. Thus, the politics of land and its loss overlay his work with Irish and Indians alike, connecting the two experiences of conquest.[30]

At times, Ireland's political questions could become uncomfortably personal: as late as 1899, Mooney would still be receiving requests from relatives in Ireland for help in paying rent. As he wrote his classic work on the Ghost Dance and other research articles in Indian ethnology in the 1890s and early 1900s, he joined the international effort to revive the Irish language, founding the Washington chapter of the Gaelic Society in 1907 and serving as its first president. He read widely in Irish social science, corresponded with founders of Ireland's newly created National Museum of Science and Art, and journeyed to Ireland, returning with a pot of earth dug from the Hill of Tara. Mooney befriended the founder of the Gaelic revival movement, the literary scholar Douglas Hyde, hosting him on a visit to the Bureau of Ethnology in 1906. (In 1938, Hyde would become the first president of the Irish Republic.)[31]

GROWING UP IRISH CATHOLIC IN A FIERCELY PROTESTANT America had burned the grievances of religious minorities into

Mooney's heart, but his religious and intellectual sensibilities also were shaped by his exposure to nonconformist belief. In Indiana, the population was overwhelmingly Methodist (a denomination with no great love for Catholics), but his home city of Richmond had been founded by Quakers. Indeed, by the time Ellen and James Mooney arrived there, it was home to the largest Quaker meeting in the world. As a young man, Mooney frequented the library of Earlham College, a Quaker institution with a reading room open to the public. The tolerance and missionary traditions of the Quakers gave him his first direct connections to Indians. There were a handful of Indian students at the college, and the Richmond Quakers were involved in opening schools among the Eastern Cherokee of North Carolina in 1880.[32]

It was in the Earlham College library that Mooney most likely first came across the thick green volumes embossed with a gold seal that announced the annual reports of Powell's newly founded Bureau of Ethnology. Perusing the wide-ranging articles by bureau researchers in those volumes, Mooney would have learned about the agency's mission "to organize anthropologic research in America."[33]

Beginning in 1882, young James Mooney began writing to the bureau, requesting a job. But repeated applications failed to elicit an offer. After three years of rejection, Mooney ventured to Washington on his own resources and presented himself at the bureau. Powell was impressed by the research the young man brought with him. Of particular interest was the newest iteration of Mooney's boyhood list of Indian tribal names, which he had now organized into an "Indian Synonymy," a catalog of cross-referenced tribal names for making sense of sources in Indian history that were often contradictory. The Zuni, for example, were also known in some sources as the Ahsheewai, the Pawnee were in various places known as the Apenanae, and the term "Blackfoot" was used to describe two completely different and linguistically distinctive peoples. Among researchers, this welter of tribal names sowed confusion and error. Powell himself had directed his employees to make a list to clarify these matters. Now, struck by the fact that this young man had accomplished the task almost without resources, the director hired him and ordered immediate publication of the synonymy.[34]

But in achieving his cherished goal—a paying job in ethnology—Mooney had also launched himself down an awkward career path. For the next thirty-six years, he would attempt simultaneously to hone a critique of assimilation and to advance his career in a bureaucracy dedicated to assimilating Indians. To meet the demands of the latter, he sometimes articulated views that veered close to the era's characteristic white supremacy. But at the same time, his willingness to identify with Indians and his admiration for Indian artistry, literature, and especially religion put him at odds with many assimilationists.

In his first five years at the bureau, Mooney researched Eastern Cherokee medicine, but he also published ethnography of Irish medicine, holidays, and funerary rites. His intellectual investigation of the struggles of his two great protagonists, the Irish and the Indians, led him to cast each in terms of the other. For his entire career he spoke of being in favor of "home rule"—for Indians and for Irish alike.[35]

He also constantly compared their cultural attributes. On at least one occasion during field research in North Carolina, Cherokee healers explained that they could reveal medicine secrets only to those who could offer secret healing arts in return. Mooney persuaded at least one of these Cherokee consultants to exchange his secrets for Irish incantations and spells that Mooney had learned among Irish immigrants. He devoted days of labor to translating the medicine books of Cherokee healers, not because he thought them scientifically valid, but because to him they were literary expressions of religion and philosophy. "So far from being a jumble of crudities," he wrote, "there is a wonderful completeness about the whole system which is not surpassed even by the ceremonial religions of the East."[36]

Mooney seldom if ever wrote about his personal experience, and he seems never to have discussed his family's assimilation in print. But it is clear that he was suspicious of social evolution and its hierarchies of achievement, no doubt in part because his own talent and expertise belied it. Even as he began his career at the bureau, he presented Irish people in his articles on Irish traditions as being at least as sophisticated and capable as the English. If they had not risen as far as fast, it was because the English had kept them in a state of bondage that undermined their many achievements. In Mooney's view, the Irish, a people of "peculiarly spiritual temper," had been a beacon of learning and piety throughout the Dark Ages, until their conquest by the English. He maintained that the imperial expansion of "civilized" nations was in fact a force for savagery; in snuffing the lamps of learning in Ireland and keeping her people in intellectual darkness, conquest had not advanced social evolution, but retarded it.[37]

This might be where science most gave way to spirit and the Romantic tradition in James Mooney's intellect. For in his view, his advantage as an ethnologist lay not in any theory of race or culture that he could advance to replace Powell's model and reveal Indian cultures in new ways, but in the mystical legacies of his Celtic ancestry, which gave him unique insights. Being a member of the Celtic race gave him a quality he believed most Anglo-Americans could not share.

He kept such romantic notions largely to himself. But clues to its importance can be seen in his passing reference to the "peculiarly spiritual temper" of the Irish and in his remarks about Washington Matthews, an Irish-born ethnologist and close friend who died in 1905. In his admiring obituary, Mooney attributed much of Matthews's scholarly success to the "spiritual vision which was his Keltic inheritance"; that vision allowed him to "look into the soul of primitive things and interpret their meaning." From an early age, Mooney seems to have believed that he possessed the same talents.[38]

And already, along these lines, in his early days at the Bureau of Ethnology, a fissure had opened between Powell and Mooney. Powell believed that the mental worlds of "savage" peoples were so completely different from those of civilized people that the two were fundamentally incompatible. Only a long period of assimilation would allow the primitive to become modern. By contrast, Mooney, who saw the "savage" Irish as modern, could question the "savagery" of Cherokees by comparing them to Irish. In direct contrast to Powell, Mooney's studies questioned whether there was any difference at all between the thought processes of peoples, be they primitive or modern.

AND IT WAS THIS CHARACTERISTIC OF HIS EARLY WORK—HIS willingness to compare Irish and Indian beliefs in ways that beggared ideas of racial superiority—that would trigger so much suspicion of his Ghost Dance study. In his book about the new religion, Mooney's writing hearkened to his Irish roots while it displayed his profound sympathy with believers. To him, the Ghost Dance represented no "craze," no primitive "superstition" but rather an expression of universal human longing. "The wise men tell us the world is growing happier—that we live longer than did our fathers, have more of comfort and less of toil, fewer wars and discords, and higher hopes and aspirations," he began. "So say the wise men; but deep in our own hearts, we know they are wrong."[39]

Mooney situated Ghost Dancers in global patterns of belief; in an approach he had first explored in his Irish writings, he makes almost no references in *Ghost Dance Religion* to stages of civilization or the evolutionary development of religion. All religions, in his view, shared certain attributes. "What tribe or people has not had its golden age, before Pandora's box was loosed, when women were nymphs and dryads and men were gods and heroes?" he asks. On the first page, he draws connections to the Irish, invoking the legendary warrior-king of the Celts who, according to legend, would rise from the dead to cast out the hated Anglo-Saxons: "And when the race lies crushed and groaning beneath an alien yoke, how natural is the dream of a redeemer, an Arthur, who shall return from exile or awake from some long sleep to drive out the usurper and win back for his people what they have lost." In a daring repudiation of the evolutionary view of religion that predominated at the bureau, Mooney dispenses with hierarchies of "savage" and "civilized" to compare religious traditions in new ways: "The doctrines of the Hindu avatar, the Hebrew Messiah, the Christian millennium, and the Hesunanin of the Indian Ghost Dance are essentially the same, and have their origin in a hope and longing common to all humanity."[40]

From this beginning, Mooney synthesizes the development of the Ghost Dance with the history of Indian uprisings, from the Pueblo

Revolt of 1680 to Pontiac's Rebellion in 1763, and on to Tecumseh's grand effort to unify the tribes of the Mississippi River Valley in the first decade of the nineteenth century. All these pan-Indian uprisings began with prophecies of an Indian world redeemed and remade; all required a return by believers to the old ways and a casting aside of the implements and religion of their white conquerors. The Shawnee prophet had even promised that his followers would be bulletproof.[41]

We can learn as much from the examples Mooney left off this list as from the ones he included. Among the notable omissions was the visionary religion of the Seneca chief Handsome Lake, who led one of the most successful Indian religious revivals and whose history Mooney undoubtedly knew. (The Bureau of Ethnology in fact archived various versions of Handsome Lake's teachings.) In 1799, Handsome Lake had received a series of divine revelations that inspired a reworking of Seneca spirituality in what became known as the Handsome Lake Religion, or the Longhouse. The new church encouraged temperance, farming, marital fidelity, the avoidance of witchcraft, and other paths to right living, in anticipation of a millennial deliverance from earthly tribulation. The Longhouse, in other words, could be seen as a fore-runner of the Ghost Dance. Both religions sought to allow believers to make measured accommodation to their conquerors while preserving a core of Indian belief and ceremony.[42]

Mooney may have left the Handsome Lake religion off his list because, in key ways, it did not fit his evidence. The Seneca still practiced the Longhouse religion in 1890 (indeed, it would have thousands of followers even in the early twenty-first century), and he may have ignored it for this very reason. For although he was sympathetic to Ghost Dancers and to Indians generally, he could not imagine them persisting as Indians for very long into the future. One of Powell's most powerful arguments in founding the Bureau of Ethnology had been that Indian languages and all that distinguished them were on the verge of disappearing without being recorded. Belief in the "vanishing Indian" was what inspired Mooney and other ethnologists of the period, who saw themselves as archivists of Indian ways that would soon exist only in history. At this stage in Mooney's career, he had no way of conceiving that Indians could continue to create new, authentic Indian religions that would help them persist as Indians. For him as for practically every other ethnologist, such achievements were literally unimaginable. In the Ghost Dance story he was telling, the new religion had to fail, just as its believers would have to accept their ultimate disappearance.

Thus, Mooney scripted this tragic story of inevitable Indian failure by comparing the Ghost Dance to other failed religious movements that culminated with uprisings that failed. This selection criterion led him to make key errors in analyzing the Ghost Dance. Foremost among them was his projection of militancy and nativism as central attributes of the new religion. To a degree, he endorsed the popular assumptions about the religion held by most white observers, who interpreted all Indian religions as frantic attempts to return to the past. As a result, he oversimplified a complicated Ghost Dance practice that underscored certain indigenous traditions but also embraced innovation to create new forms of Indianness for the reservation era.

To be sure, nativism appeared in the Ghost Dance in some places. In 1891, Mooney reported that Arapahos were "bringing out costumes not worn in years" because it was "a part of the doctrine" that "they must discard as far as possible everything white man." In being grafted onto earlier religious movements, like the Dream Dance, that had promised a return of the old ways, the Ghost Dance teachings of Wovoka were certainly invested with some degree of nativist longing. Moreover, the ritual's visions of the old life and trance reunions with ancestors helped revive older traditions of dance and ceremony.[43]

But at the same time, Ghost Dancers eschewed the trappings of white society for reasons that had little to do with rejecting the implements of white people. Among Lakotas, no person could enter the circle wearing anything made of metal, an old ritual proscription meant to ensure that no knives or guns found their way into a ceremony of peace. But other items of Western manufacture were proudly displayed, even if white eyewitnesses, captivated by the romance of Indian nativism, frequently dismissed them as unimportant. For example, Mrs. Z. A. Parker, a witness at Pine Ridge, described how Indians in the Ghost Dance "discarded everything they could which was made by the white man" shortly after observing that some of the women dancers wore expensive manufactured clothing, "beautiful brocades, and others costly shawls," purchased with wages and "given them by fathers, brothers, and husbands who had traveled with Buffalo Bill." Mooney compounded Parker's oversight in reprinting her account in *Ghost Dance Religion* by eliding the sentence that reported the shawls.[44]

Thus, nativism did not define the Ghost Dance, but it was present, varying in degree from one place to the next. "Anybody not wearing Indian clothes was not allowed in the camp," recalled Robert Higheagle, a nephew of one of the ritual leaders at the camp of the Lakota Sitting Bull, but Western clothing predominated in other camps, including those of the Northern Paiutes. There is no record of Wovoka—who would place his hat on the ground, with the crown open to the sky, as a ritual gesture—asking his followers to throw off "everything white man." In fact, Wovoka told Mooney that he "believed it was better for the Indians to follow the white man's road and to adopt the habits of civilization." The prophet appears to have been sincere, Mooney noted, "for he was dressed in a good suit of white man's clothing, and works regularly on a ranch." Even among Lakotas, "Indian dress" in the circle prominently featured blankets, which were manufactured by Americans and acquired in government rations.[45]

By overemphasizing rejection of white ways and manufactured goods in the Ghost Dance, Mooney and others construed the religion as an expression of vanishing (or perhaps vanished) Indianness. They overlooked the numerous, simultaneous references in Ghost Dance teachings to innovation and the need for new forms of work and ritual for new Indian identities. Most importantly, as Mooney himself noted, writing, literacy, and schooling were integral to the spread of the Ghost Dance and highly valued by many adherents. School graduates became ritual leaders of the religion on the Southern Plains and used their influence as Ghost Dance leaders to ease the path to allotment. When returned Carlisle student and ritual leader Paul Boynton and the Arapaho evangelist Sitting Bull helped to negotiate land cessions in 1890, they were hardly rejecting "everything white man."

In other ways, too, the ritual was profoundly innovative. As late as 1911, in an address to the Nebraska Historical Society, Mooney himself pointed out that despite the return to tradition the Ghost Dance seemed to mark, it opened up new opportunities in ritual leadership for women on the Southern Plains. Women leaders of the dance wore crow feathers, just as men did. "The fact that women were permitted to enter the circle and perform in the same way as the medicine men themselves showed that the ghost dance religion was a new departure among Indians," Mooney observed.[46]

Just as he downplayed innovation in favor of tradition, Mooney also emphasized the visions of the old life in Ghost Dance trances, largely suppressing or ignoring evidence of new kinds of religious experience, including the many encounters with Christ reported in newspapers and correspondence from the reservations. In September 1890, Special Agent E. G. Reynolds reported that a number of Lakota Ghost Dancers claimed to have met Jesus during trance visions. Reynolds's account of these visions was filed in the government's case file, on which Mooney relied extensively, but Christ appears almost not at all in his descriptions of the Lakota Ghost Dance. His own field notes seem to indicate that some of his consultants on the Southern Plains told him about meetings with Jesus. In a sheaf of handwritten pages archived in Washington, Mooney made notes about his interview with Asatitola, a Kiowa believer who during his journeys in the spirit land encountered Christ and found departed relatives who offered him a fresh buffalo feast. But Mooney mentions only Asatitola's encounter with his family in *Ghost Dance Religion;* the Kiowa's meetings with Christ did not find their way into print.[47]

These two shortcomings—the overemphasis on nativism and the presentation of the religion as exclusively devoted to restoring the old ways—were both on display in Mooney's account of the Lakota

Ghost Dance. A third shortcoming appears as well: even as he denounced the army's violence, Mooney gave strong support to the army's contention that some Lakotas had twisted the religion into a warrior movement.[48]

To be fair to Mooney, it is hard to see how he might have done otherwise. Forced to work with little testimony from Lakota Ghost Dancers, and therefore dependent on the documentary record, he resorted to two written accounts by "insiders," Indians who, though intimately familiar with events at Pine Ridge, had established themselves from the beginning as vigorous opponents of the new religion. One was the captain of the Indian police, George Sword, who led his constables in suppressing the Ghost Dance and supported the army after it arrived. Sword dictated a history of the Ghost Dance at Pine Ridge that was transcribed into Lakota and then translated into English for a missionary, who provided a copy to Mooney. We may surmise that, in composing this account, Sword found himself in a difficult position. On the one hand, he seems to have felt it his duty to record the history of these devastating events. On the other hand, Lakota custom held that as a senior man and established warrior with a position of authority, he was also responsible for maintaining unity among his people. This was no small task in the aftermath of the polarizing Ghost Dance troubles. Sword had helped to suppress the new religion, but to condemn believers outright would invite further division.

Thus, Sword included elements in his account that were sympathetic to followers of the prophet. "In the story of ghost dancing, the Ogalala heard that the Son of God was truly on earth," Sword began. He even allowed that Ghost Dance evangelists could instruct their followers to embrace reservation life. The men who met with Wovoka, he said, claimed that the prophet had told them, "My grandchildren, when you get home go to farming and send all your children to school."[49]

But in the fullness of the account, the pragmatism of the religion was lost in details that justified the suppression of believers. "They dance around in the circle," Sword explained, "until some of them become so tired and overtired that they become crazy." And "some of the dancers," according to the police chief, carried guns in the circle. (Responding to this charge sixteen years later, Short Bull retorted, "How could we have held weapons? For thus we danced, in a circle, hand to hand, each man's fingers linked with those of his neighbor.")[50]

The ethnologist would have been wise to be careful with Sword's testimony about the Ghost Dancers carrying weapons and being in a "crazed" state. He himself had collected teachings from Ghost Dance evangelists instructing believers to "work for white men." Wovoka had told him personally that his followers "must work, and not lie or steal," and Mooney had listened to the teachings of peace in Nevada and in Oklahoma. He recorded all these exhortations, and they are published in the pages of *Ghost Dance Religion*. But he had also spoken with Sword during his visit to South Dakota, and those conversations were no doubt reinforced by the policeman's written account, which Mooney accepted uncritically. He had read in that account the reference to Wovoka urging his followers to take up farming and education, but being unable to reconcile these instructions with the exclusive nativism that he imagined at the heart of the religion, he dismissed them. "Curiously enough," he remarks in *Ghost Dance Religion,* although Wovoka (as presented by Sword) had come "to restore the old life, he advised his hearers to go to work and send their children to school."[51]

Mooney's use of Sword's account was problematic, but his second source, in reinforcing the nativism and militancy that the ethnologist had already projected onto Lakotas, proved even more so. Hundreds of people contributed to the documentary record of the Ghost Dance that was archived in Washington. But of all the agents, soldiers, journalists, eyewitnesses, and outright rumormongers who wrote a letter, telegram, or other report, only one was a Dakota-speaking Indian with close connections to Pine Ridge who also could write compelling accounts of the new religion in English: William Selwyn.

The educated Yankton Dakota and onetime postmaster from Pine Ridge, who whispered dark rumors about Short Bull and other evangelists to Agent Hugh Gallagher and then helped police suppress the religion at his home reservation, became perhaps the key informant for Mooney's version of the Lakota Ghost Dance. Selwyn's suspect report from November 1890 was the ethnologist's most important source on the origins of the religion at Pine Ridge and Rosebud. Mooney credited Selwyn's warning of a "general outbreak" and published in its entirety his transcript of the incendiary interview with Kuwapi. Selwyn's tip to the agent that the Indians were following a redeemer who had returned to earth to "kill all the white people" led Mooney to conclude that the Messiah "had now returned to punish the whites for their wickedness," and that "he would wipe the whites from the face of the earth."[52]

Mooney made other mistakes that similarly pushed readers and subsequent historians toward a view of the religion as a rebel conspiracy, even though Mooney himself never quite said as much. He underplayed the Lakotas' nonbelieving majority, even, with no good evidence, referring to Red Cloud as "a firm believer in the new doctrine." He took at face value Agent James McLaughlin's condemnation of Sitting Bull, including his unsubstantiated, almost certainly scurrilous description of the old chief breaking his peace pipe and announcing that he "wanted to die and wanted to fight." Mooney denounced the chief's "irreconcilable hostility to the government" and concluded that there was "no question that Sitting Bull was plotting mischief."[53]

In contrast, Mooney valorized the "cool and reliable" leader of the Indian police, Lieutenant Bull Head, and agreed with "the warmest praise" heaped upon the arresting constables "by those most competent to judge" (presumably McLaughlin, for whom mention of Sitting Bull provoked irrational outbursts). Conceding that Sitting Bull was "honest in his hatred of the whites," Mooney nonetheless concluded that the chief "represented the past. His influence was incompatible with progress, and his death marks an era in the civilization of the Sioux." The Lakota Ghost Dance, then, had become the cause of zealots who had allowed themselves to be used by unscrupulous schemers like Sitting Bull.[54]

And yet, the study's most provocative chapter would redeem many of these errors and assumptions, not only subverting the official critique of the Ghost Dance and the rationale for its brutal suppression at Wounded Knee, but also reorienting American thought toward a broad acceptance of Indian religion.

In Mooney's hands, the Ghost Dance became, for all its supposed nativism and fixation on the past, not only a worthwhile subject for scientific study but, more importantly, a socially valid form of belief. To Mooney, the flaws in the Ghost Dance did not so much distinguish it from other religions as validate it, marking it as a religion that could and should be compared to others.

In his early articles on the Irish, Mooney drew comparisons between Irish beliefs and those of Europeans, Asians, and American Indians. Similarly, in chapter 16 of *Ghost Dance Religion,* he situates the Ghost Dance in a wide-ranging global comparison, with no reference to stages of religious development or the superiority of one belief over another, even beliefs held by peoples occupying distinctive "stages" of civilization. "The cloudy indistinctness which Wovoka and his followers ascribe to the Father as he appears to them in their trance visions has numerous parallels in both Testaments," he concludes. "Moses goes up into the mountain to receive inspiration like Wovoka of the Paiute." There were close parallels in the religious experiences of Wovoka, Christ, and every other religious visionary, for "in the agony of Gethsemane, with its mental anguish and bloody sweat, we see the same phenomena that appear in the lives of religious enthusiasts from Mohammed and Joan of Arc, down to George Fox and the prophets of the Ghost Dance."[55]

In that chapter, Mooney marches readers through the religious history of the world, pointing out parallels between the Ghost Dance and episodes of European religious ecstasy such as the fifteenth-century visions and trial of Joan of Arc and the "Dance of St. John," an "epidemic of maniacal religious dancing"—visionaries held hands and turned in circles until they collapsed in convulsions—in Germany, the Netherlands, and parts of France. Mooney also compares the Ghost Dance revivals to the seventeenth-century English ferment that birthed the Puritans. Conditions then had been not unlike what Indians suffered in 1889: "wholesale confiscations" of land

and imprisoned families suffering "insufficient food and brutal treatment." In this traumatized context, "numerous new sects sprang up, with prophecy, miracle working, hypnotism, and convulsive ecstasy as parts of the doctrine or ritual." Most famous among these sects were the followers of George Fox, prophet, clairvoyant, healer, and trance visionary. His followers became known as Quakers because they literally quaked, in convulsions so violent that on occasion the meetinghouse itself "seemed to be shaken" and believers sometimes fell to the earth "struggling as if for life."[56]

More recent developments were no less mystical. Mooney invokes the Methodists—whose early gatherings in the eighteenth century and even in some places in 1890 were characterized by "hysteric and convulsive extravagance"—and the Shakers (the "United Society of Believers in Christ's Second Appearing"), who beheld their prophetess and founder, Ann Lee, as "the actual reincarnation of Christ," and who claimed "the inspiration of prophecy, the gift of healing, and sometimes even the gift of tongues," along with ecstatic visions. Their "public dancing, shouting, and shaking" (signs of the removal of sin) led to their persecution and removal in 1789 to the United States, where they continued to receive visions—and to dance.[57]

From here Mooney dives into the rich tradition of Christian revival in the United States, repeatedly connecting the ritual practice of the Ghost Dance to American religions. He points to the Kentucky Revival, an "epidemic of religious frenzy" that erupted mostly among Methodists and Baptists around 1800 in Kentucky and Tennessee, "with accompaniments that far surpassed the wild excesses of the Ghost Dance." Excitement about the advent of the kingdom endured for five years. "The performances at the meetings of these enthusiasts were of the most exaggerated camp-meeting order," with believers, white and black and from virtually all denominations, falling to all fours and barking like dogs (those so possessed had the gift of prophecy, dreams, and visions of angels), or rolling on the ground, or taken with violent spasms, colloquially known as "the jerks." As Mooney observes, many of these expressions could still be seen in parts of the South.[58]

The Midwest was no less spiritually volatile. Mooney recalls the Millerites, or Adventists, who prepared vigorously for the Second Coming: believers donned ascension robes (not unlike ghost shirts) and disposed of their property in anticipation of the appointed date in the summer of 1843. Although the prophecy failed to materialize, in the early 1890s there were still 15,000 to 20,000 believers, most of them in southern Michigan.[59]

Even more recently, Mooney cites "various religious abnormal-isms, based on hypnotism, trances, and the messiah idea, which have sprung up and flourished in different parts of our own country even within the last twenty years," and not just "among the igno-rant classes." In 1875, Mrs. Dora Beekman, wife of a Congregational minister in Rockford, Illinois, announced that she was the reincar-nation of Jesus Christ and soon acquired followers; her successor, the Reverend George Schweinfurth, was worshiped as the risen Christ "by hundreds of followers," many of them well-to-do.[60]

And closer to home, Mooney points to the "prophecies, visions, trances, and frenzied bodily exercises" of "various local revivalists," notably Maria Woodworth, whose "Heavenly Recruits" nightly fell into trances, occasioning great interest and public concern in his home state of Indiana. "The physical and mental demoralization," Mooney notes, "at last became so great that the meetings were sup-pressed by the authorities."[61]

Embedded in Mooney's history of religion is a set of parallels that place the Ghost Dance in a universal tradition of religious expression as old as recorded history and as modern as the United States. And if the yearnings of believers in the ancient Holy Land, medieval and modern Europe, and the modern United States were broadly similar, so too was revivalist persecution across time, a coeval pattern traced by Mooney. Readers came away from his critique understanding that official and public fears concerning the Ghost Dance had been stoked by long-standing elite critiques and anxieties about enthusi-astic religion. Charismatic evangelism—from the Hebrew proph-ets and Jesus through Joan of Arc and the Methodists, the Shakers, Maria Woodworth, and the Ghost Dancers—had always disrupted social order and challenged authority in ways that made officialdom profoundly uncomfortable. Condemnation of revivals was as much a part of American culture as revivals themselves, and Mooney was intimately familiar with both; he still visited his mother in Richmond, a town where Quakers transcended their brutal persecution and Woodworth's movement achieved some of its first notoriety.

As all of his examples showed, evangelical movements often divided the most enthusiastic Methodists, Baptists, and others from their denominational leadership, many of whom were offended by uncontrolled displays of emotion, particularly shouting and falling to the floor, which they saw as a threat to order, particularly to their own authority. As in the Ghost Dance, they often blamed such behavior on the rude and the uneducated, and they also often attributed evangelism's excesses to racial minorities, particularly African Americans (as Mooney himself does here and there in *Ghost Dance Religion*).[62]

America's deep tradition of racial prejudice had added fuel to the fires of anti-revivalism and undergirded the charges of "false religion" leveled at the Ghost Dance. Thus, in undermining elite and official views of Indian religion in the assimilation era, chapter 16 was the book's most provocative section. The official line on the Ghost Dance, taken by authorities from General Nelson A. Miles to Indian agents and most of the Washington bureaucracy, was that it was not fit to be called a religion at all, but was a "craze" and a "superstition" providing cover for a conspiracy to thwart US authority. By definition, then, the gyrations of Indians, a self-evidently "primitive" people against whom all progress could ostensibly be measured, did not constitute "true religion" but rather a deceitful path away from genuine spiritual experience.[63]

Mooney's more open, comparative view of religion challenged this idea head on. Since at least the Protestant Reformation, European thought had developed a strong tradition of denouncing non-Protestant (and dissident Protestant) religions as "false religion," and this tradition had a critical influence on the formation of American culture from the beginnings of the colonial period. But during the nineteenth century a new sensibility emerged: a willingness to apply the term "true religion" to describe a category of emotion and belief that could be found in many different belief systems. By the 1840s, various scholars were attributing crowd behavior at revivals—the shouting, crying, unconsciousness, and trance visions—to mesmerism, or hypnotism. Some who invoked mesmerism were discounting the religious authenticity of these experiences, but for others, critically, mesmerism offered the key to unlocking genuine affairs of the spirit, a conduit to holiness and to God that linked all religions. From this view, hypnotically induced trances could be authentic religious experiences in their own right.

This latter, more sympathetic view of mesmerism was a sign of the growing acceptance of the concept of the subconscious mind—a force in the making of belief whose acknowledgment grew out of the development of psychology by William James, Sigmund Freud, and others. James, perhaps the foremost religious scholar of the 1880s and 1890s, saw the subconscious and its manifestations, including hypnosis, as potentially authentic, viable pathways for spiritual expressions. It was James who in 1902 began to speak of "the varieties of religious experience"; only a few decades before, the assumption had been that there could be few if any "varieties," for only one religion was "true."[64]

Mooney himself expressed no debt to James, and it is not clear whether the ethnologist ever read his work. But the increasing openness to alternative forms of religious experience that defined James's work was in any case prevalent in scholarly and popular media by 1890. In November of that year, the *New York Times* favorably compared the Ghost Dance to recent claims of revelation by white and black Christians. "The recent Indian craze is only a portion of that mysterious wave that has swept over the human emotions from the beginning of time—the Indian showing that he is neither stronger nor weaker than his brother of other hues," concluded the *Times*. (The article was subsequently excerpted in the *Journal of American Folklore*, where Mooney may first have read it.)[65]

To be sure, new psychological insights could cut either way. Social scientists often utilized the new field of psychology to criticize revival behavior, deploying a more scientific set of explanations to reinforce the old elite biases against religious enthusiasm. Some alleged that revival leaders only *seemed* to elicit spiritual responses, but that in reality they incited crowds through nefarious means of mind control. In September 1890, the same month the Ghost Dances began to grow at Pine Ridge, Woodworth's "trance revivals" seized St. Louis. Quickly, crowd behavior and the deportment of Woodworth herself became the target of two doctors who claimed to be "authorities on insanity and neurology" and who alleged that she was hypnotizing her followers. They set out to have her declared legally insane.[66]

Ultimately, Woodworth triumphed. The judge in the case dismissed the charges of insanity (although he agreed she was a nuisance). But the case reminds us that there were also white revivalists—not just trance evangelists but Methodists, Millerites, and others—who aroused public suspicion partly because the rabble that followed them threatened to dissolve the social order. By charging that Woodworth was hypnotizing her followers, some elites sought to provide a scientific explanation for crowd behavior and thus desanctify her displays of spirit.

Mooney took the opposite tack. He had seen Arapahao evangelists induce trances by waving feathers or black cloth fragments in the faces of dancers. "The most important feature of the Ghost dance, and the secret of the trances, is hypnotism," he concluded. But in his view, hypnotism only explained the technique of the trance; the use of the technique did not discount the value or meaning of the trance for the believer. Mooney maintained that mesmerism was pervasive among people who lived close to nature and that its presence among Ghost Dancers argued for the religion's authenticity. The practice bonded the Ghost Dance with other forms of religious practice, for probably all religions began with visions or trances brought on in part by mesmerism.[67]

Mooney's view that all religions had attributes that had endured for millennia and were authentically appealing to believers contrasted sharply with social evolutionary dogma, which stipulated that true religions were "advanced" from primitive origins. To some scholars, revivalist and nonconformist behaviors like ecstatic fits or the séances of Spiritualists were evidence of "survivals" of primitive instincts that had not yet been extinguished by the advance of civilization, particularly in lower-class people.[68]

Such ideas gained currency in the ongoing assault on alternative religious practice. Several months after Woodworth won her case in St. Louis, James Monroe Buckley, a leading psychologist of religion, launched another attack. Comparing the unconventional behavior of Woodworth's followers to Methodists, Baptists, Adventists, all African Americans, and "other sects holding camp meetings," Buckley derided these traditions as "survival[s] of a state to which increasingly knowledge and self-control must put an end." In other words, there was no mystery, no manifestation of spirit in any revival—merely a surrender to the savage impulse.[69]

The ease with which contemporaries ascribed revival behavior to repressed savagery compounded the purported threat of the Ghost Dance. Most of the non-Indian public, in perceiving Indian devotions through a lens of Indian primitivism, condemned it not in spite of its resemblance to Christian revivals but because of it. It is a telling contrast with the reaction to the Ghost Dance that the psychological critiques of Woodworth's revivals—the accusations of hypnotism in particular—did not gain public traction. The newspapers that covered the controversy, notably the *St. Louis Globe Democrat*, dismissed the idea that the revivals were a threat to public health, and the *Globe Democrat* spent more column inches trying to explain the views of the revivalists themselves, which the paper presented as peculiar but harmless.[70]

Generally speaking, Ghost Dancers received no such benefit of the doubt because they were Indians. As far as most Americans were concerned, Indians' dancing and unruly prayer reinforced their essential "savagery." The Ghost Dance seemed to validate the pervasive assumption that Indians could not be redeemed through their own beliefs and rituals. In fact, this kind of thinking cast the Ghost Dance as an exhibit for the essential savagery of all revivalists. In 1905 the social scientist Frederick Davenport cited Ghost Dancing as an example of the "primitive" spirit that was regrettably expressed by those white revivalists "in whom the higher cerebral processes are imperfectly organized." For Davenport, the dangers were clear. It was "the vice of democracy" that a man "who yields unquestioningly and uncritically to impassioned appeal in the crisis hour of his religious life will do it in his political life." Religious revival pointed to tyranny.[71]

Such culturally pervasive ideas made it impossible for officials to comprehend Wovoka's teachings to educate children, attend church, and cooperate with agents. The closest officials came to seeing these aspects of the Ghost Dance was to recognize the religion as one of peace. Even then, most seemed fatalistic about its prospects. After all, what Indian could remain peaceful while dancing in prayer to an Indian redeemer?

For these and other reasons, the Ghost Dance was never able to unfold as believers hoped it would at Pine Ridge and other Lakota reservations. Although Mooney did not acknowledge the more pragmatic exhortations of the religion, even he noted that much of the tension surrounding it in South Dakota had more to do with congressional perfidy in cutting rations and stealing land than with the teachings themselves. Army hostility did not develop in response to the actual content or practice of the religion. The title of his book notwithstanding, Mooney noted that there had been no "outbreak" at Lakota reservations. "It might be better designated," he concludes, "as a Sioux panic and stampede." Quoting former agent Valentine McGillycuddy's assessment of January 1891, he goes on: "Up to date there has been neither a Sioux outbreak or war. No citizen in Nebraska or Dakota has been killed, molested, or can show the scratch of a pin, and no property has been destroyed off the reservation."[72]

Even without recognizing Wovoka's exhortations to work, farm, and educate children, Mooney argued that on the Southern Plains, where the Ghost Dance had been allowed to continue, it helped to accustom Indians to the reservation era, and he gently suggested that assimilationists should accept the new religion on its own terms. "The moral code inculcated" in the Ghost Dance, with its admonitions about honesty and goodwill, "is as pure and comprehensive in its simplicity as anything found in religious systems from the days of Gautama Buddha to the time of Jesus Christ." In its instruction not to "cry" for the departed, he writes, the religion "forbids the extravagant mourning customs formerly common among the tribes," including "the burning of tipis and destruction of property" of the deceased. Mooney also notes what might have been the most "radical change" the Ghost Dance introduced: it forbade war. "Only those who have known the deadly hatred that once animated Ute, Cheyenne, and Pawnee, one toward another, and are able to contrast it with their present spirit of mutual brotherly love, can know what the Ghost-dance religion has accomplished in bringing the savage into civilization." Mooney sums up by quoting another observer, Lieutenant Hugh Scott of the US Seventh Cavalry, on the prophet Wovoka and his impact on the Southern Plains: "He has given these people a better religion than they ever had before, taught them precepts which, if faithfully carried out, will bring them in to better accord with their white neighbors, and has prepared the way for their final Christianization."[73]

Mooney's devotion to understanding the religion led him to correct his text right up until the last minute. The tone of *Ghost Dance Religion* is elegiac, as if the book is both an exposition of and a farewell to the new religion. His conviction that the Ghost Dance movement had faded left many readers believing that its history was essentially over.

But in fact, almost at that very moment, the religion had again ignited the passions of believers. Out on the Southern Plains, the circle began to turn again among Kiowas, who had abandoned it after Apiatan's denunciation of the religion three years before. Apiatan had garnered a great deal of official support for his opposition to the religion. His agent backed him, and word circulated that the government had promised him a house. No house was ever given to him, but Lieutenant Scott persuaded President Benjamin Harrison to bestow a medal on Apiatan for his help in suppressing the ritual. Subsequently, Scott intrigued among the Kiowas to remove their elderly chief, Lone Wolf, in favor of Apiatan, who was elected chief in 1894.[74]

With all the US meddling in the Kiowa Ghost Dance and support for its greatest skeptic, perhaps it was not surprising that Apiatan's opponents among the Kiowas returned to the religion, which revived about the time that he became chief. In September 1894, Kiowa believers called a great dance, and alongside several thousand Indians from neighboring tribes they turned the circle once again on the Washita River.[75]

Mooney hastily added the recent developments among the Kiowa to his report. "The dance still exists," he wrote in his introduction to the text in 1896, "and is developing new features at every performance." But he never corrected his assertions about the death of the movement, which were embedded in various places deeper in the text. Ever after, readers would interpret Mooney's postmortem of the movement as evidence for the religion's failure. In reality, the Ghost Dance continued.[76]

WHEN MOONEY SUBMITTED HIS MANUSCRIPT TO THE BUREAU, ITS title bore no mention of a "craze" or a "superstition" but read simply, "The Messiah Religion and the Ghost Dance." In those seven words, Mooney conveyed his core contention—that the Ghost Dance was exemplary of a long, global tradition of messianic faith.[77]

The degree of provocation in Mooney's arguments often passes unnoticed among Ghost Dance scholars, in part because the response to his book among his superiors, initially at least, was silence. John Wesley Powell remained dedicated to social evolutionism, particularly in matters of religion, and for the next two years Mooney's book sat on a shelf in the Bureau of Ethnology. The bureau's publication schedule was lamentably behind, but publication may have been slowed as much by Powell's ambivalence about Mooney's arguments. When the report finally appeared in print, it was the second volume of a two-volume annual report. The first volume carried a long introduction from Powell, who from the first paragraph attacked Mooney's arguments. In Powell's view, the Ghost Dance was no religion, but a "religious fantasy" that had led Indians into war and was already safely consigned to the past. "The record of this curious evanescent cult, which seems rather a travesty on religion than an expression of the most exalted concepts within human grasp, is a dark chapter in the history of the aborigines," he contended.[78]

Powell especially criticized Mooney's comparisons of the Ghost Dance with Christianity, Judaism, and other beliefs of literate peoples. To Powell, these venerable faiths could have little correspondence with the new religion. After all, people who had reached a higher stage of mental and technological development, like European Christians and Jews, possessed more complex religious faiths. The religions of Europeans and Indians, peoples widely disparate in social evolution and technological development, could not have common origins.[79]

Thus, what Mooney called a religion was, in Powell's view, "an evanescent cult," "a travesty on religion," and the product of "a mental infection." There was no way to compare the Ghost Dance to Christianity. Indians and white people were separated not only by the cultural break between the nonliterary and literary peoples, but also by "the widest known break" in the development of technology and religious faith. So vast was the difference between savage and civilized understandings of spirit that no civilized person could even understand what all that whirling and singing had been about, for the Ghost Dance was merely a product—or a symptom—of "the primitive mind."

The disagreement between the director and his employee illuminates not only the subversive qualities of Mooney's thought but the degree of intellectual freedom that reigned in Powell's bureau. Although the old explorer took the young ethnologist to task for his arguments, he did not stop him from writing them. On the contrary, he ultimately directed that Mooney's report be published in its entirety and widely distributed. "In its extent and intensity," Powell noted, "the ghost-dance fantasy of 1889–92 is a unique illustration of one of the characteristics of the aborigines which has long been under investigation in the Bureau of Ethnology, and the accompanying memoir is a contribution toward the final results of these researches." In other words, the disagreement between Mooney and Powell only proved that the bureau served as an arena of intellectual exchange and debate.[80]

If Powell delayed publication of Mooney's report out of fear of the controversy it could cause, he would not have been far wrong. Not long after the book's appearance, the director received a letter from his superior, S. P. Langley, the director of the Smithsonian Institution, warning that the content of Mooney's report was "open to grave doubt in a government publication." While he praised the ethnologist's "literary skill" and "large sympathy" with Indian believers, Langley was appalled by Mooney's "explicit statement that the doctrines of the Christian religion and the practices of its prominent sects among us, are essentially the same as those of the Indian Ghost dance, and like that, founded on the illusion of dreams." The director was particularly stricken with the parallel Mooney drew between the agonies of Christ in Gethsemane and the experiences of Ghost Dance prophets. He warned Powell that congressmen could hurt the bureau if the "dearest religious beliefs" of their constituents were thus "wounded in a Government publication." Such words, concluded Langley, "had better have been left unwritten. . . . Is it quite too late to modify this?"[81]

It was. The book was already published and distributed. Powell conceded that "the objectionable chapter" was "liable to provoke hostile criticism," but he pointed to his own introduction, which established that "ceremonial practices of different culture stages" did not have common origins.[82] As it turned out, Mooney's report would be much more widely read than Powell's introduction. The book had escaped the authorities, and like the religion that was its subject, it went forth into the world.

CHAPTER 14

CONCLUSIONS: THE GHOST DANCE AS MODERN RELIGION

MOST WHITE OBSERVERS BELIEVED THAT THE GHOST DANCE was a throwback to a savage state, but not all were so blind. Some, in fact, perceived its modernity. In February 1891, a little over a month after Short Bull and the last of his followers surrendered to the army at Pine Ridge, F. S. Kingsbury, a government farmer at Pine Ridge Reservation, toured the remains of the Lakota cabins and small fields that dotted the banks of White Clay Creek. From within a half-mile of the agency almost to the White Clay River, a distance of twenty-two miles, Kingsbury found fifty-three homes, two school-houses, and a church—all of them burned. "The windows are broken out of nearly every remaining building," reported the farmer. "A great deal of machinery and farming tools burned, a number of stoves broken, nearly all the hay burned and one bridge burned."[1]

Most of the owners had gone into the agency, in compliance with army orders, in November. Ghost Dancers, angry at the perceived betrayal and themselves in flight from the army, had then pillaged some of these homes and burned them down. But the division between these modern Indian farmers and their Ghost Dance rivals was never clear-cut. As Kingsbury pointed out, some of the owners themselves had become Ghost Dancers. Ultimately, they were "carried away by the craze" and in a fit of millennial excitement "burned their own buildings and run their machinery down high bluffs into the creek, where I find it now frozen in the ice."[2]

Unlike many other government officials, Kingsbury had sympathy for Ghost Dancers. For one thing, he pointed out, they were farming a land that received far too little rain, which was enough to drive anyone to desperation, not just Indians. In the summer of 1890, farmers across western South Dakota and Nebraska had thrown up their hands in despair. By the time Kingsbury was examining Indian properties on White Clay Creek in 1891, many whites had also abandoned their farms. Many more had joined the Farmers' Alliance and the Populist movement, demanding that the federal and state governments provide at least basic security against the conjoined threats of drought, glut, and railroad monopoly.

As far as Kingsbury was concerned, Ghost Dancers and Populists had much in common. The government, in his view, should provide Indians some security. He suggested paying them to dig irrigation ditches so that they could earn some cash while bringing water to the arid lands of Pine Ridge. "I will venture to say there is not an Indian on the reservation but what will work for money," he opined. "But they are like the farmers of Nebraska and South Dakota, they are tired of working and getting no return for their labor." Even in its most millennial moments, the Ghost Dance drew followers who labored and longed for modern success.[3]

Kingsbury was not the only one who compared Ghost Dancers and Populists. Already by 1890, political humorists had begun to criticize Populists for their seemingly outlandish demands by referring to their gatherings as "Ghost Dances." But subsequent generations would not be so dismissive. Many of the most fantastic of their proposals, such as credit unions and railroad regulation, ultimately became staples of modern economy and governance. Populists had many failings, but being premodern was not one of them.[4]

We can say the same of Ghost Dancers. As Kingsbury understood, and as we have seen throughout this book, Ghost Dancers
were thoroughly modern people. Their religion was no "last stand" of
Indian autonomy, which had vanished long before 1889, but rather
a means by which Indians anticipated, internalized, and even debated the economic and political imperatives of the rapidly advancing
twentieth century. Among the most pressing of these imperatives
was a newfound, unwelcome dependence on the federal government
for survival. Until a decade or two before the Ghost Dance revival
on the Plains, Indians of the region had survived by depending on
themselves and their kin—not only living people but also the spirits
they claimed as family, such as those who were embodied in wild
animals and plants, including Grandfather Buffalo, Bear, Elk, and
others. The loss of Indian land and the eradication of so many kin—
their people and other creatures—left virtually every tribe dependent
on federal rations, no matter how hard they tried to farm or secure
other work.

The Messiah's visitations allowed Indians to reflect on this strange,
terrifying new circumstance of being forced to depend on distant
white authorities in Washington who dictated the terms of Indian
survival. Congressmen who had never met an Indian now voted, often with devastating consequences, on whether or not to cut their
rations of flour, beef, and blankets and on whether to sell their land,
and for how much. The president appointed the bureaucrats who ran
the Office of Indian Affairs and often proved hostile to Indian pri-
orities and Indian needs. For Indians, the only route to survival was
somehow to motivate these remote figures to care about Indians—or
in the parlance of many Indian religions, to "take pity" on Indians
and show them kindness and mercy.

Indians had various ways of negotiating the vast divide between
Washington and themselves. Calling the US president "Great Father" had become an Indian tradition by the early nineteenth century, partly because it invoked a familial relation to US authority
and allowed suppliants to claim pity and mercy as dependents of

Washington. Over the course of the century, they developed other means of reaching out. By the 1880s, Indians had become increasingly adept at building friendships with people who could influence Washington on their behalf—missionaries, schoolteachers, Indian agents, anthropologists, Wild West show impresarios, and journalists, among others. To be sure, they resented the heavy hand of Congress and the Indian Office, but being Gilded Age people, they recognized the need to forge modern relationships with powerful white intermediaries in hopes of steering Indian policy.

Through the Ghost Dance, believers expressed an understandable sense of powerlessness. But Ghost Dance teachings also helped them imagine solutions to their predicament. Schooling, wage work, and farming—the commandments of the Messiah—offered paths not only to survival but also to a kind of empowerment. Following the commandments would enable Indians to read and write their own legal documents, challenge land cessions, and assert greater control over their relations not only with Washington but with Americans generally, and even with one another.

Moreover, Ghost Dance theology resonated symbolically with the political condition of Indian reservations. Just as the Messiah was an intercessor with the Great Mysteries, Indians required human intercessors in their relations with Washington. The Messiah was therefore a sign of the radical, unprecedented shift in their reduction from living in autonomous villages to becoming dependent people.

In helping believers to address the problem of dependency on distant men, the utility and popularity of the messiah figure may have come in part from his resemblance to a man. Among Lakotas and some other Indians, such figures were strikingly unusual. The Messiah was one of only two Lakota spirits (the other being White Buffalo Calf Woman) who assumed anthropomorphic form. His attractions were many, but it seems likely that for Ghost Dancers the Messiah provided a pointed counterexample, to both officials and other Indians, of the ways in which remote, immensely powerful beings should treat those who depend on them. By idealizing the Messiah's love and pity toward Indians, believers could implicitly critique the distant, powerful, and often callous congressmen and officials who left them on the verge of starvation. Thus, the Messiah of the Ghost Dance allowed believers not only to imagine restoration and renewal of their old religions, their old economy, and their families, but at the same time to contemplate and spiritually address some of the most pressing problems of the coming century.[5]

To appreciate the essential modernity of Ghost Dance teachings, it helps to keep in mind that a central appeal of any religion is how much it enables believers to resolve seemingly irresolvable contradictions. Seen in this light, the Ghost Dance taught believers how to take up key activities demanded by assimilationists (schooling, farming, and church attendance) while continuing to dance and remaining Indian, thereby rejecting assimilation. The religion thus served as a bridge straddling one of the greatest paradoxes facing Indians: the contradiction between their pre-industrial, stateless, autonomous past and their increasingly industrial, state-supervised, dependent present.[6]

This function of the Ghost Dance is one that many scholars have been hard-pressed to acknowledge. Unlike anthropologists, who became aware of the survival of the Ghost Dance by the early 1900s, historians and many other students of the religion have been bedeviled by a pervasive blindness to its two-way gaze—its way of simultaneously looking forward to the future and backward to the past. Another, only somewhat less pervasive problem has been its presentation, especially in popular media but also in some historical scholarship, as having ended at Wounded Knee. For decades after 1890, the Wounded Knee Massacre punctuated with an exclamation point the end of the frontier. In many textbooks, it still does. Such accounts of the massacre have often come to stand in for the history of the entire religion.[7]

In the aftermath of the massacre, as the prophecy failed to come to fulfillment in the spring of 1891, there was disappointment and disaffection among some believers. But as a modern religion for a modern era, the Ghost Dance still had life. It revived at Standing Rock, the Lakota Sitting Bull's home, among Yankton Lakotas in 1897. From there it traveled to Saskatchewan, Canada, where it proved most enduring among Santee Sioux refugees who had fled across the border after the Dakota Uprising of 1862. In the intervening years they had become wage workers and dryland farmers who, like Northern Paiutes, were much praised for their "judgment and industry." In what was known as the New Tidings Congregation, the central rituals became feasting and prayer. As late as the 1960s, some Santees still professed the faith.[8]

On other Lakota reservations, the massacre at Wounded Knee forced the Ghost Dance underground, but the movement continued in remote districts and largely out of sight. Kicking Bear, the Minneconjou Lakota evangelist, returned to Nevada to meet with Jack Wilson in 1902. Cloud Horse, another Brule Lakota emissary from the 1890 delegation, returned with two others, Chasing Hawk and Bear Comes Out, in 1906. Secret Ghost Dances occurred at Pine Ridge in 1909, as the tribe confronted yet more federal demands to give up land. At various times thereafter, and in keeping with its popularity among opponents of the 1889 Sioux Act, the ritual became associated with efforts to fend off land cessions.[9]

The durability of the Ghost Dance was perhaps most evident on the Southern Plains, where, as we have seen, it had played a very different role in allotment controversies. Pawnees took up the Ghost Dance in 1891. In their trances, some Pawnees met with priests who had died years before and who explained to the visionaries how to conduct religious ceremonies that had been suppressed and forgotten. This partial rebirth of Pawnee religion through the Ghost Dance made the ceremony so popular that, according to its most famous scholar, Pawnee Ghost Dancers consented to allotment partly because doing so would free them from their agent: if they became citizens, they could ignore his efforts to ban the ritual.[10]

In 1904 the Pawnees sent a delegation to meet with Jack Wilson, who advised them on various procedures to reform and advance the

Ghost Dance. The dance continued into the era of World War I and gradually was replaced by a key ritual component developed by and for the Pawnees—the sacred hand game, which, like elements of the Ghost Dance elsewhere, represented a broadening of religious access and a prayer for health. "The religion now flourishes," wrote Pawnee-mixed-blood author James Murie in 1914, having "evolved into a Christian ethical belief, demonstrated by a ritual."[11]

Elsewhere in Oklahoma, the circle continued to turn. Wovoka himself is said to have made repeated visits to Oklahoma beginning in 1906; perhaps he helped inspire Southern Arapahos, who continued to host large Ghost Dances well into the twentieth century. Among Kiowa Apaches, the Ghost Dance developed into a weekly observance. Louise Saddleblanket was born in 1893 and grew up attending services of the "Ghost Dance Church"; these were Sunday lodge meetings in which women painted their faces with crosses and prayed to God and Jesus.[12]

The Caddo devotees who brought the new teachings from Nevada in 1891 established a tradition of Ghost Dancing that endured in some form for a century. It became a regular weekend ritual, and by the 1920s (when aged and venerated emissaries to Wovoka still directed the ceremony) it was the central community gathering around which other social and political events—such as tribal council meetings—were planned. As late as the 1960s, some continued to practice it. By the 1980s, the ritual had become more of a social occasion than a strictly religious one, to the discomfiture of traditionalists. By the 1990s, Ghost Dance songs had become "church songs"—standards sung at funerals and memorial dinners—and also part of the cultural heritage regularly rehearsed by the Caddo Culture Club, which was convened to preserve traditional music and song.[13]

Among Kiowas, the Ghost Dance, or the "feather dance," carried on into the World War I era, at which point it met with severe repression at Anadarko by Agent C. V. Stinchecum. He threatened to withhold from Ghost Dancers the cash payments to which they were entitled from interest on reservation land sales. Stinchecum was supported by some anti–Ghost Dance Kiowas, especially Kiowa Christians (including the longtime opponent Apiatan). Others defended the religion, which they readily mixed with various other religions old and new. Big Tree, who professed faith simultaneously in Christianity, the Peyote Religion, and the Ghost Dance, told the agent that Ghost Dancers were "praying to the same god" as "white people in their churches," but such explanations fell on deaf ears. The agent remained steadfastly opposed to the Ghost Dance, and those who participated found themselves in dire financial straits.[14]

As a result of the persecution, the Kiowa Ghost Dance went through two transformations that offer clues as to why the religion's prescriptions to engage the world of farming, schooling, and church have become harder rather than easier for scholars to discover. Few doubted the government's hostility to the Ghost Dance after Wounded Knee. On the one hand, as that hostility mounted on the Southern Plains in the 1910s and 1920s, the dance became a marker of resistance to assimilation policies and the federal government. The religion that began by encouraging Indians to study, work, attend Christian churches, keep the peace, and dance became known ever more exclusively for the dance alone, precisely because government authorities fixated on the practice and ignored the teachings. Because they insisted that the gatherings and the turning of the circle constituted a cardinal offense against the American state, performing the Ghost Dance came to represent primarily resistance to the larger ban on all dancing. Thus, Ghost Dancers became tenacious holdouts on behalf of Indian ceremonialism.

On the other hand, agents who feared that the Ghost Dance could restore the old ways were not entirely wrong. In 1916 the anthropologist Clark Wissler observed that, since 1890, the Ghost Dance had been the central ritual of a broader reworking of ceremonial and dance traditions across the Plains. In trance visions, dancers encountered spirits who instructed them to revive older traditions and ceremonies that had vanished or faded. Between this spiritual power—the ritual's ability to open a portal to prior times—and the allure of the dance circle itself as an expression of Indianness, the Ghost Dance became a vehicle for cultural renewal and a key component of what is today known as religious traditionalism.[15]

Agents typically referred to Indians who danced or worshiped in the old ways as "nonprogressive," but this label, as we have seen, was never anything but a specter in the colonial imagination. Traditionalism, on the other hand, was a cultural movement that arose from Indian communities as individuals seeking lives both modern and traditional debated, strategized, and worked at restoring select ceremonies, crafts, songs, and other cultural attributes that had been threatened or diminished by government bans or changing culture. As the dance became a less ambiguous call to revive old ways, it may be that explicit teachings about right behavior became more implicit. By the early 1900s, after all, Indians of all religions had long since accepted the need for wage work, farming, education, and even church attendance; perhaps they no longer needed the Ghost Dance to encourage them in these directions.

Faced with the hostility of the agent, however, Kiowas at Anadarko began to hold dances less frequently. Indeed, the Ghost Dance appears to have largely ended sometime in the 1920s. Perhaps it was occasionally revived in secret, for vestiges endured long after: Kiowa singers sometimes sang Ghost Dance songs to close out pow-wows as late as the 1950s.[16]

Where did the Ghost Dance go? Perhaps some religions die, fading into oblivion once their believers pass away, or cease to have visions, or no longer feel inspired. But even as it faded in some places, the Ghost Dance has periodically revived. In 1973, activists with the American Indian Movement held a Ghost Dance during the seventy-one-day occupation of Wounded Knee. In 2006, the Walker River Paiute Tribe, downstream from Yerington, revived the Ghost Dance, partly in an effort to heal the environmental crisis created by the ongoing diversion of water from Walker River for irrigation, and the consequent decline of Walker Lake and the near-extinction of its once-abundant Lahontan cutthroat trout.[17]

Moreover, even where the dance has ceased, it often lives on in other forms. Just as the Ghost Dance itself grew out of older religious traditions and movements, it seems likely that Ghost Dancers grafted their experiences and many of their beliefs onto other religions and ceremonies.

The story of the Arapaho Sitting Bull suggests one such direction. Some years after leading the Ghost Dance revival in Oklahoma, Sitting Bull was partially paralyzed by a stroke. Like many others, he turned to Peyote and was healed. He also became a Mennonite.[18]

Sitting Bull, as we know, was also a ranking member in the medicine lodge system. His movement from medicine lodge to Ghost Dancer to Peyotist to Mennonite was less a journey through a succession of religions than a mixing and blending of at least four different traditions in a search for health and well-being, both spiritual and physical. His descendants would also make remarkable journeys in search of spirit that mingled Ghost Dance, Christian, and other Indian traditions.

This might be surprising considering that the Ghost Dance, with its prophecy of an all-Indian world, would seem to clash with established Christian orthodoxy. Perhaps no single element of Wovoka's teachings caused so much public consternation as the prophecy of white vanishment. As we have seen, many saw that teaching as a threat of antiwhite violence, or at least assumed that it predicted a dire end for white people. How could followers of any religion that promised an end to white Christians themselves become Christians?

One promising answer maintains that the fear of white destruction was always misplaced. In some versions of Wovoka's teachings the new earth would bury the whites, but in others it would push them back to Europe, where they would remain. Other versions said only that there would be no whites and Indians alone would populate the new earth. Perhaps white people would be raptured to their own heaven in a separate, segregated cosmos (which, in the age of Jim Crow, seemed their heart's desire).

There is still another meaning we could draw from this prophecy. It was certainly possible to interpret Jack Wilson's foretelling to Short Bull that "all would speak one tongue" as a warning to outsiders, especially white people. But it might also have pointed to a heavenly intervention to counter the earthly policies of the US government: a miraculous assimilation of white people, or at least good white people, into Indians.

Racial transfiguration—the miraculous rebirth of one race as another—had long been a staple of American culture. In teachings that Jack Wilson himself must have heard, Mormons prophesied that when Christ returned to earth he would appear first among the Indians, whose skins would become white as they entered his church. Such ideas had a long tradition in the beliefs of many Christian sects that invoked the original day of Pentecost as recounted in the Book of Acts: the twelve apostles and other Christians received the gift of tongues and were able to preach to all people in their own language, a miracle that secured thousands of new converts to Christ.

Of course, the rebirth of one race as another, the goal of assimilationists, could also be a distinctly secular dream. Contemporary racial theory (espoused not least by Powell and other anthropologists) postulated an ever-expanding white society that would one day absorb or annihilate all people of color, resulting in a unified, white, and presumably English-speaking world, a kind of nonreligious millennium analogous to, if not informed by, New Testament teachings.

It may be that, to Short Bull and others, Wovoka's millennium would reverse this process and a day would come when all people would become Indians instead of white and, critically, all would speak one tongue. There would be no war and no work, only a unified Indian community that was eternally prosperous, at ease, and young. This vision of the postmillennium reflected an earthly push toward pan-Indian exchange and alliance that dominated the 1880s and 1890s. The Ghost Dance movement itself grew out of preexisting networks of former allies and adversaries among the Lakota, Crow, Pawnee, Arapaho, Shoshone, and others, who visited one another and discussed how to respond to the challenges of reservation life and US Indian policy. Such discussion went on in a wide range of venues—in council meetings and private cabins, in the dressing rooms of Wild West shows, and around the wood-burning stoves of reservation trading posts.[19]

This dream of racial unity may have helped draw many Ghost Dancers to certain brands of evangelical Christianity. In 1970 one of the Arapaho Sitting Bull's granddaughters, Myrtle Lincoln, who had participated in the Ghost Dance as a child, described the emotional ecstasies of Ghost Dance visionaries as being "just like this Pentecostal way." In her adult life, Lincoln was a committed Pentecostal, and she noted that the Ghost Dance that her grandfather exhorted had more than a passing similarity to Pentecostalism. Indeed, she concluded, "We think it might be the same thing."[20]

The parallels drawn by Lincoln were not surprising. As we have seen, the Ghost Dance was contemporary with incipient Pentecostalism and its "holy rollers," the followers of the holiness movement led by Maria Woodworth and others. For all their differences, holy rollers and Ghost Dancers had much in common. Americans who took up holiness sought to free the spirit by lifting the heavy hand of scientific rationalism and engaging emotionally with Christ. Each intrusion of scientific and technical control over daily life, each application of Darwin's theories to wider and more intimate realms of understanding, each movement away from the older, organic earth of people and animals into the world of engineering and machines, each advance in the data collection of the census and other surveys, seems only to have further energized what we might call a spirit rebellion within the hearts of believers. As science and social science advanced, trust in Holy Spirit possession, faith healing, and individuals' ability to commune with God and Jesus outside of established churches grew only more ecstatic. Even though in 1905 Frederick Davenport condemned the behavior even of white revivalists as the very "savagery" on display in the Ghost Dance, the following year the Azusa Street revival in Los Angeles attracted thousands of believers who writhed on the ground, spoke in tongues, and collectively gave birth to the modern Pentecostal movement.[21]

Victorian elites insisted that true Christians abide suffering on this earth and patiently await God's reward in heaven. Rejecting such dicta, holiness followers and their Pentecostal successors embraced a belief in a Holy Spirit that could infuse the individual body with grace and healing. Parallel ideas circulated in the Ghost Dance, which advanced bodily healing and cultural resurgence through spirit intervention. Those spirits, of course, were distinctive from the Holy Spirit, but they allowed believers to escape the straitjacket of Victorian reticence imposed by missionaries.

After 1906, many holiness believers from earlier decades became Pentecostals, and many Ghost Dancers appear to have done the same. At first glance, this development seems bizarre, given that these ways of believing were unrelated and opposed. Many white Pentecostals rejected the Ghost Dance as paganism, and could any believers be more distinctive from Ghost Dancers than Pentecostals, many of whom, after all, did not dance?

But in their devotion to ecstatic spirit, clean living, hard work, and millennial deliverance, the Ghost Dance and evangelical Christianity had much in common. In fact, their connection formed early on. In 1939 the anthropologist Cora Du Bois noted that leaders of the 1870 Ghost Dance in northern California had frequently become leaders of Pentecostal and Four Square Gospel churches, often ministering to both Indians and whites. "Their influence," she concluded, "has made possible the introduction and acceptance of the many marginal Christian sects which now flourish among the Indians of this region."[22]

On the Southern Plains, in addition to Myrtle Lincoln, many other Indians noted the similarities between the ecstatic visions of Pentecostals and Ghost Dancers, with trances, bodily contortions, rolling on the ground, and shaking all common to both. Kiowa Apache women in the Ghost Dance Church behaved "just like Holy Rolly," according to Louise Saddleblanket. A Caddo believer explained to the anthropologist Elsie Clews Parsons that government opposition had taken a toll on the Ghost Dance, but that it "might come back through the influence of "Roly Rollers [*sic*]," whose beliefs were "just the same as [the] Ghost dance."[23]

In the 1930s, Myrtle Lincoln attended a multiracial Pentecostal service led by an Arapaho minister—her son, the great-grandson of Sitting Bull, the Arapaho Ghost Dance evangelist. During the service, a white woman fell to the ground, seized by the Holy Spirit. When she rose, the woman implored God, "Father in heaven, give us a blessing here. Bless our Indians. Show them the way." None of that would have been unusual at a Pentecostal service—except that the white woman was speaking fluent Arapaho.[24]

For Myrtle Lincoln, the Ghost Dance and Pentecostalism flowed together in a tradition of personal visions and a dream of a world in which "all nations will talk one tongue," just as Jack Wilson had taught Short Bull and the other evangelists decades before. For all the differences between Pentecostalism and Ghost Dancing, both religions encouraged an intimate bond with the creator, including ecstatic bodily movements and trance visions. In both religions, exhortations to live a clean life and work hard accompanied utopian dreams of a world renewed and its old racial and tribal animosities vanquished. The modernity of such beliefs and their utility for living a twentieth-century life offer a long-overlooked meaning for the Ghost Dance and may be one reason why it endured long after Wounded Knee.

The Ghost Dance, in the end, proved flexible. For the most part, it seems to have begun as a measure of accommodation to the reservation era, but when the government cracked down hard enough, as at Pine Ridge, it became one of a bundle of practices that expressed resistance. Whatever happened to the teachings about work, education, and churchgoing as the Ghost Dance developed, we should not forget that they were present in the religion's early days. To be sure, the Ghost Dance sought to restore a vanished world. But in simultaneously facilitating the recovery of traditional ceremony and dance, reinforcing Indian identity, and authorizing believers to seek success in work and school in the modern world, it also engaged the present.[25]

The Ghost Dance was a modern religion that offered believers a means to reconcile the seeming contradictions between Indian identity and twentieth-century survival. Belief is an affair of the heart, but it is hard to imagine a more sensible, rational, and spiritually authentic response to the challenges of the reservation era.

BEGINNINGS

I N January 1891, within two weeks of surrendering their guns, Short Bull, Kicking Bear, and some two dozen other Ghost Dancers were arrested by the army and placed aboard a train to Chicago. On arrival, troops escorted them to Fort Sheridan, where they were held as "hostages" against future uprisings. The lodgings were not uncomfortable, and as Short Bull recounted later that year, the Indians were often "visited by General Miles who with all the officers made us as comfortable as could be, doing all in their power for us."[1]

For all that, the Lakotas must have felt a sense of dread upon first seeing Fort Sheridan. The place comprised a 700-foot-long, two-and-a-half-story brick barracks, flanking a mock castle gatehouse, topped by a stone turret that, at 228 feet, was taller than any other building in greater Chicago. Designers patterned the turret after the bell tower in Saint Mark's Square in Venice, but with enough mock arrow loops and buttresses to resemble a medieval battement. (It actually housed the fort's water tower.)

Fort Sheridan was new—so new in fact that the imprisonment of Ghost Dancers was its first military duty. With its intentionally foreboding appearance, the architects had been commissioned to design it for enemies closer by. The looming tower guarded the shore of Lake Michigan not as an outpost of the Indian War to the west or to fend off foreign invaders from the east, but to suppress the nascent labor movement in Chicago.

In the aftermath of the Haymarket Bombing of 1886, many elites had anticipated a civil war between capital and labor. Marshall Field and other prominent businessmen of the Chicago Commercial Club had donated the land to the federal government with a petition for a fort; they wanted the army to be deployed quickly should fighting erupt between businessmen and the ranks of immigrants and union-ists in the city. Construction began in 1887, and the final tiles were installed on the tower roof in 1891, the same year the Ghost Dancers arrived.

Three years later, in 1894, as Kiowas began to turn the Ghost Dance circle in Oklahoma and James Mooney was submitting the completed manuscript of his Ghost Dance book to his employer, the prophecy of class war came true to some extent. The army, once again under the command of General Nelson A. Miles, marched out from Fort Sheridan against strikers at the company town of Pullman, seized control of the rail yards, and ended a strike and shutdown that had paralyzed much of the nation's rail network. The ensuing riots across the country killed thirty-four people.[2]

Even though Fort Sheridan had been built to crush civil insurrec-tion, its use as a prison for Ghost Dancers was fitting. As we have seen, immigration and the emergence of new ethnic groups, worker unrest, and the persistence of Indian religions and communities were interlocking social and political challenges in the last decade of the nineteenth century. Despite the continuing presence of native-born white Americans in the ranks of labor, by 1890 the increasingly im-migrant composition of the working classes seemed to signal a social crisis to many observers. The Ghost Dance had inspired panic in part because it came at a moment of profound cultural anxiety about assimilation, social order, and the alienation of the working masses from more well-to-do Americans. Fort Sheridan itself was a mon-ument to the military solution many sought for dealing with immi-grants and Indians alike.

The journey of the confined Ghost Dancers would take another turn through the workings of a popular entertainment devised both to soothe and, to a degree, exploit these profound anxieties. In the spring of 1891, William "Buffalo Bill" Cody, the onetime army scout and buffalo hunter who had achieved transatlantic celebrity as the impresario of Buffalo Bill's Wild West show, arrived at Fort Sheridan. His show was preparing for another European tour, and he invited the prisoners to join them. When his energetic publicist, John M. Burke, followed up to press the matter, he made "such grand offers to see the 'great country beyond the water' with good salary that we all consented to go," remembered Short Bull. Perhaps sealing the deal was Cody's promise to reunite them with family members. The Ghost Dancers, isolated from their kin and far from home, were thrilled when Cody brought along sixty friends and relatives from Pine Ridge to accompany them overseas.

Crossing the Atlantic to Belgium, the Ghost Dancers and their families went to work in the modern entertainment industry. Short Bull made $25 per month (far better than the wages he earned as a freighter) to enact—or "re-enact," as the show programs claimed— battlefield exploits at Little Big Horn and elsewhere. He and the others danced for paying crowds, sold handcrafts to collectors and souvenir hunters, and learned the ropes of modern show business and modern travel. After tours of Belgium, Germany, and the Netherlands, the show moved on to Britain.

It was probably during the performances in Glasgow that autumn that Short Bull dictated his memoir to the show translator George Craeger. The holy man liked Buffalo Bill's Wild West: "Ever since I have been with the Company I have been well treated and cared for, all of the promises made have been fulfilled." Cody and the show managers "are our friends, and do all they can for us in every way." There was food, clothing, work, and money, and "besides we go everywhere and see all the great works of the Country through which we travel." Whatever complaints the Indians had were addressed at once, and "if we do not feel well, a doctor comes and looks after us."

If the holy man was bitter about events in South Dakota, he did not show it. He had only one complaint about Great Britain. "I like the English people but not their weather as it rains so much."[3]

Short Bull's career in the show led to other artistic endeavors. It was probably during this European tour that he first met the German artist Carl Henckel. In 1893 the two met again when Short Bull rejoined the Wild West show to work in Chicago outside the World's Columbian Exposition. Henckel sketched a portrait of Short Bull, and the holy man sold him some of his ledger book drawings—including two of Annie Oakley. Short Bull and Cody reunited when Cody came to Pine Ridge in 1913 to reenact the Wounded Knee Massacre for his movie *The Indian Wars*. Short Bull assisted in the organizing and is said to have appeared in the film, although it is impossible to know for sure: the nitrate film degraded over time and no copy is known to exist.[4]

Cody titillated the press with tall tales of the Lakota survivors of the original massacre threatening to use real ammunition in the filming. This was pure publicity, with no basis in fact. The film departed from history in other ways as well. It contained no references to Wovoka's teachings about work, farming, and education, and to avoid stirring the undying controversy over the massacre, the filmmaker whitewashed the atrocity, staging no bodies of women and children and perpetuating the fiction that the massacre was a "battle."[5]

Back in South Dakota, in August 1891, the Wazhazha Brules had at last secured their transfer to Pine Ridge, and so Short Bull returned to Pass Creek when he left the Wild West show. In 1898 he and the other Wazhazhas moved away to join other onetime followers of Crazy Horse in founding the town of Wanblee, in the northeast corner of Pine Ridge Reservation, on Craven Creek. There in future years he spoke often about the Ghost Dance and earned money by selling paintings, drawings, and ethnographic information to visiting scholars and collectors.[6]

Although his memory of events seems to have shifted and become more mystical over time, Short Bull's rendering of the teachings

E.1. Short Bull at Saint Francis Mission, Rosebud Reservation, South Dakota, ca. 1892. Note the work gloves. Buechel Memorial Lakota Museum, Saint Francis, South Dakota.

remained remarkably consistent. In 1906 he met with Natalie Curtis, a collector of Indian music. In a lyrical, mysterious account, he related to Curtis his geographic and spiritual journeys in the Ghost Dance, his passage through both the West and the spirit world, and the impact of these travels on his life.[7]

He said nothing about the Ghost Dance code for good living. In 1909 he was sought out by the German artist Frederick Weygold, to whom he recounted his conversations with the prophet. In this interview, Short Bull almost seemed to depart from his earlier contention that the religion insisted on farming, schooling, and church. He quoted a seemingly nativist admonition from the prophet that believers should "abandon the way of the Whites" who "cursed us." As Short Bull explained, "The Indians were made by the Great Mystery and only for living in a certain way and they should (therefore) not accept the ways of another people." But it seems more likely that in relaying to Wegyold the teaching that believers should "abandon the ways of the Whites," Short Bull (and, we may assume, Wovoka himself) meant that Indians should abandon the ways of unrespectable white men, of those who "cursed us."[8]

This interpretation allows us to reconcile the command to set aside the ways of white people with the instructions that Short Bull said he delivered to followers before each Ghost Dance. As he told Weygold, all dancers were told, "Your children should go to school and learn. The old people should attend some religious worship and say prayers." He instructed his followers to "draw something [from] the earth, too [that is, do some farming or gardening] and they should build houses to live in, and take good advice from respectable white men, too. Then do not kill each other!"[9]

In 1915, Short Bull dictated a narrative of his Ghost Dance experiences for Father Eugene Buechel, a Jesuit priest at Pine Ridge. He said that a trance overtook him in the dance circle and he saw "the Son of God," who instructed him to teach the people, "under your clothes, always paint your bodies." This cryptic but suggestive instruction may have been an exhortation to remain true to Indian ceremonies and traditions, even while assuming the clothes and trappings of white society. In other words, the Ghost Dance authorized Indians to become successful in the reservation era, even as it empowered them to resist the onslaught of assimilation.[10]

He remained mystified by the violence that consumed the religion. "Who would have thought that dancing could make such trouble?"

he wondered to Buechel. "We had no thought of fighting; if we had meant to fight, would we not have carried arms? We went unarmed to the dance."[11]

Known as a gentle, retiring man, Short Bull lived so long that the date of his death is something of a mystery. One account says that he died in 1915; another says 1923. Still another claims that he lived until 1935. Family lore maintains it was 1921. Whenever Short Bull left this earth, he carried with him throughout his life a profound religiosity, a strong work ethic, and a palpable sense of injustice over what had happened at Wounded Knee and in the whole sad travail of American conquest. "In this world the Great Father has given to the white man everything and to the Indian nothing, but it will not always be thus," he prophesied to Natalie Curtis. "For ere long this world will be consumed in flame and pass away. Then, in the life after this, to the Indian shall all be given."[12]

Viewing the Ghost Dance as a religion engaged with modernity, we should not be surprised at those turns in Short Bull's biography that might otherwise seem strange—the passage of a Ghost Dance evangelist and holy man to earning wages on European tour with a Wild West show, working in the movies, and becoming a paid consultant to collectors and anthropologists. All of these pursuits were in keeping with the teachings of Wovoka, who encouraged his followers "to work all the time and not lie down in idleness," either in jobs or on their own farms, and to be true to the cause of peace. To live by a religious code is a demanding task. Short Bull was human, and therefore not perfect. But to judge by the record he left us, he lived an exemplary Ghost Dance life.

AFTER LEAVING PINE RIDGE, WILLIAM SELWYN, THE YANKTON Dakota postmaster who fed inflammatory rumors about the Ghost Dance to officials, became renowned, and in many quarters reviled, for his land dealings at his home reservation in South Dakota, 200 miles east of Pine Ridge. When he called for the sale of the Pipestone Quarry—a sacred site entrusted to Yankton Dakotas for safekeeping by other tribes in decades past—he found powerful allies in Washington. He also earned the enmity of many Yanktons. Selwyn became adept at submitting language for congressional bills to Washington officials. Some that became law benefited him at the expense of other Yanktons and even allowed him to purchase particular parcels of land. Returning by train from a negotiation in Washington, one of his fellow Yanktons denounced Selwyn as a traitor to his people. Selwyn dropped him with a single punch to the head.

The identity of Selwyn's antagonist is unknown; family lore identified him only as a maker of beautiful handwoven ropes. But others among Selwyn's opponents were well known indeed. Leading their ranks was Selwyn's own father, Chief Medicine Cow, who found himself campaigning against land cessions championed by his son.[13]

After 1900, Selwyn served as agency farmer at Yankton Reservation. He received cash payments on behalf of the tribe for rations and clothing, and he accumulated hundreds of acres of land.[14]

On August 22, 1905, Selwyn was repairing fences on his farm when a group of Dakota riders approached. According to family lore, he knew the men well. They came to deliver a traditional punishment ordered by the tribe. There was no appeal. He probably fought them, but they roped him around the middle and tied his hands behind his back. Then they galloped away, dragging Selwyn across the prairie, flaying him alive on thorn bushes, rocky outcrops, and finally against a long length of barbed-wire fence. His skin was practically gone when his family found his lifeless body—wrapped in a beautiful handwoven rope.

"We never pressed the issue," recalled his son many years later, "because Dad was in deep. He knew what he was into." His land dealings were at the root of his killing, but his part in Wounded Knee was not forgotten either. In 2009 another descendant concluded, "The Ghost Dance tragedy might not have happened at all had he kept his opinions to himself."[15]

JOSEPH HORNED CLOUD LOST MANY FAMILY MEMBERS AT Wounded Knee. With those who survived, he settled at Pine Ridge. There was not much choice: the government confiscated much of the Cheyenne River Reservation, including the land on which the Horned Clouds had built cabins and grazed their stock. Thereafter, his life was punctuated by persistence and a good deal of protest, as if he carried with him an understandable need to recall the Seventh Cavalry's brutal betrayal. Horned Cloud led the campaign for a monument to the victims of the massacre, and in 1903 he saw its dedication at the hilltop mass grave, where it yet stands. Ten years later, in 1913, he translated for Buffalo Bill Cody when the showman came to Pine Ridge to film his reenactment of Wounded Knee. Disenchanted with Cody's misleading presentation of the massacre as a battle, he would protest the film's many inaccuracies.[16]

In his life's work, Horned Cloud transcended old grievances and embraced questions of faith and justice. A man of religious devotion, he became a catechist for the Catholic Church, on whose behalf he traveled across the country. In 1920 he appeared before a US House of Representatives committee and denounced, in scathing terms, the graft and corruption associated with the leasing of Indian land at Pine Ridge. He died later that year.[17]

AFTER PUBLISHING HIS MONUMENTAL GHOST DANCE STUDY in 1896, James Mooney spent more than two decades in research mostly on the Southern Plains, primarily among Kiowas, compiling studies of Kiowa heraldry and language, publishing more work on Cherokee myth, and organizing exhibitions of Indian artifacts and history at world's fairs and expositions. By far his most captivating research was on the Peyote Religion, through which he began to imagine a very different kind of Indian history than had ever before been told.

Mooney's writing about Indians, at least in the first half of his career, had been characterized by the romantic impulses of the salvage ethnologist: an overarching sense of decline in Indian societies, an assumption that all genuinely "Indian" ways were passing as Indians were gradually assimilated into white society, and an urgency to collect "authentic" Indian customs, languages, and artifacts before they irretrievably disappeared.[18]

The Ghost Dance had opened his eyes to the possibility of a new Indian religion, as authentic as the old, and his subsequent work on the Peyote Religion took him even further in this direction. Perhaps it was the Irish rejection of assimilation that allowed Mooney to imagine Indians doing the same. In any case, the longer he spent studying Peyotism, the less certain he was that Indians were destined to vanish. Like dance, peyote ritual fascinated him in part because it represented a means of strengthening and propagating Indian community and ceremony. It allowed Indians to adapt to modern reservation life and yet remain distinctive from whites. It allowed them, in other words, to be unassimilated and forthrightly Indian, even as it helped some believers prosper in modern occupations.[19]

Two articles he published on the subject suggested that his book about the Peyote Religion would rival his work on the Ghost Dance. But after this burst of energy and some promising results, he put the Peyote Religion on the shelf—or perhaps he merely kept his research secret. For many years, it ceased to appear in the progress reports he filed with the bureau. He never said why, but the reasons seem clear. Mooney had already alienated Indian agents with his defense of the Ghost Dance and other ceremonies. In 1903 he barely managed to fend off potentially career-ending charges that he had paid a Cheyenne pledger to pierce himself at a Sun Dance near Darlington. (The man had been pierced, but Mooney had not intervened in the ceremony.)[20]

Peyote proved at least as controversial as the Ghost Dance and the Sun Dance. Despite the fact that the Peyote Religion lacked either a millenarian prophecy or a central dance ritual—two features of the Ghost Dance that caused much official anxiety—government agents came to abhor it at least as much as other forms of Indian worship. Many confused it with the more dangerous mescal bean and considered peyote a narcotic (which it was not). When officials demanded, as early as 1886, that it be banned, the popularity of the Peyote Religion among Indians only expanded. In 1899, culminating over a decade of Indian agency efforts to disrupt peyote meetings, the state of Oklahoma outlawed peyote.[21]

In this climate, Mooney's endorsement of peyote as a positive good earned him the enmity of missionaries and officials. "Mooney encourages Indians in heathenish dances and mescal dissipation," wrote J. J. Methvin, the Southern Methodist missionary at Anadarko. According to Methvin's sources, Mooney had been telling Indians that peyote was good for them and that their children should be educated at reservation schools instead of at Carlisle Indian Industrial School in Pennsylvania. Methvin passed these rumors along to Richard Henry Pratt, founder and head of the Carlisle school and still a force in the making of Indian policy. Pratt, in turn, warned Secretary of the Interior Hoke Smith that Mooney "is not a fit person to be allowed among the Indians for any purpose." Smith warned Powell to rein in Mooney.[22]

What Powell told Mooney is unknown. Apparently, the ethnologist continued to work with peyote believers on a variety of other projects, but his official reports ceased to mention peyote.

The boom finally came down in the closing days of World War I. Mooney was deeply opposed to the war. Like many Irish and American patriots, he saw the conflict as a struggle between imperial powers for world domination, and one whose effects were prejudicial to social tolerance and intellectual inquiry. In the United States, the war advanced a wave of anti-immigrant sentiment and support for the temperance cause. Late in 1917, both houses of Congress passed the Twentieth Amendment to the Constitution to ban the production, transport, and sale of alcohol, and they made similar efforts to regulate and ban other drugs, including opium, marijuana—and peyote. It was at this moment that Mooney's long interest in peyote led him into a political ambush.

In February 1918, Congress convened hearings on a proposed federal law to ban peyote. Mooney, called as a primary witness, spoke eloquently in defense of the Peyote Religion. As he explained to the congressmen, younger, educated Indians found the religion helpful in restoring health and well-being, and they were the ones—not embittered old-timers—who built churches and led the movement. Peyote was used ceremonially and, he said, medicinally, but never recreationally. He had consumed peyote as part of his research "eight or ten times," up to seven or eight buttons at once, and he had brought fifty pounds of peyote to Washington for chemical analysis. In all his time among Peyotists, he said, he had seen nothing that could be described as immorality. In fact, the religion forbade the drinking of whiskey and encouraged hard work. In his view, peyote was the sacrament of a religion that was "not a Christian religion, but a very close approximation" that might itself lead Indians to Christianity.[23]

"I favor the continuance of this peyote religion among the Indians as a religious ceremony," concluded Mooney.

"Why?" asked a hostile congressman.

"Because it is their religion," replied Mooney, adopting the language of the First Amendment. He also favored the religion, he said, "because they understand it, because it kills out whisky drinking among them, and because we have medical testimony that, as they use it, it is practically impossible to take an overdose, and because it does not result in a habit."[24]

Mooney's testimony was politely received, until he later returned to rebut the claims of several anti-peyote witnesses. As he finished, he was interrupted by another luminary in the room: Richard Henry Pratt. The founder of Carlisle Indian Industrial School had long since made it his mission to destroy Mooney's reputation, and he had been lying in wait. "I feel I would like to say something about the gentleman who has just spoken," Pratt blurted out. He then smeared Mooney with the allegation from fifteen years before that Mooney had paid a Cheyenne Indian to pierce himself in the Sun Dance at Darlington in 1903.

Mooney was furious. "General Pratt is old enough and has been in an official position long enough to know that he must investigate his statements before he declares them." His charges were "an absolute falsehood" that had been "denied on investigation by every man who asserted it and he knows that." Mooney offered to furnish documents to prove his case.

Pratt bragged that he, too, could present evidence. "You ethnologists egg on, frequent, illustrate, and exaggerate at the public expense, and so give the Indian race and their civilization a black eye in the public esteem." He suggested that Mooney himself had fomented the Ghost Dance—"white men were its promoters if not its originators." Now "this peyote craze" was "under the same impulse."

"You can not furnish proof, because there is no proof," snarled Mooney.

The chairman waved off the two antagonists and called the next witness.[25]

If the dispute seemed irrelevant to the chairman, it showcased a central disagreement between assimilationists like Pratt and the ethnologist-cum-activist James Mooney. To Pratt, Indianness had to vanish for Indians to become economic actors and citizens. Mooney had once thought the same. But by 1918 he had come to believe that while Indians would have to become workers, Indianness was flexible and adaptive, and also that Indian religion and ceremony were assets to those seeking to reconcile themselves to reservation lives through work and farming.

That fall, when Mooney returned to Oklahoma, he saw firsthand the deep appreciation of his efforts as separate delegations of Comanches, Wichitas, and Caddos traveled as far as sixty miles to see him. "My reception by my old Kiowa friends and other Indians was almost an ovation," he wrote.[26]

The congressional hearings and the impending ban on peyote had energized these peyote believers. Throughout the state, Indians were organizing to defend their religion. A group of Oto, Kiowa, and Arapaho believers, including Mooney's translator and consultant Cleaver Warden and the Ghost Dance leader Paul Boynton, convened in the town of Cheyenne, Oklahoma, to discuss the defense of peyote. Mooney joined them. Four years earlier, the peyote leader Jonathan Koshiway had led the incorporation under state law of the first peyote church—the First-Born Church of Christ—at Red Rock, Oklahoma. Now, in the summer of 1918, Koshiway attended the gathering at Cheyenne with charter in hand. According to lore within the movement, James Mooney helped persuade those present that incorporation under the law, like the First-Born Church of

Christ, would provide legal protections for peyote believers. Mooney also, it is said, originated the name for the new organization. On October 10, the charter of the Native American Church was registered with the state of Oklahoma.[27]

Mooney, Warden, Boynton, and others had all learned lessons from defending the Ghost Dance that they now applied to the Peyote Religion. In their struggles to defend the teachings of Wovoka, believers had articulated them as "their religion," and Ghost Dancers had even spoken of it as their "church." Now Peyote believers, with many Ghost Dancers among them, were organized into a legally defined church, an institution with protected status under the US Constitution.

But opposition mounted. Even before the charter went to the state, missionaries and anti-peyote activists had been put on notice by that winter's congressional hearing, and they had Mooney in their sights. In August a visiting missionary complained that one "Mr. Mooney of the Smithsonian Institute" was encouraging "old tribal customs" and the use of peyote. Church-based Indian uplift organizations began denouncing Mooney in their newsletters for "encouraging a demoralizing practice among the Indians."[28]

In Oklahoma, Indian agents eagerly joined the anti-Mooney campaign, led by the superintendent of the Kiowa, Comanche, and Wichita reservation, C. V. Stinchecum—the same man who was at that moment persecuting Kiowa Ghost Dancers. Stinchecum assailed Mooney's support for peyote and sent a telegram to his superiors demanding the anthropologist's "immediate recall" to Washington. Commissioner of Indian Affairs Cato Sells obliged, banning Mooney from all Indian reservations. On October 23, 1918, Mooney was ordered to leave the Kiowa reservation and return at once to Washington.[29]

He never returned to Oklahoma, or to any Indian reservation. Mooney's dissenting views, especially about the Peyote Religion and the role of scientists in a democratic republic, would now cost him a great deal, partly because he had few defenders in the profession. Powell had long since died. Anthropology was becoming more professional, requiring graduate training, and Mooney did not even have a college degree. Unable to hold an academic position, he never trained students, and no cadre of defenders emerged on his behalf. As a government employee in a nation gripped by assimilationist hysteria and denunciations of "foreign" influences and "un-American" thinking, Mooney, in his devotion to religious dissent and Indian autonomy, earned only unbending censure. Now effectively barred from Indian reservations, Mooney appealed twice to the Commissioner of Indian Affairs for permission to return to his research in Oklahoma. He met personally with Secretary of the Interior John Barton Payne. Early in 1921, Warren G. Harding succeeded Woodrow Wilson as president. Mooney appealed to the new commissioner of Indian affairs, Charles H. Burke. But all to no avail. Each appeal was blocked by his superiors at the Smithsonian Institution.[30]

Behind Mooney's persistence was an ironclad belief in the utility and morality of science, including social science, as a method for locating and identifying the truth. In one of his final appeals, he stated that his disbarment had "left me in the position of a condemned criminal for a period of three years, to the demoralization of my best work, the undermining of my health and the injury of my reputation built up by years of honorable service in the bureau." Not only was his heart condition "aggravated almost to suffocation point with any long confinement at the desk in the damper atmosphere of Washington," not only had no ethnologist "ever before been held to the desk for as long a period or under such conditions," but despite being "pledged before the scientific world" to investigate the Peyote Religion, the bureau was refusing to do its duty.[31]

In Mooney's view, that pledge—to explore the Peyote Religion using the tools of science—required the pursuit of the truth, whatever it turned out to be. To turn away from peyote because it challenged conventional belief and assimilation policy would have been profoundly unscientific and immoral. To Mooney, if there was anything that modern society—"civilization"—offered to the world, it was the practice of good science. His disbarment hurt as a professional slight, but it also represented the triumph of politics over scientific inquiry.

In the pursuit of truth that defined the purpose of civilization, the United States had failed.

Mooney's defense of science was stalwart, but perhaps his greatest achievement was to have realized the essential humanity of Indians, grasped their authentic, ongoing contributions to religious experience in modern America, and aided in their protection. Mooney had become an intellectual partner to Indians in developing new tools for defending their religions from assimilationists. In this two-way process, Mooney had learned from Indians the value and meaning of Indian belief. What John Wesley Powell and others called "superstitions" and "primitive" beliefs came to represent to Mooney realms of spiritual practice that should be sheltered under the First Amendment.

He made his claims based on the US Constitution and traditions of religious tolerance—which he helped to expand—but Mooney's religious sensibilities derived also from growing up Irish-American Catholic and Irish nationalist. He never articulated as theoretical positions the fundamentally anti-imperial and anti-colonial thinking about Indians that these origins helped him develop, but his form of relativistic thinking about religions came to predominate in the intellectual circles of Franz Boas, a Mooney contemporary and himself a German Jewish immigrant. Boas and his students would be a generation of "outsider" anthropologists with versions of double-consciousness even more pronounced than Mooney's. Many of Boas's students were immigrants or children of immigrants from eastern Europe, and many of them were Jewish. Among their contributions was the abandonment of racial theories of development and social evolution for what came to be called "cultural relativism," an approach in which all cultures have meaning and coherence in and of themselves and all are of equal value. Such ideas have become critical to modern American thought; what were once ominous ethnic and racial differences have now been transformed into assets of cultural diversity, which we know as a modern virtue. Mooney's work linked the old developmental models for religious thinking so favored by the generation of John Wesley Powell with the new sensibilities nurtured by Boas and his students.[32]

The Catholic who posed as an Irish healer in order to secure the medicine books of Eastern Cherokees and who became a Ghost Dancer among the Southern Arapahos, had come to identify profoundly with American Indian believers in peyote and other ceremonies and religions. When he threw down a gauntlet to the reigning doctrines of cultural evolution and assimilationism, however, he brought down upon himself the full fury of American disapproval.

Still battling to return to Oklahoma, ailing and confined to a rocking chair on the third floor of his home in Washington, James Mooney died on December 22, 1921, at the age of sixty.[33]

Upon hearing the news, the Native American Church of Clinton, Oklahoma, adopted a resolution hailing Mooney's "great work and the numerous acts of kindness rendered by this great man, to the Indians in general, and especially to our tribes." In the church's view, Mooney's life had been "spent with a view of bettering our conditions through the Native American Church . . . making us able to become better citizens and to defend our religion as he knew it."[34]

James Mooney's contributions to the Native American Church had begun in the Ghost Dance. Jack Wilson's prophecy fired Mooney's ethnological imagination. It carried him along a course on which he would embrace divergent religious traditions and even become their spokesman. The Ghost Dance inspired his greatest work, but by entering the door it opened for him, he became a pariah in Washington, where he needed elusive public approval to continue his work. The Ghost Dance made and then unmade James Mooney's career.

For all the defeat he encountered, Mooney never quailed or retreated from his convictions. The Ghost Dance and Jack Wilson's vision led him toward acknowledgment of Indian religions, defense of intellectual freedom, and a view of the world as a place of many religions—as a bigger, and dare we say it, newer world.

ABOUT 1894, JACK WILSON'S EIGHT-YEAR-OLD SON, TIMOTHY, was killed when he was run over by a wagon. Grief consumed the weather maker. The skies opened, and rivers of rain descended. Then the clouds parted, and the storm ceased.[35]

Exactly when the Ghost Dance stopped in Mason Valley is hard to say. In the fall of 1892, the Indian agent in Nevada suggested that enthusiasm for the Ghost Dance had begun to wane: "I am happy to report this craze as almost having subsided at its cradle." Part of the reason for its decline appears to have been growing reticence. That same fall of 1892, the Arapaho Sitting Bull led another delegation of Arapaho and Cheyenne to the prophet and were told by him to stop doing the dance. In October 1893, Black Coyote and others dictated a letter through James Mooney to the prophet, asking for red paint and other tokens of the prophet and inquiring if indeed he wanted them to cease their devotions; the answer, if it came, has been lost to the record.[36]

Wovoka may have been retreating from his earlier teachings, or he may have been merely lowering their public profile. As we have seen, he was still receiving Lakota believers more than a decade later. In Nevada, dances may have gone on secretly. After Mooney's visit in January 1892, Wovoka refused to speak to any other official or anthropologist. Perhaps he felt that his goals had been accomplished. Perhaps he no longer saw the point of talking to white people about his religion. Local tradition does not say when the dances stopped, only that they did.

Sometime after 1910, Jack Wilson's father died. Numu Taivo had been a powerful doctor, and now his prowess passed to Wovoka, who also became a potent healer. On the back of his Ghost Dance prophecies, his skills as a doctor became widely renowned. Indians in Oklahoma and elsewhere wrote him hundreds of letters. Wilson (who was illiterate) answered this correspondence with the help of his friend Ed Dyer, the Nevada storekeeper who spoke fluent Paiute and had served as interpreter for Wovoka and James Mooney in 1892. Many letters from Plains Indians came to Wovoka with the help of another Ghost Dance acolyte. As Ed Dyer recalled, they were "almost invariably post-marked 'Darlington, Oklahoma' and written by one Grant Left-Hand, who appeared to function as a scribe for most of the Indian Nation."[37]

Many supplicants wrote to request red ochre paint or magpie feathers. In keeping with their traditions, petitioners readily sent a "gift"—a fee in exchange for the promise of health—and Wilson made a small living from this mail-order medical practice. Among other requests, correspondents often asked for some article of Wilson's clothing, even for the large sombrero he typically wore. As Dyer recalled, "I was very often called upon to send them his hat which he would remove forthwith from his head on hearing the nature of a request in a letter." Wilson charged $20 for his hat and bought replacements from Dyer. "Although I did a steady and somewhat profitable business in hats, I envied him his mark-up which exceeded mine to a larcenous degree," wrote the storekeeper. "But somehow this very human trait made him all the more likable."[38]

Wovoka's fame extended far and wide. On at least two occasions, in 1906 and again in 1916, he traveled to Oklahoma, where he received money and gifts—mocassins, vests, belts, gloves, buckskin breeches, and "other articles of finery"—that "would have made a collector of Indian hand work green with envy," recalled Dyer. Among the Numu, too, he held a place of great esteem. His renown extended even to white doctors. In the 1920s, Dr. George Magee, the contract physician at the Walker River Reservation, often consulted with Wovoka about medical cases. Magee later recalled that Wilson "took care of the bulk of the Indians," even as he sent appendicitis cases, serious fractures, or other "severe things" to Magee. Paiutes spoke of Wovoka's magic; Magee was in awe of his "amazing" technical prowess, which enabled him to perform eyelid surgery with a piece of salt grass.[39]

Meanwhile, Americans were doing their best to remove the need for the weather maker's magic. In 1905 the massive Truckee-Carson irrigation project, the first project of the newly founded US Bureau of Reclamation, diverted the voluminous Truckee River into the Carson River just north of Walker River Reservation to fulfill dreams of irrigating 350,000 acres. Only after the first water was delivered, however, did officials test the soil, whereupon they discovered that the plains of the Carson Sink rested on a very high water table. Adding millions of gallons to the surface raised the water level so much that the roots of crops were submerged and killed. The project was plagued by decades of lawsuits from disappointed settlers, and water from the project ultimately reached only 60,000 acres. In the end, the bureau created a small fraction of the farms it had once envisioned. When it came to renewing the earth, the superiorty of the first bureau project over the Ghost Dance was not at all clear.[40]

In contrast, Paiutes could point to Wovoka's success, however limited it might be. The prophecy of a world without work was not fulfilled, but work itself improved for a time. The blizzards of 1889–1890 wiped out enough Nevada cattle to crush the open-range cattle industry. Ranchers who survived the calamity invested more money in irrigation to raise hay for winter cattle feed, which became one of the largest sectors of Paiute employment. Perhaps the earth was not renewed, but by the early 1900s Paiute wages had reached record highs as Walker River employers bid against one another for their labor.[41]

Nevertheless, the 1890s were years of continuing struggle for Northern Paiutes. As the Ghost Dance receded from public view, opium addiction bedeviled the community. Jack Wilson condemned both opium and alcohol consumption for the rest of his life.[42]

As the opium struggle made so clear, Wovoka's prophecy and his religion could not save Indians from the perils of the twentieth century. In Yerington, Numus eventually found permanent homes at a "colony"—lands purchased for them by Congress in 1916—and later, in 1936, at Campbell Ranch, an 1,100-acre tract held in trust for Yerington Paiutes on which they could farm. But in Yerington and beyond, each generation of Indians since the prophet's day has struggled against the combined threats of continuing land loss, assimilation campaigns, and racial prejudice. After Southern Arapahos accepted allotments and agreed to sell the remainder of their reservation to the government, Southern Cheyenne opposition was overcome by intimidation and fraud. Over 50 million acres passed into

US hands, and the Southern Cheyenne–Southern Arapaho reservation ceased to exist. None of these sacrifices prevented the poverty that followed. In South Dakota, Indian people did no better. To this day, Pine Ridge, Rosebud, and other Lakota reservations consistently rank among the poorest communities in the United States.[43]

For all that, Paiutes, Arapahos, Cheyennes, and Lakotas have never ceased working for a better day. Lakotas have pursued a vigorous revival of the Sun Dance; Southern Arapahos restored their Sun Dance, the Offerings Lodge, in 2006. And among all these peoples flourish continuing efforts to restore languages, ceremonies, and traditions and to secure education, work, and health. The quest for a life both traditional and modern goes on.

In his time, confronting the ongoing calamities of conquest, Jack Wilson never stopped trying to heal the wounds of others. As late as the 1920s, he doctored one Numu survivor of a car crash, who later remembered that he awoke to find Jack Wilson standing over him with an eagle feather, having miraculously removed every piece of shattered windshield glass from his body. Throughout his life, Wovoka also remained an ardent advocate of hard work and education, positions that earned him some credit with Indian agents and other officials.[44]

His fame endured among far-flung Indians. In 1924, Tim McCoy, Hollywood actor and director, filmed *The Thundering Herd* near Bishop, California. At the request of Northern Arapaho cast members, McCoy drove across the state line and returned with Wilson, who spoke to the cast about brotherhood, peace, and clean living before leading them in a dance and enjoying a feast in his honor.[45]

Late in life, the ailing healer told his followers not to worry, that when he died he would "shake the earth" to let them know he had reached heaven. He passed away in September 1932. Three months to the day after he died, a powerful earthquake rattled northern Nevada. Even his white acquaintances were awed. "Son of a gun, Jack!" remarked one. "Said he was gonna shake this world if he made it, and by God, he did!"[46]

FIGURE E.2. Jack Wilson in Yerington, Nevada, ca. 1915. Nevada Historical Society.

ALTHOUGH HE COULD NOT KNOW IT, JACK WILSON'S FIGHT against the deadening hand of assimilation was practically won. Shortly before his posthumous earthquake in Nevada, political upheaval roiled the nation when Franklin Roosevelt won the 1932 presidential election, ushering in the New Deal, which would stem the assimilation policies of his predecessors for at least a generation. For the next twenty years, the government would encourage Indians to govern their own reservations and preserve their cultures. The

FIGURE E.3. Wovoka and the Hollywood actor and director Tim McCoy, 1924. Nevada Historical Society.

tolerance that James Mooney had cultivated and that Jack Wilson and his followers had urged on the public was now official policy—at least for a time.[47]

Wilson and Mooney were not friends and did not know each other well. After their meeting at Walker River, their paths diverged, and they never met again and never corresponded. Wilson's revelation started both men down paths, however, that would not only lead to their meeting but change their lives and in the end change American society too. Following them on their journeys, we have seen that their personal concerns often reflected the broader experience of region and nation. In the end, both men envisioned a multicultural America very different from their contemporaries' ideal of a monolithic, English-speaking, Protestant country. In a sense, modern Americans who espouse pluralism as a social virtue carry on their teachings.

Although the Ghost Dance has been the coda for many stories of the frontier and Indian autonomy, we learn more by viewing it as a point of beginning. In following the entangled stories of Jack Wilson and James Mooney, Short Bull and Porcupine, Grant Left Hand and Moki, we have connected the Ghost Dance to the local crises that fomented it and the regional and national concerns that turned it into a much wider public emergency. We have also come to understand its surprising role in pushing scholars and the American public toward greater Indian autonomy and a broader acceptance of divergent religions and cultures.

The Ghost Dance events open a window on the United States at the dawn of the new century. The era saw not only a wholesale transformation in Indian policy but also an epochal shift in American understandings of the nation's future. The Ghost Dance story points to a nascent current of thought that would often be marginal but never extinguished in the century to follow: the idea that difference truly is America's great strength. Jack Wilson saw the meeting of cultures within our borders as a good thing. For James Mooney, the nation was an experimental borderland, and the lesson of the Ghost Dance was to not fear examining the results and learning the lessons of our many cross-cultural meetings. It was a teaching that would resonate through the entire century that followed.

ACKNOWLEDGMENTS

I began this book aiming to write a short essay about the weave of science and spirit in the story of the Ghost Dance. But as so often happens with historical research, I found sources I did not expect and wrote something very different from what I intended, and took much more time than I had hoped. In the years it has taken to research and write this book, I have been grateful for the generous support of fellowships from the John Simon Guggenheim Memorial Foundation, the Shelby Cullom Davis Center for Historical Studies at Princeton University, the Bill Lane Center for the American West at Stanford University, and the Rachel Carson Center for Environment and Society, Munich, Germany. I also enjoyed the benefit of membership at the Writers Room, New York City, where the desk and the coffee room were a salvation. I am grateful, too, for the faculty research grants and generous sabbatical leave policy of the University of California, Davis, and the even more generous leave extensions granted by Dean Ron Mangun.

I am forever indebted to a number of people who made extraordinary contributions along the way. Michael Hittman was an extremely generous and forthcoming guide to the world of Yerington, Nevada, where he has worked for going on five decades. In Yerington and at his home in Brooklyn, New York, Michael shared his contacts, his vast knowledge of Northern Paiute history, and his treasure trove of documents and photographs, and then offered trenchant, critical comments on multiple drafts of the manuscript.

Marlin Thompson, historian for the Yerington Paiute Tribe, gave freely of his time and his extensive knowledge of Northern Paiute cosmology, history, and lore, driving me into the hinterlands to examine petroglyphs and consider Numu spiritual geography and the world that was. Eileen Kane, too, shared key resources about Nevada during conversations in the United States and Ireland. Thanks also to Inez Jim, the late Ida Mae Valdez, and Lilius Richardson of Yerington for sharing memories of old times.

In Oklahoma, Roderick Sweezy, Mary Sweezy, and Charlotte Lumpmouth were kind and generous consultants regarding the Ghost Dance in Southern Arapaho history, and Roderick Sweezy continued to offer me counsel and advice about the Ghost Dance and the Native American Church throughout my research and writing. Mike Jordan has been a consistently helpful and generous guide in questions of Indian history and helped me get my feet on the ground on the Southern Plains.

Thank you to Max Bear and the Cheyenne and Arapaho Tribes Culture and Heritage Program for help with photo permissions.

Special thanks to Arthur Amiotte, to whom I am enormously indebted for instruction, generosity, and many years of friendship. He and Jan Murray opened their home to me on my research forays to South Dakota. Arthur not only made us magnificent dinners and shared his extensive research library with me, but also spent long hours reading the manuscript and talking with me in his studio and on his back porch about the Ghost Dance and Lakota history, patiently disabusing me of my many misconceptions about Lakota religion. It was a time so rewarding and enjoyable that I may have prolonged the research and writing to savor it (but please don't tell my publisher).

Tom Shortbull readily shared family lore and documents, and at his home he and Darlene Shortbull helped me better understand the context of many of the stories in this book.

Craig Howe and the Center for American Indian Research and Native Studies were exceedingly magnanimous with their resources and their time, putting me up on several occasions and helping me hash out key ideas over the breakfast table.

Rani-Henrik Andersson and Phil Deloria read complete drafts of the work and offered invaluable, in-depth, critical commentary. Ray DeMallie provided extremely helpful comments and saved me from embarrassing errors on an article manuscript that incorporated key components of this book. Richard White also provided critical commentary on early chapters and has been a supporter of this work throughout.

Through the generous support of the Rachel Carson Center, I was privileged to write significant parts of this book in Germany, where some very good friends helped me along. In Munich and afterward at his home in the United States, Drew Isenberg was an invaluable help in the literature of evangelism, political economy, and American history. He read multiple chapter drafts, and his constant engagement with the work helped me reshape it over several years and many iterations. Lawrence Culver, Celia Lowe, Christof Mauch, Ruth Oldenziel, Cindy Ott, and Chris Pastore all were sounding boards for ideas and problems. Thanks to all these, and especially to Melanie Arndt for her scholarly and cultural insights and for touring wine bars of Munich with me to find the very best treatment for snakebite. That a catastrophic laptop failure and data loss in the summer of 2014 did not derail this project is owed in no small measure to Andreas Kleiber at Gravis Technologies, Munich.

I was ably assisted by excellent research assistants: Matthew Reeves in Kansas City, Missouri, and Lauren Evans in Sioux Falls, South Dakota, both of whom provided critical help when the heat was on. Logan Clendening provided translations of German sources, right when I needed them. My graduate students and former graduate students have been more helpful than they know. Thanks to Lizzie Browning, Greg Brueck, Robert Chester, Rebecca Egli, Steve Fountain, Phil Garone, Cori Knudten, Nick Perrone, Miles Powell, and Josh Reid.

I have been fortunate for many years to work at an outstanding university with supportive colleagues, all of whom have discussed this work with me often and shaped it in many ways. My thanks especially to Emily Albu, Ian Campbell, Diana Davis, Ines Hernandez-Avila, Quinn Javers, Ari Kelman, Lisa Materson, Sally McKee, Kathryn Olmsted, Eric Rauchway, Andres Resendez, Mike Saler, Sudipta Sen, Alan Taylor, Chuck Walker, and Clarence Walker. A big thank you to Debbie Lyon, Grace Woods, Amanda Isaac, Lauren Thomas, and Monica Fischer for the help processing the many requests for research support. Thanks also to Basic Books, especially Dan Gerstle, Roger Labrie, and Sandra Beris for the close editing and sound advice, and Alia Massoud for her assistance.

Parts of this book appeared as "Wage Work in the Sacred Circle: The Ghost Dance as Modern Religion," *Western Historical Quarterly* 46 (Summer 2015): 141–168, and are here reproduced by permission. Many thanks to David Rich Lewis.

This book would have been impossible without documents, in libraries large and small, preserved and organized by archivists and curators who labor mostly in obscurity to defend our record of the past against tsunamis of budget cuts and the corrosive force of public apathy. Among this army of dedicated specialists, I would like to thank in particular the following: Mary Ronan at the US National Archives, Washington, DC; Candace Greene, Caitlyn Haines, Pam Henson, Daisy Njoku, and Gina Rappaport at the National Anthropological Archives and the Smithsonian Institution, Washington, DC; Steve Friesen at the Buffalo Bill Museum, Golden, Colorado; Lee Brumbaugh, Karalee Clough, Sheryln Hayes-Zorn, and Michael Maher at the Nevada Historical Society; Marty Vestecka Miller at the Nebraska State Historical Society; Marie Kills-in-Sight at the Buechel Memorial Lakota Museum, St. Francis, South Dakota; Iris Edenheiser, Kerstin Fuhrmann, and Nanette Snoep of the Grassi Museum für Völkerkunde in Leipzig, Germany; Ken Stewart at the South Dakota State Historical Society; Emma Hansen at the Plains Indian Museum, Cody, Wyoming; Eva Fognell at the Fenimore Museum, Cooperstown, New York; Su Kim Chung at Special Collections, University of Nevada, Las Vegas; and Jacquelyn Sundstrand at Special Collections, University of Nevada, Reno.

For reading or commenting on papers, presentations, and articles and for other advice and guidance, I thank Jeffrey Anderson, Thomas Andrews, Rob Campbell, Bill Cronon, Ray DeMallie, Clyde Ellis, Ann Fabian, Elizabeth Fenn, Mark Fiege, Ana Marcela Francia, Peter Gordon, Andrew Graybill, Bill Jordan, Billy Kingfisher, Howard Lamar, Sophie Lunn-Rockliffe, David Matlin, George Moses, Andrew Needham, Phil Nord, Colleen O'Neill, Sarah Payne, Mabel Picotte, Josh Reid, Matthew Restall, Diane Rothenberg, Jerome Rothenberg, Marni Sandweiss, Lise Sedrez, Gail Schneider, Julia Smith, Sherry Smith, Greg Smoak, Gary Snyder, Amara Solari, Paul Sutter, Sam Truett, Marsha Weisiger, Sean Wilentz, and Don Worster. Thanks, too, to Jennifer Goldman for helping me navigate my year in New Jersey. I want to thank my literary agent, Geri Thoma, for her unfailing support during a scholarly journey that sometimes got bumpy.

I began this book when my son Sam was starting high school. He graduated college before I was done. His older brother Jesse was finishing college back when this began and is now an established professional with artistic projects of his own. Throughout years that were full of change and challenge for them, they have been profoundly supportive of my work always. My gratitude is exceeded only by my pride in you both.

To my parents, Claude and Liz Warren, and my brother Jon Warren, and to Paulina Biggs-Sparkuhl, a huge thank-you for all the love and support. My brother Nelson and his wife Cindy Hill persuaded me to visit Ireland, where I learned a great deal more than I thought possible about James Mooney. All these, along with my nieces Kate and Libby Kunkler, my nephew Warren Kunkler, and my brother-in-law Scott Kunkler were bulwarks of support and strength. I am especially grateful to my sister Suzy, for all her help and advice on life and on work; we miss you.

Finally, Rachel St. John intercepted this work at a critical juncture on the East Coast. To her, I am grateful for the multiple readings and edits of this book, for the many, many conversations about it and all things western history. Beyond that, her sense of humor and eagerness for new adventures have continually energized me. On those occasions when I have been uncertain of my direction, she has invariably pointed the way home—and often, as she was fond of observing, there was more than one. Thank you for joining me on the journey west.

NOTES

INTRODUCTION: A HOLE IN THE DREAM

1. This account of the burial is derived from photographs of the aftermath and from William S. E. Coleman, *Voices of Wounded Knee* (Lincoln: University of Nebraska Press, 2000), 350–352; Charles A. Eastman, *From the Deep Woods to Civilization* (1916; reprint, Lincoln: University of Nebraska Press, 1977), 111–112; Jerome A. Greene, *American Carnage: Wounded Knee, 1890* (Norman: University of Oklahoma Press, 2014), 240, 299–302.

2. John Neihardt, *Black Elk Speaks: Being the Life Story of a Holy Man of the Oglala Sioux* (1932; reprint, Lincoln: University of Nebraska Press, 1979), 270.

3. Dee Brown, *Bury My Heart at Wounded Knee: An Indian History of the American West* (New York: Henry Holt and Co., 1970), 445.

4. Anthony F. C. Wallace, "Revitalization Movements," *American Anthropologist,* new series, 58, no. 2 (April 1956): 264–268; Weston La Barre, *The Ghost Dance: Origins of Religion* (1970; reprint, Prospect Heights, IL: Waveland Press, 1990), 226–254; Jennifer Wenzel, *Bulletproof: Afterlives of Colonial Prophecy in South Africa and Beyond* (Chicago: University of Chicago Press, 2009); Shelley Ann Osterreich, *The American Indian Ghost Dance, 1870 and 1890: An Annotated Bibliography* (New York: Greenwood Press, 1991).

5. For typical examples, see Heather Cox Richardson, *Wounded Knee: Party Politics and the Road to an American Massacre* (New York: Basic Books, 2010), 118; Robert M. Utley, *Last Days of the Sioux Nation* (New Haven, CT: Yale University Press, 1963), 60. Several historians have begun to push

back against the image of the religion as a cult calling for a return to the past; see Rani-Henrik Andersson, *The Lakota Ghost Dance of 1890* (Lincoln: University of Nebraska Press, 2008); Jeffrey Ostler, *The Plains Sioux and US Colonialism from Lewis and Clark to Wounded Knee* (New York: Cambridge University Press, 2004); and Gregory E. Smoak, *Ghost Dances and Identity: Prophetic Religion and American Indian Ethnogenesis in the Nineteenth Century* (Berkeley: University of California Press, 2006). In exploring how the Ghost Dance served contemporary cultural needs, anthropologists have argued that the religion's promise of a return to the past can be understood as modern, whether as militant anticolonialism or as an effort at demographic revival; see Raymond J. DeMallie, "The Lakota Ghost Dance: An Ethnohistorical Account," *Pacific Historical Review* 51 (November 1982): 385–405; Alice Beck Kehoe, *The Ghost Dance: Ethnohistory and Revitalization,* 2nd ed. (Long Grove, IL: Waveland Press, 2006); Russell Thornton, *We Shall Live Again: The 1870 and 1890 Ghost Dance Movements as Demographic Revitalization* (New York: Cambridge University Press, 1986).

6. Raymond J. DeMallie, ed., *The Sixth Grandfather: Black Elk's Teachings Given to John G. Neihardt* (Lincoln: University of Nebraska Press, 1984), 46, 266.

7. Richardson, *Wounded Knee,* 264, 273; Charles W. Allen, *From Fort Laramie to Wounded Knee: In the West That Was,* ed. Richard E. Jensen (1939; reprint, Lincoln: University of Nebraska Press, 1997), 194, 206.

8. John Sutton Lutz, *Makúk: A New History of Aboriginal-White Relations* (Vancouver, CA: UBC Press, 2008), 23–6; Joshua L. Reid, *The Sea Is My Country: The Maritime World of the Makah* (New Haven, CT: Yale University Press, 2015), 17, 197.

9. Justin R. Gage, "Intertribal Communication, Literacy, and the Ghost Dance," PhD dissertation, University of Arkansas, 2015. For newspapers, see Andersson, *The Lakota Ghost Dance of 1890,* 193; Major Wirt Davis to Asst. Adj. Gen, Dec. 23, 1890, Reel 2, Frame 854, SC 188, NARA-DC.

10. Philip J. Deloria, *Indians in Unexpected Places* (Lawrence: University Press of Kansas, 2004), 6.

11. For Indian Christianity in the colonial era, see Linford D. Fisher, *The Indian Great Awakening: Religion and the Shaping of Native Cultures in Early America* (New York: Oxford University Press, 2012), 89.

12. James Mooney, *The Ghost Dance Religion and Sioux Outbreak of 1890: Fourteenth Annual Report of the US Bureau of Ethnology, 1892–1893,* pt. 2 (Washington, DC: US Government Printing Office, 1896).

13. Tisa Wenger, *We Have a Religion: The 1920s Indian Dance Controversy and American Religious Freedom* (Chapel Hill: University of North Carolina Press, 2009), 4–5; Peter Nabokov, *Where the Lightning Strikes: The Lives of American Indian Sacred Places* (New York: Viking, 2006).

14. "Interesting to Spiritualists," *Chicago Daily Tribune,* February 27, 1885, 8; for a comparison of Ghost Dancers to Spiritualists, see John McLaughlin, *My Friend the Indian* (1910; reprint, Lincoln: University of Nebraska, 1989), 191, 193.

15. Ann Taves, *Fits, Trances, and Visions: Experiencing Religion and Explaining Experience from Wesley to James* (Princeton, NJ: Princeton University Press, 1999), 261–307; William James, *The Varieties of Religious Experience* (Cambridge, MA: Harvard University Press, 1902); see also, for example, Frederick Morgan Davenport, *Primitive Traits in Religious Revivals: A Study in Mental and Social Evolution* (New York: Macmillan, 1905). For the holiness movement, see Vinson Synan, *The Holiness-Pentecostal Tradition: Charismatic Movements in the Twentieth Century,* 2nd ed. (Grand Rapids, MI: William B. Eerdmans Publishing Co., 1997), 22–59; Randall J. Stephens, *The Fire Spreads: Holiness and Pentecostalism in the American South* (Cambridge, MA: Harvard University Press, 2008), 15–55; and Grant Wacker, *Heaven Below: Early Pentecostals and American Culture* (Cambridge, MA: Harvard University Press, 2001), 1–17.

CHAPTER 1: 1890: THE MESSIAH AND THE MACHINE

1. "Indians Expect a Savior to Appear," *Chicago Daily Tribune,* April 27, 1890, 1; "Looking for a Savior," *New York Times,* April 27, 1890, 1.

2. "Hope for the Flying Machine," *New York Times,* November 30, 1890, 7; Patricia Beard, *After the Ball: Gilded Age Secrets, Boardroom Betrayals, and the Party That Ignited the Great Wall Street Scandal of 1905* (New York: HarperCollins, 2003), 158; Mark Twain and Charles Dudley Warner, *The Gilded Age: A Tale of Today* (1873; reprint, New York: Oxford University Press, 1996). For the Gilded Age generally, see Eric Rauchway, *Murdering McKinley: The Making of Theodore Roosevelt's America* (New York: Hill and Wang, 2003); Robert Wiebe, *The Search for Order: 1877–1920* (New York: Hill and Wang, 1967); T. J. Jackson Lears, *Rebirth of a Nation: The Making of Modern America, 1877–1920* (New York: HarperCollins, 2009); and Nell Irvin Painter, *Standing at Armageddon: The United States, 1877–1919* (New York: W. W. Norton, 1987).

3. Roy Harvey Pearce, *The Savages of America: A Study of the Indian and the Idea of Civilization* (Baltimore: Johns Hopkins University Press, 1953), 49; Robert M. Utley, *Geronimo* (New Haven, CT: Yale University Press, 2012), 1823, 1838 (Kindle edition page numbers).

4. "Returned Without the Messiah," *Chicago Daily Tribune,* May 28, 1890, 1.

5. Charles L. Hyde to Secretary Noble, May 29, 1890; C. R. Crawford, W. R. Morris, and M. N. Adams to T. J. Morgan, June 21, 1890; Charles

E. W. Chesney to Commissioner of Indian Affairs (CIA), June 16, 1890, all in Reel 1, Special Case (SC) 188, Record Group (RG) 75, National Archives and Records Administration, Washington, DC (NARA-DC).

6. The following is drawn from Robertson's rendering of Porcupine's account in Redfield Proctor to Secretary of the Interior, July 7, 1890, Frames 25–30, Reel 1, SC 188, RG 75, NARA-DC; see also Mooney, *Ghost Dance Religion*, 793–796.

7. Compare Porcupine's account of his route to "A Correct Map of the United States Showing the Union Pacific, the Overland Route, and Connections" (Knight, Leonard & Co., 1892), Library of Congress, American Memory website: http://memory.loc.gov/cgi-bin/map_item.pl ?data=/home/www/data/gmd/gmd370/g3701/g3701p/rr005970.jp2&item Link=D?gmd:4:./temp/~ammem_Db3l::&title=A+correct+map+of+the +United+States+showing+the+Union+Pacific,+the+overland+route+and +connections.&style=gmd&legend= (accessed April 24, 2016); see also A. I. Chapman to John Gibbon, December 6, 1890, in *Annual Report of the Secretary of War 1891* (hereafter *ARSW [year]*) (Washington, DC: Government Printing Office, 1892), 194.

8. For another perspective on Porcupine's gospel and his extensive influence among the Northern Cheyenne, see W. S. Dudagh (or Judagh [illegible]) to T. J. Morgan, June 19, 1890, Box 635, Letters Received (LR) 1881–1907, RG 75, NARA-DC.

9. "Indians Crazed by Religion," *Chicago Daily Tribune,* July 2, 1890, 1.

10. "Census Foreshadowings," *New York Times,* June 5, 1890, 4.

11. "To Be States Soon" and "For a United Site," *Chicago Daily Tribune,* July 12, 1890, 1; "Census Foreshadowings," *New York Times,* June 5, 1890, 5; see also Geoffrey Austrian, *Herman Hollerith: Forgotten Giant of Information Processing* (New York: Columbia University Press, 1982), 58.

12. Quoted in Austrian, *Herman Hollerith,* 49–50; see also *Scientific American* 43, no. 9 (August 30, 1890): 132.

13. T. C. Martin, quoted in Austrian, *Herman Hollerith,* 70.

14. Austrian, *Herman Hollerith,* 71–72.

15. *Herman Hollerith,* 72.

16. Ibid., 97.

17. US Department of the Interior (Census Office), *Report on Transportation Business in the United States at the Eleventh Census: 1890,* pt. 1 (Washington, DC: Government Printing Office, 1895), 4, 6, 385; *Abstract of the Eleventh Census: 1890* (Washington, DC: Government Printing Office, 1894), 109–110; *Report on Manufacturing Industries at the Eleventh Census: 1890, Pt. III, Selected Industries* (Washington, DC: Government Printing Office, 1895), 383.

18. Walter F. Willcox, "The Development of the American Census Since 1890," *Political Science Quarterly* 29, no. 3 (1914): 445; "Under a Partisan Census," *New York Times,* September 15, 1890, 2; "The Census and the City," *New York Times,* September 18, 1890, 4; "The Unreliable Census," *New York Times,* September 18, 1890, 8; "The Porter Census," *New York Times,* October 19, 1890, 4.

19. T. C. Martin, quoted in Austrian, *Herman Hollerith,* 86.

20. US Department of the Interior (Census Office), *Report on Population of the United States at the Eleventh Census: 1890,* 2 vols. (Washington, DC: Government Printing Office, 1895), 1:xi–xii; Willcox, "The Development of the American Census," 444.

21. Warren K. Moorehead (unattributed), "The Red Christ," *The Illustrated American* (December 13, 1890): 11–12.

22. Ibid.

23. William J. Plumb to CIA, November 8, 1890, Reel 1, SC–188, NARA-DC.

24. *Annual Report of the Commissioner of Indian Affairs 1891* (hereafter *ARCIA*) (Washington, DC: Government Printing Office, 1892), 123; Moorehead, "The Red Christ," 13; H. D. Gallagher to T. J. Morgan, June 14, 1890, Frame 6, Reel 1, SC 188, NARA-DC.

25. Peter Matthiessen, *In the Spirit of Crazy Horse* (New York: Viking, 1983), 527–528; Jeffrey Ostler, *The Lakotas and the Black Hills: The Struggle for Sacred Ground* (New York: Penguin, 2011); *Report of the Sioux Commission of 1889,* 51st Congress, 1st Session, US Senate, Executive Document 51, 23–24; Utley, *Last Days of the Sioux Nation,* 55.

26. E. B. Reynolds to T. J. Morgan, September 28, 1890, Frames 32–36, Reel 1, SC 188, NARA-DC; Utley, *Last Days of the Sioux Nation,* 54–55, 79.

27. Ghost shirts did not appear until October 1890, and only among some Lakotas were they said to be bulletproof. Andersson, *Lakota Ghost Dance of 1890,* 67–73; Ostler, *The Plains Sioux and US Colonialism,* 279–280.

28. E. B. Reynolds to T. J. Morgan, September 23, 1890, Frames 32–36, Reel 1, SC 188, NARA-DC.

29. Mrs. Z. A. Parker, quoted in Mooney, *Ghost Dance Religion,* 917.

30. Ibid.

31. Ibid.

32. For "dance craze," see A. T. Lea to James A. Cooper, in James A. Cooper to R. V. Belt, November 22, 1890, SC 188, NARA-DC. The term "dance craze" appears periodically in these accounts; see, for example, John M. Sweeney to D. F. Royer, November 22, 1890 (copy), Box 27, Folder 391, Elmo Scott Watson Collection, Newberry Library. For

"dancing in the snow," see D. F. Royer to R. V. Belt, November 15, 1890, SC 188, NARA-DC. For "exceedingly prejudicial," see E. B. Reynolds to T. J. Morgan, September 23, 1890, Frames 32–36, Reel 1, SC 188, NARA-DC. For "fall senseless to the ground," see McLaughlin to T. J. Morgan, October 17, 1890, SC 188, NARA-DC; witness quoted in Greene, *American Carnage*, 80.

33. Little Wound, quoted in D. F. Royer to R. V. Belt, October 30, 1890, SC 188, NARA-DC; Andersson, *Lakota Ghost Dance of 1890*, 109.

34. Ostler, *The Plains Sioux and US Colonialism*, 266; Arthur Amiotte, personal communication, August 14, 2015; James R. Walker, *Lakota Belief and Ritual*, edited by Elaine A. Jahner and Raymond J. DeMallie (Lincoln: University of Nebraska Press, 1980), 101–109.

35. Mooney, *Ghost Dance Religion*, 1061, 1068, 1072.

36. For "love feast," see E. B. Reynolds to T. J. Morgan, September 23, 1890, SC 188, NARA-DC; for "séance," see McLaughlin, *My Friend the Indian*, 191, 193.

37. Synan, *Holiness-Pentecostal Tradition*, 22–59; Stephens, *The Fire Spreads*, 15–55; and Wacker, *Heaven Below*, 1–17.

38. For incipient Pentecostals and Woodworth, see Jonathan R. Baer, "Redeemed Bodies: The Functions of Divine Healing in Incipient Pentecostalism," *Church History* 70, no. 4 (December 2001): 735–771, esp. 739–748; "Religious Craze in Indiana," *Chicago Daily Tribune*, January 30, 1885, 2; "There Is a Hell," *Chicago Daily Tribune*, February 22, 1885, 3; "Electric Evangelist," *Chicago Daily Tribune*, October 4, 1885, 26. For holiness revivals and Pentecostals, see Wacker, *Heaven Below*, 1–17; Synan, *Holiness-Pentecostal Tradition*, 22–66; Stephens, *The Fire Spreads*.

39. Baer, "Redeemed Bodies"; for the Oakland riot, see "Ring the Riot Alarm!" and "Flora Briggs' Story," *San Francisco Examiner*, January 9, 1890, 1–2.

40. US Department of the Interior, *Report on Population of the United States*, pt. I, lxxix, cxc.

41. "Special Notices," *New York Times*, November 24, 1890, 5; David Leviatin, "Framing the Poor: The Irresistibility of *How the Other Half Lives*," in Jacob A. Riis, *How the Other Half Lives* (1890), edited by David Leviatin (reprint, New York: Bedford Books, 1996), 1–50.

42. Francis A. Walker, "Immigration and Degradation," *Forum* (August 11, 1891): 643, 644, quoted in Michael A. Elliott, *The Culture Concept: Writing and Difference in an Age of Realism* (Minneapolis: University of Minnesota Press, 2002), 95.

43. Rauchway, *Murdering McKinley*, 17, 89–96; Paul Avrich, *Haymarket Tragedy* (Princeton, NJ: Princeton University Press, 1984), 35–36, 45–51, 59; Lears, *Rebirth of a Nation*.

44. Lears, *Rebirth of a Nation,* 83–84; James Green, *Death in the Haymarket: A Story of Chicago, the First Labor Movement, and the Bombing That Divided Gilded Age America* (New York: Knopf, 2006); Richard Slotkin, *Gunfighter Nation: The Myth of the Frontier in Twentieth-Century America* (New York: Harper Perennial, 1992), 91–92.

45. For "every steamship," see Hjalmar H. Boyesen, "Dangers of Unrestricted Immigration," *Forum* 3, no. 5 (July 1887): 532. For "hordes of barbarians," see A. Cleveland Coxe, "Government by Aliens," *Forum* (August 1889): 600.

46. For "fear of responsibility," see Lears, *Rebirth of a Nation,* 7; George M. Beard, *A Practical Treatise on Nervous Exhaustion (Neurasthenia)* (New York: William Wood and Co., 1880), vi, xv ("the prime cause"). Another example from the period: "The nervous temperament is the creation of civilization." W. A. Hammond, "A Few Words About the Nerves," *The Galaxy* 6, no. 4 (October 1868): 493.

47. Beard quoted in Gail Bederman, *Manliness and Civilization: A Cultural History of Gender and Race in the United States, 1880–1917* (Chicago: University of Chicago Press, 1996), 84–88; Francis Amasa Walker, "The Great Count of 1890," in *Discussions in Economics and Statistics,* edited by Davis R. Dewey and Francis Amasa Walker, 2 vols. (New York: Henry Holt and Co., 1899), 2:111–126; Margo J. Anderson, *The American Census: A Social History* (New Haven, CT: Yale University Press, 1990), 106–109. US observers had warned that immigrants were having more children than native-born Americans as early as 1869. See Dr. N. Allen, "Changes in Population," *Harper's New Monthly Magazine* 38, no. 225 (February 1869): 386.

48. P. Leroy Beaulieu, "The Influence of Civilisation upon the Movement of Peoples," *Journal of the Royal Statistical Society of London* (June 1891), reprinted in Benjamin Kidd, *Social Evolution,* rev. ed. (New York: Macmillan, 1902), 381. For "the decades ending," see Austrian, *Herman Hollerith,* 85.

49. Robert H. Wiebe, *The Search for Order 1877–1920* (New York: Hill & Wang, 1967), 55. "For "one . . . common nationality," see Edward McGlynn, quoted in ibid., 57–58.

50. I owe this discussion of assimilation to Richard White, *The Republic for Which It Stands: The United States in the Gilded Age* (New York: Oxford University Press, forthcoming).

51. David S. Heidler and Jeanne T. Heidler, *Indian Removal* (New York: W. W. Norton, 2007), 39–41; see also Thurman Wilkins, *Cherokee Tragedy: The Ridge Family and the Decimation of a People,* 2d ed. (Norman: University of Oklahoma Press, 1986), 190–191.

52. Francis Paul Prucha, *The Great Father: The United States Government and the American Indians,* abridged edition (Lincoln: University of Nebraska

Press, 1984), 64–65; Frederick E. Hoxie, *A Final Promise: The Campaign to Assimilate the Indians, 1880–1920* (Lincoln: University of Nebraska Press, 1984; New York: Cambridge University Press, 1989), x–xi, 1–44; Alan Trachtenberg, *Shades of Hiawatha: Staging Indians, Making Americans 1880–1930* (New York: Hill & Wang, 2005), 39.

53. *Annual Report of the Secretary of the Interior 1883*, 48th Congress, 1st Session, 1883–1884, Executive Document 1, Pt. 5, xi.

54. Dawes quoted in Elliott, *Culture Concept*, 95.

55. Elliott, *Culture Concept*; Hoxie, *A Final Promise*, 33–34.

56. Ostler, *The Plains Sioux and US Colonialism*, 293; Richardson, *Wounded Knee*, 186–204.

57. Ostler, *The Plains Sioux and US Colonialism*, 302–306; Frank Wood to R. V. Belt, November 29, 1890, Reel 1, SC 188, NARA-DC.

58. Ostler, *The Plains Sioux and US Colonialism*, 301; Richardson, *Wounded Knee*, 235.

59. Ostler, *The Plains Sioux and US Colonialism*, 306–307; Andersson, *Lakota Ghost Dance of 1890*, 76–77, 345 n. 164, 202–209. Andersson's count of only 15,329 Lakotas excludes the 2,084 Lakotas at Lower Brule and Crow Creek Reservations, where there appears to have been little if any Ghost Dancing.

60. Coleman, *Voices of Wounded Knee*, 198–205.

61. Mooney, *Ghost Dance Religion*, 876.

62. Ibid.

63. General Miles reported 200 dead, General Colby reported 220 Indian dead on the field, and Agent Royer announced that 300 Indians had fallen at Wounded Knee. Mooney, *Ghost Dance Religion*, 871. Joseph Horn Cloud, a Wounded Knee survivor, compiled a list of 185 people who died from wounds in the massacre. Richard E. Jensen, ed., *Voices of the American West*, 2 vols. (Lincoln: University of Nebraska, 2005). This section is based primarily on vol. 1, *The Indian Interviews of Eli S. Ricker*, 204–206.

64. Rex Alan Smith, *Moon of Popping Trees: The Tragedy at Wounded Knee and the End of the Indian Wars* (Lincoln: University of Nebraska Press, 1975), 201–204; Utley, *Last Days of the Sioux Nation*, 230, 249.

65. Mooney, *Ghost Dance Religion*, 768, 879; L. G. Moses, *The Indian Man: A Biography of James Mooney* (Champaign: University of Illinois Press, 1984), 63, 96 (page before a photo of Mooney), 113.

66. Mooney, *Ghost Dance Religion*, 869, and Plate XCIX.

CHAPTER 2: GREAT BASIN APOCALYPSE

1. For Pan-a-mite, see Brigadier General A. McD. McCook to Secretary of the Interior, October 17, 1890, Frame 623; for "Bannock Jim," see K. R. Kellog to A. Ashley, October 27, 1890, Frame 125; for "designing

white man," see William Plumb to CIA, November 8, 1890, Frame 140; all in Reel 1, SC 188, NARA-DC. See also L. G. Moses, "Jack Wilson and the Indian Service: The Response of the BIA to the Ghost Dance Prophet," *American Indian Quarterly* 5, no. 4 (November 1979): 295–316.

2. Mooney, *Ghost Dance Religion,* 792; for the end of plural marriage, see Sarah Barringer Gordon, *The Mormon Question: Polygamy and Constitutional Conflict in Nineteenth-Century America* (Chapel Hill: University of North Carolina Press, 2002), 211–212, 220–221.

3. General Nelson A. Miles, quoted in "Probably a Mormon Trick," *New York Times,* November 8, 1890, 5, cited in Gregory E. Smoak, "The Mormons and the Ghost Dance of 1890," *South Dakota History* 16, no. 3 (1986): 269; and William L. Selwyn to E. W. Foster, November 25, 1890, Frames 304–310, Reel 1, SC 188, NARA-DC; see also Mrs. S. A. Crandall to President Benjamin F. Harrison, November 27, 1890, JPGs 474–475, SC 188, NARA-DC. Mooney himself would conclude that the sacred shirts of the Ghost Dancers on the Plains "may have been suggested by the 'endowment robe' of the Mormons." Mooney, *Ghost Dance Religion,* 790. For white dancers, Porcupine's view, and white settlers participating in Paiute dances, see "As Narrated by Short Bull" (hereafter ANSB), handwritten manuscript at Buffalo Bill Museum, Golden, CO, 8; Mooney, *Ghost Dance Religion,* 794; Clark J. Guild, quoted in *Wovoka and the Ghost Dance,* researched, compiled, and written by Michael Hittman, edited by Don Lynch (Lincoln: University of Nebraska Press, 1990), 307.

4. John S. Mayhugh to T. J. Morgan, November 24, 1890, Frames 275–280, Reel 1, SC 188, NARA-DC.

5. Arthur Chapman to Gen. John Gibbon, Dec. 6, 1890, in Annual Report of the Secretary of War 1891, vol. 1 (Washington, DC: GPO, 1892), 191; Mooney, *Ghost Dance Religion,* 765.

6. Gunard Solberg, *Tales of Wovoka* (Reno: Nevada Historical Society, 2012), 22.

7. Nevada remains a "laboratory" even today as federal regulators seek to balance ecological concerns with the grazing, lumbering, and mining interests on land owned or managed by the Bureau of Land Management, the US Forest Service, the US Fish and Wildlife Service, and the National Park Service—a total area of more than 53 million acres, or twice the size of Ohio. "Land Acreages by County and Land Owner/Manager," January 2012, http://www.blm.gov/style/medialib/blm/nv/information .Par.45693.File.dat/Land.Acreages.by.County.Jan2012.pdf (accessed April 21, 2016).

8. In exploring Indian investment in settler society, I have been influenced by the arguments of James H. Merrell, *The Indians' New World: Catawbas and Their Neighbors from European Contact Through the Era of Removal* (Chapel Hill: University of North Carolina Press, 1989).

9. Christopher L. Miller, *Prophetic Worlds: Indians and Whites on the Columbia Plateau* (Seattle: University of Washington Press), 71–75; Carolyn Merchant, *Reinventing Eden: The Fate of Nature in Western Culture* (New York: Routledge, 2003).

10. For the size of the Great Basin, see Richard V. Francaviglia, *Mapping and Imagination in the Great Basin: A Cartographic History* (Reno: University of Nevada Press, 2005), 5; for the aridity of the Great Basin, see Donald W. Sada and Gary L. Vinyard, "Anthropogenic Changes in Biogeography of Great Basin Aquatic Biota," in *Great Basin Aquatic Systems History: Smithsonian Contributions to the Earth Sciences* (book 33), edited by Robert Hershler, David B. Madsen, and Donald R. Currey (Washington, DC: Smithsonian Institution, 2002), 277–293. The first historian to seize upon aridity as the West's defining characteristic was Walter Prescott Webb in *The Great Plains* (Boston: Ginn & Co., 1931). More recent interpretations include Patricia Nelson Limerick, *Legacy of Conquest: The Unbroken Past of the American West* (New York: W. W. Norton, 1987); Richard White, *"It's Your Misfortune and None of My Own": A History of the American West* (Norman: University of Oklahoma, 1991); and Donald Worster, *Rivers of Empire: Water, Aridity, and the Growth of the American West* (New York: Pantheon, 1985). See also Donald Worster, "New West, True West: Interpreting the Region's History," *Western Historical Quarterly* 18, no. 2 (April 1987): 141–156.

11. For Great Basin temperatures, see Donald K. Grayson, *The Great Basin: A Natural Prehistory*, rev. ed. (Berkeley: University of California, 2011), 16–17.

12. The drum metaphor comes from Stephen Trimble, *The Sagebrush Ocean: A Natural History of the Great Basin* (Reno: University of Nevada Press, 1999), 8. For the expanding distance between Salt Lake City and Reno, see John McPhee, *Basin and Range* (New York: Farrar, Straus and Giroux, 1982), 65.

13. Margaret Wheat, *Survival Arts of the Primitive Paiutes* (Reno: University of Nevada Press, 1967), 1; Grayson, *The Great Basin*, 87–134, esp. 106.

14. Smith quoted in C. Elizabeth Raymond, "Sense of Place in the Great Basin," in *East of Eden, West of Zion: Essays on Nevada*, edited by Wilbur S. Shepperson (Reno: University of Nevada Press, 1989), 18; John C. Frémont and William Hemsley Emory, *The California Guidebook: Notes of Travel in California* (New York: D. Appleton and Co., 1849), 10.

15. For "dreary and dismal," see Raymond, "Sense of Place in the Great Basin," 17; for "poorest and most worthless," see Richard V. Francaviglia, *Believing in Place: A Spiritual Geography of the Great Basin* (Reno: University of Nevada Press, 2016), 8; for "strange, weird land," see Raymond, "Sense of Place in the Great Basin," 18, 20–21; for "Geographic purgatory," see

Rob Schultheis, *The Hidden West: Journeys in the American Outback* (1978; reprint, New York: Lyons and Burford, 1996), 138.

16. Zenas Leonard, *Leonard's Narrative: Adventures of Zenas Leonard, Fur Trader and Trapper, 1831–1836,* edited by W. F. Wagner (1839; reprint, Cleveland: Burrows Brothers, 1904), 168.

17. Frémont quoted in Julian H. Steward, *Basin-Plateau Aboriginal Sociopolitical Groups* (1938; reprint, Salt Lake City: University of Utah Press, 2002), 8–9; Abbe Emmanuel Domenech, *Seven Years' Residence in the Great Deserts of North America,* 2 vols. (London: Longman, Green, 1860), 2:64.

18. Ned Blackhawk, *Violence over the Land: Indians and Empire in the Early American West* (Cambridge, MA: Harvard University Press, 2008), 239–240. The trade in the southern Great Basin is discussed in James F. Brooks, *Captives and Cousins: Slavery, Kinship, and Community in the Southwest Borderlands* (Chapel Hill: University of North Carolina Press, 2002), 153–156, 351–353. On Paiutes as slaves, see Steward, *Basin-Plateau Aboriginal Sociopolitical Groups,* 9. Captain J. H. Simpson reports that Navajos continued to buy Paiutes from eastern Utah as late as 1859. See Simpson, *Report of Exploration Across the Great Basin of the Territory of Utah for a Direct Wagon-Route from Camp Floyd to Genoa, in Carson Valley, in 1859* (Washington, DC: Government Printing Office, 1876); Andres Resendez, *The Other Slavery: The Uncovered Story of Indian Enslavement in America* (New York: Houghton Mifflin Harcourt, 2016), 193–194.

19. California Department of Water Resources, *Walker River Atlas* (Sacramento: California Department of Water Resources, 1992), 6.

20. Willard Z. Park, *Shamanism in Western North America: A Study in Cultural Relationships* (Chicago: Northwestern University Press, 1938), 27–28, 76, 110, 115; Eileen Kane field notes, interview with Corbett Mack, July 8, 1964, 4–5, in Eileen Kane, "1964 Field Report," University of Nevada Ethnographic Archive 3, Desert Research Institute, Collection 92–09/I/1–21, Box 1, Folder 8, Special Collections, University of Nevada, Reno Libraries (hereafter "1964 Field Report"); Catherine S. Fowler, *In the Shadow of Fox Peak: An Ethnography of the Cattail-Eater Northern Paiute People of Stillwater Marsh* (Reno: Nevada Humanities Committee, 2002), 177.

21. Marlin Thompson, personal communication, August 6, 2010; Hittman, *Wovoka and the Ghost Dance,* 77, 187–91; Kane field notes, 16, in "1964 Field Report."

CHAPTER 3: THE BIRTH OF THE PROPHET

1. Wheat, *Survival Arts,* 1–2; Isabel Kelly, "Northern Paiute Tales," *Journal of American Folklore* 51, no. 202 (October–December 1938): 365–372.

2. Grayson, *The Great Basin,* 314–333. See also David B. Madsen and David Rhode, eds., *Across the West: Human Population Movement and the Expansion of the Numa* (Salt Lake City: University of Utah Press, 1994), 20–23; Jane Hill, "Proto-Uto-Aztecan: A Community of Cultivators in Central Mexico?" *American Anthropologist* 103: 913–914; Mark Q. Sutton, "Warfare and Expansion: An Ethnohistoric Perspective on the Numic Spread," *Journal of California and Great Basin Anthropology* 8 (1986): 65–82.

3. The Numic expansion is the subject of a large and sometimes contentious literature. For summaries of the main arguments and references to the principal contenders, see Steve Fountain, "Sky Dogs and Smoked Streams: Horses and Ethnocultural Change in the North American West, 1700–1850," PhD dissertation, University of California, Davis, 2007; Grayson, *The Great Basin,* 313–338.

4. Jay Miller, "Basin Religion and Theology: A Comparative Study of Power (Puha)," *Journal of California and Great Basin Anthropology* 5, nos. 1–2 (1983): 66–86; for "Water Utes," see Wallace Stegner, *Where the Bluebird Sings to the Lemonade Springs: Living and Writing in the West* (New York: Penguin, 1992), 73.

5. Michael Hittman, *The Yerington Paiute Tribe: A Numu History* (Yerington, NV: Yerington Paiute Tribe, 1984), 3–5.

6. For the history of Northern Paiute communities and territories, see Omer C. Stewart, "The Northern Paiute Bands," *Anthropological Records* 2, no. 3 (1939): 127–149. A community living nearby at Desert Creek was known as the Poo-zi Ticutta, which also translates as "Bulb Eaters," but here *poo-zi* refers to a larger bulb that grew only at Desert Creek. Inter-Tribal Council of Nevada, *Numa: A Northern Paiute History* (Salt Lake City: University of Utah Press, 1976), 11, 52, 109 n. 1. Hittman, *Yerington Paiute Tribe,* 19. The upheavals of colonization, war, and epidemic caused smaller outfits to merge with larger groups; thus, by the time scholars began looking for Paiute communities, some had disappeared, perhaps absorbed into others. Marlin Thompson, personal communication, August 6, 2010.

7. Patrick Trotter, *Cutthroat: Native Trout of the West,* 2nd ed. (Berkeley: University of California Press, 2008), 153, 155.

8. Ibid., 162; Lembi Kongas Speth, "Possible Fishing Cliques Among the Northern Paiutes of Walker River Reservation, Nevada," *Ethnohistory* 16, no. 3 (November 1969): 225–244. Except where noted, this discussion of the Numu seasonal round is derived from Wheat, *Survival Arts;* Edward C. Johnson, *Walker River Paiutes: A Tribal History* (Schurz, NV: Walker River Paiute Tribe, 1975), 7–15; and Inter-Tribal Council of Nevada, *Numa* 10–15.

9. Dan De Quille (William Wright), *The Big Bonanza* (1876; reprint, New York: Alfred A. Knopf, 1947), 208.

10. Michael Hittman, *Corbett Mack: The Life of a Northern Paiute* (Lincoln: University of Nebraska Press, 1996), 275–276.

11. Steward, *Basin-Plateau Aboriginal Sociopolitical Groups,* 27; Joel C. Janetski, "Role of Pinyon-Juniper Woodlands in Aboriginal Societies of the Desert West," in S. B. Monson and R. Stevens, *Proceedings: Ecology and Management of Pinyon-Juniper Communities Within the Interior West,* Proceedings RMRS-P-9 (Rocky Mountain Station: US Department of Agriculture, Forest Service, June 1999), 249–253, http://www.fs.fed.us/rm/pubs/rmrs_p009.pdf (accessed April 27, 2016).

12. Kane field notes, interview with Corbett Mack, July 8, 1964, 4, in "1964 Field Report."

13. Steward, *Basin-Plateau Aboriginal Sociopolitical Groups,* 28; Wheat, *Survival Arts,* 8–16; Johnson, *Walker River Paiutes,* 10–15; Robert Lowie, *Notes on Shoshonean Ethnography* (New York: American Museum Press, 1924), 311.

14. Catherine Fowler, ed., *Willard Z. Park's Ethnographic Field Notes on the Northern Paiute of Western Nevada, 1933–1940,* vol. 1, *University of Utah Anthropological Papers* 114 (1989): 54, 69–71.

15. Jay Miller, "Basin Religion and Theology: A Comparative Study of Power (Puha)," *Journal of California and Great Basin Anthropology* 5, nos. 112 (Summer–Winter 1983): 66–86; William J. Bauer Jr., "The Giant and the Waterbaby: Paiute Oral Traditions and Owens Valley Water Wars," *Boom: A Journal of California* 2, no. 4 (Winter 2012): 104–117; Alex K. Carroll, M. Nieves Zedeño, and Richard W. Stoffle, "Landscapes of the Ghost Dance: A Cartography of Numic Ritual," *Journal of Archaeological Method and Theory* 11, no. 2 (June 2004): 129.

16. Park, *Shamanism in Western North America,* 14.

17. Fowler, *In the Shadow of Fox Peak,* 171; Richard Stoffle, quoted in Bauer, "The Giant and the Waterbaby," 109. For the ubiquity of religious prescription and proscription in Northern Paiute life, see Fowler, *Willard Z. Park's Ethnographic Notes,* 20–21, 41.

18. Michael Hittman, personal communication, January 7, 2013. Far-flung kin and friends also gathered for a multiday festival and dances in the fall in a ritual of thanksgiving for the pine nut harvest. Steward, *Basin-Plateau Aboriginal Sociopolitical Groups,* 54.

19. Jedediah S. Smith, *The Southwest Expedition of Jedediah S. Smith: His Personal Account of the Journey to California 1826–1827,* edited by George R. Brooks (Glendale, IL: Arthur H. Clark Co., 977), 171–175; Leonard, *Leonard's Narrative,* 158–169; Myron Angel, *History of Nevada* (Oakland, CA: Thompson & West, 1881), 145–148. For the banding together of Paiute and Western Shoshone outfits for defensive purposes, see Steward, *Basin-Plateau Aboriginal Sociopolitical Groups,* 248–249.

20. Martha Knack, "Nineteenth-Century Great Basin Indian Wage Labor," in *Native Americans and Wage Labor: Ethnohistorical Perspectives,* edited by Alice Littlefield and Martha C. Knack (Norman: University of Oklahoma Press, 1996), 145; Merrill J. Mattes, *The Great Platte River Road: The Covered Wagon Mainline Via Fort Kearny to Fort Laramie* (Lincoln: University of Nebraska Press, 1969), 23. For emigrant reduction of grass seed and game on the Humboldt River, see Dale L. Morgan, *Shoshonean Peoples and the Overland Trails: Frontiers of the Utah Superintendency of Indian Affairs, 1849–1869,* edited by Richard L. Saunders (Logan: Utah State University Press, 2007), 102.

21. Dale Morgan reports that, for instance, the headman-talker Joaquin was on the Carson River in the late 1850s but seems to have moved to the Walker River area soon after, as we see later in this chapter. Morgan, *Shoshonean Peoples and the Overland Trail,* 116; Kane, "Field Notes," 35–38.

22. James W. Hulse, *The Silver State: Nevada's Heritage Reinterpreted,* 3rd ed. (Reno: University of Nevada, 2004), 134.

23. Ibid., 71.

24. Hittman, *Wovoka and the Ghost Dance,* 27–33; Mooney, *Ghost Dance Religion,* 773–774; Ed Dyer, "The Jack Wilson Story," 9, n.d., in Margaret M. Wheat Collection, Series III, Box 4/29, Special Collections, University of Nevada, Reno; L. G. Moses, "'The Father Tells Me So!': Wovoka, the Ghost Dance Prophet," *American Indian Quarterly* 9, no. 3 (Summer 1985): 335–351. Wovoka had at least two younger brothers: Honocha-yu, better known as Pat, and Toyanaga-a. Hittman, *Wovoka and the Ghost Dance,* 35.

25. Hittman, *Wovoka and the Ghost Dance,* 32–33; Inter-Tribal Council of Nevada, *Numa,* 55.

26. Ronald James, *The Roar and the Silence: A History of Virginia City and the Comstock Lode* (Reno: University of Nevada Press, 1998), 58, 109; Robert Neil Chester, "Comstock Creations: An Environmental History of an Industrial Watershed," PhD dissertation, University of California, Davis, 2009.

27. James, *The Roar and the Silence,* 1–118; Chester, "Comstock Creations," 1–11; George Ferdinand Becker, *Geology of the Comstock Lode and Washoe District, with Atlas,* US Geological Survey, Monograph 3 (Washington, DC: Government Printing Office, 1882), xv.

28. Forester quoted in Charles S. Sargent, *Report on the Forests of North America (Exclusive of Mexico): 10th Census of the United States,* vol. 9 (Washington, DC: Government Printing Office, 1884), 571. Agent quoted in Martha C. Knack and Omer C. Stewart, *As Long as the River Shall Run: An Ethnohistory of Pyramid Lake Indian Reservation* (Berkeley: University of California Press, 1984), 85. On the growing scarcity of pine nuts, see, for example, *ARCIA 1864* (Washington, DC: Government Printing Office, 1865), 15, 142, 145. On the impact of cattle and sheep ranching, see

James A. Young and B. Abbot Sparks, *Cattle in the Cold Desert* (1985; revised edition, Reno: University of Nevada, 2002), 135–136. It is worth observing, however, that when James Mooney spent a week at Walker River Reservation in the waning days of December 1890, he enjoyed "sampling the seed mush and roasted piñon nuts." Mooney, *Ghost Dance Religion*, 768.

29. Earl William Kersten Jr., "Settlements and Economic Life in the Walker River Country of Nevada and California," PhD dissertation, University of Nebraska, 1961, 78–84; Edward C. Johnson, *Walker River Paiutes*, 60; Hulse, *The Silver State*, 134–136; *ARCIA 1862* (Washington, DC: Government Printing Office, 1863), 215.

30. Hittman, *Yerington Paiute Tribe*, 18; Saxon E. Sharpe, Mary E. Cablk, and James M. Thomas, *The Walker Basin, Nevada and California: Physical Environment, Hydrology, and Biology* (Reno: Desert Research Institute, 2008), 13; Israel Cook Russell, *Geological History of Lake Lahontan, a Quarternary Lake of Northwestern Nevada* (Washington, DC: Government Printing Office, 1895), 46; Gary A. Horton, *Walker River Chronology: A Chronological History of the Walker River and Related Water Issues* (Carson City: Nevada Division of Water Planning, Department of Conservation and Natural Resources, 1996), available at: http://water.nv.gov/mapping /chronologies/walker/ (accessed October 3, 2016).

31. Michael Hittman, "The 1870 Ghost Dance at the Walker River Reservation: A Reconstruction," *Ethnohistory* 20, no. 3 (Summer 1973): 254, 256; *ARCIA 1864* (Washington, DC: Government Printing Office, 1865). For family labor in seed gathering, see Steward, *Basin-Plateau Aboriginal Sociopolitical Groups*, 3. Recent historians have done a superb job of exploring Indian work in the reservation era; see William J. Bauer Jr., *We Were All Like Migrant Workers: Work, Community, and Memory on California's Round Valley Reservation, 1850–1941* (Chapel Hill: University of North Carolina, 2009); Colleen O'Neill, *Working the Navajo Way: Labor and Culture in the Twentieth Century* (Lawrence: University Press of Kansas, 2005); Erika Marie Bsumek, *Indian Made: Navajo Culture in the Marketplace, 1868–1940* (Lawrence: University Press of Kansas, 2008); Paige Raibmon, *Authentic Indians: Episodes of Encounter from the Late Nineteenth-Century Northwest Coast* (Durham, NC: Duke University Press, 2005); Alexandra Harmon, *Rich Indians: Native People and the Problem of Wealth in American History* (Chapel Hill: University of North Carolina, 2010).

32. Agent quoted in *ARCIA 1866* (Washington, DC: Government Printing Office, 1867), 115; ibid., 118–119; see also H. Douglas to E. S. Parker, September 20, 1870, in *ARCIA 1870* (Washington, DC: Government Printing Office, 1871), 95.

33. J. I. Wilson testimony, September 17, 1928, vol. II, 791, Hearing Before Special Master, C-125, US v. Walker River Irrigation District, US

District Court, Reno, NV (hereafter Hearing Before Special Master); Hittman, *Wovoka and the Ghost Dance*, 53; Grace Dangberg, "Wovoka," *Nevada Historical Society Quarterly* 11, no. 2 (1968): 6, 26; Mrs. Wilson interview, Jeanne Weir Field Notes, NC 17/4/44, Nevada Historical Society.

34. Quoted in Hittman, *Corbett Mack*, 290; Hittman, *Yerington Paiute Tribe*, 22; Knack, "Nineteenth-Century Great Basin Wage Labor," 145.

35. Eugene M. Hattori, "'And Some of Them Swear Like Pirates': Acculturation of Indian Women in Nineteenth-Century Virginia City," in *Comstock Women: The Making of a Mining Community*, edited by Ronald M. James and C. Elizabeth Raymond (Reno: University of Nevada Press, 1998), 233.

36. Eugene Mitsuru Hattori, "Northern Paiutes on the Comstock: Archaeology and Ethnohistory of an American Indian Population in Virginia City, Nevada," *Nevada State Museum Occasional Papers* 2 (1975): 14–15, 18–20; De Quille, *The Big Bonanza*, 215.

37. Hattori, "'And Some of Them Swear Like Pirates,'" 242.

38. Hattori, "Northern Paiutes on the Comstock," 17–18; for fish, see Martha C. Knack, "The Effects of Nevada State Fishing Laws on the Northern Paiutes," *Nevada Historical Society Quarterly* 25, no. 4 (Winter 1982): 255.

39. Louis Bevier (agency farmer) to James E. Spencer (US Indian agent), April 13, 1880, SC 90, Special Cases 1821–1907, Box 68, RG 75, NARA-DC.

40. For the effort to renege on the free shipment deal with the Paiutes, see Henry Yerington to H. Price (CIA), May 1, 1882, SC 90, Special Cases 1821–1907, Box 68, RG 75, NARA-DC; for the figure 20,000 pounds of fish, see US Department of the Interior (Census Division), *Report on Indians Taxed and Not Taxed in the United States, at the Eleventh Census: 1890* (Washington, DC: Government Printing Office, 1894), 392; Johnson, *Walker River Paiutes*, 70; see also Chester, "Comstock Creations," 164–166, 171–178.

41. For borax, see L. H. Strother to A.A.G., June 27, 1891, in Acting Secretary of War to Secretary of the Interior, July 22, 1891, Box 758, LR 1881–1907, No. 27124, RG 75, NARA-DC; Knack, "Nineteenth-Century Great Basin Wage Labor."

42. Brad Logan, "The Ghost Dance Among the Paiute: An Ethnohistorical View of the Documentary Evidence, 1889–1893," *Ethnohistory* 27, no. 3 (Summer 1980): 16; Knack, "Nineteenth-Century Great Basin Wage Labor," passim.

43. US Department of the Interior, *Report on Indians Taxed and Not Taxed*, 392–393; for eight miles of irrigation ditch, see S. S. Sears to J. D. Atkins, July 1, 1889, No. 18152, Box 533, LR 1881–1907, RG 75, NARA-DC.

44. Steward, *Basin-Plateau Aboriginal Sociopolitical Groups,* 27–28; J. O. Gregory to S. S. Sears, September 10, 1890, Walker River Agency Press Copy Books, Box 314, RG 75, NARA, Pacific Region, San Bruno, CA (hereafter Walker River Agency Press Copy Books). See also Hittman, *Wovoka and the Ghost Dance,* 51, photographs in Numu Ya Dua.

45. Steward, *Basin-Plateau Aboriginal Sociopolitical Groups,* 20; J. I. Wilson testimony, September 17, 1928, Hearing Before Special Master.

46. J. O. Gregory to S. H. Strother, July 6, 1891, Walker River Agency Press Copy Books; see also R. G. Armstrong to Assistant Adjutant General–California, December 17, 1887, in O. O. Howard to Secretary of the Interior, December 20, 1887, Box 438, LR 1881–1907, No. 269, RG 75, NARA-DC.

47. See, for example, *ARCIA 1865* (Washington, DC: Government Printing Office, 1866), 15. For the unreliability and vindictiveness of agents, see Knack and Stewart, *As Long as the River Shall Run,* 94–95; and W. D. Gibson to CIA, April 5, 1888, Box 457, LR 1881–1907, No. 9650, RG 75, NARA-DC.

48. Michael Hittman, "The 1890 Ghost Dance in Nevada," *American Indian Culture and Research Journal* 16, no. 4 (1992): 126; Steward, *Basin-Plateau Aboriginal Sociopolitical Groups,* 54, 60; Julian Steward and Erminie Wheeler-Voegelin, *The Northern Paiute Indians* (New York: Garland Publishing Co., 1974), 48; Catherine S. Fowler and Sven Liljeblad, "Northern Paiute," in *Handbook of North American Indians,* vol. 11, *Great Basin,* edited by Walter d'Azevedo (Washington, DC: Smithsonian Institution, 1986), 453.

49. W. D. Gibson to CIA, May 2, 1888, Box 458, LR 1881–1907, RG 75, NARA-DC; Hittman, "1890 Ghost Dance in Nevada," 126.

50. Mark Aldrich, *Death Rode the Rails: American Railroad Accidents and Safety, 1825–1965* (Baltimore: Johns Hopkins University Press, 2006), 318.

51. See D. A. Bender to William Stewart, n.d., handwritten note on copy of telegram from T. J. Morgan to C. C. Warner, October 12, 1891; and Richard Clarke [?—illegible], Attorney General, to Secretary of the Interior, October 30, 1893; both in Box 68, SC 90, Special Cases 1821–1907, RG 75, NARA-DC. See also *ARCIA 1893* (Washington, DC: Government Printing Office, 1894), 30–31; Knack, "Effects of Nevada State Fishing Laws on the Northern Paiutes"; Johnson, *Walker River Paiutes,* 69–80.

52. Steward, *Basin-Plateau Aboriginal Sociopolitical Groups,* 250.

CHAPTER 4: THE GHOST DANCE ARRIVES

1. Mooney, *Ghost Dance Religion,* 702; Cora Du Bois, "The 1870 Ghost Dance," *University of California Publications in Anthropological Records* 3, no. 1 (1939): 3–7, 10.

2. For Wodziwob and his origins, see Hittman, "1870 Ghost Dance at Walker River Reservation," 265–266; for the healthfulness of the Ghost Dance, see Judith Vander, *Ghost Dance Songs and Religion of a Wind River Shoshone Woman* (Los Angeles: University of California, Department of Music, 1986), 13; see also Lowie, "Dances and Societies," 817.

3. Solberg, *Tales of Wovoka*, 74; for "They have preachers," see De Quille, *The Big Bonanza*, 209. See also Joseph G. Jorgensen, "Ghost Dance, Bear Dance, and Sun Dance," in d'Azevedo, *Handbook of North American Indians*, vol. 11, *Great Basin*, 660; E. P. Thompson, *The Making of the English Working Class* (New York: Pantheon, 1964), 350–399; Robert F. Wearmouth, *Methodism and the Working-Class Movements in England 1800–1850* (1937; reprint, Clifton, UK: Augustus M. Kelley, 1972). For "fertility and beauty of Eden," see *ARCIA 1871* (Washington, DC: Government Printing Office, 1872), 558.

4. Journalist quoted in Hattori, "'And Some of Them Swear Like Pirates,'" 243–244; see also Steward, *Basin-Plateau Aboriginal Sociopolitical Groups*, 250.

5. Mrs. Wilson interview, Weir Field Notes, NC 17/4/44; Hittman, *Wovoka and the Ghost Dance*, 29, 32–33, 97, 173; Gregory E. Smoak, *Ghost Dances and Identity: Prophetic Religion and American Indian Ethnogenesis in the Nineteenth Century* (Berkeley: University of California Press, 2008), 113–118.

6. Smoak, "Mormons and the Ghost Dance of 1890," 269–294.

7. Smoak, *Ghost Dances and Identity*, 72–73.

8. Smoak, "Mormons and the Ghost Dance of 1890"; Mooney, *Ghost Dance Religion*, 790; Gunard Solberg makes this point in Michael Hittman, "Wovoka and the 1890 Ghost Dance Religion: A Conversation with Gunard Solberg," n.d., unpublished paper in the possession of the author.

9. Sven Liljeblad, "Oral Tradition: Content and Style of Verbal Arts," in D'Azevedo, *Handbook of North American Indians*, vol. 11, *Great Basin*, 657.

10. Smoak, *Ghost Dances and Identity*, 58–67; Miller, *Prophetic Worlds*, 44; Leslie Spier, *The Prophet Dance of the Northwest and Its Derivatives: The Source of the Ghost Dance* (Menasha, WI: George Banta Publishing Co., 1935); Robert H. Ruby and John A. Brown, *Dreamer-Prophets of the Columbia Plateau: Smohalla and Skolaskin* (Norman: University of Oklahoma Press, 2002); Deward E. Walker Jr. and Helen H. Schuster, "Religious Movements," in *Handbook of North American Indians*, vol. 12, *Plateau*, edited by Deward E. Walker Jr. (Washington, DC: Smithsonian Institution, 1998), 500; Cassandra Tate, "Smohalla (1815?–1895)," July 11, 2010, History-Link.org, http://www.historylink.org/index.cfm?DisplayPage=output.cfm&file_id=9481 (accessed June 16, 2012).

11. I draw here on Gregory Smoak's discussion of the "convergence of prophecy" in the Great Basin. Smoak, *Ghost Dances and Identity*, 124–132.

12. Ibid., 63, 65.

13. George William Smart, "Mission to Nevada: A History of Nevada Indian Missions," PhD dissertation, Central Baptist Theological Seminary, Kansas City, KS, 1958, 63–81.

14. US Department of the Interior, *Report on Statistics of Churches in the United States at the Eleventh Census: 1890*, xxi, 437. Only 12 percent of Nevadans were church members.

15. US Department of the Interior, *Report on Statistics of Churches*, 421; "Methodism in Nevada, Part 1," Online Nevada Encyclopedia, http://www.onlinenevada.org/methodism_in_nevada_part_i (accessed February 26, 2013). For Wovoka quotes, see the notes from the interview with M. Wilson, Grace Dangberg Composition Notebook (GDCN), 12–20, esp. 18, in Dangberg Papers, Nevada Historical Society, Reno (hereafter Dangberg Papers); see also Hittman, "1890 Ghost Dance in Nevada," 151; Francaviglia, *Believing in Place*, 115.

16. Knack, "Nineteenth-Century Great Basin Wage Labor."

17. James, *The Roar and the Silence*, 76; US Department of the Interior, *Report on Population of the United States*, pt. I, xiii, 235; "A Dying State," *New York Times*, July 28, 1889, 4; William D. Rowley, *Reclaiming the Arid West: The Career of Francis G. Newlands* (Bloomington: Indiana University Press, 1996), 44.

18. Alexander Klein, "Personal Income of US States: Estimates for the Period 1880–1910," Warwick Economics Research Papers Series 916 (Warwick, UK: University of Warwick, Department of Economics, 2009), http://ideas.repec.org/p/wrk/warwec/916.html; see also Killeen Hanson, Peter Shannon, Erik Steiner, and Richard White, "Visualization: Per Capita Income in the United States, 1880–1910," Stanford University, Spatial History Project, http://www.stanford.edu/group/spatialhistory/cgi-bin/site/viz.php?id=259&project_id=0 (accessed October 3, 2012).

19. "A Dying State," *New York Times*, July 28, 1889, 4; "Arizona and New Mexico," *Los Angeles Times*, March 8, 1894, 6; *Territorial Enterprise*, January 23, 1881, quoted in Hittman, *Corbett Mack*, 279.

20. Young and Sparks, *Cattle in the Cold Desert*, 120–134; Richard G. Lillard, *Desert Challenge: An Interpretation of Nevada* (Westport, CT: Greenwood, 1979), 18; Hittman, *Wovoka and the Ghost Dance*, 187. See also US Department of the Interior (Census Office), *Report on Statistics of Agriculture in the United States at the Eleventh Census: 1890* (Washington, DC: Government Printing Office, 1895), 108–109. For contemporary views of ranching, see Karen R. Merrill, *Public Lands and Political Meaning: Ranchers, the Government, and the Property Between Them* (Berkeley: University of California Press, 2002).

21. For "anything to eat," see A. I. Chapman to John Gibbon, December 6, 1890, in *ARSW 1891*, 193. For "work for the white people," see Captain

George to "White Father," February 13, 1888, Box 449, LR 1881–1907, No. 5433, RG 75, NARA-DC; see also Hittman, *Wovoka and the Ghost Dance*, 71; Paiute Sam in *Territorial Enterprise*, January 23, 1881, quoted in Hittman, *Corbett Mack*, 279.

22. Sarah Winnemucca, "The Pah-Utes," *The Californian* 6, no. 33 (September 1882): 256.

23. The photograph also appears in Hittman, *Wovoka and the Ghost Dance*, 28.

24. Dyer, "Jack Wilson Story," 4.

25. Mrs. Wilson interview, Weir Field Notes, NC 17/4/44; for "began to dream," see M. Wilson interview, in GDCN, Dangberg Papers; for "wasn't shamming," see Dyer, "Jack Wilson Story," 5; see also Hittman, "1890 Ghost Dance in Nevada," 135.

26. A. I. Chapman to John Gibbon, December 6, 1890, in *ARSW 1891*, 191.

27. Ibid., 191–192; Mooney, *Ghost Dance Religion*, 771–772.

28. A. I. Chapman to John Gibbon, December 6, 1890, in *ARSW 1891*, 193.

29. Hittman, *Wovoka and the Ghost Dance*, 65–66; for a comparison to the pine nut blessing, see Wheat, *Survival Arts*, 12; for "Fog! Fog!," see Mooney, *Ghost Dance Religion*, 1054.

30. Mooney, *Ghost Dance Religion*, 772; A. I. Chapman to John Gibbon, December 6, 1890, in *ARSW 1891*, 193.

31. For the drought, see Young and Sparks, *Cattle in the Cold Desert*, 128–129. For the Walker River going dry, see US Department of the Interior (Census Office), *Report on Agriculture by Irrigation in the Western Part of the United States at the Eleventh Census: 1890* (Washington, US Government Printing Office, 1894), 184–185; and J. I. Wilson testimony, September 17, 1928, Hearing Before Special Master.

32. Park, *Shamanism in Western North America*, 59, 61. The belief in the invulnerability of shamans was also standard among Utes and Bannocks; see Lowie, *Notes on Shoshonean Ethnography*, 292–293.

33. Dyer, "Jack Wilson Story"; Hittman, *Wovoka and the Ghost Dance*, 250.

34. For practical jokes, see Stephen Powers, "Centennial Mission to the Indians of Western Nevada and California: Smithsonian Institution Annual Report for 1876," in *A Great Basin Shoshonean Source Book*, edited by David Hurst Thomas (New York: Garland Press, 1986), 450. For skepticism about shamanic powers, see Ake Hultkrantz, *Shamanic Healing and Ritual Drama: Health and Medicine in Native North American Religious Traditions* (New York: Crossroad Publishing, 1992), 87. See also Hittman, "1870 Ghost Dance," 251; Du Bois, "1870 Ghost Dance," 5.

35. Park, *Shamanism in Western North America*, 57; Maurice Snyder notes, Weir Field Notes, NC 17/4/44.

36. A. I. Chapman to John Gibbon, December 6, 1890, in *ARSW 1891*, 193. For allegations of a hoax, see Joseph I. Wilson, quoted in Robert Nathaniel Davidson, "A Study of the Ghost Dance of 1889," MA thesis, Stanford University, 1952, 46–47; and "Fieldnotes of Karl Fredericks," reprinted in Hittman, *Wovoka and the Ghost Dance*, 308–309.

37. Notes from interview with Mrs. Webster, Dangberg Papers. The problem with this tale is that Paiutes do not normally cremate their dead. For the debate over Wilson's miracles, see the documents and testimony in Hittman, *Wovoka and the Ghost Dance*, 303–312.

38. Dyer, "Jack Wilson Story"; see also Hittman, *Wovoka and the Ghost Dance*, 76.

39. Dyer, "Jack Wilson Story."

40. For the willow basket, see Kane field notes, interview with Corbett Mack, July 14, 1964, 10, in "1964 Field Report"; and Hittman, *Wovoka and the Ghost Dance*, 338. For the ice floating down the river, see Kane field notes, interview with Andy Dick, July 9, 1964, in "1964 Field Report."

41. Park, *Shamanism in Western North America*, 60; for the source of Wilson's booha, see Joe Green, quoted in ibid., 19.

42. Kane field notes, 39, 42; Kane, interview with Corbett Mack, July 27, 1964, 4; both in "1964 Field Report."

43. I have created this composite version of the event from several different accounts by Hazel Quinn, originally collected by Michael Hittman in the 1970s and retold to him with additions from Mary Lee Stevens, Russell Dick, and Ida Mae Valdez in the 1980s. See Hittman, *Wovoka and the Ghost Dance*, 163–164; see also *Numu Ya Dua'* 3, no. 28 (June 4, 1982): 1–2.

44. Kane field notes, 42, in "1964 Field Report."

45. A. I. Chapman to John Gibbon, December 6, 1890, in *ARSW 1891*, 193.

46. Mooney, *Ghost Dance Religion*, 1052–1055.

47. A. I. Chapman to John Gibbon, December 6, 1890, in *ARSW 1891*, 191–192; for Josephus's aspirations, see J. O. Gregory to S. S. Sears, October 7, 1890, Walker River Agency Press Copy Books.

48. A. I. Chapman to John Gibbon, December 6, 1890, in *ARSW 1891*, 192.

49. Ibid.; Young and Sparks, *Cattle in the Cold Desert*, 129–131.

50. J. O. Gregory to S. S. Sears, February 18, 1890, Walker River Agency Press Copy Books.

51. Corbett Mack, in Hittman, *Wovoka and the Ghost Dance*, 338–340; for the hot coal, see Hittman, "1890 Ghost Dance in Nevada," 135.

52. Hittman, "1890 Ghost Dance in Nevada," 136.

53. Notes from Wilson interview, GDCN.

54. Wier Field Notes, NC 17/4/44.

55. Wilson quoted in Chapman to Gibbon, December 6, 1890, in *ARSW 1891*, 193; correspondent quoted in Martha B. Caldwell, "Some Kansas Rainmakers," *Kansas Historical Quarterly* 7, no. 3 (August 1938): 306–324, 306.

56. Hittman, *Wovoka and the Ghost Dance*, 69; notes from interview with J. I. Wilson, Dangberg Papers.

57. J. O. Gregory to S. S. Sears, February 18, 1890, Walker River Agency Press Copy Books; Mooney, *Ghost Dance Religion*, 772.

CHAPTER 5: INDIAN PROPHECY, AMERICAN MAGIC

1. Donald Worster, *A River Running West: The Life of John Wesley Powell* (New York: Oxford University Press, 2002), 470.

2. Richard Seager and Celine Herweijer (Lamont-Doherty Earth Observatory of Columbia University), "Causes and Consequences of Nineteenth Century Droughts in North America," Drought Research, http://www.ldeo.columbia.edu/res/div/ocp/drought/nineteenth.shtml (accessed August 9, 2012); Gilbert C. Fite, *The Farmers' Last Frontier, 1865–1900* (Norman: University of Oklahoma Press, 1987), 308–309.

3. Charles Dana Wilber, *The Great Valleys and Prairies of Nebraska and the Northwest*, 3rd ed. (Omaha, NE: Daily Republican Print, 1881), 70; M. Jean Ferrill, "Rainfall Follows the Plow," Encyclopedia of the Great Plains, http://plainshumanities.unl.edu/encyclopedia/doc/egp.ii.049 (accessed February 7, 2015).

4. Thomas W. Patterson, "Hatfield the Rainmaker," *Journal of San Diego History* 16, no. 1 (Winter 1970), http://www.sandiegohistory.org/journal/1970/january/hatfield/; Caldwell, "Some Kansas Rainmakers."

5. Victoria Foth, "'Rainmakers' Didn't Deliver," *Lawrence Journal-World*, May 22, 1988, 15; "Farmers in South Dakota Meet[ing] Close Contracts," undated clipping in J. C. Ogden to Francis Newlands, October 4, 1891, Box 371/3, Francis G. Newlands Papers, Manuscripts and Archives, Yale University, New Haven, CT. The clipping refers to the Kansas Artificial Rain Company, but its correct name can be found in Caldwell, "Some Kansas Rainmakers," 311. For the Rock Island Railroad rainmaker, see Caldwell, "Some Kansas Rainmakers," 318–324.

6. Evan Zartman Vogt, *Modern Homesteaders: The Life of a Twentieth-Century Frontier Community* (Cambridge, MA: Belknap Press of Harvard University Press, 1955), 73–92; Kate Sheppard, "Rick Perry Asks Texans to Pray for Rain," *Mother Jones*, April 21, 2011; Tim Egan, "Rick Perry's Unanswered Prayers," *New York Times*, April 11, 2011.

7. A. I. Chapman to John Gibbon, December 6, 1890, in *ARSW 1891*, 193.

8. Worster, *Rivers of Empire*, 135; Worster, *A River Running West*, 476.

9. Worster, *Rivers of Empire*, 135.

10. Frank Nimmo Jr., quoted in Worster, *Rivers of Empire*, 116.

11. William E. Smythe, *The Conquest of Arid America*, 2nd ed. (New York: Macmillan, 1905), 266–267; Smythe quoted in George Wharton James, *Reclaiming the Arid West: The Story of the United States Reclamation Service* (New York: Dodd, Mead, and Co., 1917), xvi; Smythe, *Conquest of Arid America*, xiii; Worster, *Rivers of Empire*, 119.

12. Smythe himself recalled his irrigation program in religious terms: "I had taken the cross of a new crusade." Smythe, *Conquest of Arid America*, 266–267; see also Catrin Gersdorf, *The Poetics and Politics of the Desert: Landscape and the Construction of America* (New York: Rodopi, 2009), 64–67; Ian R. Tyrell, *True Gardens of the Gods: Californian-Australian Environmental Reform, 1860–1930* (Berkeley: University of California Press, 1999), 107–108; Carolyn Merchant, *Reinventing Eden: The Fate of Nature in Western Culture* (New York: Routledge, 2004), 111.

13. J. O. Gregory to S. S. Sears, February 18, 1890, Walker River Agency Press Copy Books; Kane field notes, interview with Corbett Mack, July 14, 1964, in "1964 Field Report," 8.

14. Hittman, "1890 Ghost Dance in Nevada," 123–136; A. I. Chapman to John Gibbon, December 6, 1890, in *ARSW 1891*, 193; Mooney, *Ghost Dance Religion*, 772.

15. Mooney, *Ghost Dance Religion*, 780–781.

16. Nathaniel P. Phister, "The Indian Messiah," *American Anthropologist* 4, no. 2 (April 1891): 106; Ruby and Brown, *Dreamer-Prophets of the Columbia Plateau;* Tate, "Smohalla." Mooney asserts, with little evidence, that Smohalla had traveled and perhaps taught in Nevada in the mid-1880s. Mooney, *Ghost Dance Religion*, 718, 746.

17. A. I. Chapman to John Gibbon, December 6, 1890, in *ARSW 1891*, 191.

18. Ibid., 191–193.

19. H. Douglas to E. S. Parker, September 20, 1870, *ARCIA 1870* (Washington, DC: Government Printing Office, 1871), 95.

20. Robert Fleming Heizer, *Notes on Some Paviotso Personalities and Material Culture* (Carson City: Nevada State Museum, 1960), 6–7; Steward, *Basin-Plateau Aboriginal Sociopolitical Groups*, 257–258.

21. Steward, *Basin-Plateau Aboriginal Sociopolitical Groups*, 247.

22. Female shamans appear not to have been political leaders. Kane field notes, in "1964 Field Report," 11, 35–39, 48–49.

23. Harold Olofson, "Northern Paiute Shamanism Revisited," *Anthropos* 4 (1974): 13, 19; Beatrice Blyth Whiting, *Paiute Sorcery* (New York: Viking

Fund Publications in Anthropology, 1950), 43–54; Hultkrantz, *Shamanic Healing and Ritual Drama*, 1, 15; Park, *Shamanism in Western North America*, 18, 122.

24. Hittman, "1890 Ghost Dance in Nevada," 148; Park, *Shamanism in Western North America*, 123, 294; Isabel T. Kelly, "Ethnography of the Surprise Valley Paiute," *University of California Publications in American Archaeology and Ethnology* 31, no. 3 (1932): 195; Olofson, "Northern Paiute Shamanism Revisited," 21; Hultkrantz, *Shamanic Healing*, 18–19.

25. Park, *Shamanism in Western North America*, 68; Kane field notes, in "1964 Field Report," 37.

26. Du Bois, "1870 Ghost Dance," 5–6. "Apparently," notes Park, "the more important Ghost Dance prophets were at first rebels." Park, *Shamanism in Western North America*, 70.

27. Kane field notes, in "1964 Field Report," 38–39; for an in-depth study of the phenomenon, see Whiting, *Paiute Sorcery*, passim.

28. Whiting, *Paiute Sorcery*, 48.

29. Ibid., 64–66.

30. Hittman, *Corbett Mack*, 35–36, 268–269; Kane field notes, in "1964 Field Report," 34–35.

31. Hittman, *Corbett Mack*, 15, 61, 98, 178, 186–188, 191–192, 199–200, 349, 355–358, 360; Kane field notes, 37, 43, and interview with Corbett Mack, July 14, 1964, 8, both in "1964 Field Report."

32. Hittman, *Corbett Mack*, 191, 352–353.

33. Kane field notes, in "1964 Field Report," 43.

34. Solberg, *Tales of Wovoka*, 111. The rumor was still widespread in the Yerington Paiute community in the mid-1960s. Eileen Kane, personal communication, August 12, 2013.

35. Quoted in Hittman, *Corbett Mack*, 44. For doctors confirming sorcery, see Whiting, *Paiute Sorcery*, 65; for witch killings in 1891, see William J. Plumb to CIA, June 27, 1891, Box 748, LR 1881–1907, No. 23719, RG 75, NARA-DC; see also "Getting Rid of Witches," *Daily Alta Californian*, August 3, 1885, available at California Digital Newspaper Collection, http://cdnc.ucr.edu/cgi-bin/cdnc?a=d&d=DAC18850803.2.38 (accessed November 18, 2013).

36. Du Bois, "1870 Ghost Dance," 44, 23.

37. The restorative powers of the Ghost Dance were well known; see Vander, *Ghost Dance Songs*, 10. Mrs. Z. A. Parker observed at Pine Ridge that "they believed those who were sick would be cured by joining in the dance and losing consciousness." Mooney, *Ghost Dance Religion*, 917. See also Edgar E. Siskin, *Washo Shamans and Peyotists: Religious Conflict in an American Indian Tribe* (Salt Lake City: University of Utah Press, 1983), 157–158.

38. Hittman, "The 1870 Ghost Dance at Walker River Reservation," 248.

39. According to George Sword, word of the prophecies first arrived at Pine Ridge via the Shoshone and Arapaho—that is, from Wind River Reservation. See Sword in Mooney, *Ghost Dance Religion,* 797. For boarding school correspondence, see ibid., 894; for Nakash, see ibid., 817; Jeffrey D. Anderson, *One Hundred Years of Old Man Sage: An Arapaho Life* (Lincoln: University of Nebraska Press, 2003), 60–66.

40. ANSB; Mooney, "Ghost Dance Religion," 797, 817, 774. There are alleged to have been two delegations of Lakotas in 1889, but I am in agreement with Rani-Henrik Andersson that there was only one. See Andersson, *Lakota Ghost Dance of 1890,* 32.

41. Mooney, *Ghost Dance Religion,* 816.

42. See the series of telegrams from J. A. Williamson and J. A. Miller to Frank Bell, November 7, 1890; W. D. Jones to Acting Governor Frank Bell, November 9, 1890; W. Brougher and J. R. Brotherton to Frank Bell, November 13, 1890; all in Governor Bell Incoming Correspondence, September 1–December 31, 1890, Nevada State Archives, Carson City (hereafter Governor Bell Incoming Correspondence). See also Acting Governor Frank Bell to W. S. Gage, November 7 1890, 203; Governor R. Colcord to J. T. Wright, Ruby Valley, NV, January 21, 1891, 236; Colcord to Honorable F. Bell, Cloverdale (?), NV, June 4, 1891, 351; all in Letterbook of Stevens/Bell/Colcord, Nevada State Archives (hereafter Letterbook of Stevens/Bell/Colcord). See also George Nicholl to Frank Bell, November 23, 1890, Governor Bell Incoming Correspondence.

43. A. I. Chapman to John Gibbon, December 6, 1890, in *ARSW 1891.*

44. Ibid., 191.

45. Ibid.

46. Ibid.

47. The following account of Chapman's conversation with Wilson is from ibid., 192–193.

48. Elliott West, *The Last Indian War: The Nez Perce Story* (New York: Oxford University Press, 2009), 284–285.

49. Ibid., 131, 134–135, 282, 299, 304; Solberg, *Tales of Wovoka,* 173. In addition to his service in the Nez Perce War, Chapman worked for the War Department as an "Indian Interpreter" in Nevada among the Paiutes. James H. Wilbur to US Commissioner of Indian Affairs, October 27, 1881; A. J. Chapman to General Nelson A. Miles, December 6, 1881; and Chapman to Miles, December 19, 1881; all in Special File 268, RG 75, copies in Omer C. Stewart Collection, Box 1, Folder 14, Special Collections, University of Nevada, Las Vegas.

50. A. I. Chapman to John Gibbon, December 6, 1890, in *ARSW 1891.*

51. Ibid., 194.

CHAPTER 6: SEEKERS FROM A SHATTERED LAND

1. Andrew C. Isenberg, *The Destruction of the Bison* (New York: Cambridge University Press, 2000), 50–53.

2. Elliott West, *The Contested Plains: Indians, Goldseekers, and the Rush to Colorado* (Lawrence: University Press of Kansas), 22; Richard White, "The Winning of the West: The Expansion of the Western Sioux in the Eighteenth and Nineteenth Centuries," *Journal of American History* 65, no. 2 (September 1978): 321.

3. Wilhelm W. Wildhage, "Material on Short Bull," *European Review of Native American Studies* 4, no. 1 (1990): 35; White, "Winning of the West," 321.

4. Jeffrey Ostler, "'The Last Buffalo Hunt' and Beyond: Plains Sioux Economic Strategies in the Early Reservation Period," *Great Plains Quarterly* (2001): 117; Isenberg, *Destruction of the Bison*, 143.

5. George E. Hyde, *Red Cloud's Folk: A History of the Oglala Sioux Indians*, (Norman: University of Oklahoma Press, 1979), 164–165.

6. White, "Winning of the West," 321–324; for Sitting Bull's return, see Coleman, *Voices of Wounded Knee*, 12; Hyde, *Red Cloud's Folk*, 193–194.

7. For tiyospaye organization, see Powers, *Oglala Religion*, 40–42; see also Clark Wissler, "Societies and Ceremonial Associations in the Oglala Division of the Teton-Dakota," *Anthropological Papers of the American Museum of Natural History*, vol. 11, *Societies of the Plains Indians*, pt. 1 (1912); Thomas H. Lewis, *The Medicine Men: Oglala Sioux Ceremony and Healing* (Lincoln: University of Nebraska Press, 1990), 2.

8. Short Bull was affiliated with the people of the chiefs Two Strike and Red Leaf, who settled at Pass Creek. See Richmond Lee Clow, "The Rosebud Sioux: The Federal Government and the Reservation Years, 1878–1970," PhD dissertation, University of New Mexico, 1977, 17–18; and "Letter from the Secretary of the Interior, in Relation to the Affairs of the Indians at the Pine Ridge and Rosebud Reservations in South Dakota, March 16, 1892," 52nd Congress, 1st Session, 1891–1892, Senate Executive Document 58, 84.

9. West, *Contested Plains*; Loretta Fowler, "Arapaho," in *Handbook of North American Indians*, vol. 13, *Plains*, edited by Raymond J. DeMallie (Washington, DC: Smithsonian Institution, 2001), pt. 1, 840; Pekka Hamalainen, *Comanche Empire* (New Haven, CT: Yale University Press, 2008).

10. Loretta Fowler, "Arapaho, Southern"; and John H. Moore, "Cheyenne, Southern"; both at Encyclopedia of Oklahoma History and Culture, www.okhistory.org (accessed May 17, 2015); see also Andrew C. Isenberg, *The Destruction of the Bison* (New York: Cambridge University Press, 2000), 50–53; Hamalainen, *Comanche Empire*, 18–67.

11. For the location of the tribes, see the map in Omer C. Stewart, *Peyote Religion: A History* (Norman: University of Oklahoma Press, 1987), 56.

12. For the environmental history of the Great Plains, see Isenberg, *Destruction of the Bison;* West, *Contested Plains;* Elliott West, *The Way to the West: Essays on the Central Plains* (Albuquerque: University of New Mexico Press, 1995); Webb, *Great Plains;* Dan Flores, "Bison Ecology and Bison Diplomacy: The Southern Plains from 1800 to 1850," *Journal of American History* 78, no. 2 (September 1991); and William Cronon, *Natures Metropolis: Chicago and the Great West* (New York: W. W. Norton, 2009). See also University of Virginia, Geospatial and Statistical Data Center, Historical Census Browser (2004), http://mapserver.lib.virginia .edu/ (accessed August 17, 2013); Richard White, *Railroaded: The Transcontinentals and the Making of Modern America* (New York: W. W. Norton, 2012), 484.

13. The Kansas population in 1890 stood at 1.4 million, with over 166,000 farms; Texas had 2.2 million residents and over 228,000 farms. University of Virginia, Historical Census Browser (accessed June 25, 2015).

14. John D. Hicks, *Populist Revolt: A History of the Farmers' Alliance and the People's Party* (Minneapolis: University of Minnesota Press, 1931), 32–35; Richardson, *Wounded Knee,* 148–150.

15. US Department of the Interior (Census Division), *Abstract of the Eleventh Census: 1890* (Washington, DC: Government Printing Office, 1986), 96, 102, 172.

16. George E. Hyde, *A Sioux Chronicle* (Norman: University of Oklahoma Press, 1993), 184–228; James C. Olson, *Red Cloud and the Sioux Problem* (Lincoln: University of Nebraska Press, 1974), 310; William T. Hagan, *Taking Indian Lands: The Cherokee (Jerome) Commission, 1889–1893* (Norman: University of Oklahoma Press, 2003), 61–84.

17. Ellwood House and Museum, "History of Barbed Wire" (2004), http://web.archive.org/web/20060712125058/http://www.ellwoodhouse .org/barb_wire/ (accessed August 27, 2013).

18. J. F. Wade to Assistant Adjutant General, December 26, 1891, in Assistant Adjutant General to Secretary of the Interior, January 26, 1891, SC 188, NARA-DC; "Maps Showing the Progressive Development of American Railroads: 1830 to 1950," in Association of American Railroads, *American Railroads: Their Growth and Development* (pamphlet), January 1951, available at Central Pacific Railroad Photographic History Museum, http://cprr.org/Museum/RR_Development.html (accessed August 27, 2013).

19. Alan K. Knapp et al., "The Keystone Role of Bison in North American Tall Grass Prairie," *Bioscience* 49, no. 1 (January 1999): 39–50; Allen A. Steuter and Lori Hidinger, "Comparative Ecology of Bison and Cattle on Mixed-Grass Prairie," *Great Plains Research* 9 (1999): 329–342; Steve Zack and Kevin Ellison, "Grassland Birds and the Ecological Recovery of Bison:

A Conservation Opportunity," Wildlife Conservation Society and American Bison Society, http://www.eco-index.org/search/pdfs/1354report_1 .pdf (accessed June 25, 2015).

20. *ARCIA 1889,* 153. In 1889 performers from Pine Ridge made almost $29,000 traveling with Buffalo Bill's Wild West. Louis S. Warren, *Buffalo Bill's America: William Cody and the Wild West Show* (New York: Knopf, 2005), 366.

21. Donald J. Berthrong, *The Cheyenne and Arapaho Ordeal: Reservation Life in Indian Territory, 1875–1907* (Norman: University of Oklahoma Press, 1976), 67; *ARCIA 1884,* 38; Loretta Fowler, *Arapahoe Politics, 1851– 1978: Symbols in Crises of Authority* (Lincoln: University of Nebraska Press, 1986), 88–89.

22. *ARCIA 1888,* 50; Hyde, *Sioux Chronicle,* 22–23; ANSB, 1.

23. Little Wound: "Sometimes when we have a feast we sell a little bead work or a pipe or a pair of moccasins and with the money buy some coffee and some sugar." "The Indians' Side," *Washington Evening Star,* January 28, 1891, 3. For the sale of buffalo bones, see *ARCIA 1886,* 79. For Indian efforts to tax the use of reservation land, see Thomas L. Hedglen, "Cheyenne-Arapaho Cattle Company," Encyclopedia of Oklahoma History and Culture, www.okhistory.org (accessed May 17, 2015); Donald J. Berthrong, "From Buffalo Days to Classrooms: The Southern Cheyennes and Arapahos in Kansas," *Kansas History* 12, no. 2 (Summer 1989): 104– 105; and Berthrong, "Cattlemen on the Cheyenne-Arapaho Reservation, 1883–85," *Arizona and the West* 13, no. 1 (Spring 1971): 5–32.

24. Fowler, *Arapahoe Politics,* 84; Fowler, "Arapaho, Southern," in Encyclopedia of Oklahoma History and Culture, http://www.okhistory.org /publications/enc/entry.php?entry=AR002 (accessed June 9, 2015). For the output at Rosebud and Pine Ridge Reservations, see Hyde, *Sioux Chronicle,* 23; *ARCIA 1888,* 51. For Sitting Bull's cattle, hay, and oats, see Coleman, *Voices of Wounded Knee,* 180; Berthrong, *Cheyenne and Arapaho Ordeal,* 58–59.

25. "'Kill the Indian, and Save the Man': Capt. Richard H. Pratt on the Education of Native Americans," History Matters, http://historymatters .gmu.edu/d/4929/ (accessed May 8, 2016); David Wallace Adams, *Education for Extinction: American Indians and the Boarding School Experience, 1875–1928* (Lawrence: University Press of Kansas, 1995); K. Tsainina Lomawaima, *They Called It Prairie Light: The Story of the Chilocco Indian School* (Lincoln: University of Nebraska Press, 1994).

26. Elaine Goodale to CIA, December 18, 1890, Frame 666, Reel 1, SC 188, NARA-DC. For cuts in beef rations, see Hagan, *Taking Indian Lands,* 82. The agent for the Southern Arapaho noted in 1885 the reduced beef rations resulting from a revised census. *ARCIA 1885,* 74. On Indian nutrition, see Ostler, *The Plains Sioux and US Colonialism,* 129–130; Gretchen Goetz, "Nutrition a Pressing Concern for American Indians," Food Safety

News, March 5, 2012, http://www.foodsafetynews.com/2012/03/nutrition -a-pressing-concern-for-american-indians/#.UhyqguB7TQM (accessed August 27, 2013).

27. William Selwyn, interview with Kuwapi, in Selwyn to E. W. Foster, November 25, 1890, and in Foster to T. J. Morgan, November 25, 1890, Frames 281–306, SC 188, NARA-DC.

28. Thomas H. Lewis, *The Medicine Men: Oglala Sioux Ceremony and Healing* (Lincoln: University of Nebraska Press, 1990), 43; Elaine A. Jahner, "Lakota Genesis: The Oral Tradition," in *Sioux Indian Religion: Tradition and Innovation,* edited by Raymond J. DeMallie and Douglas R. Parks (Norman: University of Oklahoma, 1987), 51–52.

29. James R. Walker, "The Sun Dance and Other Ceremonies of the Oglala Division of the Teton Dakota," *Anthropological Papers of the American Museum of Natural History* 16, pt. 2 (1917): 79; Joseph Epes Brown, *Animals of the Soul: Sacred Animals of the Oglala Sioux* (Rockport, MA: Element Books, 1992), 8; Walker, "Sun Dance and Other Ceremonies," 84, 144.

30. Arthur Amiotte, "The Lakota Sun Dance: Historical and Contemporary Perspectives," in DeMallie and Parks, *Sioux Indian Religion,* 80–84; Walker, "Sun Dance and Other Ceremonies," 60–62; Frances Densmore, *Teton Sioux Music* (Washington, DC: Government Printing Office, 1918), 131.

31. Wilhelm Wildhage, "Material on Short Bull," *European Review of Native American Studies* 4, no. 1 (1990): 35; Clow, "Rosebud Sioux," 16–18.

32. *Annual Report of the Secretary of the Interior 1883,* 48th Congress, 1st Session, 1883–1884, Executive Document 1, Pt. 5, xii; Clyde Holler, *Black Elk's Religion: The Sun Dance and Lakota Catholicism* (Syracuse, NY: Syracuse University Press, 1995), 118, 119.

33. Holler, *Black Elk's Religion,* 65–66, 68, 69, 71–72, 88.

34. Leslie Spier, "The Sun Dance of the Plains Indians, Its Development and Diffusion," *Anthropological Papers of the American Museum of Natural History* 16, no. 7 (1921); Alfred Kroeber, *The Arapaho* (1904; reprint, Lincoln: University of Nebraska Press, 1983), 279–308; Walker, *Lakota Belief and Ritual,* 176–193.

35. Holler, *Black Elk's Religion,* 63, 69, 119.

36. George A. Dorsey, *The Arapaho Sun Dance: The Ceremony of the Offerings Lodge* (Chicago: Field Columbian Museum, 1903), 3–4.

37. West, *Contested Plains,* 197–199; *ARCIA 1885,* 79.

38. *ARCIA 1887,* 83; Benjamin R. Kracht, "Kiowa Religion in Historical Perspective," *American Indian Quarterly* 21, no. 1 (Winter 1997): 23; Roderick Sweezy, personal communication, August 19, 2016.

39. Loretta Fowler, *Wives and Husbands: Gender and Age in Southern Arapaho History* (Norman: University of Oklahoma Press, 2010), 96.

40. Holler, *Black Elk's Religion,* 130.

41. Gloria A. Young, "Intertribal Religious Movements," in *Handbook of North American Indians*, vol. 13, *Plains*, pt. 2, edited by Raymond J. DeMallie (Washington, DC: Smithsonian Institution, 2001), 999–1000; James Stuart Olson and Raymond Wilson, *Native Americans in the Twentieth Century* (Champaign: University of Illinois Press, 1984), 55.

42. Mooney, *Ghost Dance Religion*, 906–907; Young, "Intertribal Religious Movements."

43. Thomas C. Maroukis, *The Peyote Road: Religious Freedom and the Native American Church* (Norman: University of Oklahoma Press, 2012), 60.

44. Stewart, *Peyote Religion*, 3–53; Ake Hultrantz, *Belief and Worship in Native North America* (Syracuse, NY: Syracuse University Press, 1981), 291; for the shortened length of the ceremony, see Kroeber, *The Arapaho*, 398–399.

45. Stewart, *Peyote Religion*, 68–79, 34.

46. Fowler, *Wives and Husbands*, 162.

47. Harvey Markowitz, "Catholic Mission and the Sioux: A Crisis in the Early Paradigm," in DeMallie and Parks, *Sioux Indian Religion*, 131.

48. Marvin E. Kroeker, "Natives and Settlers: The Mennonite Invasion of Indian Territory," *Mennonite Life* 61, no. 2 (June 2006); *ARCIA 1887*, 80; *ARCIA 1888*, 94; Herbert M. Dalke, "Seventy Five Years of Missions in Oklahoma," *Mennonite Life* 10, no. 3 (July 1955): 101; Berthrong, "From Buffalo Days to Classrooms," 107. For Southern Methodists and Baptists, see *ARCIA 1889*, 189.

49. Tash Smith, *Capture These Indians for the Lord: Indians, Methodists, and Oklahomans, 1844–1939* (Tucson: University of Arizona, 2014), 81. In 1894, the Baptists also established a mission. William Munn Colby, "Routes to Rainy Mountain: A Biography of James Mooney, Ethnologist" Ph.D. diss., University of Wisconsin, Madison, 197; Fowler, *Wives and Husbands*, 157. For Indians who took up Christianity, see Berthrong, *Cheyenne and Arapaho Ordeal*, 81; K. B. Kueteman, "From Warrior to Saint: The Journey of David Pendleton Oakerhater," Oklahoma State University Electronic Publishing Center, 2006, http://digital.library.okstate.edu/Oakerhater/bio .html (accessed May 25, 2015).

50. Hyde, *Red Cloud's Folk*, 187; Markowitz, "Catholic Mission and the Sioux," 130; Ostler, *The Plains Sioux and US Colonialism*, 188.

51. Ostler, *The Plains Sioux and US Colonialism*, 188; Andersson, *Lakota Ghost Dance of 1890*, 164.

52. Douglas Barrows, "Congregational Dakotah Churches," in *History of the United Church of Christ in South Dakota, 1869–1976*, edited by Edward C. Ehrensperger (Freeman, SD: Pine Hill Press, 1977), 167.

53. Virginia Driving Hawk Sneve, *That They May Have Life: The Episcopal Church in South Dakota, 1859–1976* (New York: Seabury Press, 1977),

19–20, 35; Vine Deloria Jr., *Singing for a Spirit: A Portrait of the Dakota Sioux* (Santa Fe, NM: Clear Light Publishers, 2000), 39–48; Vine Deloria Sr., "The Establishment of Christianity Among the Sioux," in DeMallie and Parks, *Sioux Indian Religion*, 105–106; Andersson, *Lakota Ghost Dance of 1890*, 166; Douglas Barrows, "Congregational Dakotah Churches," in *History of the United Church of Christ in South Dakota, 1869–1976*, edited by Edward C. Ehrensperger (Freeman, SD: Pine Hill Press, 1977), 167; James Constantine Pilling, *Bibliography of the Siouan Languages* (Washington, DC: Government Printing Office, 1887), 20, 69.

54. "The Indians' Side," *Washington Evening Star*, January 28, 1891, 3; Andersson, *Lakota Ghost Dance of 1890*, 164.

55. William K. Powers, *Oglala Religion* (Lincoln: University of Nebraska Press, 1977), 115; Ostler, *The Plains Sioux and US Colonialism*, 188.

56. See Walker, *Lakota Belief and Ritual*, 74–75; Sneve, *That They May Have Life*, 59; Mark R. Ellis, "Reservation Akicitas: The Pine Ridge Indian Police, 1879–1885," *South Dakota History* 29 (1999): 184, 195.

57. Hittman, *Corbett Mack*, 182; A. I. Chapman to John Gibbon, December 6, 1890, in *ARSW 1891*.

58. George Bird Grinnell, "The Messiah Superstition Among the Northern Cheyenne," *Journal of American Folklore* 4, no. 12 (January–March 1891): 62; Hugh Lenox Scott, *Some Memories of a Soldier* (New York: Century Co., 1928), 155.

59. Wildhage, "Material on Short Bull," 38; Amiotte, "Lakota Sun Dance," 80–84. In what is probably artistic license (perhaps a response to German enthusiasm for Lakota regalia), some of Short Bull's dancers wear eagle headdresses, which the pledgers in this ceremony probably would not have worn.

60. Young, "Intertribal Religious Movements," 1000.

CHAPTER 7: PLAINS PASSAGE

1. General Nelson A. Miles to Adjutant General, November 28, 1890, M 983, vol. 1, p. 283, RG 94, NARA-DC; see also Andersson, *Lakota Ghost Dance of 1890*, 141–142.

2. Short Bull quoted in James P. Boyd, *Recent Indian Wars* (Philadelphia: Publishers Union, 1891), 208; Utley, *Last Days of the Sioux Nation*, 141. Historian Robert Utley, for instance, concluded that Short Bull and a fellow apostle, Kicking Bear, "perverted Wovoka's doctrine into a militant crusade against the white man." Utley, *Last Days of the Sioux Nation*, 87. See also Robert M. Utley, *Frontier Regulars: The United States Army and the Indian, 1866–1890* (New York: Macmillan, 1973), 402–403; Paul Hedren, *After Custer: Loss and Transformation in Sioux Country* (Norman: University

of Oklahoma, 2011), 170; Greene, *American Carnage,* 69, 74. Others have squared the circle by arguing that Lakotas did not need to change the religion because Wovoka himself was a militant. Thus, according to Jeffrey Ostler, Wovoka preached rebellion as part of "an anticolonial movement" and Lakotas did not stray "in any fundamental way" from his teachings. Ostler, *The Plains Sioux and US Colonialism,* 261–262.

3. Wildhage, "Material on Short Bull," 35–42; Ronald McCoy, "Short Bull: Lakota Visionary, Historian and Artist," *American Indian Art Magazine* (Summer 1992): 54–65, 57; George Wright to CIA, December 5, 1890, JPG 547, SC 188, NARA-DC.

4. Sam A. Maddra, *Hostiles?: The Lakota Ghost Dance and Buffalo Bill's Wild West* (Norman: University of Oklahoma Press, 2006), 29–31.

5. See Holler, *Black Elk's Religion,* 150–151, 204–223.

6. ANSB; Maddra, *Hostiles?,* 192–205.

7. Craeger was planning to write a book about Short Bull as early as 1891, which is the likely date of the narrative. Maddra, *Hostiles?,* 27–44. As far as I have been able to determine, the first history to use ANSB was Coleman, *Voices of Wounded Knee.*

8. The Omaha dance originated among Pawnees and spread to other Plains peoples during the nineteenth century. By 1889, among Lakotas, it had become primarily a social dance. Clyde Ellis, *A Dancing People: Powwow Culture on the Southern Plains* (Lawrence: University Press of Kansas, 2003), 50–54; James R. Murie, "Pawnee Indian Societies," in Clark Wissler, ed., *Societies of the Plains Indians* (New York: American Museum of Natural History, 1916), 629.

9. ANSB, 1–2.

10. Ibid., 2, 5.

11. Greene, *American Carnage,* 26.

12. ANSB, 4.

13. Ibid., 5; see also Mooney, *Ghost Dance Religion,* 818; A. I. Chapman to John Gibbon, December 6, 1890, in *ARSW 1891,* 192.

14. ANSB, 7.

15. Boyd, *Recent Indian Wars,* 209; Utley, *Last Days of the Sioux Nation,* 62.

16. ANSB, 7.

17. Ibid., 7–8.

18. One example of the criticism directed at the holy man is the remark of the unknown interpreter in Walker's *Lakota Belief and Ritual* who alleged that Short Bull "wants to prove that he was not the cause of the trouble of 1890–91." Walker, *Lakota Belief and Ritual,* 142.

19. A. I. Chapman to John Gibbon, December 6, 1890, in *ARSW 1891;* Stewart Indian School, "Stewart Indian School History," http://stewart indianschool.com/history/; Omer C. Stewart, "Contemporary Document

on Wovoka (Jack Wilson), Prophet of the Ghost Dance in 1890," *Ethnohistory* 24, no. 3 (Summer 1977): 222.

20. J. O. Gregory to S. S. Sears, February 18, 1890, Walker River Agency Press Copy Books; Mooney, *Ghost Dance Religion*, 772.

21. Mooney, *Ghost Dance Religion*, 788–789.

22. *ARSW 1891*, vol. 1, 142–143; Utley, *Last Days of the Sioux Nation*, 106; Greene, *American Carnage*, 74.

23. Ostler, *The Plains Sioux and US Colonialism*, 295–297.

24. A. T. Lea to Jas. A. Cooper, in Cooper to Honorable R. V. Belt, November 22, 1890, SC 188, NARA-DC; Hyde, *Sioux Chronicle*, 79, 282.

25. "The Indians' Side," *Washington Evening Star*, January 28, 1891, 3. For the description of Little Wound, see D. F. Royer to T. J. Morgan, November 8, 1890, M 983, vol. 1, pp. 62–66, RG 94, NARA-DC.

26. "The Indians' Side," *Washington Evening Star*, January 28, 1891, 3 (emphasis added).

27. Sword quoted in Mooney, *Ghost Dance Religion*, 797.

28. "Proceedings of a Council with the Cheyennes on Tongue River, Montana, Nov. 18, 1890," in Redfield Proctor to Secretary of the Interior, December 10, 1890, Reel 1, JPGs 657–662, SC 188, NARA-DC.

29. David Rich Lewis, "Reservation Leadership and the Progressive-Traditional Dichotomy: William Wash and the Northern Utes, 1865–1928," *Ethnohistory* 38 (Spring 1991): 124–148; Alexandra Harmon, *Indians in the Making: Ethnic Relations and Indian Identities Around Puget Sound* (Berkeley: University of California Press, 1998), 178; Andrew H. Fisher, *Shadow Tribe: The Making of Columbia River Indian Identity* (Seattle: University of Washington Press, 2010), 122.

30. Loretta Fowler says that Sitting Bull was born in 1853. Fowler, *Wives and Husbands*, 39, 159–160; see also Fowler, *Arapahoe Politics;* Mooney, *Ghost Dance Religion*, 895–896; Scott, *Some Memories of a Soldier*, 150; Julia A. Jordan, continuation of interview of November 2, 1967, with Jess Rowlodge, T-159:7, Doris Duke Collection, University of Oklahoma, University Libraries, Norman (hereafter Doris Duke Collection); Hugh Scott to Post Adjutant, February 10, 1891, in Redfield Proctor to Secretary of the Interior, March 3, 1891, Reel 2, SC 188, NARA-DC.

31. Mooney, *Ghost Dance Religion*, 894–895.

32. Ibid., 894–898; Fowler, *Wives and Husbands*, 158–159.

33. Mooney, *Ghost Dance Religion*, 899.

34. Ibid., 977.

35. Jack Wilson explicitly asserted that only he, not the dancers, had the trance experience. Mooney, *Ghost Dance Religion*, 772.

36. Ibid., 901, 1032, 1038–1039. An 1887 census records Grant Left Hand and Little Woman as a married couple without children. See "Census of Arapahoe Indians, Cheyenne and Arapahoe Agency, Darlington, Indian

Territory, 30 June, 1887," Cheyenne-Arapaho Lands of Oklahoma Gene-alogy, http://www.rootsweb.ancestry.com/~itcheyen/1887ArapahoeCensus.html (accessed July 15, 2013).

37. Mooney, *Ghost Dance Religion*, 1069.

38. Ibid., 921, 964–965, 974–975, 1074–1075; see also Kroeber, *The Arapaho*, 368–397.

39. Mooney, *Ghost Dance Religion*, 1070.

40. "Until the Ghost dance came to the prairie tribes [Kiowa] women had never before been raised to such dignity as to be allowed to wear feathers in their hair." Ibid., 909; James Mooney, "The Indian Ghost Dance," in *Collections of the Nebraska Historical Society*, vol. 16 (Lincoln: Nebraska Historical Society, 1911), 174. For Pawnee women in the Ghost Dance, see Alexander Lesser, *Pawnee Ghost Dance Hand Game: Ghost Dance Revival and Ethnic Identity* (Lincoln: University of Nebraska Press, 1996).

41. Mooney, *Ghost Dance Religion*, 895; Lesser, *Pawnee Ghost Dance Hand Game*.

42. Hugh L. Scott, in Mooney, *Ghost Dance Religion*, 897; Mrs. Z. A. Parker, in ibid., 917; Judith Vander, *Shoshone Ghost Dance Religion: Poetry Songs and Great Basin Context* (Chicago: University of Illinois, 1997), 65–66.

43. Mooney, *Ghost Dance Religion*, 1072.

44. Powers, *Oglala Religion*, 133; Mooney, *Ghost Dance Religion*, 903; H. L. Scott to Post Adjutant, January 5, 1891, in Secretary of War to Secretary of the Interior, January 21, 1891, Frames 87–92, esp. 92, Reel 2, SC 188, NARA-DC; see also Mooney, *Ghost Dance Religion*, 903 (Caddo), 909 (Kiowa); and Fowler, *Wives and Husbands*, 160.

45. Kroeber, *The Arapaho*, 154–155; Fowler, *Wives and Husbands*, 61; Jeffrey D. Anderson, *The Four Hills of Life: Northern Arapaho Knowledge and Life Movement* (Lincoln: University of Nebraska Press, 2008), 3.

46. On the well-lived Arapaho life, see Fowler, *Wives and Husbands*, 30, 79–80; Mooney, *Ghost Dance Religion*, 986–989; Kroeber, *The Arapaho*, 153–154, 156. For parallels among Northern Arapahos, see Anderson, *Four Hills of Life*, 137–161. For the work and contributions of wives, see Fowler, *Wives and Husbands*, 62, 77; Jeffrey D. Anderson, *Arapaho Women's Quillwork: Motion, Life, and Creativity* (Norman: University of Oklahoma Press, 2013), 116–117.

47. Anderson, *Four Hills of Life*, 160; Fowler, *Wives and Husbands*, 62–63.

48. Fowler, *Wives and Husbands*, 73–74; Kroeber, *The Arapaho*, 156–157.

49. Fowler, *Wives and Husbands*, 39, 156, 158–159; Fowler, *Arapahoe Politics*, 122; Mooney, *Ghost Dance Religion*, 896; H. L. Scott to Post Adjutant, January 4, 1891, in Secretary of War to Secretary of the Interior, January 21, 1891, SC 188. NARA-DC.

50. Fowler, *Wives and Husbands,* 162.

51. Ibid., 160–161.

52. Grant Left Hand student file, Carlisle Indian Industrial School, Carlisle Indian Industrial School Digital Resource Center, http://carlisle indian.dickinson.edu/student_files/grant-lefthand-student-file (accessed October 8, 2016).

53. Hugh L. Scott to Post Adjutant, January 18, 1891, in Hugh Lenox Scott Papers, Box 6, Library of Congress, Washington, DC. For Boynton, see Andrew Cowell, Alonzo Moss Sr., and William J. C'Hair, *Arapaho Stories, Songs, and Prayers: A Bilingual Anthology* (Norman: University of Oklahoma Press, 2014) 9, 517–519. Hugh Scott claimed that Smith Curley was a Carlisle graduate, but I have been unable to find any record of a Smith Curley (or Curly) at the school. Hugh L. Scott to Post Adjutant, Fort Sill, Oklahoma Territory, January 30, 1891, in L. A. Grant (Acting Secretary of War) to Secretary of the Interior, February 13, 1891, Reel 2, SC 188, NARA-DC; Mooney, *Ghost Dance Religion,* 820.

54. Grant Left Hand student file, Carlisle Indian Industrial School.

55. Fowler, *Wives and Husbands,* 130, 132, 137.

56. H. L. Scott to Post Adjutant, December 16, 1890, in Assistant Adjutant General to Redfield Proctor, January 7, 1891, Frame 1129, Reel 1, SC 188, NARA-DC; Mooney, *Ghost Dance Religion,* 780–781.

57. Luther Standing Bear, *My People the Sioux* (Lincoln: University of Nebraska Press, 1975), 217–230; Mooney, *Ghost Dance Religion,* 808; Hyde, *Sioux Chronicle,* 270; ANSB. The most famous (or notorious) educated Lakota Ghost Dancer was Plenty Horses, a boarding school graduate who, in January 1891, during the period of skirmishing that followed the massacre at Wounded Knee, shot and killed an army officer who was attempting to negotiate a peace. Deloria, *Indians in Unexpected Places,* 29–32.

58. Fowler, *Arapahoe Politics,* 122; Anderson, *Four Hills of Life,* 206; Anderson, *One Hundred Years of Old Man Sage,* 62–63. Reinforcing such ideas, Arapahos taught that the Ghost Dance was "another Pipe"; all Arapaho rituals and ceremonies derived authority from the tradition of the sacred Flat Pipe, a gift from the Creator. Cowell, Moss, and C'Hair, *Arapaho Stories, Songs, and Prayers,* 3.

59. Fowler, *Wives and Husbands,* 164; Stewart, "Contemporary Document on Wovoka," 222.

60. Maroukis, *Peyote Road,* 34–35; Fowler, *Wives and Husbands,* 295; Kroeber, *The Arapaho,* 158. For Young Bear and Heap of Crows, see Fowler, *Wives and Husbands,* 161–163. For Cleaver Warden and Paul Boynton, see Stewart, *Peyote Religion,* 106–107, 189–191.

61. *ARCIA 1890,* 178; T. J. Morgan to Bell, Indian Office, November 25, 1890, in SC 188, NARA-DC. Charles Ashley even reported on

November 25 that the Ghost Dance excitement was subsiding. Ashley to CIA, November 25, 1890, SC 188, NARA-DC.

62. *ARCIA 1891*, 1:350.

63. ANSB, 8.

CHAPTER 8: LAKOTA ORDEAL

1. ANSB, 8; *ARCIA 1891*, 411; Utley, *Last Days of the Sioux Nation*, 74; Mooney, *Ghost Dance Religion*, 820; Maddra, *Hostiles?*, 32.

2. For the significance of Sioux "outbreaks" in American policy, see Deloria, *Indians in Unexpected Places*, 15–51, esp. 21, 27.

3. D. F. Royer to T. J. Morgan, November 8, 1890, M 983, vol. 1, p. 65, RG 94, NARA-DC.

4. As Jerome Greene summarizes the consensus, the Ghost Dance sought (in the anthropologist Jack Goody's phrase) to "bend time backwards" to recover an ideal past, or alternatively, "to quicken its movement forward" to utopian resolution. Lakotas performed the Ghost Dance to "encourage the anticipated millennium and its promised rejection of white civilization." Greene, *American Carnage*, 65–66,71; 72–73, 440 n. 19.

5. Perain Palmer to T. J. Morgan, October 25, 1890, Frame 66, Reel 1; and D. F. Royer to R. V. Belt, October 30, 1890, Frame 71, Reel 1; both at SC 188, NARA-DC; Charles Eastman to Frank Wood, November 11, 1890, copy in Frank Wood to R. V. Belt, November 17, 1890, Frames 145–149, Reel 1, SC 188, NARA-DC; James McLaughlin to T. J. Morgan, October 17, 1890, Frames 49–61, Reel 1, SC 188, NARA-DC; F. S. Kingsbury to CIA, February 24, 1891, Frames 116–119, Reel 2, SC 188, NARA-DC; Philip F. Wells to James McLaughlin, October 19, 1890, in *New Sources of Indian History, 1850–1891*, edited by Stanley Vestal (Norman: University of Oklahoma Press, 1934); Anonymous [Warren K. Moorhead], "The Red Christ," *The Illustrated American*, December 13, 1890, 8; Andersson, *Lakota Ghost Dance of 1890*, 168.

6. Andersson, *Lakota Ghost Dance of 1890*, 76. The notion of religion as a means of reconciling cultural contradictions is widespread in religious studies. For a useful example, see Anthony A. Lee, "Reconciling the Other: The Baha'I Faith in America as a Successful Synthesis of Christianity and Islam," *Occasional Papers in Shayki, Babi, and Baha'i Studies* 7 (March 2003), http://www.h-net.org/~bahai/bhpapers.htm.

7. Hyde, *Sioux Chronicle*, 110–144, 189–192.

8. Ibid., 194–201.

9. Ibid., 202–208, 224.

10. Ibid., 209–213, 224–228, 202–228; Ostler, *Plains Sioux and US Colonialism*, 217–239.

11. *ARCIA 1890,* 49.

12. Hyde, *Sioux Chronicle,* 212, 236; Coleman, *Voices of Wounded Knee,* 154. According to Bishop William Hare of the Protestant Episcopal Church, many Lakotas died in the epidemics of 1889–1890 "not so much from disease as for want of food." Mooney, *Ghost Dance Religion,* 827–828.

13. *ARCIA 1889,* 152, 184.

14. Charles L. Hyde to Secretary Noble, May 29, 1890, Frame 2, Reel 1, SC 188, NARA-DC; McChesney to CIA, June 16, 1890, Frames 8–9, Reel 1, SC 188, NARA-DC.

15. Gallagher to T. J. Morgan, June 14, 1890, Frame 6, Reel 1, SC 188, RG 75, NARA-DC; Wright to CIA, June 16, 1890, RG 75, NARA, Kansas City, MO (NARA-KC). Gallagher seems to have believed that his superiors knew what he was talking about, although there is no surviving record of a prior report to Washington about the Ghost Dance; Gallagher's mention in this letter is the first.

16. Utley, *Last Days of the Sioux Nation,* 54–55, 79.

17. Wright to CIA, June 16, 1890, Frames 11–13, Reel 1, SC 188, RG 75, NARA-DC; Wright to CIA, January 23, 1891, Letters Sent from Rosebud Agency, RG 75, NARA-KC.

18. Clow says that there were 500 Wazhazhas at Pass Creek, but the agent counted 358. Clow, "Rosebud Sioux," 72; Wright to CIA, February 1, 1890, and Wright to CIA, February 11, 1890, both in Letters Sent from Rosebud Agency, RG 75, NARA-KC.

19. Clow, "Rosebud Sioux," 71–74; "An act to divide a portion of the reservation of the Sioux Nation of Indians in Dakota into separate reservations and to secure the relinquishment of the Indian title to the remainder, and for other purposes," March 2, 1889, 25 Stat. 888, in *Indian Affairs: Laws and Treaties,* vol. 1, compiled and edited by Charles J. Kappler (Washington, DC: Government Printing Office, 1902), http://digital .library.okstate.edu/kappler/vol1/html_files/SES0328.html#sec2a (accessed September 7, 2015); Wright to CIA, March 27, 1889, Wright to CIA, May 14, 1890, Wright to CIA, July 22, 1890, and Wright to CIA, August 7, 1890, all in Letters Sent from Rosebud Agency, RG 75, NARA-KC.

20. E. G. Bettelyoun to Eliza McHenry Cox, December 6, 1890, Frame 515, Reel 1, SC 188, NARA-DC; Clow, "Rosebud Sioux," 74; see also ANSB, 15.

21. Mooney, *Ghost Dance Religion,* 826; Utley, *Last Days of the Sioux Nation,* 40–55.

22. J. O. Gregory to S. S. Sears, February 18, 1890, RG 75, Walker River Agency Press Copy Books, Box 314, NARA–Pacific Region, San Bruno, CA.

23. Hugh L. Scott, quoted in Mooney, *Ghost Dance Religion,* 896.

24. Ibid., 899; Julia A. Jordan, interview with Jess Rowlodge, April 4, 1968, T-235–2, Doris Duke Collection.

25. Cherokee Commission Report, Entry 310, Irregularly Shaped Papers, Item 78, Box 45A, Folder 5, 39–40, RG 75, NARA-DC.

26. Hagan, *Taking Indian Lands,* 73–74; Cherokee Commission Report, Entry 310, Irregularly Shaped Papers, Item 78, Box 45A, Folder 4, 57, Folder 5, 40–41, RG 75, NARA-DC.

27. *ARCIA 1891,* 341–342; quote from Jordan, interview with Jess Rowlodge, April 4, 1968, Doris Duke Collection.

28. Fowler, *Arapahoe Politics,* 297; Anderson, *Four Hills of Life,* 17.

29. Wissler, "Societies and Ceremonial Associations," 7–27, 62.

30. Jeffrey Ostler, "Conquest and the State: Why the United States Deployed Massive Military Force to Suppress the Lakota Ghost Dance," *Pacific Historical Review* 65(2) May, 1996: 217–48.

31. *ARCIA 1889,* 184.

32. For Spotted Tail and Pratt, see Hyde, *Sioux Chronicle,* 51–56.

33. Robert M. Utley, "The Ordeal of Plenty Horses," *American Heritage* 26, no. 1 (December 1974), http://www.americanheritage.com/content /ordeal-plenty-horses?page=show (accessed September 28, 2013).

34. P. P. Palmer to CIA, December 1, 1890, JPGs 417–421, Reel 1, SC 188, NARA-DC.

35. W. T. Selwyn to E. W. Foster, November 25, 1890, Frames 301–306, Reel 1, SC 188, NARA-DC.

36. Pilling, *Bibliography of the Siouan Languages,* 69; W. Fletcher Johnson, *Life of Sitting Bull and History of the Indian War of 1890–91* (Edgewood Publishing Co., 1891), 162; V. Edward Bates, *In Search of Spirit: A Sioux Family Memoir* (Spokane, WA: Marquette Books, 2009), 178–179, 183–185.

37. Bates, *In Search of Spirit.*

38. Ibid.

39. Little Wound quoted in "The Indians' Side," *Washington Evening Star,* January 28, 1891, 3.

40. E. W. Foster to T. J. Morgan, November 25, 1890, Frame 282, Reel 1, SC 188, NARA-DC.

41. The details of Cook's account of Gallagher's confrontation with Ghost Dancers on September 7 are exactly the same as those in the report of E. B. Reynolds, who got those details from Gallagher. E. B. Reynolds to T. J. Morgan, September 25, 1890, Frames 32–36, Reel 1, SC 188, NARA-DC. Cook also says that Gallagher was his source: "The Agent told me this morning that yesterday he went down to see with his own eyes the dance." Excerpt from Cook to Hare, September 8, 1890, in W. H.

Hare to T. J. Morgan, September 11, 1890, Frames 37–40, Reel 1, SC 188, NARA-DC. For Cook's education, see Pilling, *Bibliography of the Siouan Languages*, 20.

CHAPTER 9: TIN STARS AND HOLY POWER

1. ANSB, 1.

2. Ibid., 2.

3. Utley, *Last Days of the Sioux Nation*, 26–30.

4. The Lime Crazy Lodge continued to meet as late as 1906. Loretta Fowler, *Arapahoe Politics*, 121.

5. Anderson, *Four Hills of Life*, 154; Fowler, *Wives and Husbands*, 150.

6. Red Cloud eventually parlayed his leadership into federal recognition as head chief of all the Lakotas (an office that did not exist in Lakota custom) during treaty negotiations with the United States in 1868. Hyde, *Red Cloud's Folk*, 52–53, 313–314. Little Wound quoted in Walker, *Lakota Belief and Ritual*, 67.

7. Hyde, *Red Cloud's Folk*, 315.

8. Thomas Powers, *The Killing of Crazy Horse* (New York: Random House/Vintage, 2010), 224.

9. Ellis, "Reservation Akicitas," 200.

10. For instance, among Brules, Crow Dog was chief of police when he began to feud with Spotted Tail, the leading chief. After he was forced out of the police force (for other reasons), Crow Dog continued the feud, and in 1881, in a brazen, daylight shooting, he assassinated Spotted Tail. Utley, *Last Days of the Sioux Nation*, 150; Stanley Vestal, *Sitting Bull, Champion of the Sioux: A Biography* (1932; revised edition, Norman: University of Oklahoma Press, 1957), 251–533, 272, 287; Hyde, *Sioux Chronicle*, 47–63, 205; Frank Bennett Fiske, *Life and Death of Sitting Bull* (Fort Yates, ND: Pioneer-Arrow Print, 1933), 50.

11. William T. Hagan, *Indian Police and Judges: Experiments in Acculturation and Control* (New Haven, CT: Yale University Press, 1966), esp. 43; Robert Utley, "Indian Police and Judges," *Pacific Northwest Quarterly* 57, no. 3 (July 1966): 129–130. For "the multitude are bitterly opposed," see *ARCIA 1885*, 22; for "will not serve," see McChesney in *ARCIA 1890*, 45; for George Sword, see Walker, *Lakota Belief and Ritual*, 74–75. See also Utley, *Last Days of the Sioux Nation*, 28; Ellis, "Reservation Akicitas," 195 n. 17. For the percentage of the force remaining in 1890, see Ellis, "Reservation Akicitas," 200.

12. Greene, *American Carnage*, 72–74.

13. Utley, *Last Days of the Sioux Nation*, 84. Utley claims that Short Bull did not begin dancing again until September, but Short Bull himself recalls

that he began in May, following the lead of Scatter and others. ANSB, 9. Kicking Bear allegedly collaborated with Good Thunder to initiate the dances at Pine Ridge. See D. F. Royer to T. J. Morgan, November 8, 1890, Frames 95–99, Reel 1, SC 188, NARA-DC.

14. George Wright to CIA, December 5, 1890, JPG 545, Reel 1, SC 188, NARA-DC; Utley, *Last Days of the Sioux Nation*, 94.

15. Royer to CIA, November 27, 1890, JPGs 366–367, Reel 1, SC 188, NARA-DC.

16. Utley, *Last Days of the Sioux Nation*, 97; Perain Palmer to CIA, October 11 and 25, November 10 and 28, 1890, Reel 1, SC 188, NARA-DC.

17. McLaughlin to CIA, October 17, 1890, Frames 49–61, Reel 1, SC 188, NARA-DC; Utley, *Last Days of the Sioux Nation*, 98. Carignan reported that school attendance fell from "about 40" students to "8 or 9" in two months. "Report of John M. Carignan" (undated), in Vestal, *New Sources of Indian History*, 1. Years later, Carignan recalled attendance dropping from ninety to three. Carignan, in Fiske, *Life and Death of Sitting Bull*, 32; Mary C. Collins, "A Short Autobiography," in Vestal, *New Sources of Indian History*, 61–72.

18. McLaughlin to T. J. Morgan, November 29, 1890, Entry 310, Irregularly Shaped Papers, Item 128, Box 76, Folder 1, RG 75, NARA-DC.

19. For the camps, see D. F. Royer to T. J. Morgan, November 8, 1890, M 983, vol. 1, pp. 62–66, RG 94, NARA-DC; Utley, *Last Days of the Sioux Nation*, 103, 105.

20. Hyde, *Sioux Chronicle*, 235, 250; "Dr. V. T. McGillycuddy on the Ghost Dance," in Vestal, *New Sources of Indian History*, 87–89; D. F. Royer to T. J. Morgan, November 8, 1890, M 983, vol. 1, pp. 62–66, RG 94, NARA-DC. Little Wound's Ghost Dance vision itself is in Boyd, *Recent Indian Wars*, 189–191.

21. E. B. Reynolds to T. J. Morgan, September 25, 1890, Reel 1, SC 188, NARA-DC; *ARCIA 1890*, 49.

22. Utley conflates these two events into one. But a close reading of the sources reveals that Gallagher arrived at Torn Belly's camp shortly before he made his annual report in late August and Reynolds arrived on September 21. Utley, *Last Days of the Sioux Nation*, 92–94; E. B. Reynolds to T. J. Morgan, September 25, 1890, Reel 1, SC 188, NARA-DC; *ARCIA 1890*, 49.

23. Perain P. Palmer to T. J. Morgan, October 11, 1890, Frames 135–136, Reel 1, SC 188, NARA-DC.

24. Royer to CIA, November 11, 1890, Frames 135–136, Reel 1, SC 188, NARA-DC; Eastman, *From the Deep Woods to Civilization*, 94–95.

25. Utley, *Last Days of the Sioux Nation*, 108.

26. Not all wicasa wakan took up the Ghost Dance; American Horse, who, as we have seen, was a leading "progressive" chief at Pine Ridge, was

also a holy man who opposed the new religion throughout 1890. For American Horse as a holy man, see Walker, *Lakota Belief and Ritual*, xiv, 68, 283.

27. Mooney, *Ghost Dance Religion*, 823; Boyd, *Recent Indian Wars*, 186; Holler, *Black Elk's Religion*, 135–136; Mary Collins, [no title], *The Word Carrier*, November 27, 1890, fragment of a clipping in Collins Papers, Box 2, Accession H80–014-F38, South Dakota State Archives, Pierre.

28. For a description of religious seizures, see E. B. Reynolds to T. J. Morgan, September 25, 1890, Reel 1, SC 188, NARA-DC; and Mrs. Z. A. Parker's account in "Ghost Dance at Pine Ridge," *Journal of American Folklore* 4, no. 13 (April–June 1891): 160–162.

29. McLaughlin, *My Friend the Indian*, 201–207.

30. Marla N. Powers, *Oglala Women: Myth, Ritual, and Reality* (Chicago: University of Chicago Press, 2010), 72; Amiotte, "Lakota Sun Dance," 77.

31. At the October Ghost Dance on White Clay Creek observed by Mrs. Z. A. Parker, only about 110 dancers—of some 300 to 400—wore ghost shirts or dresses. According to Mrs. Parker, a woman visionary made garments for women in the dance. Mrs. Z. A. Parker, in Mooney, *Ghost Dance Religion*, 916; see also "Ghost Dance at Pine Ridge," *Journal of American Folklore* 4, no. 13 (April–June 1891): 160.

32. Arthur Amiotte, personal communication, October 25, 2014. With so many participants, the sweat lodges of the Ghost Dance were not small structures, but as James Mooney noted, they were "made sufficiently large to accommodate a considerable number of persons standing inside at the same time." Mooney, *Ghost Dance Religion*, 823.

33. Mooney, *Ghost Dance Religion*, 1064, 1072–1073.

34. Karl Markus Kreis, ed. *Lakotas, Black Robes, and Holy Women: German Reports from the Indian Mission in South Dakota, 1886–1900* (Lincoln: University of Nebraska Press, 2007), 159.

35. Sword quoted in Walker, *Lakota Belief and Ritual*, 80, 161–163. See also Lewis, *The Medicine Men*, 43; McLaughlin to T. J. Morgan, October 17, 1890, Frame 58, Reel 1, SC 188, NARA-DC.

CHAPTER 10: SPIRIT OF THE GHOST DANCE

1. Quoted in Vestal, *New Sources of Indian History*, 342.

2. For Little Wound and American Horse, see "The Indians' Side," *Washington Evening Star*, January 28, 1891, 3; Josephine Waggoner, *Witness: A Hunkpapha Historian's Strong-Heart Song of the Lakotas* (Lincoln: University of Nebraska Press, 2013), 222.

3. Utley, *Last Days of the Sioux Nation*, 110.

4. President Benjamin Harrison to Honorable Secretary of the Interior, November 13, 1890, SC 188, NARA-DC.

5. "The Indian Situation," extract from the *Sioux Falls Press*, December 2, 1890, in Bishop Hare to Morgan, December 5, 1890, JPGs 556–558, Reel 1, SC 188, NARA-DC; W. Hare to Morgan, December 5, 1890, Frame 553, Reel 1, SC 188, NARA-DC.

6. M. A. DeWolfe Howe, *Life and Labors of Bishop Hare: Apostle to the Sioux* (New York: Sturgis & Walton, 1914), 237. For the schools established by Episcopalian missionaries, see Andersson, *Lakota Ghost Dance of 1890*, 163.

7. *Sioux Falls Press*, "The Indian Situation."

8. Ibid.

9. E. B. Reynolds to CIA, November 26, 1890, JPGs 331–333, Reel 1, SC 188, NARA-DC.

10. For a summary of the boundary controversy, see Utley, *Last Days of the Sioux Nation*, 78.

11. *Sioux Falls Press*, "The Indian Situation."

12. Ibid.

13. Palmer to T. J. Morgan, December 9, 1890, JPG 561, Reel 2, SC 188, NARA-DC.

14. Palmer to T. J. Morgan, November 10, 1890, SC 188, NARA-DC.

15. Andersson, *Lakota Ghost Dance of 1890*, 168, 273; Perain Palmer to T. J. Morgan, November 10, 1890, JPG 125, Reel 1, and Perain Palmer to T. J. Morgan, December 9, 1890, JPG 560–562, Reel 1, SC 188, NARA-DC.

16. DeMallie, "Lakota Ghost Dance," 399.

17. Reynolds to CIA, September 25, 1890, Frames 31–36, Reel 1, SC 188, NARA-DC; DeMallie, *Sixth Grandfather*, 266. For Kicking Bear, see Edward Ashley journal typescript, entry for September 3, 1890, Center for Western History, Augustana College, Sioux Falls, SD; Mooney, *Ghost Dance Religion*, 824.

18. Ashley journal typescript, entry for September 2, 1890.

19. Kreis, *Lakotas, Black Robes, and Holy Women*, 40.

20. Ashley journal typescript, entry for September 14, 1890.

21. Reynolds to CIA, September 25, 1890. Little Horse also related being carried to the Messiah by "two holy eagles." See Boyd, *Recent Indian Wars*, 193.

22. Andersson, *Lakota Ghost Dance of 1890*, 165.

23. For converts' incomplete understanding of Christianity, see Howe, *Life and Labors of Bishop Hare*, 236.

24. Ostler, *Plains Sioux and US Colonialism*, 189; Andersson, *Lakota Ghost Dance of 1890*, 164; Utley, *Last Days of the Sioux Nation*, 38–39.

25. Ostler, *Plains Sioux and US Colonialism*, 188–189. For the duty of chiefs, see Wissler, "Societies and Ceremonial Associations," 11.

26. Quoted in Andersson, *Lakota Ghost Dance of 1890*, 169.

27. Eugene Buechel and Paul Manhart, eds., *Lakota Dictionary* (Lincoln: University of Nebraska Press, 1990), 384, 445.

28. Powers, *Oglala Religion*, 128.

29. Ashley journal typescript, entry for October 26, 1890.

30. *ARCIA 1891*, 1:350.

31. Craft quoted in Andersson, *Lakota Ghost Dance of 1890*, 182; "In Darkest America," *The Times* (Philadelphia), January 8, 1891, clipping in Reel 1, JPG 90, SC 188, NARA-DC; John Gray to CIA, December 20, 1890, Reel 1, JPGs 674–675, SC 188, RG 75, NARA-DC.

CHAPTER 11: INVASION AND ATROCITY

1. Emphasis in original, Royer to Belt, November 15, 1890, Frame 156, Reel 1, SC 188, NARA-DC; Utley, *Last Days of the Sioux Nation*, 111. The exact dates of the tour by Ashley and Clark are unknown, but given that most of the Wazhazhas fled Pass Creek on November 20, when the army invaded, the tour must have taken place before then. November 20 was also the day that Bishop William Hare gave an interview to the press about his recent trip to Rosebud Reservation. Hare left Rosebud the day Ashley left on his journey with Clark, which I estimate to have been about November 13. See *Sioux Falls Press*, "The Indian Situation."

2. Utley, *Last Days of the Sioux Nation*, 114–115.

3. ANSB, 10; Utley, *Last Days of the Sioux Nation*, 78. According to Short Bull, these Brules had received word that they were to move to Pine Ridge and settle there and were preparing to move about the time the army arrived.

4. Utley, *Last Days of the Sioux Nation*, 118; ANSB, 11–12.

5. Interview transcript in William Selwyn to E. W. Foster, November 25, 1890, in Foster to T. J. Morgan, November 25, 1890, Frames 281–306, SC 188, NARA-DC; Mooney, *Ghost Dance Religion*, 799–801, quote on 801.

6. Selwyn to E. W. Foster, November 25, 1890, in Foster to T. J. Morgan, November 25, 1890, Frames 281–306, SC 188, NARA-DC.

7. Vestal, *New Sources of Indian History*, 39, 42. The letters may not be credible. Although there was no widespread killing or looting in the fall of 1890, one of the correspondents, Brings Plenty, claimed in an undated letter: "There is lots fight going on at Black Hill I am in it all of them. We Kill lots white people and take away everything they got." On December 7, 1890, Spotted Sheep advised his brother-in-law Kills Standing, "There are 20 companies of soldiers at this place. And we thought fighting them but gave it up until spring. Then is the time we decided on fighting."

8. ANSB, 12.

9. C. H. Carlton to Assistant Adjutant General, January 11, 1891, in Wesley Merrit to Adjutant General, January 21, 1891, Reel 2, JPGs 83–96, SC 188, RG 75, NARA-DC; Charles Adams to CIA, November 5, 1890, Frames 90–92, Reel 1, SC 188, RG 75, NARA-DC. For Lakota and Arapaho letters, see Grinnell, "Messiah Superstition," 63.

10. Utley, *Last Days of the Sioux Nation*, 121.

11. ANSB, 12.

12. Utley, *Last Days of the Sioux Nation*, 121–122.

13. Ibid., 127.

14. Ibid., 130–131.

15. Ibid., 132.

16. ANSB, 13.

17. "Lo the Poor Indian Has Census Troubles, Too!" *New York Herald,* December 7, 1890, 16; Utley, *Last Days of the Sioux Nation,* 137; Kreis, *Lakotas, Black Robes, and Holy Women,* 143.

18. Mooney, *Ghost Dance Religion,* 867.

19. Shangreau quoted in Warren K. Moorehead (unattributed), "Sioux on the Warpath," *Illustrated American,* January 10, 1891, 269–270 (my thanks to Rani-Henrik Andersson for this source); Short Bull letter in Greene, *American Carnage,* 160, 164–165; Mooney, *Ghost Dance Religion,* 867.

20. Sitting Bull quoted in Coleman, *Voices of Wounded Knee,* 77; "Note on Kicking Bear," in Vestal, *New Sources of Indian History,* 341.

21. McLaughlin to CIA, November 19, 1890, Frames 185–194, Reel 1, SC 188, NARA-DC.

22. James McLaughlin to T. J. Morgan, October 17, 1890, Frames 49–61, Reel 1, SC 188, RG 75, NARA-DC.

23. Walker, *Lakota Belief and Ritual,* 96.

24. Quoted in Greene, *American Carnage,* 179.

25. McLaughlin to CIA, October 17, 1890, Frame 59, Reel 1, SC 188, NARA-DC.

26. Robert M. Utley, *The Lance and the Shield: The Life and Times of Sitting Bull* (New York: Ballantine, 1994), 32–33.

27. Greene, *American Carnage,* 179–181; Coleman, *Voices of Wounded Knee,* 204–210; John Lone Man, as told to Robert Higheagle, in Vestal, *New Sources of Indian History,* 45–55; Utley, *Last Days of the Sioux Nation,* 146–166; Mooney, *Ghost Dance Religion,* 857–859.

28. Mooney, *Ghost Dance Religion,* 857–858.

29. Utley, *Last Days of the Sioux Nation,* 174; Greene, *American Carnage,* 199; Coleman, *Voices of Wounded Knee,* 247; Mooney, *Ghost Dance Religion,* 861, 867.

30. Utley, *Last Days of the Sioux Nation,* 167–186.

31. ANSB, 15.

32. Ibid.

33. Utley, *Last Days of the Sioux Nation*, 140–142; Moorehead, "Sioux on the Warpath."

34. For the camp at Drexel Mission, see Mooney, *Ghost Dance Religion*, 868. Short Bull's memoir departs from the official history in the one small detail of his staying behind. See, for example, ibid., 866–867.

35. Coleman, *Voices of Wounded Knee*, 250; Jensen, ed., *Voices of the American West*, 1:214–215.

36. Utley, *Last Days of the Sioux Nation*, 187–199.

37. The foregoing description of the massacre is based primarily on Richardson, *Wounded Knee*, 259–274. Rough Feather and White Lance quoted in Smith, *Moon of Popping Trees*, 190–191. See also Utley, *Last Days*, 200–230; Greene, *American Carnage*, 220–243.

38. On the supposed invulnerability felt by young Indians, some refer to the alleged exhortation by a holy man named Yellow Bird during the search for guns that army bullets "cannot penetrate us . . . they will not penetrate you." See Utley, *Last Days of the Sioux Nation*, 210; Hyde, *Sioux Chronicle*, 301.

39. Horn Cloud quoted in Jensen, ed., *Voices of the Amerian West*, 1:192, 194–195; Richardson, *Wounded Knee*, 258–259.

40. Horn Cloud quoted in Jensen, *Voices of the American West*, 1:191, 425 n. 4; Philip Burnham, *Song of Dewey Beard: Last Survivor of the Little Bighorn* (Lincoln: University of Nebraska Press, 2014), 58–59.

41. ANSB, 16.

42. Utley, *Last Days of the Sioux Nation*, 226–227, 231; Greene, *American Carnage*, 334.

43. ANSB, 18.

44. Red Cloud in T. A. Bland, *A Brief History of the Late Military Invasion of the Home of the Sioux* (Washington, DC: National Indian Defence Association, 1891), 22; Utley, *Last Days of the Sioux Nation*, 231, 233–234, 251.

45. Utley, *Last Days of the Sioux Nation*, 232, 239–240, 253–254; Greene, *American Carnage*, 324.

46. ANSB, 18–19.

47. Utley, *Last Days of the Sioux Nation*, 260; ANSB, 19.

CHAPTER 12: THE ROAD FROM WOUNDED KNEE

1. Mooney, *Ghost Dance Religion*, 913.

2. The tale of Wovoka's disillusionment is a popular story. See for example, Paul Bailey, *Wovoka, The Indian Messiah* (Los Angeles: Westernlore Press, 1957); Utley, *Last Days of the Sioux Nation*, 284–285.

3. *ARCIA 1891,* 301.

4. Mooney, *Ghost Dance Religion,* 903.

5. Dangberg, "Wovoka," 34, 49; Maddra, *Hostiles?,* 187; Hittman, *Wovoka and the Ghost Dance,* 265.

6. Alice Beck Kehoe, *The Ghost Dance: Ethnohistory and Revitalization* (New York: Holt, Rinehart, and Winston, 1989), 44.

7. Mooney, *Ghost Dance Religion,* 653, 927.

8. Mooney to Henshaw, January 19, 1891, Records of the Bureau of American Ethnology (BAE), Series 1, Correspondence, Letters Received, 1888–1906, Box 109, National Anthropological Archives (NAA), Washington, DC.

9. James Mooney, "The Indian Ghost Dance," in Albert Watkins, ed., Collections of the Nebraska Historical Society, 16 (1911): 171.

10. Mooney to Henshaw, January 27, 1891, Records of the BAE, Series 1, Correspondence, Letters Received, 1888–1906, Box 109, NAA.

11. Moses, *The Indian Man,* 18–51; Colby, "Routes to Rainy Mountain," 63–121.

12. Moses, *The Indian Man,* 51.

13. Hugh L. Scott to Post Adjutant, January 18, 1891, Hugh Lenox Scott Papers, Box 6, Library of Congress, Washington, DC.

14. Scott, *Some Memories of a Soldier,* 148.

15. Mooney, "The Indian Ghost Dance."

16. Ibid., 171–172.

17. Warden became a longtime consultant for anthropologists and would coauthor several studies. See Fowler, *Arapahoe Politics,* 325, n. 67.

18. Mooney, "The Indian Ghost Dance," 172; Mooney, *Ghost Dance Religion,* 918.

19. "It is awful," he reported, using the word in its original sense as a synonym for "sacred" or "awe-inspiring." Mooney to Henshaw, January 27, 1891, Records of the BAE, Series 1, Correspondence, Letters Received, 1888–1906, Box 109, NAA.

20. Quoted in Hattori, "'And Some of Them Swear Like Pirates,'" 243–244.

21. Mooney, *Ghost Dance Religion,* 908–909.

22. Ibid., 911.

23. Ibid., 911–914.

24. Ibid., 913–914; Louise Saddleblanket, interview with William Bittle, June 27, 1967, T-56–2, Doris Duke Collection.

25. Mooney, *Ghost Dance Religion,* 903.

26. Ibid., 900.

27. Ibid.

28. "The Messiah Letter (Free Rendering)," in ibid., 781.

29. Mooney, *Ghost Dance Religion*, 903; Cowell, Moss, and C'Hair, *Arapaho Stories, Songs, and Prayers*, 481, 516.

30. "The Messiah Letter," in Mooney, *Ghost Dance Religion*, 780–781.

31. Ibid., 781.

32. Ibid. The Messiah Letter is a rare example of Wovoka invoking the name of Jesus, and one wonders if he did so by way of explaining his teachings to Plains believers, who had much exposure to Christian teachings and perhaps were curious to know if the promised Messiah was Christ or some other messiah. Ibid., 781.

33. Cowell, Moss, and C'Hair, *Arapaho Stories, Songs, and Poetry*, 478.

34. Mooney, *Ghost Dance Religion*, 901.

35. Ibid., 767, 816.

36. Richmond L. Clow, "The Lakota Ghost Dance After 1890," *South Dakota History* 20 (Winter 1990): 324–327.

37. Mooney, *Ghost Dance Religion*, 1059–1060.

38. Ibid., 655. Mooney mentions that he consulted with Fire Thunder, whom he describes as an emissary to Nevada, but no other source names Fire Thunder as an emissary. Ibid., 1060. I am indebted to Sam Maddra for this argument about Mooney's problematic sources at Pine Ridge. Maddra, *Hostiles?*, 30–34.

39. Mooney, *Ghost Dance Religion*, 869, 879, plate XCIX (between pages 872–873); Moses, *The Indian Man*, 63.

40. Although the army scout Arthur Chapman had interviewed Wovoka, Chapman's report was not published until sometime in 1891, and it is not clear whether Mooney had seen it. Mooney, *Ghost Dance Religion*, 766.

41. C. C. Warner to James Mooney, October 12, 1891, in Mooney, *Ghost Dance Religion*, 767.

42. Mooney, *Ghost Dance Religion*, 767–768.

43. Ibid., 768.

44. Ibid.

45. Ibid.

46. Ibid., 768–769.

47. Colby, "Routes to Rainy Mountain," 227.

48. Mooney, "The Indian Ghost Dance," 179; Mooney, *Ghost Dance Religion*, 768.

49. Mooney, *Ghost Dance Religion*, 768–770.

50. Hittman, *Wovoka and the Ghost Dance*, 118.

51. Mooney, *Ghost Dance Religion*, 771.

52. Ibid., 772.

53. Ibid., 773.

54. Ibid., 774.

55. Ibid., 774–775.

56. For "spiritual stock in trade," see ibid., 775. In *The Ghost Dance Religion* (775), Mooney implies that he left the same night, but in "The Indian Ghost Dance" (179), he explains that he took the photo the next morning. The photograph is in the Smithsonian digital collections, http://sirismm .si.edu/naa/baegn/gn_01659a.jpg (accessed July 9, 2010).

57. Mooney, *Ghost Dance Religion,* 775.

58. Ibid., 778.

59. Ibid., 778.

60. Ibid., 778–779; Hittman, *Wovoka and the Ghost Dance,* 185.

61. Mooney, *Ghost Dance Religion,* 779.

62. Ibid., 779.

63. Ibid., 778.

64. Ibid., 780.

65. James Mooney, report of November 1893, BAE Monthly Reports, MS 4733, NAA; Mooney, *Ghost Dance Religion,* 903.

CHAPTER 13: WRITING *THE GHOST DANCE RELIGION AND SIOUX OUTBREAK OF 1890*

1. Regna Darnell, *And Along Came Boas: Continuity and Revolution in Americanist Anthropology* (Philadelphia: John Benjamins, 1998), 78.

2. Worster, *A River Running West,* 109–382; Wallace Stegner, *Beyond the Hundredth Meridian: John Wesley Powell and the Second Opening of the American West* (1953; reprint, Lincoln: University of Nebraska Press, 1982).

3. John Wesley Powell in "Surveys of the Territories," 45th Congress, 3rd Session, 1878–1879, House Miscellaneous Document 5, 26–27.

4. Thomas L. Haskell, *The Emergence of Professional Social Science: The American Social Science Association and the Nineteenth-Century Crisis of Authority* (1977; revised edition, Baltimore: Johns Hopkins University Press, 2000), 24–47; Dorothy Ross, *The Origins of American Social Science* (New York: Cambridge University Press, 1991), 53–57.

5. Neil M. Judd, *The Bureau of American Ethnology: A Partial History* (Norman: University of Oklahoma Press, 1967); Virginia H. M. Noelke, "The Origins and Early History of the Bureau of American Ethnology," PhD dissertation, University of Texas, 1974.

6. Curtis M. Hinsley, *Savages and Scientists: The Smithsonian Institution and the Development of American Anthropology, 1846–1910* (Washington, DC: Smithsonian Institution Press, 1981), 167.

7. Worster, *A River Running West,* 560–562.

8. Hinsley, *Savages and Scientists,* 190–230; Darnell, *And Along Came Boas,* 76.

9. Ross, *Origins of American Social Science,* 53–57; Haskell, *Emergence of Professional Social Science,* 63, esp. n. 2.

10. Ross, *Origins of American Social Science,* 61; Haskell, *Emergence of Professional Social Science,* 117.

11. Worster, *A River Running West,* 437–440; James Kirkpatrick Flack, *Desideratum in Washington: The Intellectual Community in the Capital City, 1870–1900* (Cambridge, MA: Schenkman, 1975).

12. Worster, *A River Running West,* 420.

13. John Wesley Powell, quoted in Worster, *A River Running West,* 456.

14. Powell in "Surveys of the Territories," 26–27; J. W. Powell, "Sketch of the Mythology of North American Indians," in *First Annual Report of the Bureau of Ethnology 1879–80* (Washington, DC: Government Printing Office, 1881), 30–31, 40, 42–43.

15. Moses, *The Indian Man,* 2; Colby, "Routes to Rainy Mountain," 35.

16. Luke Gibbons, "Unapproved Roads: Post-Colonialism and Irish Identity," in *Distant Relations: Cercanías Distantes/Clann I gCéin,* edited by Trisha Ziff (Santa Monica, CA: Smart Art Press, 1995), 5–6; Nicholas P. Canny, "Ideology of English Colonization: From Ireland to America," *William and Mary Quarterly* 30, no. 4 (October 1973): 597–598; Noel Ignatiev, *How the Irish Became White* (New York: Routledge, 1995); *The Times* quoted in Kerby A. Miller, *Emigrants and Exiles: Ireland the Irish Exodus to North America* (New York: Oxford University Press), 307.

17. Charles Mann, "How the Potato Changed the World," Smithsonian .com, November 2011, http://www.smithsonianmag.com/history/how-the -potato-changed-the-world-108470605/?page=6 (accessed July 25, 2016).

18. Miller, *Emigrants and Exiles,* 323; Matthew Frye Jacobson, *Whiteness of a Different Color: European Immigrants and the Alchemy of Race* (Cambridge, MA: Harvard University Press, 1998), 48–52; Ignatiev, *How the Irish Became White,* passim.

19. Pádraig Siadhail, "'The Indian Man' and the Irishman: James Mooney and Irish Folklore," *New Hibernia Review* 14, no. 2 (Summer 2010): 22.

20. Moses, *The Indian Man,* 4. The concept of the immigrant as exile comes from Matthew Frye Jacobsen, *Special Sorrows: The Diasporic Imagination of Irish, Polish, and Jewish Immigrants to the United States* (Cambridge, MA: Harvard University Press, 1995).

21. Eire Stevens to "Mr. M.," n.d., shorthand notes in Mooney Papers, Box 1, NAA; Moses, *The Indian Man,* 5.

22. "The 'Indian Man,'" *Chicago Inter-Ocean,* August 20, 1893, clipping in James Mooney vertical file, NAA.

23. O'Toole quoted in Joy Porter, "'Primitive' Discourse: Aspects of Contemporary North American Indian Representations of the Irish and of Contemporary Irish Representations of North American Indians,"

American Studies 49, nos. 3–4 (Fall–Winter 2008): 65; Jacobson, *Whiteness of a Different Color,* 51, 53–54; Blackhawk, *Violence over the Land,* 263; Alexander Saxton, *The Indispensable Enemy: Labor and the Anti-Chinese Movement in California* (Berkeley: University of California Press, 1971), 117–121; Brigham D. Madsen, *The Shoshone Frontier and the Bear River Massacre* (Salt Lake: University of Utah Press, 1985), 59.

24. James Jeffrey Roche, *Life of John Boyle O'Reilly, Together with His Complete Poems and Speeches* (New York: Mershon Co., 1891), 142; see also Jacobsen, *Special Sorrows,* 57–58.

25. 1870 US census data for Wayne County, IN, University of Virginia, Historical Census Browser.

26. Norman Dunbar Palmer, *The Irish Land League Crisis* (London: Octagon, 1978), 34; Mann, "How the Potato Changed the World."

27. Roche quoted in Jacobsen, *Special Sorrows,* 181.

28. Gelya Frank, "Jews, Multiculturalism, and Boasian Anthropology," *American Anthropologist* 99, no. 4 (December 1997): 740.

29. Moses, *The Indian Man,* 4–5; Colby, "Routes to Rainy Mountain," 38.

30. Mooney to J. W. Powell, June 9, 1882; Mooney to Garrick Mallery, July 8, 1882; Mooney to Powell, February 14, 1883; all in Records of the BAE, Series 1, Correspondence, Letters Received 1879–1887, Box 80, NAA.

31. Daniel Mooney to James Mooney, January 4, 1899, James Mooney Papers, Box 1, Folder "Letters," NAA; "James Mooney," *American Anthropologist,* new series (1922): 209–213; Moses, *The Indian Man,* 163. For Irish social science and the national museum, see M. C. Knowles to James Mooney, December 13, 1911, James Mooney Papers, Box 1, Folder "Letters," NAA; Siadhail, "'The Indian Man,'" 28. The National Museum of Science and Art succeeded the earlier Dublin Museum of Science and Art. See National Museum of Ireland, "History of the Museum," http://www.museum.ie/en /list/history-of-the-museum.aspx (accessed August 21, 2015).

32. Earlham College, "History," http://www.earlham.edu/about/campus -history/history/ (accessed August 17, 2015); Moses, *The Indian Man,* 11.

33. Powell, *First Annual Report of the Bureau of Ethnology,* xxxiii.

34. Moses, *The Indian Man,* 17.

35. Ibid., 175–176; James Mooney, "The Medical Mythology of Ireland," *Proceedings of the American Philosophical Society* 24, no. 125 (1887): 136–166; "The Funeral Customs of Ireland," *Proceedings of the American Philosophical Society* 25, no. 128 (1888): 243–296; "Holiday Customs of Ireland," *Proceedings of the American Philosophical Society* 26, no. 130 (1889): 377–427.

36. James Mooney, "Sacred Formulas of the Cherokees," in *Seventh Annual Report of the Bureau of Ethnology, 1891* (Washington, DC: Government

Printing Office, 1892), 313, 318–319; Mooney to Henshaw, October 29, 1887, and Mooney to Powell, September 19, 1888, Records of the BAE, Series 1, Correspondence, Letters Received 1879–1887, Box 80, NAA; Moses, *The Indian Man,* 24; Colby, "Routes to Rainy Mountain," 82.

37. Mooney, "Medical Mythology of Ireland," 136. Ideas of Irish superiority took on new salience as Irish immigrants and their leaders responded to the mania for Anglo-Saxonism and resurgent American nativism in the United States in the 1890s. Jacobsen, *Special Sorrows,* 31.

38. Mooney, "Medical Mythology of Ireland," 136; James Mooney, "In Memoriam: Washington Matthews," *American Anthropologist,* new series 7, no. 3 (July–September 1905): 520; see also Colby, "Routes to Rainy Mountain," 53.

39. MS 3249, NAA; Mooney, "Ghost Dance Religion," 657.

40. Mooney, *Ghost Dance Religion,* 657.

41. Ibid., 659–691.

42. For the bureau's archiving of the Code of Handsome Lake, see Anthony F. C. Wallace, *The Death and Rebirth of the Seneca* (New York: Alfred A. Knopf, 1970), 342 n. 2.

43. Mooney to Henshaw, January 19, 1891, NAA.

44. Parker's account appeared originally in the *New York Times* and was reprinted in the *Journal of American Folklore.* Mrs. Z. A. Parker quoted in "Ghost Dance at Pine Ridge," *Journal of American Folklore* 4, no. 13 (April–June 1891): 160; Mooney, *Ghost Dance Religion,* 916.

45. Vestal, *New Sources of Indian History,* 44; Mooney, *Ghost Dance Religion,* 772.

46. "Address of Mr. James Mooney," 174.

47. Compare Mooney's field notes of his interview with Asatitola in Mooney, "Vocabulary," MS 1915, 16–18, NAA, with his account of the man's vision in *Ghost Dance Religion,* 911.

48. General Nelson A. Miles to Adjutant General, November 28, 1890, M 983, vol. 1, p. 283, RG 94, NARA-DC. Mooney attributes the initial eruption of gunfire at Wounded Knee to a misunderstanding, but labels the use of Hotchkiss guns and the pursuit of fleeing Indians as "simply a massacre." Mooney, *Ghost Dance Religion,* 869.

49. Sword quoted in Mooney, *Ghost Dance Religion,* 797.

50. Ibid., 797–798; Short Bull, in Natalie Curtis, *The Indians' Book: An Offering by the American Indians of Indian Lore, Musical and Narrative, to Form a Record of the Songs and Legends of Their Race* (1907), reprinted in Maddra, *Hostiles?,* 208.

51. Mooney, *Ghost Dance Religion,* 821.

52. Ibid., 819–821.

53. Ibid., 848, 854–855.

54. Ibid., 857, 859, 861.

55. Ibid., 929–930.

56. Ibid., 936–938.

57. Ibid., 939, 941–942.

58. Ibid., 942–944.

59. Ibid., 945.

60. Ibid., 946–947.

61. Ibid., 947.

62. Taves, *Fits, Trances, and Visions*, 77. Indeed, in the United States fears of how religious spirit possessed dark-skinned people lingered behind much of the elite critique that Mooney relays. At the revival tent of Maria Woodworth in Oakland in January 1890, shortly before the riot broke out, the mostly white crowds were attending the harangues of a black preacher. "Ring the Riot Alarm!" *San Francisco Examiner*, January 9, 1890, 2.

63. Taves, *Fits, Trances, and Visions*, 349.

64. Ibid., 348–349; William James, *The Varieties of Religious Experience* (1902; reprint, New York: Penguin, 1982).

65. "Plenty of False Christs," *New York Times*, November 30, 1890; "Messianic Excitements Among White Americans," *Journal of American Folklore* 4, no. 13 (April–June 1891): 163–165.

66. Taves, *Fits, Trances, and Visions*, 241–242.

67. Mooney, *Ghost Dance Religion*, 922.

68. This view was first formulated in 1871 by the famed British anthropologist E. B. Tylor. Spiritualism—the contacting of spirits of the deceased through ritualistic séances—had been a subject of popular controversy and fascination for much of the nineteenth century. Tylor explained it as a remnant of ancient animist religion that lingered exclusively in lower-class people (even though he met Spiritualists from all classes at the séances he attended for his research). Taves, *Fits, Trances, and Visions*, 199–200.

69. Buckley quoted in ibid., 245.

70. Ibid., 245–247.

71. Frederick Morgan Davenport, *Primitive Traits in Religious Revivals* (1905; reprint, New York: Negro Universities Press, 1968), 32–44, 285–286.

72. Mooney, *Ghost Dance Religion*, 888.

73. Ibid., 782–783.

74. Scott, *Some Memories of a Soldier*, 151, 157–158; Mooney, *Ghost Dance Religion*, 914; Julia Jordan, interview with Cecil Horse, July 26, 1967, T-25, Doris Duke Collection; Louise Saddleblanket, interview with William Bittle, June 27, 1967, T-56-2, Doris Duke Collection.

75. Mooney, *Ghost Dance Religion*, 914.

76. Ibid., 653, 927.

77. BAE Monthly Reports, MS 4733, NAA.

78. J. W. Powell, "Introduction," in *Fourteenth Annual Report of the Bureau of Ethnology 1892–93*, 2 vols. (Washington, DC: Government Printing Office, 1896), vol. 1, ix.

79. Ibid., lx–lxi.

80. Ibid., lxi.

81. Langley to Powell, May 25, 1897, Collection RU 34, vol. 44, pp. 60–61, Smithsonian Institution Archives.

82. Powell to Langley, May 26, 1897, RU 31, Box 75, Folder 9, Smithsonian Institution Archives.

CHAPTER 14: CONCLUSIONS:
THE GHOST DANCE AS MODERN RELIGION

1. F. S. Kingsbury to CIA, February 24, 1891, Frames 116–119, Reel 2, SC 188, NARA-DC.

2. Ibid.

3. Ibid.

4. See, for example, the cartoon available through the Library of Congress at http://cdn.loc.gov/service/pnp/ppmsca/28800/28855v.jpg (accessed July 28, 2016); Charles Postel, *The Populist Vision* (New York: Oxford University Press, 2007).

5. The historian Peter Brown points out that saints became a mainstay in Christian theology only in the fourth century A.D., when Romans realized that praying to them provided an idealized reflection of their need for high-placed "friends" who could secure them favors with the imperial court. The saints allowed Christians to "articulate and render manageable urgent, muffled debates on the nature of power in their own world, and to examine in the searching light of ideal relationships with ideal figures, the relation between power, mercy, and justice as practiced around them." Peter Brown, *The Cult of the Saints: Its Rise and Function in Latin Christianity* (Chicago: University of Chicago Press, 1981), 63.

6. The notion of religion as a means of "reconciling the unreconcilable" and dissolving or resolving contradictions is widespread in religious studies. See, for example, Anthony A. Lee, "Reconciling the Other: The Baha'i Faith in America as Successful Synthesis of Christianity and Islam," *Occasional Papers in Shayki, Babi and Baha'i Studies* 7, no. 2 (March 2003), http://www.h-net.org/~bahai/bhpapers.htm (accessed August 28, 2014).

7. See, for example, David M. Kennedy and Lizabeth Cohen, *The American Pageant*, 16th ed. (New York: Wadsworth, 2016), 579; John Murrin et al., *Liberty, Equality, Power: A History of the American People*, 6th ed. (Boston: Wadsworth Cengage, 2011), 501.

8. Clow, "Lakota Ghost Dance After 1890," 332–333; Thomas H. Lewis, *The Medicine Men: Oglala Sioux Ceremony and Healing* (Lincoln: University of Nebraska Press, 1990), 112–113; James H. Howard, *The Canadian Sioux* (Lincoln: University of Nebraska Press, 1984), 174–175, 182; Alice Beck Kehoe, *The Ghost Dance: Ethnohistory and Revitalization* (Long Grove, IL: Waveland Press, 2006), 50.

9. Clow, "Lakota Ghost Dance After 1890"; Solberg, *Tales of Wovoka,* 76; Dangberg, "Wovoka," 34, 49; Maddra, *Hostiles?,* 187; Hittman, *Wovoka and the Ghost Dance,* 265; Lewis, *The Medicine Men,* 112–113.

10. Lesser, *Pawnee Ghost Dance Hand Game,* 67, 77; Murie, "Pawnee Indian Societies," 636.

11. Lesser, *Pawnee Ghost Dance Hand Game,* 68; Murie, "Pawnee Indian Societies," 636.

12. Solberg, *Tales of Wovoka,* 87; Louise Saddleblanket, interview with William Bittle, June 27, 1967, T-56–2, Doris Duke Collection.

13. Dayna Bowker Lee, "A Social History of Caddoan Peoples: Cultural Adaptation and Persistence in a Native American Community," PhD dissertation, University of Oklahoma, 1998, 260–264; Elsie Clews Parson, "Notes on the Caddo," *Memoirs of the American Anthropological Association* 57 (1941): 47–48.

14. Benjamin R. Kracht, "The Kiowa Ghost Dance, 1894–1916: An Unheralded Revitalization Movement," *Ethnohistory* 39, no. 4 (Autumn 1992): 466–468.

15. Clark Wissler, "General Discussion of Shamanistic and Dancing Societies," *Anthropological Papers of the American Museum of Natural History,* vol. 11, *Societies of the Plains Indians,* pt. 12 (1916): 868–871; see also Lesser, *Pawnee Ghost Dance Hand Game.*

16. Kracht, "Kiowa Ghost Dance," 469.

17. Solberg, *Tales of Wovoka,* 154, 160–164.

18. Stewart, *Peyote Religion,* 106.

19. Frank Rzeczkowski, *Uniting the Tribes: The Rise and Fall of Pan-Indian Community on the Crow Reservation* (Lawrence: University Press of Kansas, 2012).

20. Julia A. Jordan, interview with Myrtle Lincoln, July 30, 1970, T-613, 1, 20, Doris Duke Collection.

21. Wacker, *Heaven Below,* 6; Cecil M. Robeck Jr., *The Azusa Street Mission and Revival: The Birth of the Global Pentecostal Movement* (Nashville: Thomas Nelson, 2006).

22. Du Bois, "1870 Ghost Dance," 2.

23. Parsons, "Notes on the Caddo," 49–50. For similar remarks by Kiowa Christians, see Kracht, "Kiowa Ghost Dance," 470–471.

24. Julia A. Jordan, interview with Myrtle Lincoln, July 30, 1970, T-613, Doris Duke Collection.

25. Smoak, *Ghost Dances and Identity*, 118.

EPILOGUE

1. ANSB, 19.

2. Eleanor Hannah, "Fort Sheridan," Encyclopedia of Chicago, http://www.encyclopedia.chicagohistory.org/pages/478.html (accessed December 28, 2014); "Nelson Appleton Miles," US Army History Center, http://www.history.army.mil/books/cg&csa/miles-na (accessed October 10, 2016). A useful source is the "National Register of Historic Places Inventory—Nomination Form" for the tower, available at: http://ihpa.greatarc.com/pdfs/200797.pdf (accessed December 28, 2014).

3. ANSB, 20; Warren, *Buffalo Bill's America*, 417.

4. McCoy, "Short Bull," 60; Wildhage, "Material on Short Bull," 35–36, 38.

5. Warren, *Buffalo Bill's America*, 538–540.

6. Utley, *Last Days of the Sioux Nation*, 283; Students and Faculty of Crazy Horse School, *Pute Tiyospaye (Lip's Camp): The History and Culture of a Sioux Indian Village* (Wanblee, SD: Crazy Horse School, 1978), 9.

7. Maddra, *Hostiles?*, 209.

8. Ibid., 211.

9. Ibid., 210.

10. Ibid., 209.

11. Ibid.

12. McCoy, "Short Bull," 61; Lothar Dräger, "Short Bull, Apostel der Ghost Dance Religion bei den Lakota, als Showman und Maler," *Amerindian Research* (2012): 92; Tom Shortbull, personal communication, August 2, 2016; Maddra, *Hostiles?*, 209.

13. Bates, *In Search of Spirit*, 226–229.

14. Ibid., 229, 232–233.

15. Ibid., 218, 235–236, 192.

16. Burnham, *Song of Dewey Beard*, 104–105.

17. Ibid., 136.

18. See, for example, Mooney, "Myths of the Cherokee (1908)," in *James Mooney's History, Myths, and Sacred Formulas of the Cherokees*, edited by George Ellison (Fairview, NC: Bright Mountain Books, 1992), 181. "The older people still cling to their ancient rites and sacred traditions, but the dance and the ballplay wither and the Indian day is nearly spent."

19. Colby, "Routes to Rainy Mountain," 477–478.

20. James Mooney, "The Mescal Plant and Ceremony," *Therapeutic Gazette*, 3rd series, 12 (1896): 7–11; "The Kiowa Peyote Rite," *Am Ur-Quell*, new series 1 (1897): 329–333; Moses, *The Indian Man*, 145–154.

21. *ARCIA 1886*, 130; *ARCIA 1888*, 98–99; quotes from *ARCIA 1889*, 191; Colby, "Routes to Rainy Mountain," 474.

22. Colby, "Routes to Rainy Mountain," 475.

23. *Peyote: Hearings Before a Subcommittee of the Committee on Indian Affairs of the House of Representatives on HR 2614* (Washington, DC: Government Printing Office, 1918), I:58–63; I:61–63, 89, 107, 111.

24. Ibid., I:111.

25. Ibid., I:147.

26. Mooney to J. Walter Fewkes, July 26, 1918, Records of the BAE, Series 1, Correspondence, Letters Recd., 1909–1949, Box 200, NAA.

27. James Sydney Slotkin, *The Peyote Religion: A Study in Indian-White Relations* (Glencoe, IL: Free Press, 1956), 58; Weston La Barre, *The Peyote Cult* (Norman: University of Oklahoma Press, 2012), 168–169; Moses, *The Indian Man*, 207; Julia Jordan, interview with Jess Rowlodge, December 12, 1967, T-172-11, Doris Duke Collection.

28. Moses, *The Indian Man*, 206.

29. Stinchecum to Indian Office, telegram copy, n.d.; Cato Sells to Charles D. Walcott, October 22, 1918; Mooney to J. Walter Fewkes, November 19, 1918; all in "Mooney, James 1916–1934," Records of the BAE, Box 200, NAA.

30. Moses, *The Indian Man*, 217–218.

31. James Mooney, draft letter protesting disbarment, n.d. [1921], James Mooney Papers, Box 1, NAA.

32. Frank, "Jews, Multiculturalism, and Boasian Anthropology," 734, 736; Darnell, *And Along Came Boas*, 89, 93, 296–297.

33. Moses, *The Indian Man*, 219.

34. "Resolutions Adopted by the Native American Church of Clinton, Okla. on the Death of James Mooney" (spelling corrected), in "Biographical Materials," James Mooney Papers, Box 1, NAA.

35. Another account claims that a wind blew so strong that "nobody could stand up against it." Hittman, *Wovoka and the Ghost Dance*, 204–206.

36. *ARCIA 1892*, 322; Mooney, *Ghost Dance Religion*, 901; L. G. Moses, "Jack Wilson and the Indian Service: The Response of the BIA to the Ghost Dance Prophet," *American Indian Quarterly* 5, no. 4 (November 1979): 311.

37. Dyer, "Jack Wilson Story," 11.

38. Ibid., 11–12.

39. Ibid., 16; Solberg, *Tales of Wovoka*, 88–89.

40. Knack and Stewart, *As Long as the River Shall Run*, 269–270; John M. Townley, "Soil Saturation Problems on the Truckee-Carson Project, Nevada," *Agricultural History* 52, no. 2 (April 1978): 283, 290.

41. For the effects of the "white winter" of 1889–1890, see Young and Sparks, *Cattle in the Cold Desert*, 154–179; for the Paiute labor shortage, see Knack, "Nineteenth-Century Great Basin Wage Labor,"172.

42. Solberg, *Tales of Wovoka*, 91.

43. Hittman, *Yerington Paiute Tribe*, 34, 41; Hagan, *Taking Indian Lands*, 78–84; "Nation's Top Three Poorest Counties in Western South Dakota," *Rapid City (South Dakota) Journal*, January 22, 2012, http://rapid cityjournal.com/news/nation-s-top-three-poorest-counties-in-western -south-dakota/article_2d5bb0bc-44bf-11e1-bbc9–0019bb2963f4.html (accessed October 10, 2016).

44. Michael Hittman, personal communication, July 25, 2016; Stewart, "Contemporary Document on Wovoka."

45. Hittman, *Wovoka and the Ghost Dance*, 129–133.

46. Ibid., 173.

47. Francis Paul Prucha, *The Great Father: The United States Government and the American Indians*, 2 vols. (Lincoln: University of Nebraska Press, 1984), 2:918–919.

INDEX

Louis S. Warren is the W. Turrentine Jackson Professor of Western US History at the University of California, Davis, and the multiple-award-winning author of *Buffalo Bill's America* and *The Hunter's Game*. He lives in Davis, California.